The Prevention of Humanitarian Emergencies

UNU WORLD INSTITUTE FOR DEVELOPMENT ECONOMICS RESEARCH (UNU/WIDER) was established by the United Nations University as its first research and training centre and started work in Helsinki, Finland, in 1985. The purpose of the Institute is to undertake applied research and policy analysis on structural changes affecting the developing and transitional economies, to provide a forum for the advocacy of policies leading to robust, equitable and environmentally sustainable growth, and to promote capacity strengthening and training in the field of economic and social policy-making. Its work is carried out by staff researchers and visiting scholars in Helsinki and through networks of collaborating scholars and institutions around the world.

UNU World Institute for Development Economics Research (UNU/WIDER)
Katajanokanlaituri 6 B, FIN-00160 Helsinki, Finland

The Prevention of Humanitarian Emergencies

Edited by

E. Wayne Nafziger
University Distinguished Professor of Economics
Kansas State University
USA

and

Raimo Väyrynen
Professor of Government and International Studies
Director, Joan B. Kroc Institute for International Peace Studies
University of Notre Dame
Indiana
USA

in association with
The United Nations University/World
Institute for Development Economics
Research (UNU/WIDER)

0300429

First published 2002 by
PALGRAVE
Houndmills, Basingstoke, Hampshire RG21 6XS and
175 Fifth Avenue, New York, N.Y. 10010
Companies and representatives throughout the world

PALGRAVE is the new global academic imprint of
St. Martin's Press LLC Scholarly and Reference Division and
Palgrave Publishers Ltd (formerly Macmillan Press Ltd).

ISBN 0-333-96438-1

This book is printed on paper suitable for recycling and
made from fully managed and sustained forest sources.

A catalogue record for this book is available
from the British Library.

Library of Congress cataloging-in-publication data
has been applied for.

10 9 8 7 6 5 4 3 2 1
11 10 09 08 07 06 05 04 03 02

Printed and bound in Great Britain by
Antony Rowe Ltd, Chippenham, Wiltshire

Contents

List of Tables

Foreword

During the last fifteen years, the number of humanitarian crises and social conflicts has escalated abruptly, resulting in scores of people dying, starving and homeless. And at the dawn of the third millennium there is no sign that the frequency of such crises is about to subside. Indeed, numerous countries could be affected by this scourge in the not-too-distant future, unless preventative corrective measures are introduced as a matter of urgency. This surge in emergencies – the most important source of human suffering in the world today – cannot be attributed to an increase in natural disasters but rather to factors which are man-made.

Until recently, most analyses of the causes of such emergencies have focused on factors including sudden outbursts of ethnic animosity, deteriorating environmental conditions, the collapse of the Soviet Union, the decline of aid to 'ugly dictators', and structural adjustment. While not irrelevant, these explanations are partial and overlook the impact of failed development policies and institutional collapse. Moreover, traditional responses to this new scourge have focused on ex-post interventions, that is, interventions carried out after the conflicts have arisen.

This work emphasizes that in several cases humanitarian emergencies can be prevented by means of balanced and equitable development policies, which would remove the deep-seated distortions responsible for the outburst of social conflicts and humanitarian emergencies. While conflict mediation and reconstruction during and after war are important components of a strategy aimed at avoiding, containing and ending such emergencies, ex-post interventions appear often far less efficient in terms of losses of human life and human sufferings, destruction of infrastructure, long-term disruption of even basic economic activities (due, for instance, to land mines) and requirements of external aid. This volume argues, therefore, in favour of shifting the policy focus to the ex-ante prevention of humanitarian emergencies by means of appropriate economic and social development policies. These include strengthening civil society and democratic governance, reforming political institutions, improving the capability of the state to collect taxes and provide basic services, undergoing agrarian reform and land redistribution, accelerating economic growth through domestically planned macroeconomic stabilization and structural adjustment, protecting the position of weaker segments of the population, and redesigning aid to be more stable, predictable and oriented to a coherent national plan and to long-term, locally oriented agricultural research and technology.

Preventive measures can be undertaken by a rich variety of actors – the country's civil society and government, transnational non-governmental organizations (NGOs), rich-country governments and international agencies. As will be shown, for preventive strategies to be effective, international economic and political agencies involved in prevention (such as the United Nations (UN) Security Council, Secretariat and Development Programme) need to monitor the situation carefully, giving highest priority to the promotion and maintenance of peace and coordinating their actions at early and critical phases of crisis development.

Future researchers will look to this volume as an innovative effort in identifying how to prevent humanitarian emergencies. The study is strongly recommended to researchers and policy-makers with an interest in reducing war and destitution in developing countries.

GIOVANNI ANDREA CORNIA
University of Florence
and
former Director, UNU/WIDER

Acknowledgements

We owe a great debt to Giovanni Andrea Cornia, former Director of UNU/WIDER, for his vision in initiating this research, and for his support and guidance throughout. We thank the UNU/WIDER staff for its tireless effort. In particular, we thank Janis Vehmaan-Kreula, who spent many hours word-processing, editing, and arranging travel and housing for meetings in Helsinki, Oxford and Stockholm, Liisa Roponen for her word-processing and copyediting, Barbara Fagerman for helping to plan the Stockholm conference, Tuula Haarla and Adam Swallow for organizing reporting and publishing, and Anthony Shorrocks and Matti Pohjola for facilitating publishing.

UNU/WIDER and the editors gratefully acknowledge the financial contributions to the research project by the Ministry for Foreign Affairs of Finland and the Government of Sweden (Swedish International Development Agency – Sida). We hope that our work will influence the world community in providing resources for preventing wars through tackling the roots of conflict, while continuing to fund reconstruction, humanitarian aid and peace-building after wars occur.

The contributors wish to thank Tony Atkinson, Cindy Collins, Jose Cuesta-Leiva, Degol Hailu, Dina Kiwan, Helinä Melkas and Larry Minear for their help. We also wish to acknowledge Eric Weisbander and the Kansas State University Department of Geography for cartography. While we are grateful to all who have contributed to this work, we, the editors, remain solely responsible for its errors.

E. Wayne Nafziger and Raimo Väyrynen
Helsinki

Notes on the Contributors

R. A. Berry is Professor of Economics at the University of Toronto. His research has focused primarily on agrarian structure and reform, income distribution and labour markets, and small and medium enterprise. He is co-author with William Cline of *Agrarian Structure and Productivity in Developing Countries* (1979), co-author with Miguel Urrutia of *Income Distribution in Colombia* (1976), editor of *Poverty, Economic Reforms, and Income Distribution in Latin America* (1998), and author of various other articles and books. He has been a consultant for the UN Development Programme, the World Bank, the International Fund for Agricultural Development (IFAD), the InterAmerican Development Bank and other international agencies.

Andrew Clapham is Associate Professor of Public International Law at the Graduate Institute of International Studies, Geneva. He was the representative of Amnesty International to the United Nations (UN) in New York from 1991 to 1997. He is a barrister and an associate academic member of Matrix Chambers, Grays Inn, London. His publications include *European Union: the Human Rights Challenge* (vol. 1) (1991) and *Human Rights and the Private Sphere* (1993).

Christopher Cramer works at the School of Oriental and African Studies (SOAS) in the University of London. He is also the Convenor of the MSc on Violence, Conflict and Development at SOAS, and teaches the political economy of development and the applied economics of Africa. He has lived and worked in Mozambique and South Africa, and his current research interests are in the following fields: the political economy of conflict; rural poverty and labour markets; privatization; and the scope for processing primary commodities such as cashew across different developing economies.

William E. DeMars has taught International Relations at the American University in Cairo and the University of Notre Dame, and is currently writing a book, *Alchemists of World Politics: NGOs and Their Partners*. He has published several articles on the politics of the humanitarian network in internal wars, and is co-author of *Breaking Cycles of Violence: Conflict Prevention in Intrastate Crises* (1999).

Antonio Donini has worked for the UN at Headquarters and in the field for more than 20 years. He is Deputy Coordinator of the Office for the

Coordination of Humanitarian Assistance in Afghanistan. He was Chief of the Lessons Learned Unit at the UN Department of Humanitarian Affairs (UNDHA), which prepares independent studies assessing the effectiveness of international relief efforts in complex emergencies. Before joining the DHA, he worked in the UN Joint Inspection Unit and in the executive office of the Secretary-General. He served in and around Afghanistan from 1989 to 1992, where he was Deputy Chief of Mission in the UN Office for the Coordination of Humanitarian Assistance to Afghanistan (UNOCA) in Islamabad and Chief of Mission of UNOCA in Kabul. In 1995 he was awarded a sabbatical at the Watson Institute for International Studies, which allowed him to prepare a monograph, 'The Policies of Mercy: UN Coordination in Afghanistan, Rwanda and Mozambique', published in June 1996. He has recently co-authored a 'lessons learned' report on coordination of humanitarian assistance in Afghanistan, and is the author of several studies and articles on humanitarian and UN coordination issues.

Valpy FitzGerald is Director of the Finance and Trade Policy Research Centre at Queen Elizabeth House, University of Oxford. He is also a Professorial Fellow of St Antony's College, Oxford. He holds a PhD in Economics from Cambridge University, and has worked as an economic advisor in Central America and Cambodia, as well as to the United Nations Conference on Trade and Development (UNCTAD), International Labour Office (ILO), Organization for Economic Cooperation and Development (OECD) and the European Commission (EC). He is currently working on the issue of macroeconomic vulnerability and the place of poor countries in global capital markets.

Helge Hveem is Professor of Political Science at the Department of Political Science, University of Oslo. He was Research Fellow at the International Peace Research Institute, Oslo (1968–81). He has been Research Director at the Centre on Development and the Environment, University of Oslo (1990–99) and, in the 1960s and 1970s, Research Fellow at Makerere College, University of East Africa, L'Université des Sciences Sociales, Grenoble, and at the Center for International Affairs, Harvard University. He has often worked as a consultant to UNCTAD, and has been Visiting Professor at the European University Institute, Florence, and the Institut de Sciences Politiques, Bordeaux. He has published numerous books and articles on international political economy and international development studies.

Gaim Kibreab was a Senior Research Fellow at Uppsala University until the beginning of 1999. He is now a Senior Lecturer in Development Studies, Faculty of Humanities and Social Sciences at the South Bank University, London. His research interests include general development issues with particular emphasis on forced migration, resettlement, environment and post-conflict reconstruction, on which he has written several books and articles. He is currently studying (re)-integration of displaced populations in postwar Eritrea.

E. Wayne Nafziger is University Distinguished Professor of Economics at Kansas State University. He is editor (with Frances Stewart and Raimo Väyrynen) of *War, Hunger, and Displacement: the Origins of Humanitarian Emergencies* (2 vols) (2000), and author of *The Economics of Developing Countries* (1997); *The Debt Crisis in Africa* (1993); *Inequality in Africa: Political elites, Proletariat, Peasants and the Poor* (1988); *The Economics of Political Instability* (1983), and numerous other books and articles on developing nations. Dr Nafziger has been Research Fellow at the University of Nigeria; Visiting Fulbright Professor at Andhra University, India; Fellow at the East-West Center (Honolulu); Visiting Professor at the International University of Japan; Visiting Scholar at Cambridge University and the Nigerian Institute for Social and Economic Research; Hewlett Visiting Fellow at the Carter Center; and Senior Research Fellow at UNU/WIDER.

Richard Sandbrook is a Professor of Political Science at the University of Toronto, and has written and edited eight books on Africa. He has conducted field research in East, West and Southern Africa on topics ranging from union–government relations, urban poverty, new social movements, democratization, and the political economy of economic stagnation and market-oriented recovery programmes. He is currently engaged in a comparative study of the survival of social-democratic regimes in the North and the South in the context of globalization.

John Toye is a Visiting Professor at the University of Oxford, and Director of the Centre for the Study of African Economies. Between 1987 and 1997 he was Director of the Institute of Development Studies at the University of Sussex, and then spent two years as a Director of UNCTAD. He is the author of *Dilemmas of Development* (2nd edn, 1993) *and Keynes on Population* (2000), and co-author of *Aid and Power* (2nd edn, 1995).

Raimo Väyrynen is a Professor of Government and International Studies at the University of Notre Dame, Indiana, and served from 1993 to 1998 as Regan Director of its Joan B. Kroc Institute for International Peace Studies. In addition to several books in Finnish on security issues, globalization and other topics, he has recently authored, co-authored or edited *Globalization and Global Governance, Breaking the Cycles of Violence* (1999); *Global Transformation: Economics, Politics, and Culture* (1997); *Military Industrialization and Economic Development* (1992), and *New Directions in Conflict Theory* (1991). Dr Väyrynen has been Senior Research Fellow at

UNU/WIDER, Visiting Professor at Princeton University and the University of Minnesota, Visiting Scholar at Harvard University and Massachusetts Institute of Technology (MIT), Dean of Social Sciences and Professor of International Relations at the University of Helsinki, Director of the Tampere Peace Research Institute, and Secretary-General of the International Peace Research Association.

John Weeks is Professor of Development Economics at the School of Oriental and African Studies, and Director of the Centre for Development Policy and Research. He has served as a consultant to numerous UN organizations, including the ILO and the Food and Agriculture Organization (FAO). His current work focuses on macroeconomic policy in developing countries. He is author or editor of numerous books, most recently *Restructuring the Labour Market: the South African Challenge* (with Guy Standing and John Sender) (1996).

Thomas G. Weiss is Presidential Professor of Political Science at The Graduate Center of The City University of New York, where he is also Research Director of the International Commission on Intervention and State Sovereignty, editor of the journal *Global Governance,* and co-director of the UN Intellectual History Project. From 1990 to 1998 as a Research Professor at Brown University's Thomas J. Watson Jr Institute for International Studies, he also held a number of administrative assignments (Director of the Global Security Program, Associate Dean of the Faculty, Associate Director), served as the Executive Director of the Academic Council on the UN System, and co-directed the Humanitarianism and War Project. Previously he was Executive Director of the International Peace Academy and held a number of UN posts. He has authored or edited some thirty books on various aspects of international relations and organization, including *Military–Civilian Interactions: Intervening in Humanitarian Crises* (1999) and *Humanitarian Challenges and Intervention* (2nd edn, 2000).

List of Abbreviations

ACP	Africa, the Caribbean and the Pacific
ASEAN	Association of South East Asian Nations
CHE	complex humanitarian emergency
DAC	Development Assistance Committee of the OECD
DCs	developed (industrialized) countries
EC	European Commission
ECA	UN Economic Commission for Africa
EPRDF	Ethiopian Peoples' Revolutionary Democratic Front
EU	European Union
FAO	Food and Agriculture Organization of the UN
FDI	foreign direct investment
FY	fiscal year
G8	Meetings of the seven major DCs: the US, Canada, Japan, the UK, Germany, France and Italy, plus Russia, together the Group of Eight.
GATT	General Agreements on Tariffs and Trade, the predecessor to the WTO
GDP	gross domestic product
GNP	gross national product
GSP	generalized system of (tariff) preferences
HIPCs	highly indebted poor countries
ICRC	International Committee of the Red Cross
IDPs	internally displaced persons
IDS	Institute of Development Studies, Sussex University, UK
IFIs	international financial institutions (the IMF and World Bank)
IFPRI	International Food Policy Research Institute
ILO	International Labour Office
IMF	International Monetary Fund
LDCs	less-developed (developing) countries
LICs	low-income countries
LLDCs	least developed countries
MEP	Minister of European Parliament
MICs	middle-income countries
MNCs	multinational corporations
MSF	Médecins Sans Frontières
NATO	North Atlantic Treaty Organization
NGOs	non-governmental organizations
NICs	newly industrializing countries

NUPI	Norwegian Institute for International Affairs
OAS	Organization of American States
OAU	Organization for African Unity
ODA	official development assistance
ODI	Overseas Development Institute
OECD	Organization for Economic Cooperation and Development
PRIO	International Peace Research Institute, Oslo
RFA	Research for Action
SDRs	Special drawing rights, bookkeeping entries in the accounts of member countries of the IMF used as an internationalized currency by central banks for official transactions (with the IMF and other central banks).
Sida	Swedish International Development Cooperation
SIPRI	Stockholm International Peace Research Institute
SOEs	state-owned enterprises
SSA	sub-Saharan Africa
UK	United Kingdom
UN	United Nations
UNCTAD	United Nations Conference on Trade and Development
UNDHA	United Nations Department of Humanitarian Affairs
UNDP	United Nations Development Programme
UNGA	United Nations General Assembly
UNHCHR	Office of the United Nations High Commissioner for Human Rights
UNHCR	Office of the United Nations High Commissioner for Refugees
UNICEF	United Nations Children's Fund
UNRISD	United Nations Research Institute for Social Development
UNSC	United Nations Security Council
UNSG	United Nations Secretary-General
US	United States of America
USAID	United States Agency for International Development
VAT	value-added tax
WFP	World Food Programme
WHO	World Health Organization
WIDER	United Nations University/World Institute for Development Economics Research, Helsinki, Finland
WB	World Bank
WP	Working Paper
WTO	World Trade Organization, established in 1995, to administer rules of conduct in international trade.

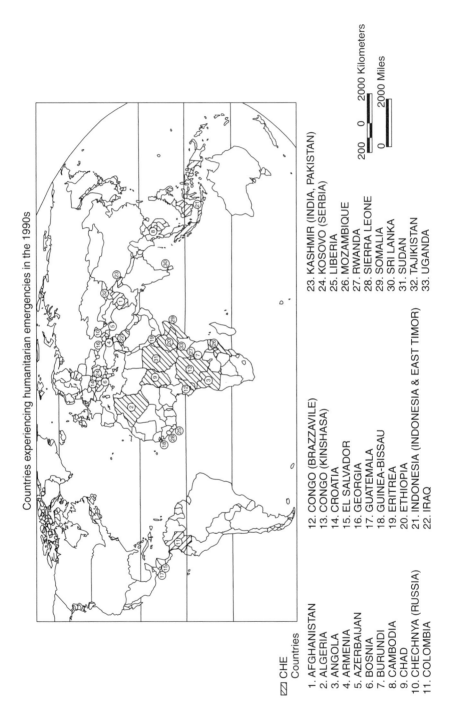

Countries experiencing humanitarian emergencies in the 1990s

CHE
Countries

1. AFGHANISTAN
2. ALGERIA
3. ANGOLA
4. ARMENIA
5. AZERBAIJAN
6. BOSNIA
7. BURUNDI
8. CAMBODIA
9. CHAD
10. CHECHNYA (RUSSIA)
11. COLOMBIA

12. CONGO (BRAZZAVILE)
13. CONGO (KINSHASA)
14. CROATIA
15. EL SALVADOR
16. GEORGIA
17. GUATEMALA
18. GUINEA-BISSAU
19. ERITREA
20. ETHIOPIA
21. INDONESIA (INDONESIA & EAST TIMOR)
22. IRAQ

23. KASHMIR (INDIA, PAKISTAN)
24. KOSOVO (SERBIA)
25. LIBERIA
26. MOZAMBIQUE
27. RWANDA
28. SIERRA LEONE
29. SOMALIA
30. SRI LANKA
31. SUDAN
32. TAJIKISTAN
33. UGANDA

200   0   2000 Kilometers

0   2000 Miles

Introduction: Preventing Humanitarian Emergencies – Asking the Questions

E. Wayne Nafziger

A complex humanitarian emergency (CHE) is a man-made crisis, whereby large numbers of people die or suffer from war, physical violence (often by the state), or displacement (Väyrynen 2000a). This volume identifies mechanisms for preventing CHEs. The focus is on the less-developed countries (LDCs) of Africa, Asia, Latin America and Eastern and Central Europe, where virtually all CHEs take place (Nafziger *et al.* 2000).

The volume does not focus on the immediate delivery of food and medicine to refugee camps or the repatriation of displaced people. Rather the contributors concentrate on long-term or immediate policies linked to the research project's analysis of root causes (ibid.).

Preventing conflict by reducing its causes costs less than crisis management after the emergency begins. Stewart *et al.* (2000a: I) calculate that the economic cost of the cumulated lost income of wars since 1980 was nearly six times El Salvador's national income in 1995, four times that of Ethiopia, and perhaps thirteen times that of Nicaragua.

Nafziger (1983) estimates that federal Nigeria forwent 27.4 per cent of real gross domestic product (GDP) (and an even larger share of *civilian* real GDP) during the three fiscal years of the war, 1967/68–1969/70; secessionist Biafra's *percentage* loss (some double counted among Nigeria's loss) was two to three times greater during the same period. GDP estimates understate Nigeria's losses, since a conservative estimate for capital destruction[1] from the war as a percentage of GDP was 5–10 per cent. Perhaps four million people died from hunger and other war-related causes and several million people were displaced.

I The roots of CHEs

Emergencies have numerous sources. Important economic elements are low average income, protracted economic stagnation and decline (especially in food output), high income inequality, and conflict over the control of mineral exports. Political elements include government exclusion of particular ethnic or social communities, rule by entrenched minorities, weak state legitimacy, and a tradition of violent conflict. Only a portion of violence results from insurgent action. In fact, the majority of casualties from CHEs are from government sponsored or organized politicides. Amid war and scarcity, ruling elites may benefit from spearheading genocide or tolerating crime or mass murder by allies among militias, war profiteers and ethnic champions. Indeed, some interests derive economic advantage by war and state violence; stopping deadly political violence requires changing the balance between benefits and costs among belligerents (Nafziger *et al.* 2000).

The early stages of famines and other CHEs are not easily distinguishable from endemic poverty (Green 1986). War and emergency may merely entail a deepening of conflict and exploitation existing during 'peacetime' (Keen 2000). Thus the causes and prevention of poverty (Nafziger 1997) overlap substantially with the causes and prevention of CHEs.

II   Africa as an example

The increase in intrastate political conflict and CHEs in the 1990s was linked to the disastrous growth record of LDCs (except Asia) in the 1970s and 1980s; moreover, sub-Saharan Africa's (SSA's) economy was virtually stagnant throughout the 1990s. In SSA, which is disproportionately represented both among countries with slow growth[2] and chronic external deficits, and major CHEs,[3] falling average incomes and growing political consciousness added pressures to national leaders, whose response was usually not only anti-egalitarian but also anti-growth, hurting small farmers' incentives, appropriating peasant surplus for parastatal industry, building parastatal enterprises beyond management capacity, and using these inefficient firms to give benefits to clients. Regime survival in a politically fragile system required expanding patronage to marshal elite support, at the expense of economic growth (Nafziger 1988).[4] Spurring peasant production through market prices and exchange rates would have interfered with state leaders' ability to build political support, especially in cities.

Africa's economic crisis originated from its inability to adjust to the 1973–74 oil shock, exacerbated by a credit cycle, in which states overborrowed at negative real interest rates in the mid- to late 1970s, but faced high positive rates during debt servicing or loan renewal in the 1980s. African leaders' statist economic policies during the 1970s and early 1980s (OAU 1980) emphasized detailed state planning, expansion of government-owned enterprises, heavy-industry development, and government intervention in exchange rates and agricultural price-setting. These policies contributed to economic regress and growing poverty (especially in rural areas) and inequality. The political elites used the state to pursue economic policies that supported their interests at the expense of Africa's poor and working classes (Nafziger 1993).

This stagnation and decline contributed to political decay in the 1980s and early 1990s in such African countries as Nigeria, Sierra Leone, Zaire and Liberia, where ethnic and regional competition for the bounties of the state gave way to a predatory state, in which the ruling elite and their clients 'use their positions and access to resources to plunder the national economy through graft, corruption, and extortion, and to participate in private business activities' (Holsti 2000: 251). Ake (1996: 42) contends that 'instead of being a public force, the state in Africa tends to be privatized, that is, appropriated to the service of private interests by the dominant faction of the elite'. People use state funds for systematized corruption, from petty survival venality at the lower echelons of government to kleptocracy at the top.

Väyrynen (2000b: 440) shows that CHEs are more likely to occur in societies where the state is weak and venal, and thus subject to extensive rent-seeking, 'an omnipresent policy to obtain private benefit from public action and resources'. Cause and effect between state failure and rent-seeking are not always clear. State failure need not necessarily result from the incapacity of public institutions. Instead, while 'state failure can harm a great number of people, it can also benefit others' (ibid.: 442), especially governing elites and their allies. These elites may not benefit from avoiding political decay through nurturing free entry and the rule of law and reducing corruption and exploitation. Instead, political leaders may gain more from extensive unproductive, profit-seeking activities in a political system they control than from long-term efforts to build a well functioning state in which economic progress and democratic institutions flourish (ibid; Keen 1998, 2000).[5] These activities tend to be pervasive in countries that have abundant mineral exports (for example diamonds,[6] columbite-tantalite and petroleum), such as Sierra Leone, Angola and Congo, but predatory economic behaviour is much less viable in mineral-export-poor economies such as Ghana and Tanzania (Väyrynen 2000b).

III The major questions of the study

What political and economic policies are most likely to reduce LDCs' vulnerability to emergencies and their reoccurrence? What political and economic levers can LDCs and their supporters in the international community pull to reduce the probability of CHEs?

Both initial emergencies and their reoccurrences are included, because research indicates that emergencies often persist. Populations adapt to a certain, acceptable level of violence through its cultural experience (Gurr 1970). A tradition of deadly political violence makes societies more susceptible to its return. Past violence, as in Colombia, is likely to lower the threshold for using violence to express dissent, making intensive forms of political conflict normatively justifiable. During 1980–2000, numerous countries, such as Ethiopia and Uganda, moved in and out of CHEs and sometimes, as in Burundi, Somalia and Liberia, back again. Indeed, Auvinen and Nafziger's (1999: 286) econometrics indicate that, other things equal, a doubling 'in deaths from political violence [1963–77] would have increased an emergency's probability [in any given year, 1980–94] by 4.4%'.

The research question is set in probabilistic terms. Even the statement linking deaths from prior political violence to subsequent emergencies is tied to particular datasets (Singer and Small 1994 and update, and SIPRI's 1996 database on war deaths), time periods and concepts of CHEs (Auvinen and Nafziger 1999). As Holsti (2000: 239, 250, 264) points out,

> If...there are certain conditions and/or processes that increase the likeli-hood of a humanitarian emergency, there is no certainty that such an emergency will in fact ensue. ...Why, for example, was there wide-spread bloodshed in 1965 Indonesia, or in Burma since 1962, but not in Malaysia or Singapore at the same time? ...For this reason I have avoided causal terminology and emphasized correlates, risks, and probabilities.

What long-term structural economic and political changes can reduce LDCs' risks of CHEs? What short-term operational measures can diminish countries' vulnera-bility to emergencies? What roles can national policymakers, DCs, international agencies and NGOs play in these preventive efforts?

The volume distinguishes between short-term and long-term prevention. The earlier chapters stress reducing structural vulnerabilities and inequali-ties, and strengthening the preconditions for stability, while the later chap-ters concentrate on short-term diplomatic or military operations or medium-term political or constitutional arrangements. The differences in perspectives are between longer-term economic approaches and shorter-term military or political actions.

Long-term efforts include undertaking structural and institutional change, building capacity and spurring economic and political develop-ment. Much of the longer-term focus of this volume is on economic approaches, for example in chapters 1 to 6. Long-run political changes include democratization, which is discussed in Chapter 8. Human-rights monitoring and intelligence (Chapter 12) not only have the potential to lead to preventive action but can also serve as an early-warning device.

Short-term measures are usually political and military, and include con-stitutional arrangements to share power, pressures by regional organiza-tions (such as the Organization for African Unity (OAU) and the Organization of American States (OAS)), conflict transformation, partition, diplomatic mediation, arms bans, sanctions (Chapter 7), peacekeeping operations and military intervention (Chapter 11). Short-term development and humanitarian aid may also help ameliorate potential conflict.

The earlier chapters of this volume emphasize long-term economic policies and are more optimistic than later chapters. Väyrynen (Chapter 7) feels that short-term strategies are generally not promising, as third parties are unwilling to become involved, especially in military approaches, or their policies are ineffectual in preventing the outbreak of a crisis. Indeed, short-term actions in which options are limited are often too late to eliminate or modify the underlying causes.

IV   The focus of the volume

This section summarizes the policy issues raised by contributors. In Chapter 1, I focus on a long-term politico-economic approach to prevention in which policies are linked to the research project's analysis of root causes. Domestic responses include accelerating economic growth through domestically planned macroeconomic stabilization and structural adjustment, designing appropriate economic and political institutions, improving the capability of the state to collect taxes and provide basic services, undergoing agrarian reform and land redistribution, and secure property and usufruct rights for traditional community or village land-rights systems. These responses need to examine the effect of policies on the weaker segments of the population – the poor, minorities, rural and working people, and women and children.

Enhancing growth and improving income distribution to reduce the risk of CHEs may require changes in the international economic order. This order encompasses economic relations and institutions linking people from different nations, including the World Bank (WB) and United Nations Development Programme (UNDP) that lend capital to LDCs; the International Monetary Fund (IMF), which provides credit to ease short-term international payments imbalances; the World Trade Organization (WTO), which administers international-trade rules; bilateral and multilateral trade, aid, banking services, currency rates, capital movements and technological transfers; aid consortiums; and international commodity stabilization agreements. The premise is that modifying international trade, foreign investment, aid (especially for agriculture and for cushioning external shocks), debt rescheduling and capital movements would be mutually advantageous, enhancing the economic development of LDCs and, through economic linkages, the prosperity of developed countries (DCs). However, even where the economic interests of DCs and LDCs conflict, DCs may benefit from cooperation in international economic institutions by facilitating democracy and development in poor countries, so that they can contribute to global peace and stability.

In Chapter 2, Cramer and Weeks evaluate how macroeconomic stabilization (monetary, fiscal and exchange-rate policies) and structural adjustment (privatization, deregulation, wage and price decontrol and trade and financial liberalization) programmes affect vulnerability to CHEs. These

programmes, almost universal among LDCs (1979–2000) were mostly introduced in response to chronic macroeconomic imbalances and external
deficits, often associated with negative or slow growth. The primary
emphasis is on programmes of the IMF and WB, which set conditions and
provide financing for stabilization and adjustment, and whether changes in
these programmes can reduce the risk of CHEs.

The research by Cramer and Weeks examines the suitability of orthodox
macroeconomic policies, often required by the IMF, WB and the US
Treasury as conditions for loans to countries in international economic
crises. What are the goals of the policies prescribed by international
financial institutions (IFIs): returns to lenders and other creditors, inflation
reduction, economic growth or widespread improvement of economic
welfare? In highly vulnerable states, do IMF and WB policies counter or
reinforce tendencies towards tensions and social conflict?

In Chapter 3, FitzGerald examines the effects of globalization on the risk
of conflict, especially among least developed countries (LLDCs), the poorest
countries of the world. For these vulnerable countries, globalization has
entailed growing trade liberalization, increased capital mobility, rising debt,
falling export commodity prices and purchasing power, declining foreign
aid, small shares of foreign direct investment (FDI), and more stringent
policy conditions set by international economic institutions. FitzGerald
asks whether these international economic factors have exacerbated the
likelihood of emergencies among vulnerable countries and, if so, what
resulting changes should be made in the international economic system.
To what extent do external influences exacerbate wealth inequality, economic disintegration, economic insecurity and state failure that are the
roots of conflict? Can we use information about external linkages and vulnerability to predict where CHEs are most likely to occur?

In Chapter 4, Toye asks whether a lack of basic services reduces the legitimacy of the state and increases the risk of CHEs. Providing more services
requires an increase in tax revenues, a difficult concern given the administrative and political constraints in LDCs. Toye assumes that fiscal strength,
together with corresponding expenditures on health, education, infrastructure and defence, promotes economic growth and state legitimacy and
cohesion. These outcomes reduce the likelihood of rebellion and increase
loyalty to the state.

Toye assumes a poor and vulnerable economy, similar to Ethiopia, with a
history of rampant corruption, development failure and political instability. His central question is: How can government increase tax revenues and
enhance state legitimacy? The author proposes value-added tax (VAT), a tax
on the difference between the sales of a firm and its purchases from other
firms, as a solution.

Berry (Chapter 5) argues that a major economic source of CHEs is conflict
over agricultural land. For Berry, famines result from production shortfalls
combined with conflict over the distribution of goods. Rural political vio-

lence often originates from land disputes or restiveness from the landless. Moreover, unequal land distribution contributes to poverty and inequality, which correlate with poor infrastructure, poor health and educational services and other variables that increase the probabilities of emergencies. Accordingly, one potential preventive measure is equitable land distribution together with policies supporting small-scale agriculture. Where land distribution is highly unequal, reducing vulnerability to CHEs may require agrarian reform. Berry discusses agrarian reform, land distribution and what pitfalls to avoid, indicating also the political prerequisites for successful reform and conflict reduction. He draws on a wide array of cases, including Korea, Taiwan, Japan, China, India (Kerala and West Bengal), Bangladesh, Vietnam, Cambodia, Egypt, Iran, Rwanda, Burundi, Kenya, Nigeria, Ethiopia, Central America, Cuba, Colombia, Bolivia, Peru and Mexico.

After an extensive discussion of degradation, sustainability and vulnerability, Kibreab (Chapter 6) asks whether protecting environmental resources reduces the vulnerability of low-income countries (LICs) to potential CHEs. He argues that the welfare of rural people is inextricably linked with the well-being of the environment. The myriad consequences of land degradation, such as decline in crop yields, forest produce and pasture resulting from overcultivation, overgrazing, deforestation, siltation and waterlogging, constitute vulnerability that threatens those living on the edge of disaster. These people are stripped of their safety net, the buffer against the slow onset of CHEs triggered by natural or man-made misfortunes. Protected environmental resources constitute bulwarks against stress. Indeed, these resources do not prevent man-made or natural crises. Nevertheless, protected resources reinforce the ecological resilience of users, enabling them to withstand, cope with and recuperate from crises.

Kibreab also identifies specific environmental protection or regeneration programmes that can reduce the vulnerability to emergencies of individuals, households and communities. In his last section he examines whether policy-makers can reduce vulnerability to deadly conflict by protecting the productive capability of the environment.

In Chapter 7, Väyrynen distinguishes between short-term and long-term strategies to prevent the outbreak and escalation of CHEs. While both types of strategies need to be based on adequate early warning of deadly political violence, the effective implementation of preventive action is the requirement for success. He also distinguishes between 'remote' and 'hands-on' strategies. Remote approaches, such as military deterrence and economic sanctions, are imposed from the outside, while hands-on strategies require engagement in the zone of conflict.

For Väyrynen, short-term measures usually rely on political and military means (for example diplomatic mediation and preventive deployment of military forces). Long-term strategies of prevention call for a systematic involvement in the economic and institutional peace-building of the country vulnerable to war and political violence. Important elements of long-term strategies include the strengthening of democratic institutions and power-sharing, control of the spread of weapons, redistribution of land and its ownership, and stabilization of the external economic position of the target country. However, none of these strategies will be successful unless local civil society resists authoritarian government, becomes strong and pluralistic, and takes responsibility for putting the country back on track.

Sandbrook, in Chapter 8, probes the efficacy of democratization in forestalling CHEs in poor and deeply divided societies. He analyses the pathology of a particular syndrome of a CHE with four mutually reinforcing processes: rising communal tensions, an increasingly predatory and incapacitated state, a stagnating economy with growing levels of absolute poverty, and environmental degradation. This syndrome suggests institutional challenges that democratization may help threatened societies to overcome. In principle, democratization promotes institutional reforms through constitutionally prescribing procedural norms and organization and empowering civil society to defend its cherished formal institutions. Whether new democracies survive and foster institutional reform depends heavily on astute statesmanship, as well as a country's structural conditions and historical legacy. Nonetheless, Sandbrook's discussion of failures, such as Sudan, and relative successes, such as Ghana, yields a few guidelines on the conditions under which democratization, as one element of a larger preventive programme, may mitigate a downward spiral into a CHE.

Hveem's contribution in Chapter 9 focuses on the policy-making processes and institutions of the major donors: the European Union (EU) (with emphasis on France), the US, Japan and Norway. Hveem investigates and compares which factors and actors shape the policies of those that experience CHEs. He argues that policies need to be evaluated according to their response to demands for efficacy, justice and legitimacy. The chapter pays particular attention to how actors handle issues such as multilateral and national coordination of policy-making and implementation, early warning and preparedness, and setting priorities for assistance among crisis theatres. Furthermore, Hveem examines whether humanitarian aid is a supplement or substitute for development assistance, and vice versa.

Hveem finds that donor willingness to provide resources for emergency aid has levelled off or receded after its peak in the early 1990s. This trend can be attributed to donors' negative experiences with past emergency operations (the 'Somalia syndrome' in the US), a general aid fatigue caused by tighter finances, and the failure of NGOs or the media to raise awareness. Donor plans have little meaning without a willingness to intervene. The chapter ends with policy recommendations.

Chapter 10, by DeMars, asks whether international NGOs promote early warning and conflict prevention. The answer varies, depending on the ability of NGOs to analyse information, the unintended effects of actions by NGOs with objectives other than conflict prevention, whether the Third

World state is collapsing, and the inadvertent power of NGOs relative to combatants in collapsing states. The first section argues that NGO roles are essential to the new conflict prevention agenda in the foreign policy of major powers and the UN. Their bureaucracies rely on NGO alliances to control downsizing, maintain global scope and innovate techniques for confronting new problems. The second section identifies structural limitations on NGO effectiveness, suggesting that the inadvertent side-effect of NGO action in collapsing states may be more important than the intended effects. The third section summarizes the challenge for achieving effective conflict prevention. Despite their limitations, promoting NGO involvement in emerging crises allows policy-makers to limit cost and risk, maintain engagement, gather information and generate future policy options. As a consequence, DeMars contends that some variant of 'throwing NGOs at the problem' is often the best available policy option for conflict prevention.

Weiss, in Chapter 11, develops a theoretical framework of costs and benefits of outside military interventions after massive human tragedies. According to Weiss, most discussions of 'military-civilian humanitarianism' (the coming together of military forces and civilian aid agencies to deal with the human suffering from emergencies) consist more of exchanging invectives than arguments. Weiss addresses the following question: Is it possible and worthwhile to use the military in conjunction with humanitarian action to thwart violence and mitigate civilian suffering? Evidence from the first half-decade after the Cold War indicates that, despite the lack of political will, the level of multilateral military operations could change to the benefit of war victims. The author examines success in northern Iraq and Haiti, and valuable contributions in Rwanda and (arguably) Somalia and Bosnia. These five cases of multilateral military operations and humanitarian action in war zones after the Cold War lay the groundwork for an inductive framework to assess outside military involvement and its accompanying costs for intervening countries; in this assessment, Weiss considers the magnitude of a country's humanitarian tragedy and the impact on civilians after the intervention.

In Chapter 12, Clapham defines a role for human rights and human-rights workers in preventing CHEs. Human-rights law, monitoring and information can be useful in two ways: first to warn of an impending emergency, and second as part of resolving the crisis. Too often scholars and policy-makers assume that human-rights issues should drop out of the picture. Clapham shows *why* human rights are downgraded as imperatives at certain stages of the discussion, and *how* using human-rights principles and reports can assist in tackling emergencies effectively. While human-rights violations are clearly important indicators of a potential CHE, the human-rights and humanitarian aid communities remain worlds apart. The chapter examines problems faced by human-rights personnel in Rwanda, Liberia, Mozambique and the former Yugoslavia. The author looks at how to enhance rapid response at the beginning of a crisis, report on human rights and tackle impunity and the legacy of the past. He indicates that the human-rights movement is a crucial resource in analysing CHEs. UN reform opens up the possibilities for integrating human-rights work into global efforts to prevent CHEs.

The rise and fall of humanitarianism as a paradigm in international relations is examined by Donini in Chapter 13. Donini looks at humanitarianism as an imperative, as a 'mobilizing myth', and as a contemporary form of containment. He shows how these three dimensions have altered our conceptualization of North–South relations. Using concrete examples from Afghanistan, Liberia, Sierra Leone and elsewhere, he reviews the evolution of humanitarian practice in the post-Cold War years, attempts to define the function of humanitarian assistance in the context of globalization of the economy and the failure of development models, and proposes paths for policy-makers and practitioners. The chapter analyses the role of humanitarian aid in peace operations and discusses the advantages and disadvantages of mixing politics and relief, particularly during delicate peace consolidation. Furthermore, Donini argues that short-term strategies in countries of crisis are recipes for failure and that the new paradigm, which is waiting to emerge, must be based on a strategic vision integrating politics, relief and development for the long haul.

Finally, in Chapter 14, Väyrynen summarizes major strategies for preventing emergencies. According to Väyrynen, the most effective approach to prevention is to address the domestic causes of CHEs through socioeconomic development, environmental protection, low income and land inequality, secure usufruct and property rights, tax reform to finance social services, inclusive and participatory political systems, and accountable public administration and political institutions. A major obstacle to socioeconomic progress is a root cause of humanitarian emergencies, undemocratic and predatory rule.

International preventive strategies, although secondary to domestic policies, may still be indispensable for providing financial and political support to internal reforms or intervening where those controlling the state are the source of deadly political violence. For Väyrynen, the toolbox for DCs, the UN and other international agencies includes human-rights monitoring, well targeted economic sanctions, development aid to reduce export instability, IMF and WB policies oriented towards growth and equity, debt reduction for heavily indebted LDCs, and the opening of DC markets to LDCs.

Väyrynen reiterates Chapter 7's emphasis on long-term strategies, arguing that too often governments and multilateral agencies do not focus on a conflict until after it is already too late for effective prevention. DCs and international agencies need to tackle the root causes of emergencies early. Both domestic governments and the international community need to create a 'culture of prevention' in national and international decision-making.

Notes

1. GDP is output before subtracting either capital consumption or destruction. Net domestic product figures, by convention, include capital consumption but *not* capital destruction.
2. SSA's real GDP per capita was lower in the late 1990s than it was at the end of the 1960s. Moreover, since 1990, the sub-Saharan life expectancy has stagnated, primarily due to the high adult prevalence of HIV/AIDS (World Bank 2000).
3. Stewart *et al.* (2000b) indicate that Africa had by far the greatest number of deaths (direct and indirect) from conflict, from 1960 to 1995, as a proportion of the 1995 population, 1.5 per cent, compared to 0.5 per cent in the Middle East, 0.3 per cent in Asia and 0.1 per cent in Latin America.
4. Ake (1996: 1, 18) reinforces this contention when he states that for Africa, 'the problem is not so much that development has failed as that it was never really on the agenda in the first place. ...[W]ith independence African leaders were in no position to pursue development; they were too engrossed in the struggle for survival'.
5. Felipe (2000) indicates that parts of East and Southeast Asia experienced a 'lost decade' centred on the Asian financial crisis (1997–99), similar to Latin America's lost decade of the 1980s and that of SSA in the 1980s (perhaps extending to the 1990s). The question is whether the most vulnerable Asian economies – Indonesia, Lao PDR, Vietnam, Cambodia, Myanmar and the Philippines – will face the downward spiral of negative growth, political decay and further negative growth that parts of SSA have faced.
6. The new international system, created in 2000, to certify all diamonds sold on international markets is an example of cooperative action intended to reduce the access of warlords to money financing their military operations. However, as of early 2001, international sanctions are weak and legislation by major consuming nations, such as the United States, is riddled with loopholes. Vested interests opposed to or ambivalent about an effective global agreement include Ukraine and African countries that launder diamonds smuggled from war zones, producing nations that fear damage to legitimate producers, and an industry concerned about controlling supply.

1
The Political Economy of Preventing Humanitarian Emergencies

E. Wayne Nafziger

1.1 The scope of this chapter

This chapter focuses on long-term policies to prevent emergencies, linked to an analysis of root causes. It emphasizes economic approaches: stabilization, adjustment and reform; aid and debt relief; foreign investment; institutional change; safety nets for the poor; reduction of inequalities; and food and agriculture. A political economy approach includes economic analysis but also examines the interests of political leaders and policy-makers who make economic decisions, and of members of the population (domestic or foreign) who are affected by these decisions.

While the chapter discusses policies to reduce the risk of emergencies in LDCs, it recommends concentrating resources on SSA and other highly vulnerable economies (see Table 1.1). Many measures that prevent CHEs are also worthwhile for other reasons, such as increasing economic growth and reducing poverty.

1.2 Long-term preventive responses

Sections 1.3–1.5, on international factors, discuss the policies of international agencies, bilateral donors, private firms and NGOs, in concert with LDCs, in reducing the risk of emergencies. Section 1.6 focuses on how building economic and political institutions, including democratic governance, tax collection, infrastructure and land and capital markets diminishes the likelihood of CHEs. Sections 1.7–1.9 examine how LDCs' policies to affect income distribution, poverty reduction and food security can reduce vulnerability to emergencies.

The discussion of international factors in reducing LDC vulnerability to CHEs does not imply that the world community is the major source of the problem.[1] Indeed, Auvinen and Nafziger (1999) find[2] that World Bank (WB) funding as a percentage of GNP is unassociated with CHEs, and IMF funding as a percentage of GNP inversely related or not associated with CHEs.

Table 1.1   Economically most vulnerable countries (GNP per capita (1995) less than US$3100, with negative per capita growth (1985–95))

GNP per capita, less than US$750	*GNP per capita, US$750 to less than US$3100*
Afghanistan*	Algeria
Albania	Belarus
Angola	Bulgaria
Armenia	Estonia
Azerbaijan	Iran*
Benin	Iraq*
Bosnia & Herzegovina	Jordan
Burkina Faso	Kazakhstan
Burundi	Korea, Dem. Rep.*
Cambodia	Latvia
Cameroon	Lebanon*
Central African Republic	Lithuania
Congo-Brazzaville*	Macedonia*
Congo-Kinshasa	Moldova*
Côte d'Ivoire*	Panama
Eritrea*	Peru
Ethiopia	Russia
The Gambia*	Romania*
Georgia	Slovak Republic
Haiti	Turkmenistan*
Kyrgyz Republic	Ukraine
Liberia*	Uzbekistan
Madagascar	Yugoslavia*
Malawi	
Mongolia	
Myanmar*	
Nicaragua	
Niger*	
Rwanda	
Sierra Leone	
Somalia*	
Sudan*	
Tajikistan*	
Togo	
Vietnam*	
Yemen, Rep. of*	
Zambia	
Zimbabwe	

Note
* growth estimated by author
Source: World Bank (1997b: 214–15, 248)

1.3   Stabilization, adjustment and reform

1.3.1   Greater international support for domestically planned macroeconomic stabilization and structural adjustment

Stagnation and decline in incomes exacerbate the feeling of relative deprivation, defined as peoples' perception of social injustice from a deprivation relative to other groups in society or a discrepancy between goods and conditions they expect and those they can get or keep (Nafziger and Auvinen 2000; Gurr 1970). Slow or negative growth puts ruling coalitions on the horns of a dilemma. They can expand rent-seeking opportunities for existing political elites, contributing to further economic stagnation that can threaten the legitimacy of the regime and future stability. Or they can reduce the number of allies and clients they support, risking opposition by those no longer sharing in the benefit of rule. Either strategy, amid economic crises, can exacerbate the potential for repression and insurgency and, ultimately, CHEs.

Economic stagnation, frequently accompanied by chronic international balance on goods and services deficits and growing external debts, intensifies the need for economic adjustment and stabilization. A persistent external disequilibrium has costs whether countries adjust or not. But non-adjustment has the greater cost;[3] the longer the disequilibrium, the greater is the social damage and the more painful the adjustment. Nafziger and Auvinen (2000) indicate that countries that failed to adjust were more vulnerable to a CHE. Non-adjustment can contribute to poverty, displacement and humanitarian crises, as in the former Yugoslavia and Algeria in the 1980s and early 1990s. Woodward (1995) blames the Yugoslav conflict on the disintegration of government authority and breakdown of political and civil order from the inability to adjust to a market economy and democracy. Yugoslavia's rapid growth during the 1960s and 1970s, fuelled by foreign borrowing, was reversed by more than a decade of an external debt crisis amid declining terms of trade and global credit tightening, forcing austerity and declining living standards. In Algeria, the lack of adjustment, stabilization and growth in the 1980s strengthened Islamist party opposition, which recruited substantially among discontented unemployed young men for terrorism (Morrisson 2000).

More than a decade of slow growth, rising borrowing costs, reduced concessional aid, a mounting debt crisis, and the increased economic liberalism of donors and IFIs, compelled LDC elites to change their strategies during the 1980s and 1990s. Widespread economic liberalization and adjustment provided chances for challenging existing elites, threatening their positions and contributing to increased opportunistic rent-seeking and overt repression. And cuts in spending reduced the funds to distribute to clients and required greater military and police support to remain in power.

Political elites in Africa and other LDCs faced increasing pressure from slow growth and international debt crises, as well as external pressure by donors and IFIs to liberalize and privatize. Pressures to cut the size of the state, amid shrinking resources, put substantial constraints on the ability of elites, particularly in Africa, to reward and sanction political actors, contributing to greater instability and the potential for CHEs.

All these changes increased the potential for political instability and a CHE. More FDI and more coherent long-term aid programmes to increase the LDCs' own planning for macroeconomic stabilization, structural adjustment and government spending would reduce the vulnerability of these countries' leaders to domestic discontent.

1.3.2 Changes in the Bretton Woods institutions' goals, instruments and openness

This section discusses changes in goals, instruments (especially trade and external capital-market liberalization), and the transparency of adjustment programmes of the Bretton Woods institutions, the IMF, and the WB. In these institutions, the collective vote of high-income OECD countries comprises a substantial majority of the total.[4]

i) **Goals** Although stagnation, a current-account deficit and inflation are components of a macroeconomic disequilibrium, IMF stabilization programmes in LDCs focus on the last two components, while neglecting stagnation.[5] Bruno and Easterly's (1998) study for the WB shows no negative correlation between inflation and economic growth for inflation rates under 40 per cent annually. Indeed Stiglitz (1998: 8) argues that below this level, *'there is little evidence that inflation is costly'* [his italics]. This implies, as Cramer and Weeks (Chapter 2) argue, that the focus of IMF orthodox programmes on inflation (often draconian monetary measures) is usually unnecessary, and that reviving growth should generally take precedence over monetary and fiscal orthodoxy.

Indeed, as long as the IMF continues its orthodox emphasis, one essential reform is to strengthen independent financial power within the world economy – independent of the IMF Good Housekeeping seal for stabilization programmes required before the WB, OECD governments or commercial banks will provide loans, debt writeoffs and writedowns and concessional aid. Stiglitz (1998), as a WB economist, argues against stabilization programmes designed to reduce annual inflation below 15 per cent, simple rules for deciding the optimal level of budget deficits, financial liberalization without the construction of a well-functioning regulatory system, and adjustment without paying attention to building new economic institutions.

For Cramer and Weeks, the 'evidence [is] that adjustment did not stimu-late recovery in LICs'. The WB, in its 1992 overview of adjustment, identified growth as the 'long-term objective' and discussed 'moving from adjustment to growth'. Indeed, for the Bank, the aim of adjustment loans 'is to support programs of policy and institutional change to modify the structure of an economy so that it can maintain its growth rates and the viability of its balance of payments' (ibid.).

The poorest countries, primarily SSA, that are most vulnerable to conflict and war, would benefit from the expansion of funding from Japan, the EU or its member states, or from banks or regional development banks inde-pendent of two sides (the IMF and US government) of the triangle of the Washington institutions' lending and policy cartel.[6] Official donors and lenders, with their emphasis on democratization, political stability and socioeconomic development, and their provision of project and humani-tarian aid, have a broader agenda than the IMF's priority on the balance of payments (or even the WB on development and adjustment). Thus, donors should not condition funds on the recipient country's stabilization agree-ment with the IMF. Bilateral agencies (and the EU) need to be more active in designing and monitoring the programmes they co-finance with the IMF and WB. In addition, the monitoring by bilaterals should be separate, or at least supplementary, to that of the IFIs (Aguilar 1997).[7]

ii) Trade liberalization In the long run, liberal international trade is a source of growth (Sachs and Warner 1997;[8] Frankel and Romer 1999; and Nafziger 1997). However, Greenaway *et al.* (1997) show that, in the short run, trade liberalization by LDCs in the 1980s and 1990s is associated with a deterioration in growth.[9] Trade liberalization amid stabilization, even if politically possible, may perpetuate a government budget crisis. As Mosley *et al.* (1991) argue, given labour and resource immobility, early liberaliza-tion of external trade and supply-side stimulation in 'one glorious burst' results in rising unemployment, inflation and capital flight, and the subse-quent undermining of adjustment programmes. Frequently, the WB has asked for liberalizing trade early without limiting the imports that it should be applied to. For example, in Kenya in 1980 the foreign-exchange require-ments associated with trade liberalization, the major component of the Bank's first structural adjustment loan, became unsustainable, thus liberal-ization had to be abandoned.

Trade-reform failures such as these are consistent with the theory of the second best. An application of this theory suggests that trade liberalization while other prices are still controlled may be worse than having all prices distorted. Trade liberalization, a desirable goal over time, needs optimal sequencing to contribute to growth.

iii) External capital-market liberalization The IMF pressures LICs for rapid external capital-account liberalization (Fisher 1997). Mosley *et al.* (1991) and FAO (1991) suggest the following more gradual sequence for trade, exchange and capital-market liberalization: i) devaluing domestic currency to a competitive level, while simultaneously restraining monetary and fiscal expansion to curb inflation and convert a nominal devaluation to a real devaluation, ii) liberalizing imports of critical capital and other inputs, iii) promoting exports through liberalizing commodity markets, subsidies and other schemes, iv) instituting prudential regulations and other financial-sector reforms, v) allocating foreign exchange for maintaining and repairing infrastructure for production increases, vi) removing controls on internal interest rates to achieve positive real rates, and expanding loans agencies to include farmers and small business people, vii) reducing public sector deficits to eliminate reliance on foreign loans at banking standards without decreasing real development spending, and reforming agricultural marketing to spur farmers to sell their surplus, viii) liberalizing other imports, rationalizing the tariff structure, and removing price controls and subsidies to the private sector, and ix) reducing external capital-account controls.

This sequence recognizes the necessity of reforming internal capital markets before liberalizing international capital movements. Despite the IMF recognition of exceptions (Mussa *et al.* 1999), IMF recommendations and implementation put too much emphasis on opening capital markets to external flows in early stages of capital-market reforms. Taiwan, Colombia (Cardeñas and Barrera 1997), Chile, and Malaysia have used a prudential and regulatory framework, together with controls or surcharges on short-term capital to decrease reverse capital flows, thus reducing the cuts in import capacity, government budget and social expenditures that threaten the stability of ruling political coalitions. On the other hand, abrupt financial liberalization, with its increased vulnerability to short-term capital flights and non-performing bank loans, rarely provides the short-term vehicle for rapid growth that helps support LDC regimes to maintain political power (Cornia and Lipumba 1999; Mkandawire 1999; and Mosley 1999).

iv) Open debate Cramer and Weeks contend that the Bretton Woods institutions' programmes need to be subject to open debate before agreements with governments, so as to reflect the priorities and perceptions of the host country. Avramovic (1991) argues that: 'Adjustment and development programmes should be prepared, and seen to be prepared, by national authorities of [the] countries rather than by foreign advisors and international organizations. Otherwise commitment will be lacking'. Transparency and substantial local contribution should reduce the social tension accompanying adjustment that sometimes contributes to the political instability that portends CHEs.

Aguilar (1997: 13) finds that 'experience suggests that programs with a high degree of ownership on the part of the government have a higher probability of success'. Still, he recognizes that the host country, with a shortage of skills, may lack the qualified people to analyse the programme.

Or the government, under pressure from donors, may lack the political will to be accountable for designing the structural programme, and would prefer for IFIs to be the scapegoats for essential contraction, reallocation and restructuring. Open discussion with ministers, civil servants, parliamentarians and the public so that they are aware of the contents of the programme increases the responsibility of the host country and the probability of its success.[10]

v) High-income OECD countries' interests These modifications of goals, instruments and policies regarding openness of Bretton Woods institutions, especially for the IMF, would not only enhance the economic development of LDCs but also, through economic linkages, the prosperity of DCs as well. An IMF and international economic system that emphasize economic growth rather than price stability (that is, less than 15 per cent inflation annually), abrupt trade and financial liberalization and short-term adjustment[11] would potentially reduce economic stagnation and collapse, and the risk of CHEs. The most important catalyst for this shift in emphasis would be the IMF and its majority shareholders, the US and other DCs.

1.3.3 Reduction in trade barriers against Africa and other LDCs, to reduce external vulnerability and provide more scope for export-led growth, thus decreasing vulnerability to political instability and potential emergencies

LICs face constraints on expanded international trade and integration to spur growth and stability. While the IFIs often require that individual countries undertaking adjustment expand the export of existing primary products, low price and income elasticities of demand for these exports limit the potential growth for all adjusting countries combined. Moreover, even after the Uruguay Round of 1986–94, the DCs' effective rates of protection against LDC agricultural, manufacturing and processing exports are still high (World Bank 2001). Indeed, the higher the stage of processing, the greater the DCs' effective protection against LDCs. Furthermore, the Multifiber Arrangement (MFA) allows DCs to limit 'disruptive' textile and clothing imports from LDCs through 2005. And in agriculture, the net producer subsidy equivalents for wheat exports were 44 per cent in the US, 46 per cent in the EU, and 99 per cent in Japan, with even higher rates for rice, milk and other basic farm products (UNCTAD 1994).[12]

The Lomé conventions between the EU and 66 ACP countries included reductions in trade barriers against an important component of the developing world. These agreements were implemented in 1975, 1980, 1985, 1989 and 1995 (expired in 2000). The conventions have allowed freer access to the EU for many ACP products, mechanisms for stabilizing foreign exchange earnings from certain commodities and minerals, and a channel for EU aid.

EU trade preferences to ACP under Lomé, however, breached the rules of the WTO, established in 1995, which administers rules of conduct in international trade. But even if the EU could have obtained a waiver for a new Lomé, its renewal would only be beneficial under limited circumstances. For liberalization under the WTO/GATT's Uruguay Round of tariff reductions and textile quota elimination from 1992 to 2005 was eroding ACP's Lomé convention privileges. The Uruguay Round, while generally beneficial to LDCs because of the lowered trade barriers against their exports, resulted in the displacement of African exports in EU markets by Asian competitors (Hertel *et al.* 1998). After 2000, post-Lomé agreements, consistent with WTO rules, provide trade preferences to ACP LLDCs but not to other ACP countries, which are required to negotiate reciprocal trade preferences.[13]

1.4 Aid and debt relief

1.4.1 Aid to vulnerable economies

Since the late 1980s, the real value of aid – that is, official development assistance (ODA), bilateral or multilateral funds with at least a 25 per cent grant element – has fallen overall, but at an even faster rate in the case of that to LLDCs (OECD 1997a). Still, as FitzGerald (this volume) indicates, ODA/GDP in LLDCs from 1988 to 1994 was 25 per cent, equal to 111 per cent of the LLDCs' domestic capital formation.

Auvinen and Nafziger (1999) find that ODA is not associated either positively or negatively with CHEs. Indeed many poor countries are hampered by a high dependence on aid.[14] This dependency includes food and commodity aid that competes with domestic production and, for some LLDCs, aid-flows large enough to contribute to an overvalued domestic currency that is biased against exports.

When donors underwrite most of the development budget, they insist on continual, extensive project supervision and review, so that recipient government agencies are more answerable to them than to their own senior policy officials. Donors frequently recommend and supervise poorly conceived projects. But even when well conceived, officials in poor countries fail to learn how to do something until they have the power to make their own decisions. The proliferation of donors and requirements has resulted in weakened institutions and reduced management capacity. For example, in 1981 Malawi, lacking the indigenous capacity to manage 188 projects from 50 different donors, hired donor-country personnel (sometimes with donor-salary supplements) to take government line positions to manage projects. However, Malawi was not able to increase its capacity to run its own affairs and establish its own policies (Morss 1984). Tanzania, on the other hand, retained its best economic analysts at home in the late 1980s and early 1990s, but 'the price of keeping top professionals at home [was] to see them absorbed into the domestic consultancy market, sustained by donor-driven programmes of [technical assistance]' (Sobhan 1996: 119). Sobhan (1996) points out that the opportunity cost of this co-option by the donors was diversion from contributions to teaching and domestic policy debate and initiative. But the cost of aid in reduced domestic initiative and technical learning may be even greater for other highly vulnerable LICs than for Malawi or Tanzania.

However, the problem is not so much the size of aid-flows as the manner in which ODA is given and utilized. Aid-flows to poor countries are complicated by high conditionality, and 'are both volatile and unpredictable' (FitzGerald, this volume). To reduce the risk of conflict, aid needs donor coordination reflecting long-term programme coherence and an orientation toward increasing productive capacity, providing infrastructure and reducing poverty and communal inequality. Donors also need to emphasize aid to ruling groups, economic classes and communities that have strong economic incentives to increase political integration and reduce the potential for conflict and repression (ibid.; Edgren 1996).

1.4.2   Cushioning the effects of sudden external shocks

Research shows that abrupt external shocks can contribute to stagnation or precipitous slumps, increasing vulnerability to political disintegration and CHEs (FitzGerald, this volume).[15] An external debt crisis, with declining terms of trade, global credit tightening, and falling debt relief and concessional aid from the West, forced austerity and declining living standards in Africa in the 1980s and early 1990s, putting additional pressure on its government authority and its political and civil order.

The IMF's compensatory and contingency financing facility is used to finance a temporary shortfall in export earnings or to bolster IMF-supported adjustment programmes. However, this facility is a drop in the bucket compared to the need to rescue countries such as African LICs that experience temporary external shocks. Despite limited funding, the EU's Stabex, which covered primary products from 66 ACP countries from 1975 to 2000, was a more effective programme for cushioning external shocks. But in 2000, the EU discontinued Stabex, folding it into a general aid programme combining support for adjustment, project aid, good governance and price stabilization (Brown 2000). Discontinuance was wrong, as DCs need to provide a larger share of loans and concessional aid to reduce the vulnerability of LICs to external shocks and potential political instability.

1.4.3 Rescheduling and writing-down debt

Highly indebted poor countries (HIPCs) owe almost their entire debt to official bilateral or multilateral creditors. HIPC creditors can probably reduce relative deprivation from the distress of the poor and vulnerability to CHEs by decreasing the HIPC's high debt–service ratio. The HIPCs' 1985–94 *scheduled* debt–service ratio was 64 per cent, with the ratio *actually paid* at 22.2 per cent (UNCTAD 1997a), meaning that more than one-fifth of annual export receipts was used to pay debt servicing. Reducing the debt overhang not only removes a major barrier to investment (Deshpande 1997), but also increases the adjustment time horizon, so that political elites, many of whom have inherited their debt burden from previous regimes,[16] have time to plan more stable structural changes.

Since 1990, Chancellor and (subsequently) Prime Minister John Major and Prime Minister Tony Blair (with Chancellor Gordon Brown) have taken the initiative, in advance of other G8 nations, in rescheduling the entire stock of debt owed by African LICs to Britain in one stroke, increasing their debt cancellation, and stretching and increasing the flexibility of the repayment schedule of the fraction of their debt remaining. NGOs and churches in Britain, and subsequently its government, with Brown's 1997 presentation of a Commonwealth 'Mauritius Mandate' calling for firm decisions on debt relief for at least three-quarters of the eligible HIPCs by 2000, helped spur a movement for the Jubilee 2000 debt remission for selected HIPCs.[17] In 2000, the US approved debt relief of US$435 million for HIPC nations.

The WB/IMF HIPC initiative, begun in 1997, usually required successful adjustment programmes for three to six years, after which Paris Club official creditors would provide relief through rescheduling up to 80 per cent of the present value of official debt (UNCTAD 1997a). In 1999, an enhanced HIPC initiative reduced the requisite successful adjustment programme to three years before promising relief. The WB and IMF, in principle, maintained the conditions (sound macroeconomic policies and improved governance) for debt writeoffs. Still, by the end of 2000, the IMF and WB, with a flurry of activity and under pressure from Jubilee 2000, had provided (or were scheduled to provide) concessional funds based on profits from lending and the sales of gold to begin the three-year process of reducing the debt of Benin, Bolivia, Burkina Faso, Cameroon, Gambia, Guyana, Guinea, Guinea-Bissau, Honduras, Madagascar, Malawi, Mali, Mauritania, Mozambique, Nicaragua, Niger, Rwanda, São Tomé and Principe, Senegal, Tanzania, Uganda and Zambia. However, since the G8 failed to commit to front loading debt writedowns, the immediate effect in decreasing actual debt-service payments, once the debtor meets conditions, is small. Moreover, reducing debt payments in later years will depend on uncertain private and government donations to HIPC funds.

The DCs' and IFIs' continuation of writing-down debt, liberalizing trade and increasing aid to counter external shocks could spur HIPC leaders to undertake further political and economic reforms, at least in some of the countries listed above, if not to Sierra Leone, Liberia, Sudan, Congo (Kinshasa) and Côte d'Ivoire, where political conflict or blatant corruption precludes even minimally effective capital utilization. Indeed, in predatory states such as Sudan and Sierra Leone, the ruling elite and their clients 'use their positions and access to resources to plunder the national economy through graft, corruption, and extortion, and to participate in private business activities' (Holsti 2000: 251).

The immediate cost to DCs of a programme similar to Jubilee 2000 for non-predatory states is negligible. Efforts to 'wipe the slate clean' for selected HIPCs could free political leaders, especially in Africa, of their inherited debts, and provide some breathing space to enable them to focus on long-range planning and investment to improve general welfare and reduce their vulnerability to CHEs.[18]

1.5   Investment

As discussed previously, external deficits are costly, increasing pressures on LDC political elites to reduce government expenditures, thus limiting the ability of elites to attain stable ruling coalitions. As real aid to LDCs fell during the 1990s, FDI and other private flows have comprised an increasing portion of resource flows to LDCs. Indeed, in 1995 private flows consisted of 56 per cent (of which FDI was 21 per cent) of total net resource flows by OECD countries to LDCs (OECD 1997a).

The WB (1997a: 2) states that 'participation in the global production networks established by multinational corporations (MNCs) provides LDCs with new means to enhance their economic performance by accessing global know-how and expanding their integration into world markets'. Indeed, private capital flows to LDCs soared to US$245 billion, or 4.5 per cent of their GDP, in 1996, a four- to five-fold increase as a percentage of GDP since 1990. But the share of the poorest countries with low credit ratings (especially SSA), fell during the same period (World Bank 1997a), a continuation of a fall that began in the early 1980s (FitzGerald, this volume). In addition, private capital flows are highly volatile, especially in countries that have liberalized their financial markets. After the 1997–98 Asian crisis, for example, private capital flows to LDCs fell substantially.

More than half of private capital flows to LDCs are loans, which contribute to future debt service, and portfolio investments, which are subject to reverse capital flows. FDI does not generate debt servicing or capital outflows, and can potentially finance a savings or balance-of-payments deficit, transfer technology to increase productivity, fill some shortages of high-level skills, provide training for domestic managers and technicians, generate tax revenue from income and corporate profits tax, and complement local entrepreneurship by subcontracting to ancillary industries, component makers or repair shops, or by creating forward and backward linkages.

Investment inflows as a percentage of gross fixed capital investment in Africa were 7 per cent in 1995. However, while annual FDI flows to LLDCs (those highly vulnerable to CHEs) tripled between 1986 and 1990, and 1991 and 1996, LLDCs' share of LDC inflows was only 1.8 per cent (UNCTAD 1997a). Moreover, LICs other than China accounted for only 5.9 per cent of the US$99 670 million FDI flows to LDCs of 1995 (ODI 1997).

Still, there is a possibility of attracting FDI to LICs, not just to those with potentially large markets, such as China and India, but with non-resident nationals, as China or India, with resident nationals managing cross-border investments, as in Malaysia, Mozambique, South Africa or East Africa,[19] or with extractive industries like Nigeria or Angola. Vietnam introduced FDI legislation in 1987–88, which together with the lifting of US economic sanctions in 1994 increased FDI inflows from US$8 million in 1988 to US$150 million in 1995. Bangladesh's FDI reforms in 1991, which facilitated the establishment of foreign-owned subsidiaries, increased inflows from just a trickle in the 1980s to US$125 million in 1995. Ghana, as a result of Ashanti goldfield privatization, increased annual FDI inflows seventeen-fold from a US$11.7 million average during 1986–92 to an average of US$201 million in 1993–95 (ODI 1997). Chad could receive substantial investment in petroleum, pending a WB loan facilitating an 1100-kilometre pipeline from landlocked Chad through Cameroon to an Atlantic Coast terminal. Even Cambodia, which created a legal framework and the necessary institutions to promote FDI after 1993, increased its FDI capital inflows from virtually nothing in 1990 to US$656 million in 1996 (UNCTAD 1997a).

Since the mid-1980s, with falling trade, transport and communication barriers, MNCs have increased their international outsourcing, importing components from low-cost production locations abroad and exporting to overseas assembly or processing locations. As an example, following the rise of the yen after 1985, Japan's major electronics manufacturers outsourced assembly and other final stages of output to Asian countries (World Bank 1997a). Japanese companies' borderless economic system of trade and investment selected sophisticated activities, including R&D-intensive industries for the newly industrializing countries (NICs) (South Korea, Taiwan, Hong Kong and Singapore), while assigning labour-intensive production and assembly with standardized technologies to China and the ASEAN four (Indonesia, Malaysia, the Philippines, and Thailand). Indeed, in 1993, Malaysia was third to the US and Japan in producing semiconductors, and the world's leading exporter of computer chips. These companies used a flying-geese pattern, with Japan at the lead, the NICs toward the front, and the ASEAN four close behind (Nafziger 1997).

An example of this global seamless network, Sony, has factories for audio, television and video products and parts in the NICs, Thailand and Malaysia, its major distribution warehouse in Singapore, and linkage of these units online with Japanese, US, European and Southeast Asian companies as well as important cooperating firms (Shojiro 1992). In a similar fashion, an automobile produced in the US embodies labour, assembly operations, small and advanced components, styling and design engineering, advertising and marketing services and data processing from scores of units, in both LDCs and DCs, around the world.

With institutional changes (see below), a number of LICs could begin participating in the new international division of labour created by outsourcing by high-income OECD countries. But this flying-geese pattern may also apply to non-OECD leader countries. ECA (1989) estimates that, during the 1980s, Southern African Development Community (SADC) countries other than South Africa lost one-quarter of their GDP from South Africa's destabilization. However, since 1994 a democratic and prosperous South Africa should provide the economic leadership to spur SADC's economic development. South Africa, with its trade and FDI (including from MNCs), could serve as a 'growth pole' for other SADC members of the region – Angola, Botswana, Lesotho, Malawi, Mauritius, Mozambique, Namibia, Swaziland, Tanzania, Zambia and Zimbabwe (UNCTAD 1997b).

Of course, FDI is not a panacea. Malaysia and Thailand have sacrificed their economic autonomy to participate in producing less sophisticated, labour-intensive, low value-added production in an internationally organized division of knowledge. Their short-run prosperity from integration within this external system came at the expense of the technological learning and skill acquisition essential for rapid growth near the turn of the twenty-first century. Aoki (1992) mentions the lack of indigenous mastery of industrial technology, the few Malay entrepreneurs and the substantial shortage of skilled workers, technicians, and engineers as major obstacles to Malaysia's future growth. For Morris-Suzuki (1992), some major barriers to Thailand's prospective development are the concentration of technological transfer within MNCs, the lack of innovation and adaptation by Thais, and the falling R&D capability. Indeed, Malaysia and Thailand have emphasized peripheral intermediation in technologically complex industrial industry rather than indigenous innovation and technology generation in less complex industry that provides more scope for gains from learning.[20]

However, LDCs need a policy to increase FDI and other external resources. In 1988, the WB established the Multilateral Investment Guarantee Agency (MIGA) to help LDCs attract foreign investment. MIGA provides investors with marketing services, legal advice and guarantees against non-commercial risk, such as expropriation and war (Aguilar 1997). In addition, LDCs need to undertake major institutional changes, not only to facilitate foreign and domestic investment but also to provide the scaffolding for other economic policies that reduce a country's vulnerability to CHEs.

1.6   Economic and political institutions

1.6.1   Institutions

Economic policies are no better than the institutions that design, implement and monitor them (Aguilar 1997). Stabilization and adjustment programmes, foreign aid and foreign investment are not likely to be effective in spurring a country's economic development and reducing the risk of CHEs if economic and political institutions are poorly developed. Building institutions and investing in infrastructure are essential to spur investment by nationals and foreigners in directly productive investment projects. LICs and other vulnerable countries need to develop a legal and judicial system, monetary and fiscal institutions, capital, land and exchange markets, a statistical system, and a civil society independent of the state to achieve the development to reduce the risk of CHEs.

North (1997: 2) indicates that 'institutions are the rules of the game of a society composed of the formal rules (constitutions, statute and common law, regulations), the informal constraints (norms, conventions and internally devised codes of conduct) and the enforcement characteristics of each. Together they define the way the game is played'. Sandbrook (this volume) defines political institutions as the 'rules of the game that shape the behaviour of people when they contest and exercise power, as well as their, and the general public's, expectations regarding the actions of others.'

Many LDCs lack the economic institutions and governance structures (efficient and transparent administration and legislature, enforcement of contracts and property rights) of highly institutionalized democratic countries that reduce capriciousness, predatory behaviour and potential conflict. Sandbrook stresses building the rule of law, constructing an effective, efficient and non-partisan civil service, circumscribing the patronage system so that it does not destroy the productive economy, and instituting accountability at all levels, a daunting task of reform. LDCs need a legal and judicial system with such components as trademarks, registration of signed contracts, letters of credit, contract law with stipulated penalties for non-performance, product liability suits, corporate and enterprise legislation, and a police force to enforce against theft, fraud and violation of contracts (Lin and Nugent 1995).[21] Certainly, neo-patrimonial or predatory rulers may not be interested in this reform, as it would eliminate an important source of patronage (Sandbrook, this volume). But a political elite interested in accelerating growth and reducing vulnerability to emergencies should put a priority on legal and bureaucratic reform.[22]

In most LICs, land, capital and credit, insurance, and forward and other exchange-rate markets are poorly developed. As discussed below, land markets should assign property rights to cultivators, but without undermining usufruct rights for traditional community or village land-rights systems. Exchange markets that increase the efficiency of transactions not only enhance growth but external adjustment, thus reducing political instability.

Macroeconomic stability is enhanced by a robust capital market and financial system, which select 'the most productive recipient for [capital] resources [and] monitor the use of funds, ensuring that they [continue] to be used productively' (Stiglitz 1998: 14). Government needs to develop a bond market to facilitate raising resources for social spending and economic development. Also important is a central bank, with a director and staff chosen for their technical qualifications, and who use economic criteria for making decisions about monetary expansion (Uche 1997). However, Singh (1999: 341, 352) argues that while improving the banking system is important for increasing LICs' savings and investment, a stock market is 'a costly irrelevance which they can ill afford'; for most others, 'it is likely to do more harm than good', as its volatility may contribute to 'financial fragility for the whole economy', increasing 'the riskiness of investments and [discouraging] risk-averse corporations from financing their growth by equity issues'.

LICs need to expand social overhead capital to increase the productivity and attractiveness of both domestic and foreign private investment. This includes investments in infrastructure such as transport (roads, railways, coastal shipping, ports, harbours, bridges and river improvement), communication (telegraph, telephone and postal services), electronics, power, water supply, education, extension, research in science and applications of technology to commercial practice, and trade fairs and exhibitions. A high-quality communications system with competitive prices is essential to increase the productivity and propensity to invest. The state plays a major role in making investments in transport, communication, education and science.

A major investment in infrastructure is the development of a statistical service, with timely, accurate and comprehensive data, which is widely accessible to relevant publics. For example, LDCs need poverty and income distribution data to provide safety nets and more even development (see below). The database should be national in coverage, comparable across time and place, and include household surveys or censuses, with information on non-cash income such as food and other goods produced at home (Fields 1994; Nafziger 1997). In addition, if investors and the public had access to better information, LDCs would not continue unsustainable policies of bad debts to banks or exchange transactions of the banking system (Fischer 1998).

1.6.2   Improving the state's capability to collect taxes and provide basic services

One important institutional capability is the capacity to raise revenue and provide basic services. In several LICs, such as Sierra Leone, Liberia, Sudan and Somalia, the state has failed to provide minimal functions such as defence, law and order, property rights, public health (potable water and sewage disposal), macroeconomic stability and protection of the destitute, to say nothing of intermediate functions such as basic education, transport and communication, pollution control, pensions, family allowances and health, life and unemployment insurance (World Bank 1997b). Countries whose fiscal positions are deteriorating and can no longer provide basic functions face an increasing risk of CHEs. A vicious circle of declining legitimacy, fiscal mismanagement and the further erosion of legitimacy from a decline in public services can contribute to a country's emergency; examples include Russia, Georgia, Tajikistan and Mengistu's Ethiopia. Governments need to maintain or re-establish a social compact with all their citizens, including the poor, in which some basic needs are met in return for tax contributions according to the ability to pay. One way to increase legitimacy and raise tax revenue is to replace widely evaded direct taxes, such as personal income taxes, with indirect taxes, such as a VAT. The appeals of the VAT are simplicity, uniformity, the generation of buoyant revenues (from a high income elasticity), and the enabling of a gradual lowering of other tax rates throughout the system (for example, the lowering or elimination of the distortions of a cascade tax, such as the simple sales tax that takes a straightforward percentage of all business turnover, so that tax on tax occurs as a taxed product passes from manufacturer to wholesaler to retailer).

The most frequently used approach for levying the VAT is the subtractive-indirect (the invoice and credit) method. Under this approach, the firm issues invoices for all taxable transactions, using these invoices to compute the tax on total sales. But the firm is given credit for the VAT paid by its suppliers. To a substantial degree, the VAT is self-enforcing, as the firm has an incentive to present invoices to subtract the VAT on purchases from the VAT on sales; these invoices provide a check on VAT payments at earlier stages, and reduce leakage from cheating or corruption. In Turkey, an additional cross-match is by consumers who, with receipts for purchases, can offset a proportion of the VAT paid on their retail purchases against their income-tax liability.

However, VAT faces administrative problems, especially among the numerous retailers in LICs. The costs of compelling compliance among these retailers, who may pay for their purchases out of the till and keep no records of cash transactions, are substantial relative to the tax collected. So despite the distorting effect on capital, enterprise and resource allocation, LICs often have to levy taxes that are simpler to administer such as corporate taxes, taxes on international trade, where goods pass through a limited number of ports and border crossings, taxes on sales by manufacturers, where numbers are fewer and control is easier, or taxes on luxuries,[23] as many of these countries lack the capability to administer, collect, audit, monitor and hear appeals from VAT payers and evaders (Nafziger 1997). In the final analysis, governmental legitimacy requires the capability of levying taxes and providing basic services, even when, at the margin, this is at the expense of efficiency and private savings (Toye, this volume).

Building economic institutions and infrastructure, including a well-regulated tax system, is essential for spurring investment to increase the economic growth and stability to reduce the risk of CHEs.

1.6.3   Democratization

CHEs often result from the abuse of political power and are virtually non-existent in established democratic societies. But emergencies occur in societies making the transition from authoritarianism to democracy (Collier 1998; Väyrynen 2000a; Sandbrook, this volume), including the electoral democracies with few civil and political freedoms that have abounded in Africa in the 1990s as 'virtual democrac[ies],...deliberately contrived to satisfy international norms of "presentability"' (Joseph 1998: 3–4). The opposition parties, free press, labour unions and strong civil society needed to support a transparent, accountable democratic society were still lacking (Joseph 1998).

Indeed, democratically elected regimes 'are routinely ignoring constitutional limits on their power and depriving their citizens of basic rights and freedoms' (Zakaria 1997: 22). Strongmen in these illiberal democracies create electoral rules of the game to divide, co-opt and subdue the opposition, maintain private armed forces and death squads, and detain political opponents in ways that distort democratic institutions (Zakaria 1997; Joseph 1998; Barkan and Njuguna 1998; Gyimah-Boadi 1998).

Clientalism or patrimonialism, the dominant pattern in Africa, is a personalized relationship between patrons and clients, commanding unequal wealth, status or influence, based on conditional loyalties and involving mutual benefits (Nafziger and Auvinen 2000). For Sandbrook and Oelbaum (1997), patrimonialism is associated with the power of government used to reward the rent-seeking behaviour of political insiders, the ruler's acquiescence in the misappropriation of state funds and the non-payment of taxes by political cronies, the distribution of state jobs by political patrons to followers (with corresponding incompetence, indiscipline and unpredictability in government positions), and the non-existence of the rule of law.

While 'even at its best, liberal democracy is inimical to...people having effective decisionmaking power', Ake (1996: 42, 130) argues that in many LICs, the state tends to become privatized, appropriated by the political elite.

Amid state-building in Africa and other socially heterogeneous patrimonial societies, Ake (1997: 2) sees widespread conflict and emergencies (including famine) as almost inevitable, since:

State-making is perhaps best understood as the political equivalent of primitive accumulation, except that it is more violent still. It entails conquest and subjugation – conquest, because the state power which is projected in the process is arbitrary power since those on whom it is projected originally owed no political allegiance to the state makers. State-making entails revoking the autonomy of communities and subjecting them to alien rulership within a bigger political order, laying claim to the resources of the subordinated territory including claims over the lives of those who live there. To effect these claims, the state must appropriate and monopolize the means of violence.

Given this process of state building, Sandbrook (this volume) contends that democratization, the movement from authoritarian to democratic rule, is a highly disruptive process. Democratization, or the 'process of getting to stable democracy', can trigger conflicts 'to manifest themselves freely, but without the restraints of the checks and balances, and of agreement on the basic rules that regulate conflict' (Ottaway 1995: 235–6). Democratic contestation can heighten inter-ethnic mistrust, animosity and polarization (Sandbrook, this volume), contributing to a CHE.[24] However, one-party and military governments are even less adept than newly democratizing states at avoiding ethnic conflict. Moreover, democracies can manage ethnic divisions, facilitating compromise, inclusion and cooperation across cleavages, if their institutions encourage consensual governance rather than 'winner-take-all' approaches (ibid.). For Kohli (1997), the key is for democracies to accommodate movements for communal or ethnic self-determination. While mobilized groups in a well-established democratic state with firm but accommodating leaders are likely to confront state authority, 'such movements eventually decline as exhaustion sets in, some leaders are repressed, others are co-opted, and a modicum of genuine power sharing and mutual accommodation between the movement and the central state authorities is reached' (ibid.: 326).

Democratization includes the growth of institutions independent of the state: private and non-governmental entities such as labour unions, religious organizations, educational and scientific communities, and the media. These components of civil society are crucial in developing mediation and problem-solving for reducing the risk of CHEs (Carnegie Commission 1997).

Sandbrook and Oelbaum (1997: 643–6), while conceding that 'institutional performance is shaped by traditions established over many years', contend that donor pressure for liberalization and democratic governance, even with deeply rooted patrimonialism, may facilitate the gradual institutional change essential to support economic development. In a democratic society, where power is dispersed and 'there is rule of law, equal opportunity, accountability of power, and a leadership sensitive to social needs, primary group identities [and enmities] will be less appealing. In such circumstances, [economic collapse and] humanitarian emergencies are less likely to occur' (Ake 1997: ix).[25]

1.7   Safety nets for the poor

As indicated in the Introduction, there may be a fine line between an emergency and endemic poverty. Indeed, Morrisson (2000) shows that where there is already serious poverty, CHEs can occur during stabilization programmes that include high price increases for food bought by poor households and the absence of a safety net in the adjustment programme. Moreover, harsh repression of political discontent following an adjustment programme can trigger a limited humanitarian emergency, which however can be avoided by improving the sequence of timing (for example, avoiding abrupt changes reducing the living standards of the poor) of adjustment and by compensatory transfers to poor households.

Adjustment and stabilization programmes need to provide compensatory transfers or other safety nets for the incomes and livelihoods of weaker segments of the population – the poor, minorities, rural and working people, and women and children – to avoid pushing them below the line between endemic poverty and an emergency. Funds to reduce the short-term costs of adjustment need to be expanded, including moneys for public works, food-for-work projects and retrenched public-sector workers, as well as nutrition, potable water and healthcare for disadvantaged classes. These programmes, if timely and well targeted, will help garner popular support for the necessary adjustment and reduce the society's vulnerability to hunger, disease, displacement and even CHEs.

Therefore, it might be expected that donor or lender support (through IFIs or OECD government concessional funds) for provision of social funds can contribute to poverty reduction and the political sustainability of the adjustment process. For example, under the WB structural adjustment programme in Ghana in 1988, a Programme of Action to Mitigate the Social Costs of Adjustment (PAMSCAD) provided funds for public works and food-for-work projects to reduce the immediate harm to retrenched public-sector workers from privatization programmes, designed to increase productivity in the long run (Nafziger 1993; Morrisson 2000). Yet as Stewart and van der Geest (1998) show, retrenched and redeployed public-sector employees who were relatively well off benefited substantially, while poor households benefited little.

Indeed, a survey (ibid.) of ten LDCs undergoing adjustment during the 1970s and 1980s indicates that only social funds programmes designed and funded domestically have been successful in reducing vulnerability to hunger, disease and displacement. In contrast, external programmes have usually failed.

Those schemes that have succeeded (all in the 1970s) included Botswana's employment programme during severe drought, Chile's emergency employment effort during economic stagnation and rising unemployment and poverty, Costa Rica's social spending targeted at the poorer segments of the population, and in India, Maharastra state's employment guarantees on demand. These schemes, which utilized self-targeting through low wage payments for unskilled work, were effective in alleviating poverty and reducing vulnerability to hunger, disease and displacement from adjustment. Yet, while these programmes were funded domestically, the success of externally funded programmes if domestically designed and sensitive to locally specific needs should not be ruled out.

1.8 Reduction of inequalities

1.8.1 Uneven development between regions and ethnic communities

Communal factors contributing to conflict include educational differentials, regional and ethnic employment differentials, inter-regional revenue allocation and language discrimination, which disadvantages minority language communities. Examples include the struggle for petroleum tax revenues and employment in the civil service and modern sector in Nigeria in the early to mid-1960s, the distribution of resources from East to West and employment discrimination against Bengalis in Pakistan in the 1950s and 1960s, the conflict between Hutu and Tutsi for control of the state and access to employment in Burundi and Rwanda, the conflicts over the distribution of falling economic resources and rising debt obligations in Yugoslavia in the 1980s and early 1990s, and the language, employment and educational discrimination by the state against Tamils in post-independent Sri Lanka.[26]

In Africa, differences in regional and ethnic opportunities for employment and asset acquisition during the waves of indigenization of the 1960s and the 1970s, and privatization of the 1980s and the 1990s have been important sources of conflict.

Policies include targeting programmes for the poorest regions and communities and employment and educational preferences for disadvantaged communities. India has an affirmative action programme favouring the placement of outcastes and other economically 'backward castes and tribes' in educational institutions and government positions. A number of countries, including India, use industrial incentives and subsidies to help economically backward regions and train business persons from underprivileged groups. Upgrading housing in blighted urban areas can increase real income among the poor. Finally, some LDCs, in a reversal of the policies of the 1950s, 1960s and 1970s, have stressed development in the rural areas where most poor live. Undertaking these policies to reduce the risk of conflict requires not only economically feasible programmes, but also coalitions of interest groups – employers, government agencies, educators and members benefiting directly – to support economic opportunities for members of disadvantaged communities.

1.8.2   Educational inequality

The World Bank (1996a) shows that, on average, LICs, particularly SSA, spend substantially more on education for households in the richest quintiles than those in the poorest ones. Although secondary and (especially) university education is highly subsidized, the private cost is still often a barrier to the poor. Providing free, universal primary education is the most effective policy for reducing the educational inequality that contributes to income inequality and political discontent. Near-universal primary education in Kenya, Uganda, Ghana, Nigeria and Zambia has dampened some discontent in these countries, while the low rates of primary school enrolment in Ethiopia, Mozambique, Angola, Sierra Leone, Rwanda, Burundi, Congo, Somalia and Sudan have perpetuated class, ethnic and regional divisions and grievances in educational and employment opportunities.

Still, virtually universal basic education is not a panacea. In Sri Lanka, with continuing high enrolment rates in primary and secondary schools, the majority Sinhalese perception of Tamil economic success as a threat to their own economic opportunities increased during the period of slow growth and high unemployment after independence in 1948. This perception contributed to governmental policies of educational, language and employment discrimination against Tamils, beginning in the mid-1950s, which contributed to the Sri Lankan civil war of the last quarter of the twentieth century. Thus, in Sri Lanka educational policy favoured the majority community.

Generally, however, expanding educational opportunities for low-income minority regions and communities can reduce social tension, political instability and the potential for a CHE. Politically, the support for expansion in education, especially basic schooling, can come from educators and peasant and working-class constituents whose children lack access to education, and nationalists who recognize the importance of universal literacy for national unity and labour skills for modernization. Examples of these coalitions supporting universal basic education include Meiji Japan (Nafziger 1995) and Africa in the 1960s.[27]

1.9   Food and agriculture

1.9.1   Agrarian reform and land redistribution

In most societies, land is the most important asset that families either have or aspire to having. Land inequality contributes to low incomes and income inequality (Binswanger *et al.* 1995), which are major sources of CHEs in LDCs. A long-simmering set of tensions due to inequality in the distribution of land provided the tinder for internal wars in El Salvador, Guatemala and Nicaragua. As Pastor and Boyce (2000) show, El Salvador's agrarian structure is indicative of the tensions that contribute to political

violence: a highly unequal land distribution combined with a proletarian-
ized labour force, maintained in the face of popular resistance by 'intimida-
tion, bloodshed, and other forms of organized violence' perpetuated by the
ruling oligarchy that controlled the state (ibid.: 368). El Salvador's 1992
peace accords included a land-transfer programme to benefit ex-combatants
for both the government and the rebel Farabundo Martí National
Liberation Front (FMLN), but unfortunately the programme was delayed
and too small to serve as a model for other countries.

Land reform and redistribution, with relatively low ceilings on parcel size,
the inclusion of tenants and landless workers, and a good package of complementary measures such as infrastructure credit and technical assistance, can
potentially reduce rural discontent. Indeed, land distribution in the early
1950s in Japan, Taiwan and South Korea, coupled with credit and extension
services for small farmers, contributed to the later widespread rural prosperity
that reduced vulnerability to political violence. In India, in contrast to the
states of Punjab, Haryana, Bihar, Orissa, Andhra Pradesh, Assam, Meghalaya
and Nagaland where rural unrest festered in the midst of the absence of
significant land reform and redistribution, Kerala undertook radical, comprehensive land reform and redistribution in the 1970s that reduced the number
of discontented landless or land-poor people (Berry 1997).

Land reform has frequently failed because of the political opposition of
landlords, the transfer of holdings to relatives, or because the new
landowners lacked access to credit, water, fertilizer, extension assistance
and other services. The WB and many OECD donors are willing to support
market-assisted land reform, where willing buyers negotiate deals with
willing sellers, in the hope, usually illusory, that 'government would facilitate the process by providing incentives to potential sellers and by helping
potential buyers to acquire the means to buy.' The WB also sees market-
assisted reform as feasible during a 'farm debt crisis when land prices are
depressed' (World Bank 1996a: 15). But, besides these situations, which are
rare, for political reasons the WB and external donors have usually failed to
support this most fundamental 'structural' adjustment in agricultural land
redistribution.

Frequently, however, land redistribution is not to the cultivator, the
landless worker or tenant, but to urban elites and affluent farmers who are
influential with political elites. Distributions by East African governments
from Europeans to Africans are examples of this problem. Zimbabwe's
current land distribution emphasises the politically connected rather than
the cultivators. And from 1954 to 1974, Kenya replaced the colonial land
tenure system with a new system whereby Africans acquired land from
whites in the central and western highlands. The government purchased
land from the former owners and redistributed land to Africans under the
'one million acre settlement programme'. Thousands of hectares were
transferred to Africans through land settlement schemes, large-scale indi-

vidual purchases, land buying companies and cooperatives. The landless, however, were not the main beneficiaries. Indeed, many tenants, squatters and other landless peasants were evicted with land privatization. For the political leadership redistributed most of the land to itself, allies and clients, many of whom had no experience in farming. The Kenyan case illustrates how politics can limit the success of programmes that ostensibly redistribute land to the cultivator.

Still, the examples of Japan, Taiwan and Korea indicate the potential for land reform, if accompanied by non-farm output and employment growth, to reduce agrarian discontent. Where there is political will, land redistribution, along with credit and services for small farmers, can reduce poverty and inequality in agrarian societies and their vulnerability to CHEs. Moreover, Besley and Burgess (2000) show that where vested interests block land redistribution, more modest agrarian reform, such as reform of the terms of tenancy and the abolition of intermediaries between owner and tenant, has a major impact in reducing rural poverty. In addition, donors and international agencies can often provide the necessary extra resources, making land redistribution or at least tenancy reforms feasible.

1.9.2   Secure property and usufruct rights for traditional community or village land-rights systems

Property rights usually assign the rights to and rewards from using resources to individuals, thus providing incentives to invest in resources and use them efficiently. Given the high cost of supervising agricultural wage labour, allocating land rights to owner-operators would generally increase the efficiency of farm production (Binswanger and Deininger 1997).

However, private property rights do not always produce the most efficient farming arrangements where information costs are high and markets for finance and insurance are imperfect (ibid.). Moreover, the emphasis by IFIs and African elites on the abrupt shift from traditional use rights to individualized titling from purchases and sales in a land market has reduced agricultural efficiency, torn safety nets for the poor, and increased risk. Under most traditional community or village systems, farm families not only have inheritable use rights to cropland, pastures and forests, but these land rights are highly transferable. These systems provide tenure security at low cost, therefore not discouraging individuals from investing in the operation (ibid.). Agricultural intensification from population growth gives rise to pressure for increasingly formal private property rights. But the precipitate registering of individualized land titles, in the name of modernizing land-rights systems, reduces tenure security in the short run, as the number of land disputes surges, as rural masses, unaware of the implications of registration, are outjockeyed by clever, well-informed and powerful individuals. Women especially face difficulties in having their customary rights recognized by political authorities. And in the longer run, the high costs of land registration and lack of familiarity with the government bureaucracy displace weak or politically marginalized groups, and redistribute land to the commercial and estate sectors, increasing the concentration of land holdings. As an example, Kenya's systematic, compulsory individualized titling of all farmlands since the 1950s contributed to a substantial gap between the control of rights reflected in the land register and recognized by most local communities, providing opportunities for affluent town-dwellers to establish property rights through land registration. In Nigeria, since 1960, under cover of national development projects, state officials granted extensive land tracts to friends, dispossessing many villagers from their customary lands. Redistribution through individualized titling on demand not only increased inequality but also reduced labour intensity, capital formation and innovation contributing to the inverse relationship between farm size and yields (Berry, this volume; Platteau 1996; Cornia 1994), and the potential for agrarian discontent and humanitarian crisis.[28]

In Ethiopia, political conflict, land insecurity and environmental degradation form a vicious circle, which contributes to further conflict. The insecurity and conflict of the past quarter of a century has compelled people to concentrate in safer zones, thus intensifying the process of degradation of the available local resources, particulary for those living on the razor-edge of survival (Kibreab, this volume).

In light of these problems, in SSA secure property and use rights usually mean maintaining the tenure security but highly transferable land rights of traditional community or village land systems. Secure property and usufruct rights not only contribute to safeguarding environmental resources and agricultural land productivity but also reduce the potential for CHEs (ibid.).

1.9.3 Aid for food and agricultural development

Auvinen and Nafziger's (1999) econometric analysis shows that slow food production per-capita growth is a source of CHEs,[29] with some feedback from emergencies to reduced food production. From 1960 through the early 1990s, food output per capita declined almost 1 per cent annually in SSA, contributing to Africa's vulnerability to hunger and famine. The real value of food aid dropped from the 1960s to the 1970s and 1980s, falling even further during the 1990s (Nafziger 1997; Pinstrup-Andersen *et al.* 1997). Given the reduction in other aid, the International Food Policy Research Institute (IFPRI) contends that:

> The substantial reduction in food aid deliveries...has disturbing implications for food security. The need for aid to combat food insecurity has not diminished. ...Food aid will have an important role for some years, not only in addressing humanitarian emergencies but also in directing

resources to many of the world's most vulnerable food-insecure people to help them permanently escape poverty and assure food security (Pinstrup-Andersen *et al.* 1997: 26).

Given these findings, DCs, especially the US, need to restore the real value of food aid to the levels of 1970–90 (or even the 1960s), with a priority to LLDCs. However, as IFPRI argues, donors should consider 'gradually replacing program food aid with increasing cash assistance for commercial food import', because of the high transaction costs of most food aid (ibid.).

Perhaps even more important than food assistance is long-term agricultural research and technology in LDCs. Only a small fraction of global agricultural research is spent on these countries. LDCs need their own research, since many of their ecological zones (particularly the arid and semi-arid tropics) are quite different from those of North America and Europe. Food grain growth in India, Pakistan, the Philippines and Mexico would not have exceeded population growth in the 1960s through the early 1990s without the investment in improved packages of high-yielding seed varieties, fertilizers, pesticides, irrigation, improved transport and extension.[30] LICs vulnerable to emergencies also need substantial agricultural investments. However, agriculture suffered disproportionately from the decline in LDC aid in the late 1980s and the 1990s as real aid to LDC agriculture declined from US\$19 billion in 1986 to US\$10 billion in 1994 (ibid.: 27). A priority for reducing long-term food insecurity and vulnerability to emergencies is for DCs to restore their agricultural technical aid to real levels in the 1970s and 1980s.

1.10 Conclusion

This chapter stresses long-term policies to reduce the risk of CHEs. International and domestic actors must take early preventive action, since options narrow and become more expensive once the conflict or emergency starts. As low average income, slow economic growth, and high income-inequality are important contributors to emergencies, policies need to strengthen and restructure the political economy of poor, economically stagnant and inegalitarian countries.

Preventive measures can be undertaken by a wide variety of actors – the country's civil society and government, transnational NGOs, DC governments and international agencies. OECD governments, the UN and IFIs must lead in providing support to reduce the risk of emergencies to SSA and other LLDCs where political elites are subject to the rule of law and accountability of power. In the late 1990s, providing international support for predatory rulers similar to Zaire's Mobutu Sese Seko and Nigeria's Sani Abacha proved harmful.

The major changes that LDC governments need to make are economic and political institutional changes – the development of a legal system, enhanced financial institutions, increased taxing capacity, greater investment in basic education and other forms of social capital, well-functioning resource and exchange markets, programmes to target weaker segments of the population and democratic institutions that accommodate and co-opt the country's various ethnic and regional communities. Institutional and infrastructural development increases the productivity of private investment and public spending, and enhances the effectiveness of governance.

DC governments, MNCs and transnational NGOs, as well as international agencies such as the UN, Bretton Woods institutions and the WTO, disproportionately dominated by DCs, bear substantial responsibility for modifying the international economic order to enhance economic growth and adjustment. While LDCs have lacked the power to compel DCs and international agencies to adhere to the declaration on principles and programmes of the United Nations General Assembly's (UNGA's) sixth and seventh special sessions (1974–75), LDCs can demand greater voice and consideration of their economic interests within present international economic and political institutions. LDCs, by working with their allies within the Nordic countries, the EU, Japan and the G8, the IFIs and WTO, and within UN agencies such as UNGA, UNCTAD, UNDP, UNICEF and regional agencies, can ensure that LDC economic and political interests are more strongly considered. These interests can generally be served by enhanced LDC flexibility and self-determination in designing paths toward adjustment and liberalization, a shift in the goals and openness of the Bretton Woods institutions (particularly the IMF), the restructuring of the international economic system for trade and capital flows, more technological transfer by foreign companies, bilateral donors and international agencies, a greater coherence of aid programmes, and increased international funding to reduce food crises, directly help the poor, ameliorate external shocks and write-down debt burdens. LDCs can use the Group of 15, Group of 20, Group of 77 UN and other fora to take initiatives and apply pressure to DCs to undertake these changes in the international order.

Since the policies of governing elites are at the root of most CHEs, and since usually some powerful factions in society benefit from emergencies, there may be a number of countries vulnerable to emergencies not amenable to political economy solutions. Yet a large number of countries vulnerable to emergencies have the will to change. Thus, there is substantial scope for international, national and non-governmental economic and political actors to coordinate their long-term policies to reduce the developing world's vulnerability to humanitarian emergencies.

Notes

1. While Nafziger (1988 and 1995) discuss how colonialism and imperialism in Africa and Asia contributed to their underdevelopment and political instability,

this issue is less relevant when we discuss policy and prevention. Henderson and Singer (2000) and Ayoob (1995) contend that contemporary CHEs emerge largely from the internal vulnerabilities of LDCs rather than from international factors.

2. Reinforced by Morrisson (2000).
3. A major contributor to non-adjustment is the distortion to both internationally and domestically traded goods from an overvalued domestic currency (Nafziger 1988).
4. The US view of policy for LDCs is the most dominant among high-income OECD countries. The US view (Summers 1998) corresponds closely to IMF policy, as the US alone has veto power over IMF loans. Indeed Thacker's econometrics (1999) provides 'strong evidence that the political interests of the US drive much of the behavior' of the IMF. See Nafziger (1995) on the OECD model for LDCs and the US's role in that model.
5. FAO (1991: 89) contends: 'An important aspect of [IMF] loans and their associated policies is that they do not present a growth package as such, ... [but] their primary role is to serve as a balance-of-payments support'.
6. The third side of the triangle is the WB (Nafziger 1993).
7. Ehrenpreis (1997) indicates that the Swedish International Development Cooperation Agency or 'Sida is planning to integrate [program-aid] support more closely with the over-all country strategy planning of development cooperation'. Sida is to define criteria related to the policy reform process without, however, setting the same conditions as the World Bank or IMF.
8. International trade is liberal if average tariff rates are below 40 per cent, average quota and licensing coverage of imports are less than 40 per cent, the black market exchange-rate premium is less than 20 per cent, and there are no extreme controls (taxes, quotas or state monopolies) on exports (ibid.). Rodriguez and Rodrik (1999) criticize the Sachs-Warner approach.
9. Lundberg and Squire (1999), who use Sachs and Warner's measure for openness, find that openness is negatively correlated with income growth among the poorest 40 per cent of the population of LDCs but positively correlated with growth among higher-income groups.
10. An open process may mean less draconian measures more fully supported by elites and the public, a trade-off probably beneficial for both the IFIs and the host country. See Dessus *et al.* (1998).
11. Nafziger (1993) discusses the short time-horizon of the IMF and, to a lesser extent, the WB.
12. Since 2000, the US has provided trade access to African countries, which open their markets to US trade and investment. While opening markets, especially for trade, should be part of a long-term policy goal, immediate trade and capital liberalization is likely to trigger further external economic crises, which increase the risk of political instability.
13. France and the EU also need to help the 14 francophone African countries that are members of the franc de la Communauté financièrede l'Afrique (CFA franc) zone to adapt to the introduction of the European Monetary Union (EMU), with its euro currency.
14. Riddell (1996) defines aid dependency as the process by which aid makes no significant contribution to self-sustained development. For my purposes, I would add that the aid makes no contribution to reducing vulnerability to war or CHEs.
15. FitzGerald shows the relationship between external shocks and CHEs, but is more sceptical than myself about the intermediate variable, per capita income stagnation or decline.

16. Ndikumana and Boyce (1998) argue that successor governments, such as those in Congo, should be able to repudiate their liabilities for prior predatory regimes' debts (for example, the spiriting by Mobutu of official borrowed capital for his personal accounts overseas) on the basis of creditor complicity in odious debt.

17. For a discussion of the various initiatives for debt reduction, conversion or rescheduling, see Nafziger (1993) and OECD (1997a).

18. UN Secretary-General Kofi Annan (1998: 6) has 'suggested that creditors consider clearing the entire debt stock of the poorest African countries while expanding the Highly Indebted Poor Countries program of the World Bank'.

19. See FitzGerald, this volume, on non-resident nationals and cross-border investments.

20. For a discussion of the costs and benefits of FDI, see Nafziger (1997).

21. Posner (1998) argues that poor countries that lack the resources for a costly, ambitious creation of a first-class judiciary or extensive system of civil liberties can support economic reform with more modest expenditures on substantive and procedurally efficient rules of contract and property.

22. See Ndikumana (1998).

23. Nafziger (1997) provides some cautionary notes, including a warning against a tax levied only on imports, which would stimulate domestic investment in luxury goods.

24. Raknerud and Hegre (1997) show that while democracies almost never engage in war against each other, in LDCs democracies are as prone as authoritarian countries to experience intrastate war.

25. Based on their empirical study and the citation of numerous others, Henderson and Singer (2000: 295) indicate 'that semi-democracy is associated with an increased likelihood of civil war'. They contend that 'full-fledged democracies...are less prone to civil warfare due to the availability of legitimate channels for dispute resolution' while '[a]utocracies are also resistant to civil war because their use of repression often stifles dissent and undermines potential insurgency' (ibid.: 279).

26. Urban unemployment is linked with ethnic conflict and CHEs in Sri Lanka, Somalia, the former Yugoslavia and late-1960s Nigeria (Nafziger 1996). In the 1960s, political thugs in Nigeria, including those used by the old Northern elite in September–October 1966, were recruited largely from the ranks of the unemployed. And the large number of unemployed, displaced and destitute persons in Eastern Nigeria, who were driven by pogroms in the North to their ethnic homelands, constituted a combustible and easily manipulated group for the pursuit of military mobilization, secession and territorial extension. However, because LDC unemployment data, where they exist, have large margins of error and are difficult to compare cross-nationally, and underemployment figures are virtually meaningless (Nafziger 1997), global generalizations concerning the relationship between underemployment and CHEs is lacking. Most likely, policies to increase growth and improve labour-market effectiveness (ibid.) will reduce the threat of unemployment as a tinderbox to war and emergencies.

27. Nafziger (1988: ch. 10) discusses the political barriers to universal quality education.

28. To avoid undesirable effects, Binswanger et al. (1995: 2721) recommend that 'titling programs should be accompanied by publicity campaigns to ensure widespread knowledge of the rules and procedures. Both equity and efficiency considerations argue that titling programs be systematic rather than on demand'.

29. When the growth of food production per capita in lieu of GDP growth was introduced into multiple regression models, it was found that the lack of availability

of food was important in generating wars or refugee flows. To preclude circularity, hunger or malnourishment was not included as a component of the dependent variable, CHEs.

30. In some regions of these countries, R&D of high-yielding varieties of wheat and rice in the 'green revolution' has had negative effects on income distribution, farm labour displacement, rural unemployment and environmental degradation. However, the overall impact, including the effect on incomes and food supplies, has generally been positive (Nafziger 1997). Pinstrup-Andersen *et al.* (1997) warn against misapplying environmental concerns about chemicals and fertilizers in DCs to LDCs. These countries, especially SSA, need expansion in their use of fertilizers.

Part I
International Economic Responses

2
Macroeconomic Stabilization and Structural Adjustment

Christopher Cramer and John Weeks

2.1 Analytical basis for policy recommendations

Claims that structural adjustment and stabilization (henceforth 'adjustment') programmes are directly responsible for conflict lack empirical support[1] and smack of economism. Yet, to the extent that economic forces contribute to the origins of CHEs, policy will affect the likelihood of such crises.[2] This chapter explores the role of adjustment policies in the origins of conflict, and the implications for economic policies, especially for designing WB and IMF adjustment.

The roots of CHEs are complex and historical. Isolating policy mechanisms or packages, either as cause or cure, is unlikely to enlighten policymakers, and is superficial. Using simple empirical laws is further clouded because the analytical categories of adjustment are ambiguous. As examples, inequality and outward orientation are too vague for intrastate or international comparisons, and CHEs cover a range of social instabilities.[3] Thus empirical laws of the effects of inequality on conflict, or ethnicity on economic performance, are flawed.[4]

The roots of CHEs are also multiple and historically deep. From protracted civil war in Afghanistan and Angola to localized urban and rural violence throughout India, LDC conflicts express the contradictions and tensions of late capitalist development. The spread of capitalism has always been uneven and has provoked social upheavals (Warren 1980). Capitalist development contains progressive potential, but also the seeds of conflict, because social development and major historical change are by their nature conflictual.[5] The origins and spread of capitalism have been closely associated with conflict – from the ties between war, state-making and capitalism in Europe (Tilly 1990) to the alleged role of capitalism in provoking peasant wars (Moore 1966; Wolf 1969; Scott 1976). The upheaval involved in capitalist development is intensified by its 'late' development.[6] In the industrializing economies of the late 20th century, there are two common tensions: those created by economic backwardness between the promise of industrialization and obstacles to spreading its benefits; and those from weak nation-ness, between a political entity conforming to international norms and the obstacles presented by social diversity (Anderson 1983). Conflicts often arise from this tension and response, taking the shape of rival coalitions based on appeals (sometimes coercive) to shared material interest and collective identity. Collective identity is not reducible to 'revealed' ethnicity, but may include clan, class, region, religion, or specific manipulations of ethnic histories or myths.

Tensions and varied responses have different outcomes. The social differentiation of capitalist development might undermine categories of 'belonging' or reduce identity-based rivalry.

Alternatively, differentiation might prove so disruptive that it generates regressive dependency on collective identities. While conflict is not a necessary outcome of given tensions in a society, the potential for conflict results from late capitalist development, material experience and identity ties, which preclude attributing the problem to methodological individualism or positivist models of causality. Conflict depends on government, for example, offering inclusive benefits or acknowledging claims arising from centralized resource mobilization. The scope for 'exit' from and 'voice' within a society largely determines the upheaval and increased tensions. Above all, every conflict and its origins are specific to historical conditions and particular relationships between structure and human agency. Thus appropriate conflict-averting economic policies are highly specific and difficult to predict. Nevertheless, we should identify general policy guidelines, which provide the start for analysing a country's economic policy.

Policy discussions arise from combining our analysis of late capitalist development with case studies. The next section critically examines links between IMF/WB policies and CHEs. Subsequently, links between IMF policies and low growth and conflict in SSA are examined. The case studies examine the effect of IMF/WB interventions on conflicts in Sierra Leone and Yugoslavia. The chapter's conceptual, cross-country and case-study analyses indicate how adjustment might be adjusted to minimize the fuelling of CHE fires.

The principal measures that reduce the likelihood of conflict are associated with raising growth rates (not merely 'getting prices right', as IFIs stress) and providing exit and voice. Exit and voice ensure that economic policy is not top-down, with exhortations to improve 'governance', but bottoms-up, through creating institutions for channelling participation upwards, as through trade unions.

2.2   Adjustment and the origins of conflict

The difficulties of generalizing about the effect of adjustment on cross-country economic performance include: unreliable or missing data, differences among countries undergoing adjustment, variations in the intensity of adjustment, variations in programmes, unpredictable timelags, and the impact of causal factors other than adjustment. Both proponents and critics of adjustment have exploited these difficulties. Given these, one must be wary of unsubstantiated claims that adjustment policies are likely to increase a country's risk of CHEs. Such claims, for example Mosley *et al.* (1995), typically derive from a general preconception that LDC economic problems have external causes. Here it is assumed that LDC conflicts, while constrained externally, have internal origins, and that CHEs result partly from economic causes, implying the need for reforming adjustment to minimize its exacerbating socioeconomic tensions as has been suggested in a WB report.[7]

The argument that IMF/WB adjustment contributes to CHEs has two parts: an association between IMF-type policies and political instability, and a link of CHEs to economic factors, which are associated with IMF and WB programmes. The causal link in Auvinen's (1996a, b) test of the link between IMF policies and instability is presumed to be IMF austerity in response to balance-of-payments crises. Auvinen suggests that IMF interventions contribute to political instability, and the longer the IMF involvement in a country the more extensive the instability. He further suggests that IMF interventions challenge the interests of politically influential groups. Similarly, Morrisson *et al.* (1994) argue, with qualification, that most measures associated with IMF/WB adjustment 'run the risk' of causing political tensions. Subsidy reductions, taxation increases, privatization and removal of commercial protection are measures that threaten the income and employment of either large numbers of people or, at least, of significant well-organized groups.

Auvinen and Nafziger (1999) suggest support for CHEs occurring in LICs that have been growing slowly, have high Gini coefficients, and a recent tradition of violence. They test hypotheses, rather than causality, both in the statistical sense and because of the complexities in assessing measures of cross-country inequality. Moreover, they find that IMF adjustment funding as a percentage of GNP is inversely correlated with CHEs, although causality may run from emergencies to low IMF assistance, rather than the other way round. Further, the evidence suggests complex interactions among variables, although their methodology cannot consider missing variables with potentially important causal effects. After correcting for auto-correlation, 'the relationship between growth and CHEs is weakened', the authors indicate, 'which may reflect the two-way causality between CHEs and growth; some of the impact of economic growth on [a variable measuring war deaths and refugees] is carried over from past interactions between war, refugees and economic growth' (ibid.: 280).

The literature on IFIs and political instability suggests economic outcomes or policies associated with the outbreak or deepening of conflict. Among the important factors are prolonged economic stagnation, relative deprivation, sharp declines in living standards, and undermining the privileges of elites (Nafziger and Auvinen 2000), each of which can be associated with IMF and WB adjustment. This evidence indicates that stabilization (through demand restrictions and other austerity measures) and adjustment (through the changes brought about by liberalization of markets and reduction of the role of the state), increase mobilization by threatened elites, which can take the form of populist, anti-democratic regimes. More generally, adjustment programmes undermine patronage within the state, which weakens political cohesion. Woodward argues that Bretton Woods' conditionality contributed to political upheavals in the former Yugoslavia, provoked by the shift towards a market economy during high external indebtedness, declining terms of trade, a reflux of previous emigrants and global credit tightening:

> [The] primary problem...lay in the lack of recognition and accommodation for the socially polarizing and politically disintegrating consequences of [the 1980s] IMF-conditionality program...The austerities of policies of demand-repression led to conditions that could not easily foster a political culture of tolerance and compromise (Woodward 1995: 383).

However, the argument that adjustment programmes contribute to CHEs might not withstand close inspection. First, the argument suggests that political instability is at one end of a continuum towards extreme social conflict such as civil war. This need not be the case. Food riots in Lusaka during the 1980s, in protest against cuts in subsidies conditional for an IMF programme, are not equivalent to the genocide and mass population displacement in Rwanda in the 1990s, or to prolonged warfare in Sudan. IMF and WB interventions may trigger riots or transitory protest without contributing to more serious emergencies. Indeed, transitory protests may serve as a one-off release of tension.[8]

Further, to always oppose political instability as bad indicates a defence of the status quo. 'Political instability' may be the prelude to overthrowing an oppressive regime. Had political stability been maintained, the apartheid regime might still rule South Africa, and Marcos or his successors might yet control the Philippines. Thus, when outside interests intervene in conflict, they cannot avoid value judgements about political legitimacy, equity and justice.

Second, it is expected that inequality generates conflict through relative deprivation or polarization, and that adjustment, when it increases inequality, contributes to conflict. But comparable and trustworthy cross-country data on inequality is lacking. Overemphasizing the relationship between polarization and conflict can obscure the nature of conflicts by suggesting that they are primarily class phenomena. Despite the rhetoric of participants, violence in the name of redressing inequities may involve localized retribution in the absence of increased wealth inequality (Cramer 1997).

Third, adjustment, especially by the IMF, challenges the interests of the politically powerful and well organized, such as the urban working-class.

Still, generalizations are difficult; for example, privatization may not under-mine elites but merely alter the form of their control, such as shifting rent-seeking from the public to the private sector (Castel-Branco and Cramer, forthcoming; Bayliss and Cramer 2001). Privatization and other measures associated with adjustment may undermine formal sector real wages and employment, but the effects vary across countries and may not be severe, depending partly on alternative opportunities in the informal sector.

Fourth, to assert that IMF programmes are at the expense of poverty pro-grammes and social safety nets is to overdramatize the contrast between IMF austerity (and regressive social policy) and pre-adjustment inclusive social policy and financial overheating. Often growth is slow and social programmes are in crisis before IMF reforms, thus weakening the argument for adjustment causing CHEs.

Fifth, whether stagnation and economic decline contribute to CHEs depends on the strength and direction of causality of other factors less amenable to measurement. Thus extended economic stagnation that weakens sections of the elite may provide both 'exit' and 'voice' strategies to mediate accumulating tensions (Hirschman 1970). Institutionalized mechanisms for channelling resentment into political and economic deci-sion-making may avert the violent expression of tension. When economic factors are combined with coercive mobilization of resources and groups attribute their disadvantage to collective identity, there will be a greater tendency towards conflict.

Were economic stagnation and severe declines in living standards sufficiently powerful causes of conflict, outbreaks of violence in Tanzania in the 1980s, Congo before 1997, and Cuba in the early 1990s would have been expected. Explaining why tensions there did not ripen into violence requires an analysis of a country's historical conditions. Indeed, as Trotsky (1996) argues, if deprivation or oppression were sufficient to cause rebel-lion, much of the world would be in permanent rebellion.

2.3 Evidence on IMF programmes and growth

The key question here is whether IMF programmes result in demand com-pression, and, therefore, lower economic growth. If they do not, then the link of IMF programmes and conditionality with conflict is weakened, unless programmes generate negative side-effects, such as a cornered elite or greater inequality. However, the link between conditionality and inequality is difficult to establish, given the complexity of distribution rela-tionships. If negative growth is demonstrated, then several Nafziger-Auvinen conflict-inducing mechanisms might follow: slow or stagnant growth and a decline in living standards.

To examine growth, Table 2.1 presents IMF programmes in SSA, which has a high incidence of conflict (see note 3 of the Introduction).[9] From 1979 to 1996, 40 countries had one or more programmes, with a total of

Table 2.1 IMF 'arrangements' in sub-Saharan countries (millions of SDRs), 1979–96

	1979	1980	1981	1982	1983	1984	1985	1986	1987	1988	1989	1990	1991	1992	1993	1994	1995	1996	Total SDRs (millions) by country	No. of years with IMF programme (of 18)
Benin											15.7				42.8			27.2	85.7	8
Burkina Faso													6.3		42.2			39.3	87.8	6
Burundi								27.1					19.2						46.3	6
Cameroon										46.4				8.0		21.9	28.2		104.5	9
Central African Rep.		4.0			4.5	11.5	7.5		16.2							10.7			54.4	11
Chad									21.4							10.3	49.6		81.3	6
Comoros													2.3						2.3	3
Congo								9.5				4.0				12.5		69.5	97.5	9
Côte d'Ivoire			484.5			30.1	53.0	24.0		7.0	117.4		33.1			333.5			1082.5	15
Djibouti																		4.6	4.6	1
Equatorial Guinea		3.0					5.4			3.7					4.6				16.7	8
Ethiopia			44.0											49.4				88.5	181.9	6
Gabon		0.0						73.1			7.5		4.0			23.2			107.8	11
Gambia	0.0			16.9		2.6		11.6		17.1									48.3	10
Ghana					238.5	150.0		16.4	138.5	729.1							164.4		1436.8	10
Guinea				11.5				15.0	29.0				46.3					70.8	172.6	11
Guinea Bissau									3.8								9.5		13.2	5
Kenya	0.0	90.0		90.0	176.0		85.0			82.0	216.2				45.2			149.6	933.9	15
Lesotho										10.6			18.1			0.0	-0.5	-0.5	27.7	7
Liberia	9.3	18.6	11.0	35.0	55.0	8.5													137.4	8
Madagascar		10.0	39.0	40.8		33.0			13.3	2.8	51.3							81.4	322.8	11
Malawi	3.1	22.0		22.0	76.0		26.3	25.0		70.6							45.8		239.5	15
Mali				30.4	40.5		16.3			38.1				79.2				62.0	266.5	14

Table 2.1 IMF arrangements in sub-Saharan countries (millions of SDRs), 1979–96 (*continued*)

	1979	1980	1981	1982	1983	1984	1985	1986	1987	1988	1989	1990	1991	1992	1993	1994	1995	1996	Total SDRs (millions) by country	No. of years with IMF programme (of 18)
Mauritania		8.9	10.3				9.6	29.0	10.0		17.0				33.9		42.8		161.4	14
Mauritius	20.0	15.0	7.5		49.5		49.0												141.0	7
Mozambique									42.7			115.4						75.6	233.7	10
Niger					5.2	12.8	10.8	22.9		47.2			0.0			11.1		58.0	177.9	11
Nigeria											0.0								0.0	0
Rwanda	0.0												8.8						8.8	3
São Tomé & Príncipe										0.8									0.8	4
Senegal	10.5	41.1	15.7	5.9	63.0		76.6	69.1	21.3	144.7						161.7			609.5	17
Sierra Leone	7.5		33.5			19.0		19.6								27.0			106.6	14
Somalia		6.0	25.9	60.0			2.0		5.5			8.8							108.3	9
Sudan	281.0			70.0	144.5	20.0													515.5	7
Tanzania		25.0						45.5	74.9				85.6					161.6	392.6	9
Togo	0.0	7.3		19.4		19.0	15.4	12.6		18.0	38.4					43.4			173.5	16
Uganda			77.5	112.5	65.0				49.8		219.1					120.5			644.4	12
Zaire	20.0		175.0		198.0		162.0	47.6	170.0		75.0								847.6	12
Zambia		300.0	0.0		76.5	80.0		35.0									181.8	701.7	1374.9	8
Zimbabwe					175.0									238.8					413.8	5
Total SDRs (millions) by year	2332.3	2223.6	3212.2	2477.0	3379.5	2370.5	2503.8	2468.9	2583.3	3205.2	2747.2	2118.2	2214.7	2401.4	2127.9	2769.9	2516.4	3585.1	47 236.9	
Countries per year	7	12	18	18	20	20	19	20	18	26	28	26	22	20	20	25	20	23		9.1 (average)

Notes: Shaded years indicate conflict. Dark borders indicate that the country had an IMF programme for more than six months. A dashed border indicates less than six months (these are omitted from the year count). Zeros indicate that a programme was agreed, but no funds used.

Source: Table provided with the research assistance of Degol Hailu

special drawing rights (SDRs) 47.2 billion. On average, each country operated under IMF conditionality for 9.1 years, slightly over half the period. For most of the 1980s and 1990s, most SSA governments operated under the conditionality of the IMF, its largest role in the domestic policy-making of any world region. IMF programmes are central to analysing SSA policy, as many countries operated under IMF conditionality for virtually the entire 18-year period, raising questions about the improvement of economic performance from the programmes.

2.4 Multilateral intervention and conflict: concrete examples[10]

2.4.1 Sierra Leone

Events in Sierra Leone and Yugoslavia cast doubt upon arguments that adjustment leads to CHEs in any predictable way. The experience of these countries has policy implications for preventing conflict elsewhere, though identifying these is complex. The Sierra Leonean conflict had its roots in a slow deterioration of economic performance and social services, combined with a weakening of transport (Richards 1996) that was especially serious in the regions of rebellion, where populations viewed themselves as having unique collective identities.

A second conflict-inducing factor was the decline of the country's education system.[11] In Sierra Leone, compared to most of SSA, educational provision was a defining feature of the nation, the 'imagined community', in the making. Moreover, worsening economic conditions, amid a potentially rich resource base, heightened the tension between the promise of and obstacles to economic growth. In the early 1980s, ill-conceived IMF stabilization transformed economic stagnation into rapid collapse.

The IMF's (and WB's) diagnosis was excess demand caused by excessive government expenditure amid an overvalued exchange rate. This diagnosis, contrary to actual conditions (Weeks 1992), prompted the standard prescriptions: sharp cuts in government expenditure and nominal devaluation. While a moderate real depreciation of the exchange rate may have improved the external current account in the medium term,[12] the mechanism for devaluation proved disastrous. In June 1986 the IMF urged a 'clean' (non-interventionist) exchange rate float. Within three months, despite the government's strict monetary policy, the number of Leones (the local currency) exchanged for US$1 increased by more than 500 per cent, catastrophically destabilizing the money economy. The collapse of the Leone spurred accelerating inflation leading to increasing credit demands; when the IMF-set credit limits were reached, private banks refused to accept deposits (they could not lend beyond the credit limits), provoking capital flight facilitated by IMF-required capital account deregulation. Per capita GDP declined by over 6 per cent from mid-1986 to mid-1987. A brief fixed exchange rate arrested the growth of inflation and brought positive growth for the next 12 months. This respite was followed by negative growth for the rest of the decade and into the 1990s (Weeks 1992).

While the political regime of the 1980s was corrupt and inefficient, ill-planned and inflexible stabilization and adjustment provoked an unnecessarily severe economic decline that undermined the population's confidence in government economic management. IMF and WB policies did not create regional tensions, which arose from long-run social factors. However, economic mismanagement associated with adjustment left the government without resources to manage the accumulating tensions.

The trigger for conflict was the spillover of violence from neighbouring Liberia in the early 1990s. Marginalized groups in the two countries, such as Sierran youth excluded from education and labour market opportunities, were mobilized by disaffected sections of the elite. In summary, the underlying cause of conflict in Sierra Leone arose from economic stagnation and poor policy undermining the population's faith in the government's development, which, together with failed nation-building, weakened government legitimacy. This underlying cause gave rise to the immediate possibility of conflict resulting from economic mismanagement associated with adjustment, which turned stagnation into sharp decline.[13] The immediate possibility of conflict was triggered into widespread violence by the civil war that raged in a neighbouring country.[14]

We can only speculate about whether a different set of IMF/WB policies might have weakened the risk of Sierran conflict. Our framework provides little reason to believe that different policies would have averted the conflict by overcoming structurally entrenched tendencies and the events spilling over from Liberia. Still, different IFI policies could have worked more positively to ameliorate tensions, especially if IFI intervention had focused more on reviving output and employment and less on reducing budget and current account deficits. Specifically, a more gradual approach, such as a 'crawling peg', could have been taken to achieving a more competitive exchange rate. Also, conditionality could have placed priority on infrastructure maintenance and renewal, and reviving the education system. The public sector could have been strengthened through increased resources and training. Multilateral advice might have focused on maximizing the technology and employment gains from foreign companies. The overall aim of policy reforms would still have been to overcome entrenched stagnation; the means would not have been imposed from an abstract model that failed to consider local conditions and tensions.

2.4.2 Yugoslavia

Yugoslavia's disintegration was largely generated by structural conditions and policy decisions, especially from the mid-1960s onwards. Initially, the socialist state-led industrialization after the Second World War held promise that federal Yugoslavia could overcome economic tensions of relative backwardness and fragmented nation-ness.[15] Reforms to planning in 1950–51 effectively accelerated productive forces, raising living standards and increasing nation-state legitimacy (Ellman 1979). By the early 1960s most of Yugoslavia had experienced rapid industrial development (Schierup 1992). While unification of the federation's postal and rail services helped submerge regional distinctions, other factors steadily undermined national integration. Country identity weakened, as the threats of fascism during the Second World War and subsequent Soviet domination faded. From the late 1960s onwards, administrative and economic decisions spurred competitive political and bureaucratic fragmentation and economic decline. Massive foreign borrowing (1976–81) was not effectively channelled into productive expansion or export growth. This poorly managed borrowing exposed Yugoslavia to harsh adjustment associated with the international response to the 1980s debt crisis. Increasingly, local bureaucracies shored up the legitimacy of economically threatened domains in the republics with populist appeals to 'ethnic nationalism'.

Economic expectations built up during the initial postwar period were undermined in the 1970s by decreasing labour productivity and diminishing investment returns. In the 1980s hyperinflation, falling real wages, rising unemployment and discriminatory employment practices during economic austerity destroyed faith in the federation's government (Schierup 1992, 1993b). The transition to a market economy had begun in the mid-1960s. The 1965 economic reforms that ended centrally directed investment were a precursor for the 'shock therapy' of the 1990s. Federal institutions that fostered research and development were dismantled. Inter-republic capital transfers 'dwindled continuously from the mid-1960s' (Schierup 1993b: 95). As a result, the Yugoslav 'national' market and policy became increasingly fragmented. During reform, the federal post and telecommunications, transport and energy systems fell apart, replaced by separate organizations in the republics and autonomous provinces. During the 1970s and 1980s different Yugoslav rail corporations showed less cooperation. To vitalize a sclerotic bureaucratic system, more populist administrative reforms were undertaken, but these brought more anarchy than efficiency.

Thus, the Yugoslav federation began disintegrating before the ethnically based political and military warfare of the 1990s. There was little 'education in civil society' (Hroch 1993: 16). Nationalist ideologues called on identity myths to mobilize people with no voice in federal regulation, and whose economic survival was threatened. 'Civil war became the final source of legitimacy left for local state elites and the last political outlet for increasingly impoverished populations void of apparent alternatives' (Schierup 1993a: 8). In this build-up to conflict, international demands for rapid deflation and liberalization undermined the credibility and military authority of the last federal government under Ante Markovic (Schierup 1993a; Blackburn 1993).[16] Like Sierra Leone, adjustment did not cause conflict but added further discontent with the federal government. A more constructive engagement by the WB and IMF in Yugoslavia is unlikely to have prevented the descent into conflict. Nonetheless, many, including some at the WB, blamed the drastic IMF-enforced deflation in 1990 for the timing of the break-up of Yugoslavia. In summary, the IFIs could have used their case-by-case approach to the debt crisis but still facilitated reforms to aid the government to manage the economy to facilitate flexibility in dealing with competing claims by ethnic groups.

Sierra Leone and Yugoslavia suggest that adjustment is unlikely to do more than work in the same direction as other factors contributing to conflict. If the goal is to prevent CHEs, the key is timely recognition of other conditions, with the expectation that these programmes can only facilitate this goal. Nevertheless, the discussion here provides support for the potential role of economic stagnation or sharp declines in the origins of conflicts under particular conditions.[17] Inequality, as measured by the Gini coefficient, isolated from other factors of specific societies, may be less useful in this analysis than the application of the concepts of social exclusion.[18]

2.5 Adjusting adjustment

Despite variations, it is argued here that there is an identifiable analytical and ideological core to prevailing orthodox packages. 'Structural adjustment' came into use in the early 1980s to distinguish 'efficiency-raising policies' from stabilization programmes. Stabilization seeks to control demand to reduce inflation and achieve a sustainable balance of payments. Structural adjustment is directed to the supply side, to remove 'market imperfections' to growth (Corbo *et al.* 1992; Khan 1987). IMF stabilization seeks to achieve external and internal equilibrium, while WB structural adjustment tries to foster growth. The distinction between the two was central to the policy debate in the 1980s. Adjustment programmes to stimulate growth were the core justification of the WB's increased policy-based lending during the 1980s (Mosley *et al.* 1991). In the early 1990s, the distinction between stabilization and adjustment disappeared. The heart of our critique of Bretton Woods macro programmes is that, despite rhetoric, they do not emphasize economic growth, and thus are inappropriate for reducing potential conflict.

Given the increasing evidence that adjustment did not stimulate recovery in LICs,[19] the World Bank (1992a) issued an 'overview' of adjustment programmes, redefining their context and purpose. The Executive Summary stated that the aim of adjustment loans 'is to support programs of policy and institutional change to modify the structure of an economy so it can *maintain* its growth rate and the viability of its balance of payments' (ibid.: 1, emphasis added). Six objectives follow, the first being 'stabilizing the macroeconomic environment'. In summary, the report:

uses a simplified macroeconomic framework that assigns fiscal policy to reducing inflation, the real exchange rate to the current account, and monetary policy to the external balance in terms of foreign exchange reserves.[20]

According to the report, fiscal and monetary policies involve an emphasis on demand management rather than economic growth.[21] If one accepts that fiscal deficits are the cause of inflation, then using tax and expenditure instruments implies a strict trade-off between growth and inflation. The report notes later that adjustment countries that maintained levels of social expenditure 'have generally seen improvement...in social indicators', and Mosley and Weeks (1993: 1591–2) show that cuts in public investment reduce growth. Therefore, to 'assign fiscal policy to reducing inflation' is to give fiscal policy no role in stimulating growth. The trade-off is more obvious for monetary policy, namely, the setting of interest rates. Here, the WB prescribes that the domestic central bank rate be set above international interest rates to attract an inflow of short-term capital.[22] The WB's neoclassicism assumes that investment should be sensitive to the interest rate. Raising interest rates would depress investment, thereby trading a short-term improvement in foreign exchange holdings for a lower rate of growth.[23]

Such an interest rate policy would represent a major government distortion of financial markets. The efficient time structure of interest rates is that short-term rates should be below long-term rates, which should approximate the social rate of time-preference. Only by chance would the central bank rate that satisfied the short-run goal of attracting reserves be equal to that which would equate saving and investment in the long term. The 1992 report unambiguously relocates adjustment in the stabilization camp.

This report has been reviewed to justify the conclusion that with respect to macro policy there is little, if any difference between stabilization (the IMF) and structural adjustment (the WB), though the latter programmes include 'meso' and micro policies not given prominence by the IMF. The macro policy framework of the Bretton Woods institutions is summarized in Table 2.2. Both fiscal and monetary policies are demand reducing: increased revenue, in effect, finances deficit reduction; monetary policy aims to increase real interest rates, which would depress investment. Taken alone, a real depreciation has an ambiguous effect. If the IMF's monetary approach to the balance of payments is accepted, a real devaluation is contractionary (Agénor and Montiel 1996), although it shifts relative prices in favour of tradables. Even in an alternative framework, where the law of one price does not hold, tight monetary policy would negate any expansionary effect from increased exchange rate competitiveness. Whatever the theory, recent research, commissioned by the WB, suggests no compelling reason to emphasize price stability: only for rates over 40 per cent per annum is there a negative correlation between inflation and economic growth.[24]

Table 2.2 Policy areas and goals, stabilization and adjustment programmes

Policy areas	Overall goal*	Instruments/outcomes**
1. Fiscal policy	Reduce inflation	a. Fiscal balance: Reduce deficit b. Government revenue: Increase revenue
2. Exchange rate policy	Improve the current account	a. Exchange rate: Real depreciation b. Parallel market: Reduce official/parallel gap
3. Monetary policy	Increase foreign exchange reserves, reduce inflation, increase saving	a. Interest rate: Real interest rates above real rate of growth, and above international money market rates b. Money growth: Equate to real economic growth c. Inflation: Reduce rate of inflation

Sources: * World Bank (1992a: 2)
    ** World Bank (1992a: 2 and 1994: *passim*).

This macro framework is inappropriate and unnecessary for countries at risk from conflict. It assigns government a neutral role in the macroeconomy, leaving the growth stimulus to the private sector amid demand contraction. Yet, in conflict-prone countries, the confidence of the private sector, especially its motivation to invest, is likely to be weak. Further, conflict-prone countries are likely to be suffering from slow or stagnant growth. In effect, this policy framework makes that problem worse.[25]

The IMF and WB need to incorporate into their programmes the circumstances of conflict: that reviving growth should take priority over fiscal and monetary orthodoxy. This means a shift away from the growth depressing effect of IMF programmes.

A more subtle, case by case approach is necessary, influenced by a historical understanding of capitalism. Nafziger and Auvinen suggest that a strategy to avoid CHEs should include inclusive growth. Other factors besides short-term stabilization undermine a long-term adjustment to higher growth. First, diminishing the state, especially in investment, weakens the potential for the public-sector crowding in private-sector investment (Greene and Villanueva 1991; Mosley *et al.* 1995). At a microeconomic level, successful industrialization results not from stressing competition between the private and public sectors, but constructive relationships between the two sectors (Amsden 1997; Chang 1993; Chandler *et al.* 1997); development derives from collaboration as well as competition.[26] Institutions that encourage collaboration and constructive competition help generate growth and *manageable* social conflict. But there is no blueprint for identifying competition strategy. Indeed sometimes the government may have an important role in avoiding 'excess competition', similar to the period of rapid ascent of industrial and technological learning curves during Korean industrialization (Chang 1993).[27] Other microeconomic policies important for pursuing stability and investment might include careful creation of well-regulated financial sectors (Stiglitz 1998).

Along with contractionary macro policy, adjustment invariably includes trade liberalization, justified by efficiency gains arising from equating internal prices to 'border prices'. Changing pricing may be appropriate sometimes, but 'getting prices right' cannot be the central objectives of policy, especially if we acknowledge that competition is never perfect and that the theoretically right price is elusive. Even proponents of liberalization find it difficult to support claims that trade liberalization stimulates growth. Greenaway *et al.*'s (1997) statistical analysis suggests that trade liberalization often has a negative impact on growth, because of a 'J-curve' response in which liberalization losses in the short run are recovered in the long run. Trade liberalization can spur growth-oriented improvements, especially in export manufactures. Yet these manufactures are as likely to result from industrial policy and increased capacity utilization, fuelled by improved access to foreign exchange, rather than liberalization policies (Mulaga and Weiss 1996; Lall 1995).

This discussion implies several changes to adjustment programmes so that they are more appropriate for conflict affected countries. First, macro policy should accommodate growth. For *fiscal policy*, this means maintaining or increasing government investment (see below). Current expenditure should focus on social sectors, education and health, plus programmes to reintegrate displaced populations in post-conflict (Cramer and Weeks 1998). Reduction of military expenditure in post-conflict countries should be transferred to social sectors, rather than used for deficit reduction.

Monetary policy should foster investment, which implies positive, but low, real interest rates that should not exceed the 'golden rule', the economy's long-run sustainable growth rate. Governments should avoid distorting investment by setting high real interest rates. In some countries, directed and subsidized credit should be encouraged, for example for modern inputs in agriculture, or to stimulate employment-intensive sectors. These measures are consistent with moderate monetary expansion. The efficacy of selection is critical to whether cheap credit is associated with productive failure or phenomenal success. Subsidized credit based on performance, in a regime of moderate monetary expansion, is more fruitful for WB policy and research than total liberalization of financial markets and abandoning industrial policy.

Countries in or at risk from conflict have volatile foreign exchange markets, especially from capital flight. Governments must regulate the exchange rate to prevent nominal exchange rate instability, perhaps leading to uncontrolled devaluations, which can be prevented only by large inflows of ODA, as in Mozambique in the mid-1990s (Weeks 1997).[28] A 'floating' rate sustained by official capital flows is not market determined but an administered price supported by ODA, so that government should set the rate purposefully. A politically unstable country may need exchange controls to minimize the negative effect on capital inflow.

While WB adjustment, similar to IMF stabilization, has little emphasis on growth, the WB has pushed political advice, such as improved 'governance' and reducing corruption. Behind the WB's interest is its predilection for the 'new political economy' of development, an economic theory of politics built on assumptions of methodological individualism, utility maximization and choice that underpins neoliberal economics. The new political economy is badly flawed, ahistorical and highly cynical in its implications, and a poor basis for understanding CHEs. The implications of this chapter (which differ significantly from the new political economy) for the WB's lending and policy advice to LDCs are highlighted below.

First, IFI loans should be adjusted towards infrastructure spending directed towards areas most likely to generate rapid growth of output, employment and exports. Accordingly infrastructure must be improved to facilitate migration from remote regions to emerging 'growth poles', offering an 'exit' option. Migration by effective transport facilitates plural identities and a national 'imagination of the community', relieving a population 'trapped' in a zone prone to drought and hunger. Population movement and intermingling of different identity groups may weaken sharp inter-group antagonism. [29]

Second, industrial and trade policies should be more inclusive and effective than they are likely to be under trade liberalization, industry deregulation and privatization. Productivity and international competitiveness need not rely exclusively on real wage repression, but should be nurtured through policies spurring technological change and improving industrial skills.[30] Growth-oriented industrial policies will also require less distinction between public and private sectors and a less cynical view of the public sector than the 'new political economy' allows. Institutions are needed that generate constructive relationships between public and private sectors.

Third, societies need greater options for exit and voice to manage tension. Policies should include not only infrastructure development but also support to employee and employer organizations, such as trade unions and employer associations. Furthermore, the UN system should consider developing institutions that resolve conflict, or manage tensions that arise from ethnic, regional or other collective identities. Quota systems based on ethnicity (such as *bumiputra* policies in Malaysia) and regional cross-subsidization (for example, India or Yugoslavia), while often inefficient or inflexible, have contributed to political stability and national cohesion. Institutions need to be appropriate to that country's history and needs. We can learn lessons from analysing not only policies in Malaysia, India and Yugoslavia but also in Mauritius, which has managed ethnic diversity effectively.

Finally, these objectives are more feasible if the IFIs subject their programmes to open debate before agreements with governments. Governments, independent economic analysts, businesses, unions and representatives from the informal sector and rural society should influence stabilization and adjustment. For where economic reforms and policy advice are based on specific conditions and needs, there is a greater likelihood that the IFIs will avoid the failures of 1980–2000.

The IMF and WB should not only adjust LDC programmes but also themselves. The inflexibility of adjustment owes much to the intellectual insularity and rigidity of Washington economic models. One example is the narrowness of perspective of most WB studies, whose references are typically to WB documents or commissioned research. An apparent shift to a 'post-Washington consensus' does not overcome this weakness. The shortcomings of WB structural adjustment, the damaging consequences of IMF stabilization (Radelet and Sachs 1998), and the links between slow growth and CHEs provide evidence that the IFIs should be open to more diverse influence and advice, and more accountable to donors, borrowers and the academic community. There might be a role for a new advisory board for each institution to institutionalize i) historical memory and ii) learning from experience and openness to independent research. The advisory board might give weight to representatives from LICs, NICs and countries involved in CHEs during the twentieth century. It is also necessary to redefine the relationship between the WTO and LDCs, because excessively rapid compliance with post-Uruguay Round regulations could threaten output and employment stability.

Furthermore, given the shortcomings of conditionality during the 1980s and 1990s, donors must consider how far to make resources conditional upon a government's signature of a letter of intent with the IMF. Economic activity, when expanding during adjustment periods, probably owes more to an influx of foreign exchange than to the efficiency reforms of the Washington consensus.

2.6 Conclusion

This chapter has shown that IMF and WB conditionality cannot by itself create CHEs. Conditionality may not even be an immediate trigger. But conditionality works in the same causal direction as other factors common to CHEs in LDCs. In particular, stabilization policies restrict growth, while adjustment policies are inept at stimulating growth. Yet economic stagnation or sharp declines in incomes are critical economic factors often associated with conflict or descent towards CHEs. Thus, policies typical of IMF and WB conditional lending can aggravate a key problem that intensifies social tensions leading to CHEs. Moreover, the idea that adjustment programmes take politics out of economic interactions is manifestly groundless (Hibou 1999). It is also argued that there can be no effective predictive model of CHEs. These crises cannot be reduced to causal mechanisms, with the same empirical outcome occurring whenever they are operative. Understanding and preventing such crises requires a historical political economy not dependent on the 'closure' assumptions of positivist methodologies such as econometrics.

The lack of predictability strengthens rather than weakens the case for changing economic reform, as there are not just one or two cases where we can confidently anticipate an emergency, and hence recommend a different set of policies. There are many such cases, in LICs and even MICs, whose economies have frail structures that expose them to sharp income declines. The tensions typical of conflict countries are common to late capitalist development in general. CHEs are the most extreme manifestation of these tensions. There is an urgent need for policies that enable governments and societies to manage those tensions. This will be done by policies that promote growth that is rapid and inclusive: but not necessarily always equal and equitable. The objective should not be social and economic change without tension, as this is impossible, but change and development that can contain ever shifting tensions and social conflicts.

Notes

1. See, for example, Nafziger and Auvinen (2000).
2. Bardhan (1997) points to the tendency to 'throw up our hands'; but the momentum within economics has really been in the opposite direction – from an initial disinterest of economists in conflict to a creeping colonization of the problem, accompanied by a rising confidence in economic policy to stop the irrationalities of conflict. This may lead to over-reach common to mainstream economics.
3. ILO (1997) discusses the diversity of conflicts and their impacts, Väyrynen (2000a) the range of CHEs, and Pritchett (1996) the uselessness of 'outward orientation' as a comparable indicator for trade policy's contribution to economic growth.
4. See Cramer (1997) and Collier and Hoeffler (1998) on inequality, and Easterly and Levine (1997) on ethnicity and SSA growth.
5. Hirschman (1995) surveys contributions to the idea that conflict can play a constructive role in social relationships.
6. Gerschenkron (1962) is a more formal analysis of conflict than de Tocqueville (1955), who suggests that many conflicts erupt when expectations just begin to rise with a breath of prosperity.
7. The WB report, when discussing loans to countries 'at risk' of future conflict, states:

> [With regard to] prevention in 'at risk' countries...[t]he [World] Bank needs to integrate concern for conflict into development operations. It must ensure that its interventions do not aggravate existing inequities...and that they ameliorate potential conflict situations, through judicious social analysis and adequate attention to distributive policies... (World Bank 1997c: iii).

8. The fact that IMF conditions are associated with instability and protest does not establish causality, as there may be scapegoating, for protests may partly express discontent with the government and its policies.

9. The dating of conflicts is from Nafziger *et al.* (2000) and Melkas (1996).

10. Other examples include Angola and Mozambique from Cramer (1994) and Birmingham (1992).

11. An indication of this was the ransom demand for college places by the 'West Side Boys', who took a group of British soldiers hostage in mid-2000.

12. This would not have been straightforward, because a large proportion of imports were financed by aid-flows and were therefore not exchange-rate sensitive. On the export side the problem was largely structural, with stagnation the result of a US company closing its iron ore operations, and the depletion of alluvial diamonds (Weeks 1992).

13. Deregulation, liberalization and a public-sector squeeze also provided new means of organizing the contest for material and political control: the post-privatization relationship between the elite and foreign firms has produced a tragic parody of the way that privatization and foreign investment can increase rather than decrease social exclusion and can encourage the state to relocate the pursuit of legitimacy away from the nation-state constituency and towards external sources of capital, technology, know-how and, ultimately, the reproduction of power (see Reno 2000).

14. The descent of Rwanda into genocide followed a similar sequence: the underlying cause lay in a dual crisis of the nation-state and of economic constraints; the shift towards possible conflict was facilitated by financial tightening in the aftermath of sharp falls in coffee prices; and the trigger for actual conflict came partly from changes in Uganda that prompted the Rwandan Patriotic Front (RPF) invasion and partly from international pressure on the government to 'democratize' (Austin 1996; African Rights 1994a).

15. The tension was extreme in Yugoslavia because no 'other Communist state was as intimately acquainted with Western lifestyles as Yugoslavia. Tourists going one way, and migrant workers the other, helped to dramatize the failings of an economic order where average GNP was still less than a fifth of that in Western Europe' (Blackburn 1993: 102).

16. Public expenditure cuts left Markovic's government unable, by late 1990, to pay wages to the Yugoslavian army.

17. The two case studies reviewed here suggest that deaths in the prior six years, a variable used by Auvinen and Nafziger (1999), may be too blunt an instrument to pick up the history or tradition of violence. Political memories of violence and fear can be longer: for example, in Rwanda an undoubted influence on the catastrophe of the 1990s was the memory of earlier mass violence and displacement, such as that following the 1959 social revolution.

18. On social exclusion, see Richards (1996) on Sierra Leone; Paus (1995) on El Salvador after the peace accord of 1992; and Breman (1997) on the political economy of Surat.

19. An EC study indicates: 'The major reason for the continuing debate on adjustment...is that the results achieved have remained well below expectations' (Guillaumont and Guillaumont 1994: 32).

20. To this is added: 'Tightening the overall fiscal position was a central component of the macroeconomic adjustment program...' (World Bank 1992a: 2).

21. Fine (1994) and White (1996) rigorously demonstrate the inconsistency between stabilization policy and long-term growth.

22. 'Of the 42 countries [covered in the study], 37 increased their differential [between domestic and international interest rates] (or reduced a negative differential) across the adjustment period' (World Bank 1992a: 3).
23. Most of SSA would gain little in foreign reserves from a higher interest rate differential, because financial markets are narrow and undeveloped. Econometrics suggest no correlation between the domestic/international interest rate differential and foreign exchange flows for the region during the 1980s (Weeks 2001). The World Bank (1992a: 27) also finds foreign exchange inflows inelastic with respect to the interest rate differential: 'Ten of the 18 [sub-Saharan] countries increased their international-domestic interest rate differential or reduced negative differentials, but only two...had their foreign exchange reserves increase...'.
24. Bruno and Easterly (1998) conclude:

> After excluding countries with high-inflation crises – periods when annual inflation is above forty per cent – the data reveal no evidence of a consistent relationship between growth and inflation, at any frequency.

25. A World Bank document (1992a: 3, 20–1) concedes that adjustment policies might cause declines in investment:

> ...*an adjustment period is almost inevitably a period of public investment cuts and heightened uncertainty for private investment*...An investment pause is therefore to be expected during the adjustment period [emphasis added].

26. Cf Milne (1997).
27. We differ from Stiglitz (1998), who stresses an over-simplified notion of competition abstract from sectoral or country conditions and needs.
28. Mozambique, after the 1992 peace settlement, showed an ODA commitment by donors to protect peace and thus their own investment of aid and advice.
29. See Richards (1996) on eastern Sierra Leone; infrastructure development may blur the distinction in Bardhan's (1997) matrix of sources of secession, which argues that its greatest scope is among backward groups in backward areas.
30. Paus (1995) argues for more inclusive trade and industrial policies in El Salvador, in contrast to those adopted in the aftermath of the 1992 peace agreement.

3
Global Linkages, Vulnerable Economies and the Outbreak of Conflict

Valpy FitzGerald

3.1 Introduction

Among LDCs that comprise almost half the world economy and three-quarters of the world population, a considerable proportion have recently experienced armed conflict. During the past twenty years, half of the poorest countries have been seriously affected by civil strife or war; one-third of them since 1990. Despite expectations to the contrary, these conflicts are probably increasing: they are predominantly *within* rather than *between* established states, and often involve state failure or territorial secession. Nonetheless, until recently academics have paid little attention to the impact of armed conflict on economic and social conditions (FitzGerald and Stewart 1997) and the role of changes in the world economy.

The international context of these conflicts has some relationship to their outbreak and intensity; two obvious historical factors being the colonial independence struggle and the geopolitics of the Cold War. While these are hopefully problems of the past, conflicts may continue as the legacy of state structures created during the past fifty years adjusts to a new world geopolity, including economic globalization. To maintain living standards, poor economies are dependent on access to international commodity markets and aid, and their changes strongly influence survival. It is argued here that low per capita incomes, or even widespread absolute poverty, are not in themselves the primary causes of conflict. Sudden changes in economic circumstances contribute to uncertainty among social groups, weaken the state's capacity to deliver public goods underpinning the 'social contract', and create a perceived injustice by particular groups or regions – and it is these factors which lead to conflict. This instability is characteristic of economic globalization, to which poor countries are particularly vulnerable.

This chapter examines how current patterns of trade and foreign investment as well as renegotiation of debt and development cooperation affect state failure and social conflict. This is then used to assess the current role of international economic institutions with respect to poor and vulnerable countries, and to draw tentative policy conclusions. Section 3.2 opens with a summary of the literature on major causes of conflict. Section 3.3 considers the effects of primary commodity market instability, trade liberalization and FDI – particularly natural resource sectors – on conflicts and their duration. Section 3.4 discusses the effects of debt burdens in causing insolvency and repeated renegotiation through undermining state capacity and increasing business uncertainty, and aid-flows which account for nearly all imports and investment. In Section 3.5, the effect of IFIs' policy conditionality imposed on vulnerable economies (extending a model of integration to global markets) and whether this conditionality reduces vulnerability and prevents conflict, is examined. Section 3.6 concludes by suggesting how the effects of globalization on conflict might be mitigated, particularly by reducing the economic vulnerability of poor countries and avoiding state collapse that promotes social disintegration.

3.2 The political economy of the outbreak of conflict

The literature does not directly address the relationship between international economic arrangements and domestic conflict[1] but rather assumes that conflict results indirectly from domestic social conditions related to integration of the world economy.

The World Bank (1996b) and IMF (1997) appear to claim a positive relationship between world economic integration and reduced conflict. This is attributed to two developments expected from the structural adjustment of integration into the world economy: an increase in economic growth that generates more employment and increased expenditure on social services, and privatisation that reduces the state's discretionary powers. These developments should be reinforced by refocusing welfare programmes through targeting of limited public expenditure on the poor alone. Conflict is seen as arising from 'state failure' associated with corruption, rent-seeking behaviour, neglect of small-scale agriculture, government control over the economy and financial repression, meaning that the problem is domestic and political, although aid donors can use conditionality to make the state more efficient and democratic.

The IFIs' position contrasts sharply with UN agencies, such as the United Nations Research Institute for Social Development (UNRISD) (1995) and UNCTAD (1996), the views of which are that rapid integration into the world economy reduces social cohesion and makes conflict more likely. The mechanisms are increased open unemployment as firms recover competitiveness by shedding labour, government reduction of the civil service to service debt, and reduced social services, especially for marginal social groups or rural regions, as the state is scaled back. Privatization may worsen this, as state managers become private entrepreneurs. Moreover, income distribution worsens from globalization, and solidarity within communities and neighbourhoods weakens. Under social regress, effective and legitimized government is almost impossible as the state becomes increasingly less relevant to satisfying everyday needs.

Development economists generally assume that conflict will arise from 'failed economic development' or low (or declining) per capita GNP growth, increased poverty from population growth or widening income disparities, and increased competition over scarce resources such as land or water (Sen 1994).[2] This extends the competitive 'market' model of society where a 'zero sum game' creates more conflict than growth because the gains of one player can be made only at the expense of another. Moreover, under 'economic regress' tax revenues decline and thus the ability to deliver welfare services to the population, particularly the poor. This leads not only to a large welfare loss but also to a loss of state legitimacy as the terms of the 'social contract' break.

If economic regress is attributed to external economic factors, such as debt service or deteriorating terms of trade, then causality goes from the world economy to domestic conflict. However, there is little empirical evidence that conflict is located in poor or slow-growing economies, or even in countries where household absolute poverty is rising (Stewart *et al.* 1997). Moreover, a broadly based government could 'share poverty' without a breakdown in social institutions.

The 'political economy' approach is different, and identifies the source of armed conflict as state failure born of a lack of political legitimacy (for example, Keen 1997). Intrastate conflict, arising from community identity and central government legitimacy, is now far more common than interstate conflict. Large income or wealth discrepancies between groups are regarded as 'unjust' by the poor majority and social cohesion requires the state to redistribute resources to command support from the whole community. Differential access to positional and distributional public goods, especially in states based on ethnic, language or religious legitimacy, means that subordinate groups face real restrictions on access. When the state fails in its most important functions – guaranteeing property and safety – insecurity between groups increases and 'aggressive self-defence' becomes increasingly common. State failure can occur when a newly independent country fails to achieve full statehood, or when the state is undermined from without, or led by a predatory regime. This approach suggests that the policies of governing elites (and their external supporters) lie at the root of most domestic armed conflicts (Holsti 2000).

This view implies that the relevance of changes in the global economy to intrastate conflict is how these changes promote perceived injustice between social groups or geographical regions, increase uncertainty and insecurity, or contribute to state failure.

Of 48 LLDCs,[3] 24 have undergone serious conflicts during the past three decades. The WB's LICs[4] include 64, of which over one-third have experienced serious conflict. Some countries in the Bank's 'lower middle-income' group are also conflictive, such as Colombia, Peru, Guatemala, Lebanon, Iraq, Iran and Angola – and even upper-middle income countries such as Yugoslavia – but the main grouping of conflict-prone countries is clearly among poor economies.

LLDCs/LICs are defined here as 'vulnerable economies', in that a large part of their population suffers from absolute poverty and most of the rest are near the poverty line, they have poor levels of economic and social infrastructure, and their public institutions have few resources to resolve internal conflicts. Thus exogenous shocks that can be absorbed by MICs or DCs may engender large changes in LICs/LLDCs: in the average level of inter-regional or inter-group distribution of income; in expected relative to perceived survival incomes, or in the state's capacity to provide public goods. Such exogenous shocks include changes in terms of trade, foreign investment, aid or debt and external policy conditionality. In addition, a considerable proportion of vulnerable economies have suffered from armed conflict, which further increases their vulnerability.

The LLDCs' average annual income per capita was approximately US$400, and the LICs' US$380 in 1994 (World Bank 1996b); US$380 is roughly equivalent to the WB's absolute poverty level, US$1 per person per day. The LICs' income is about a quarter of that of LDCs. Further, both LICs' and LLDCs' averages fell over the long term, while the gap with other LDCs has widened. The LICs/LLDCs thus exhibit considerable economic stress and absolute economic regress (see Table 3.1 on the LLDCs).[5]

Nonetheless, although the means for income levels and growth in conflict countries appear lower than for non-conflict economies – consistent with intuition – detailed examination shows that *there is no statistically significant difference between the means and variances of the two sub-groups.* In other words, these levels of income and growth are characteristic of LLDCs generally, not of conflict as such – either as cause or effect. This result may be attributed to selection bias, in that the sample contains only 'failures', and the 'successful' poor countries have previously graduated out of the LLDC category. Indeed evidence indicates a growing divergence between

Table 3.1   Level and growth or per capita GDP in LLDCs

		LLDCs		Sig. Diff.			
		Conflict	*Non-conflict*	*Means?*	*Variance?*	*All LLDCs*	*All LDCs*
1994 US$:	1980	373	588	no	no	488	828
	1994	304	486	no	no	395	984
Growth rate:	1980–90	–0.5	–0.1	no	no	–0.2	1.2
	1990–94	–1.8	0.2	no	yes	–0.7	1.8

Source: Computations from UNCTAD (1996)

LLDCs and other LDCs, the MICs having achieved some convergence in per capita incomes and other development indicators with DCs (UNDP 1997).

This finding underscores the difficulties of measuring causal relationships between conflict and economic growth. For instance, both direct inspection of the data and detailed econometric tests indicate that conflicts in LDCs are preceded by periods of slow and declining growth (Auvinen and Nafziger 1999).[6] However, if this is a general characteristic of vulnerability (and thus a necessary but not sufficient cause of conflict) this is hardly surprising. Again, intuitively one would expect conflicts to lower GDP per capita or at least reduce rates of growth, but this does not appear to be so in practice.[7] The explanation is that conflict economies often attract very high levels of aid relative to domestic economic output, so that national 'income' can actually rise even though tradable output is falling – a point taken up again below.[8] This is partly a measurement problem (using expenditure rather than earnings, which measures welfare rather than income) but also reflects a deeper issue – whether aid, by maintaining incomes, also prolongs the conflict. As shall be demonstrated, this phenomenon is common to all external linkages other than aid. Thus, it is necessary to proceed largely by deduction (from general to particulars) rather than by induction (inferring a general law from particular facts).

In this chapter, it is thus assumed that the main causal *economic* factors creating conflict in vulnerable economies are:

i)   the sudden widening of disparities in income or wealth within a society, which can arise from both the impoverishment of some groups or the enrichment of others. The disparities can be vertical (between social groups) leading to what is sometimes termed 'class conflict' or horizontal (between territorial groups) which leads to 'regional conflict'. In both cases the creation of a collective sense of injustice and resentment undermines the legitimacy of existing institutions, and makes violence appear as the only solution; but vertical tensions usually lead to attempts to overthrow the government while horizontal tensions lead to attempts at secession and an independent state.

ii) an increased uncertainty of the economic prospects of dominant or subordinate groups (or both) in real incomes and asset ownership (including access to common resources), which generates collective insecurity. This insecurity may be subjective, but is perceived as real, and increases aggressive behaviour in wealth accumulation (that is de facto or de jure theft) and 'self defence', which challenges the legitimacy of the state monopoly over military force. Again, this can lead towards either a collapse of central authority or the constitution of separate territorial entities; but can also lead to suppressed conflict under an increasingly authoritarian state.

iii) the weakening of the economic capacity of the state to provide public goods, which undermines the legitimacy of the existing administration.

Lack of financial resources can mean that the government no longer provides all social and territorial groups with acceptable access to social services and economic infrastructure, nor mediates between 'winners' and 'losers' in the economic development (particularly during major economic reforms) by appropriate resource transfers, nor even maintains law and order. In consequence, the 'social contract' no longer receives wide support, and allegiance is transferred to actors (ranging from security companies to warlords) who can fulfil more limited 'group contracts'.

It is stressed here that the interaction between these three factors, in economies which are already vulnerable, brings about armed conflict. A weak state in an economy without sudden changes in equity or security can survive for long periods without conflict – as in Rwanda or Cambodia after independence. In contrast, a strong state perceived as 'fair' by the majority of the population (particularly by the poor) can survive considerable shocks and group insecurity, as in Tanzania, or even attempts at secession such as Sri Lanka. In other cases legitimate states with low inequality can be destabilized by external intervention which increases insecurity – as in Mozambique or Nicaragua. This chapter explores how much the international economic linkages of vulnerable economies affect these three conditions.

3.3 Trade and foreign investment

Poor countries, except India and China, are marginal to the world economy. LLDCs comprise one-half of 1 per cent of world production and less than 1 per cent of world trade and investment. Moreover, their shares in world trade, investment and output are declining over time as they diverge from global trends (Table 3.2). Indeed, exports per capita in LLDCs reached only US$28 per capita in 1994.[9] However, although vulnerable economies are marginal to the world economy, the world economy is far from marginal to vulnerable economies. Their extreme reliance on foreign exchange to maintain vital sectors and strategic investment, means that small variations in export or aid receipts can have significant effects on economic inequality, social uncertainty and state capacity.

Table 3.2 Vulnerable economies in world trade and private investment

LLDC share (%)	1980	1993
World exports	0.7	0.4
World imports	1.1	0.7
Foreign direct investment	0.9	0.4
World GDP	0.6	0.4

Source: UNCTAD (1996)

3.3.1 Exports

The real value of LLDCs' export purchasing power[10] is not only low but declining (Table 3.3). Export purchasing power per capita fell 37 per cent from 1980 to 1993, an external constraint representing the major single obstacle to growth and thus 'escape' from economic vulnerability and LLDC status. However, despite a priori expectations, conflict and non-conflict countries show no systematic statistical difference in export purchasing power. The external constraint applies not only to manufacturing, transport, communications, health and education but also to exports – both in the supply of inputs (such as herbicides, pesticides, tools, spare parts and transport equipment) essential to maintain the existing level of exports, and the investment in mines, irrigation, roads and processing plants necessary to raise export capacity.

The trend in exports reflects a combination of low investment (see Section 3.5) and declining terms of trade for primary exporters. The social strain that leads to conflict also reduces the volume and price of exports even when armed conflict does not occur. The reasons are the gradual deterioration of poorly maintained export capacity, lack of production inputs and transport systems, and reduced producer profitability due to increased costs and reduced productivity – which can be exacerbated by currency over-valuation. These factors reduce the quality and quantity of exports, and thus prices received fall too. In addition, geopolitical factors may interrupt external transport and trade links, closing markets and increasing freight costs. Contemporary armed conflict probably involves deliberate destruction of export capacities in mines and plantations, displacement of skilled labour and the disruption of marketing channels; but data do not indicate these but rather economic vulnerability as the main explanation for deteriorating export purchasing power.

Further, most LDCs, and particularly LLDCs, are critically dependent on external finance to sustain working capital for the export sector and to increase export capacity. Borrowing from international commercial banks (beyond a small amount of pre-export finance) and FDI are not likely to be significant in light of country risk, so these economies rely heavily on aid

Table 3.3   Trends in the purchasing power of vulnerable economies' exports

Annual change in the income terms of trade (%)	*1980–90*	*1990–93*
All LLDCs	0.1	4.8
Conflict LLDCs	–1.3	1.5
Non-conflict LLDCs	8.9	0.7
Sig. Diff. Means?	No	No
Sig. Diff. Variance?	No	Yes
All LDCs	1.8	8.0

Source: UNCTAD (1996)

to capitalize their export sectors. However, as Section 3.5 argues, the funding for traded goods sector investment is difficult to obtain, particularly for small domestic producers. These factors also imply that exports are not highly responsive to the real (let alone the nominal) exchange rate unless supported by specific measures to increase export capacity directly.

The export structure of LLDCs compounds their external fragility, as they are much more dependent on primary products than LDCs generally. Why is the external vulnerability of LLDCs increased? First there is the long-run downward trend in LDCs' real prices,[11] with LLDCs' real prices deteriorating even faster. Second is the fact that primary commodity prices are much more volatile around the trend than manufactured prices, so that LLDCs' export prices are much more volatile than those of LDCs generally. These trends decrease profitability of and employment in the primary sector, thus reducing income and investment. Price volatility makes incomes more uncertain and further reduces investment in the sector.[12]

In addition, the importance of mining, oil and agro-industrial ('plantation') exports has implications for foreign investors (see below). Moreover, the weakness of the rule of law in vulnerable economies opens up a whole series of 'informal' exports. First, small-scale smuggling of exportable 'legal' products, such as grains, coffee or cattle, expands rapidly in border regions as border controls and local markets collapse. Second, the opportunities for the export by larger operators (including institutions such as the armed forces) of 'illegal' exports – such as drugs, gems or timber – expand as state control of particular regions declines and is replaced by local power centres, which may include opposition movements or potentially secessionist regions.

Reliance on these income sources probably increases the probability of armed conflict because illegal income increases the power of independent 'warlords' (or army commanders) and organized groups located in key territories. In the case of drugs, due to the large international externalities associated with this trade, domestic conflict is complicated by pressures from importing DCs to suppress these exports from LDCs. This leads to more violent military interventions in remote rural areas and the strengthening of the defensive capabilities of non-state actors involved as scarcity rents rise.

The differences between the LLDCs' shares of exports in primary products (non-manufacturing) (75 per cent) and the shares of LDCs generally (40 per cent) are striking. However, the difference in the share of manufactures in the exports of conflict and non-conflict countries is not statistically significant (calculated from UNCTAD 1996).

3.3.2 Imports

LLDCs' imports, largely determined by ODA (largely exogenous) and primary exports, have grown slowly (Table 3.5). Moreover, the increased imports during the 1990s may be related to trade liberalization under the structural adjustment programmes, which form the condition for new loans. However, although import/GDP for conflict economies is much lower than for non-conflict economies, neither the means nor the variances are significantly different from non-conflict economies (calculated from UNCTAD 1996).

The marked dependence of vulnerable economies on imported food and fuels is evident from Table 3.4. Thus, a decline in import volume cannot easily be met by expenditure switching or by reducing non-essential consumption: production levels fall or real levels of essential consumption have to be cut. Further, insofar as almost all imports are funded by aid donors (Table 3.7), they will have a determinate though usually uncoordinated effect on the composition of imports and their use. While aid-funded imports are fungible (releasing the government's 'own' foreign exchange for other uses that may be socially undesirable or at least undesired by donors), the scale of aid for LLDCs' imports indicates that they are not marginal, but rather affect overall import composition.

Imports under these circumstances are determined by the sum of exports and net external finance. A considerable proportion is determined by debt servicing and pre-determined by import support schemes, that is, tied to programmed supplies of food, medicines, etc. decided by donors. Further, while high-tech items such as aircraft are often financed by aid donors, much of the current expenditure needed for security enforcement and counter-insurgency campaigns (munitions, fuel, uniforms, spares etc.) must be provided from the government's own scarce foreign exchange reserves.

Moreover, the scarcity of foreign exchange may create a parallel market, fed by leakages from official and aid agencies, family remittances from overseas and export smuggling. These finance non-official imports, either permitted by the authorities as 'self funded' without an official exchange allocation from the central bank, or simply smuggled as customs control declines. There thus emerges a dual price structure reflecting the parallel exchange rate, which then feeds back into reduced profitability for exporters selling through state marketing boards at the official rates, and

Table 3.4   Composition of vulnerable countries' imports, 1992

		LLDCs	*Sig. Diff.*			
	Conflict	*Non-conflict*	*Means?*	*Variance?*	*All LLDCs*	*All LDCs*
Food products	22.2	23.6	no	no	22.9	8.6
Agricultural raw materials	5.8	2.0	no	yes	3.8	2.7
Fuels	11.2	12.2	no	yes	11.7	7.9
Ores and metals	0.5	1.0	no	no	0.7	2.6
Manufactured goods	56.2	58.1	no	yes	57.1	75.8

Source: UNCTAD (1996)

further diversion of foreign exchange incomes from official channels. However, because this segmentation results from a mismatch between market demand for imports and the public allocation of them (hopefully responding to social needs) rather than a misguided exchange rate policy alone, it cannot be remedied by devaluation.

3.3.3 Foreign investment

Vulnerable economies lack the conditions that attract FDI, such as large domestic markets, skilled labour force, good infrastructure, supportive economic policies, transparent and reliable legal systems, etc. Private foreign investment in LLDCs is thus small and a declining share of global FDI (Table 3.2). Inherited assets and new FDI are mainly in the primary export sector, although foreign firms may be significant in the distribution of imported goods, the provision of 'modern' services such as telecommunications and hotels, and some import-substituting industries such as petroleum refining, cigarette production and soft drinks.[13]

Three types of foreign investors can be distinguished, with different modes of operation, in LLDCs. First are MNCs involved in oil and mining or residually in plantation agriculture, which are major sources of revenue and foreign exchange for the state, but also require adequate physical security and predictable contract arrangements. Thus, MNCs' relationships with the state and local society are inevitably complex and potentially conflictive. The state's dependence on revenue from MNCs gives these firms considerable influence on policy or even government composition. In addition, opposition groups often establish direct relationships with MNCs, which may encourage the relationship to ensure future security.

Second are smaller foreign investors (often from neighbouring countries) engaged in predatory 'projects' such as gems mining or logging which does not require substantial infrastructure. These investors generally operate outside the law – indeed may establish private 'armies' – and their disintegrative effect is probably greater than that of MNCs, which have longer-term objectives. Thus while the predatory foreign investors have less power, their opportunities are greater as they bear no external costs from their activities, nor do their shareholders place limits on their actions.

Third are non-resident or resident nationals managing cross-border investments, who enjoy considerable capital mobility and may concentrate investment on hotels, import distribution, and such activities. They may exercise considerable influence on the government through their access to international trading and financial networks. Whether they increase vulnerability or not is unclear, but arguably their only alternative to local investment may be capital flight.

3.3.4 Trade, investment and conflict

Foreign trade and investment have close relationships to the three factors defined above as increasing vulnerability and the risk of CHEs.

Export sector changes can increase inequality, at least if one adopts the widespread assumption of development economists that primary exports are more labour-intensive than manufacturing, so that LLDCs fail to create employment. But export fragility has three other consequences in LLDCs. First, slow real export income growth means slow GDP growth and rising aid dependency so that, with rapidly rising population, employment prospects are generally poor, further worsening income dispersion and increasing the attraction of 'parallel' activities such as smuggling, drug-running, petty crime, prostitution and armed gangs.

Second, the location of primary exports – often in underdeveloped regions – means that price changes or new investment contribute to sudden fluctuations in regional income distribution, spurring feelings of injustice among regions not benefiting. A state limited in inter-regional income distribution may face an undermining of legitimacy or pressure for secession.

Third, export income instability may engender uncertainty, low investment and capital flight. LLDCs rely heavily on export taxes and royalties, which are negotiated shares of natural resource rents in return for exploitation rights rather than profits taxes. Revenue fluctuations from volatile global commodity prices inhibit infrastructure and social services planning, while the casino-like nature of fiscal income encourages corruption and short-term spending.

With import compression, government increases its preference for official imports and contributes to reduced and higher-priced imported inputs and consumer goods. The indirect effect of import shortages on the state's ability to provide basic social services and ensure adequate food in remote areas erodes local support for the administration, thus weakening the state and breaking the 'social contract,' as regional inequality increases. Further, low imports lead to reduced tariff revenue and falling production in the 'fiscal industries' (refining, alcohol, tobacco and soft drinks), therefore undermining the government's revenue base.

Trade liberalization amid extreme foreign exchange shortage is unlikely to reduce these inequalities. Import composition shifts towards that dictated by market demand, largely reflecting the disposable incomes of better-off and politically influential urban dwellers, while the real incomes of the poor and rural inhabitants may actually fall, causing widespread resentment. Thus trade liberalization should be accompanied by concessional finance to meet basic needs until exports recover. Trade liberalization, with its price shift between tradables and non-tradables, causes uncertainty among particular groups, especially if they feel others (for example, immigrants) are the main beneficiaries, or among commercial groups if they expect reversal. In principle, trade liberalization reduces the discretion and corruption of government officials, but in practice it may just shift rents arising from import scarcity from the public to the private sector.[14]

The financing of much of imports by aid ameliorates the disruptive effects of import compression and trade liberalization. However, future imports are still uncertain in LLDCs, since aid disbursements are rarely certain for more than a year or so. This uncertainty has negative effects on both the public and private sectors.

In the public sector, forward planning becomes impossible and thus social services such as health and education, and infrastructure such as road maintenance, cannot be guaranteed and their quality deteriorates. In the private sector, productive investments – even by small farmers in (say) pasture improvement – become risky with no guarantee of inputs. Moreover, consumers have an incentive to buy and hoard durables and non-perishable food to avoid future shortages. Uncertainty abounds, spurring speculation and reducing longer-term commitments to production and employment, thus increasing tension in a fragile society.

Finally, as indicated above, FDI in LLDCs creates considerable potential for increasing inequality, rising uncertainty and a weakened state. While LLDC economic success depends considerably on foreign investors, the three types discussed above, in contrast to FDI in manufacturing or services in MICs, have little shareholder interest in broad-based investment to reduce the economy's vulnerability. Even basic utilities (such as telecommunications, water, power and highways) and the required labour skills can be provided directly by the investor for its project alone.

3.4 Debt and aid

3.4.1 Debt

LLDCs are highly indebted economies, with debt/GDP 74 per cent in 1983 and 114 per cent in 1993, high and rising. Moreover, debt/GDP varies between the 11 'strong growth' LLDCs (growth rate 1.7 per cent annually) with 65 per cent in 1994; the 21 'stagnant' LLDCs (growth rate 0.3 per cent) with 44 per cent; and the 16 'civil strife/war affected' LLDCs (growth rate –5.7 per cent) with 126 per cent (statistics and definitions from UNCTAD 1996). Very high debt ratios seem associated *either* with wars, which reduce GDP *or* with growth, which encourages creditor lending (calculated from UNCTAD 1996).

Vulnerable economies are insolvent in two ways: having liabilities in excess of (marketable) assets, and lacking the ability to generate prospective current account surpluses to pay back the debt. This is why the debt–service ratio for LLDCs is relatively low and falling, with actual debt–service payments less than half scheduled payments.

The debt–service ratio in 1993 varied from 14 per cent for 'strong-growth' LLDCs (whose export growth from 1990 to 1993, was 11 per cent annually); 21 per cent for 'stagnant' LLDCs (with export growth of 2 per cent), and 11 per cent for the 'conflict group' (with export growth of –8 per cent) (ibid.). That rapid export growth decreases the ratio is arithmetically logical, but the low ratio for conflict economies presumably reflects inability to pay (and tolerance by donors) rather than low debt. Indeed, for LLDCs generally, the 1993 *scheduled* debt service was 37 per cent compared to

16 per cent actually paid, often with new lending designed to pay debt service.[15] Nonetheless, conflict and non-conflict economies show no statistically significant differences in debt and debt–service ratios, although the process of debt repayment may be more orderly in economies without conflict (calculated from UNCTAD 1996).

The composition of LLDC debt has changed, as the concessional share increased from 48 per cent in 1983 to 67 per cent in 1993, reflecting both the reliance on aid-flows after the debt crisis of the 1980s to finance trade deficits and the refinancing of commercial debts by aid donors, so that liabilities change owners (calculated from UNCTAD 1996). The multilateral institutions hold one-half of all concessional debt, a proportion that is rising, making debt renegotiation more difficult as they cannot cancel debt. Debt service, in contrast, is still skewed towards non-concessional commercial debt, as interest rates are generally higher. However, the proportion of non-concessional debt guaranteed by donor governments has risen from one-third to a half of the total, implying both that private lending relies on public support, and that further reductions may be politically negotiable.

Given this, the logic of the conditionality rules for current debt relief is difficult to understand. At best, the HIPC initiative is characterized by long qualifying periods of macroeconomic rigour, a relatively small proportion of total debt relieved, no cancellation of multilateral debt, and the charging of the capital cost to current aid budgets. The Paris Club argues that strict terms and a limited write-off are justified by the danger of 'moral hazard'. On the one hand, to maintain incentives, donors, who fear recipients might abandon reform once their debts are cancelled, want most structural reforms completed and irreversible before cancelling debt. On the other hand, countries already repaying debt under previous restructuring exercises might be encouraged to cease payment to attain new terms, if countries unable (or unwilling) to meet their repayments were to receive debt relief. This is true, even after the G8's 1999 Cologne Debt Initiative, which slightly relaxed the conditions and adjustment time for debt relief.

In view of the debt burden on vulnerable economies, both these arguments seem disingenuous, if not irresponsible. The total debt of LLDCs is small – some US$15 billion out of total LDCs' debt of some US$2000 billion in 1996 – and a separate category not affecting repayment by other LDCs. Donors can avoid LLDC macroeconomic incontinence after debt relief by making fresh aid commitments part of an agreed long-term financial programme. If anything, the present arrangement is a disincentive to increasing exports due to contingent obligations to renew full debt service on the remaining debt. For countries undergoing or recovering from conflict, a temporary suspension of payments (as in commercial insolvency) and (at best) the writing-off of debts against specific social expenditure targets would seem logical.

Debt insolvency has several negative effects on vulnerability, which further increase the risk of conflict. First, the pressure on the balance of payments increases import compression, as discussed above. Second, a large part of the government budget is devoted to debt service,[16] which amplifies external revenue shocks in reducing infrastructure and social services spending. Third, public service provision and administrative reform are made more difficult owing to frequent debt renegotiations that create uncertainty regarding future resources. Fourth, private investment (both domestic and foreign) and thus employment are depressed by the uncertainty of the debt overhang in the form of 'sovereign risk'.

3.4.2 Aid

Further external finance is ODA available from IFIs and bilateral aid agencies. Neither source is determined economically, having been related during the Cold War to geostrategic objectives. Since 1989, ODA has been changed by i) 'aid fatigue' among DC taxpayers, meaning declining real aid in the 1990s, which is expected to continue in the first decade of the 2000s, ii) a focus on integrating aid recipients to world markets and relying on private finance, and iii) an increasing proportion assigned to humanitarian assistance in emergency relief and security interventions (Chapter 9). Consequently, ODA is no longer oriented towards increasing productive capacity or even providing infrastructure. Thus both balance-of-payments support and humanitarian aid received by vulnerable economies tend to maintain household consumption and central government activities rather than capital formation or longer-term development objectives.

Curiously, despite official statements to reorientate aid towards LLDCs, they receive little over a quarter of all ODA (OECD 1997b), due to geopolitical commitments to client states and continued balance of payments support to MICs as part of structural adjustment.

ODA/GDP averages about 25 per cent, or 111 per cent of domestic capital formation, in vulnerable economies, implying that savings is negative and that investment and its composition is essentially determined by aid donors. Moreover, a rising proportion of imports, about 85 per cent of the total, are financed (and determined) by aid. Nonetheless, the absence of coordination between donors means that investment and imports do not reflect a coherent long-term programme to reduce vulnerability and prevent conflict.

The large differences in the means for aid per capita and the various aid ratios are statistically significant (Table 3.5), but per capita aid rates are actually higher in non-conflict than conflict economies, presumably because regular development cooperation programmes break down and are replaced by humanitarian assistance. Only the ratio of aid to imports is higher in conflict economies than in non-conflict economies, reflecting a high level of 'aid dependency' in the level of current economic activity itself as opposed to the development effort.

ODA to vulnerable economies has not become globalized since 1980: only two-fifths now come from the multilaterals, principally the Bretton

Table 3.5   Aid to vulnerable economies

Aid ratios in LLDCs (1988–94)	LLDCs		Sig. Diff.		All LLDCs
	Conflict	*Non-conflict*	*Means?*	*Variance?*	
ODA per capita (US$)	119.7	159.0	yes	no	97.5
ODA/GDP	16.4	32.8	yes	no	24.6
ODA/investment	104.9	117.1	no	no	111.2
ODA/imports	90.1	78.9	no	no	84.6
Bilateral/total ODA	57.6	63.5	yes	no	60.6
ODA Grant Element:					
Bilateral	53.0	60.0	yes	no	56.5
Multilateral	25.0	18.6	yes	no	22.7

Source: UNCTAD (1996)

Woods institutions and regional development banks. Of the total, approximately one-quarter takes the form of technical assistance, and a further quarter food aid and humanitarian relief. The grant element in total ODA – which does not generate debt – has risen slightly due to the shift away from development projects, but is mainly associated with bilateral donors and their humanitarian relief efforts.

The high aid dependency of vulnerable economies is complicated by aid being volatile and unpredictable. Due to donor budgeting, protracted negotiations over debt and recipients' difficulties in fulfilling policy conditions, both aid commitments and actual disbursements vary considerably from one year to another. This additional source of uncertainty in a vulnerable economy has serious consequences for the stability of imports and public expenditure.

In vulnerable economies, aid agencies play a major part through import support programmes, humanitarian projects and the local expenditures of their personnel. Aid operations play a crucial role, albeit unwittingly, in the way the macroeconomy works. Import support for LLDCs is not intended to raise investment or government expenditure, but to use existing productive capacity more effectively (raising employment and incomes) and sustain nutrition, health and other essential services. In a vulnerable

Table 3.6   Sources of aid to vulnerable economies

Composition of ODA to LLDCs (%)	1981–87	1988–94
Technical assistance	32.5	28.1
Bilateral ODA	60.6	58.1
Multilateral ODA	39.3	39.4

Source: UNCTAD (1996)

economy, where large development projects are difficult to implement, import support is the major resource inflow and frequently the greater part of imports. Programme aid is largely commodity (or food) aid, although fuel from non-DAC donors can be significant. Commodity aid, which is usually required to prevent displacing normal trade, has the advantage of generating counterpart funds as a revenue source.

For the donor, the advantages of import support are the relative absence of absorptive capacity limits, using existing processing plants and adminis-tration, rapid disbursement, and the countervalue from the sale of goods to support social expenditures.[17] Moreover, import support, which can be 'switched on or off' quickly, is ideal for policy conditionality. Imports can be allocated administratively, but donors often prefer an auction to mini-mize corruption and strengthen the private sector. However, an auction system needs an efficient banking system to administer the licenses and a transparent private sector, neither of which are available in most LLDCs, particularly conflict LLDCs.

The debate over the macroeconomic impact of aid (specifically import support) is considerable. Traditionally economists argue that aid ('external saving') reduces domestic saving, and that capital inflows lead to an over-valued exchange rate biased against exports. However, while import support significantly displaces demand, the positive effect on supply can increase domestic savings and investment, while monetary policy counter-acts the overvalued exchange rate. Nonetheless, achieving these positive macroeconomic outcomes in LLDCs is difficult unless aid is oriented towards increasing export capacity and strengthening the financial system, usually not done by bilateral donors concentrating on human development and humanitarian relief.

3.4.3 Debt, aid and conflict

Do debt management and aid distribution affect social inequality, eco-nomic uncertainty and state strength (and thus reduce conflict)? Not neces-sarily. How debt is renegotiated affects private investment and export growth. Government expenditure compression is likely to increase inequal-ities of access to employment and consumption, although the injustice and resentment generated depends on state capacity to redistribute resources in a way perceived 'fair'. Probably more important is the uncertainty caused by the repeated renegotiation of debt and insolvency. Inability to repay debt implies that major fiscal shift and import restrictions will be needed to generate the resources required for repayment, or that default will occur with serious effects on creditworthiness. This uncertainty reduces private investment and makes planned provision of public services more difficult. Finally, the fiscal resources required to service debt reduce state capacity to mediate between opposing social groups; although this could be compen-sated by reductions in other expenditures.

The present criteria of the HIPC initiative (OECD 1997b) of low per capita income, debt/GDP of over 200 per cent, and a prolonged record of successful stabilization programmes do not consider the recent experience or risk of conflict and other vulnerability. HIPCs' limited scope is difficult to understand, given the small absolute size of LLDC debt and the even smaller proportion that might never be repaid.

Aid is designed to reduce poverty and strengthen social services, which should reduce vulnerability and state weakness. Nonetheless, substantial aid dependency may not reduce vulnerability unless regional or inter-group inequalities are addressed and productive capacity is increased, particularly in exports. In addition, relying on ODA to finance the public sector through counterpart funds reduces the need for tax reform. As suggested above, the uncertainty from volatile ODA disbursements has a negative effect on public services and probity. While in principle aid donors wish to reduce vulnerability and conflict, the small proportion of ODA allocated to LLDCs and the lack of donor coordination and effective policy conditionality throw doubt on this goal in practice.

3.5 International economic institutions and policy conditionality

This section does not provide a detailed critique of policy lending or structural adjustment but rather examines the effect on LLDCs of the standard policy model that emphasizes external balance and international economic integration. Aid agencies tend to leave macroeconomic policy to the IFIs. However, the role of the IFIs, supported by regional development banks, in vulnerable economies is ambiguous. The IFIs prescribe adjustment, central to vulnerable economies, without consideration of supply response, state capacity or social conflict.[18]

Three factors lead to more frequent IFI intervention in vulnerable economies than in the more 'reformable' MICs.[19] First, rising debt burdens, default on repayment schedules, exhaustion of reserves and need for urgent balance-of-payments equilibration make a comprehensive approach necessary. Interestingly, the main creditors are often the IFIs, because commercial debtors write off their losses (or transfer them to their home governments) and bilateral donors are more willing to tolerate delays or to roll over debt. Second, aid agencies concerned by mounting inflation, collapse of public administration, black markets and rising poverty turn to IFIs to 'straighten out the economic situation'. Third, the government, unable to resolve the situation, may call on IFIs to determine the economic reforms required to renew access to foreign funds.

The IMF's main concern is a short-term stabilization programme to restore external payments capacity – both a convertible currency and reasonable debt service. This programme is defined as a nominal exchange-rate devaluation, sharp reduction in the growth of the money supply, positive real interest rates and reduced government expenditure and thus the budget deficit. The aim is to reduce inflation, restore currency convertibility and renew debt service. However, applying this monetary adjustment to a vulnerable economy with the structural constraints discussed above can have effects contrary to policy-makers' expectations.

Large nominal devaluations require considering import demand and export supply elasticities, and the income effect of the downward adjustment of household consumption. However, LLDCs' imports are largely debt-financed and administratively allocated, so devaluation will be passed through almost entirely to domestic prices. Although export profitability will increase, export volume – constrained by investment and imported input shortages – may not rise. Thus the real exchange rate is not a policy variable.

The main macroeconomic consequence of nominal devaluation is therefore to reduce domestic demand. The fiscal impact of devaluation depends on the foreign-exchange composition of revenue and expenditure: only heavily aid-dependent governments would reduce the budget deficit with devaluation, but even if nominal budgets are incompletely adjusted, if public-sector imports are covered by aid, then increased counterpart funds cover the difference. Private sector real demand will only fall if firms reduce investment or households consumption, but among households inflation's impact is not evenly distributed, with the poor particularly vulnerable.

Reduced real government expenditures under stabilization are usually spread across the whole budget, and are manifested in investment cuts and real wage reductions by civil servants. However, reduced government credit requirements, combined with a lower overall credit ceiling, can reduce inflation considerably. But credit reductions and high nominal interest rates harm production, particularly that of small producers, and thus reduce food supply. Real interest rates do not increase bank deposits due to exchange risk, while the increased profitability of exporters cannot be immediately translated into growth, employment and import capacity.

There is no doubt that price stability, fiscal solvency and a manageable balance of payments are desirable objectives; the problem is the cost of assuming that macroeconomic imbalances are monetary in nature when private and public-sector behaviour in LLDCs is so different than in MICs with a strong private sector, sound fiscal structure and rising incomes.

Is structural adjustment required? The WB suggests permanently reducing the fiscal deficit by privatization, import liberalization and credit deregulation to force efficiency on domestic firms, real devaluation to promote exports and deregulating farm prices to stimulate food supply. Similar to IMF programmes, the objectives are reasonable and the methods effective for MICs with a strong private sector, however LLDC structural adjustment is more ambiguous.

For vulnerable economies, orthodox structural adjustment may be counterproductive. Import liberalization can undermine the supply of essential goods and services and stimulate capital flight; privatization can be impossible or enrich senior government officials; and real devaluation can generate distributional problems, compounded by fiscal deficits unless public investment and social services are abandoned. Farm price deregulation may not increase peasant output without improved credit and an adequate supply of rural producer goods. Above all, private investment may not increase enough to restore employment, given the uncertainty about profits or even asset ownership. In sum, deregulation assumes the existence of a new market equilibrium towards which the economy will naturally move, and that supply and demand are responsive to relative price changes without unacceptable increased inequality. Under conflict (and post-conflict) conditions this is an unwarranted and even dangerous assumption.

For adjustment to be successful in reducing vulnerability, exports and productivity need sustained growth, requiring a permanent rise in investment (and to reduce aid dependency) saving rates. Investment rates and growth have fallen in both LLDCs and LICs (Table 3.7), and the rate of investment has also declined. Any hope of successful integration to world markets depends on higher investment rates.

Finally, other international economic institutions that do not intervene directly affect LLDC vulnerability. The WTO's international trade liberalization since the Uruguay Round is reducing LLDCs (especially SSA preferences) under the GSP and Lomé Convention, increasing critical import prices, especially in food-deficit countries, as world grain surpluses decline, and increasing LLDC compliance and administrative costs. The potential for increased LLDC trade under the Uruguay Round depends on LLDCs overcoming supply-side constraints and becoming more competitive internationally. Meanwhile, LLDCs will lose preferential market access for tropical products, textiles and garments. The international property rights agreements, while providing greater protection to LDC owners of capital, may increase importers' pharmaceutical, agrochemical and technology costs.

Table 3.7   Gross domestic investment in vulnerable economies

	LLDCs (UNCTAD)	LICs (World Bank)
Investment/GDP		
1980	16	20
1994	15	17
Investment growth		
1980–90	–0.4	–0.4
1990–94	0.6	–1.8

Source: UNCTAD (1996)

The IMF, WB and WTO do not inherently increase inequality, worsen insecurity or weaken LLDCs, and thus raise the risk of conflict. Indeed measures to force fiscal consolidation and reduce inflation should strengthen the state and reduce uncertainty. Rather, these three institutions must consider how liberalization increases LLDCs' exposure to volatile markets and how adjustment programmes affect LLDCs' redistribution of income and assets.

3.6 Conclusions and policy implications

LLDCs include 550 million people, while LICs contain over one-third of the world's population. The purpose here has been to show how the linkages of vulnerable economies to the global economy – through trade, investment, debt, aid and multilateral institutions – may increase inequality, uncertainty and state weakness.

This chapter is not about domestic economic policy or institutions, but about the international influences on conflict. Nor has it suggested that international arrangements are 'the cause of conflicts', but rather that they may affect political tensions and state failures that lead to conflict. Conflict is not merely a local problem that the international community tries to resolve. We also need to examine how vulnerable societies are integrated into the global economy and ensure that this integration does not increase intrastate tensions, thus undermining the capacity of local institutions to mediate during the process of modernization.

Vulnerability is not inevitable: countries can increase growth, exports and human development without excessive debt or social inequality; but they can get into a recessive cycle of debt, foreign exchange shortages and import compression which exacerbates inequality and uncertainty. Vulnerability need not necessarily lead to conflict if the state is strong and broadly based enough to provide public goods and ensure minority-group security. However, if increased vulnerability coincides with a weak state and a divided society, then conflict can break out. When this happens, the recessive cycle is exacerbated, making conflict difficult to resolve.

The main lesson here is that international linkages can worsen the combination of economic vulnerability and a weak state that can trigger conflict. Economic vulnerability is not just low per capita income or high debt/GDP, but rather perceived inequality between groups, their uncertainties, and the lack of resolving social stress by public action. It is not 'underdevelopment' that increases the likelihood of conflict, but rather sudden economic change, often from exogenous shocks. The general consensus of historians is that rising expectations among key social groups and the loss of social legitimacy rather than economic deprivation have been at the root of most revolutions (Davies 1962).

It is argued here that the influence of international economic arrangements on LLDC armed conflict is to be found in the impact of an increased sense of injustice generated by trade and financial liberalization; an increased insecurity generated by international market shocks affecting domestic income and assets; and the effect of aid conditionality on the state's ability to mediate the conflict. External vulnerability is more than just the characteristic of economies affected by armed conflict.

There is a strong case for reconsidering international economic arrangements for vulnerable countries, not necessarily through a large resource transfer to these countries (probably politically infeasible anyway) but by creating special provisions to reduce the effects of economic globalization on distributive injustice, economic uncertainty and state weakness. The international community has the tasks of reducing the economic vulnerability and risk of conflict of poor economies, and ensuring that vulnerable countries do not slide into conflict.

Reducing economic vulnerability and conflict proneness is not merely an issue of domestic 'development policy'. The following international policy measures logically derive from this chapter's argument:

i)   Export primary commodity stabilization schemes for LLDCs to reduce uncertainty about foreign exchange income; and preferential access to regional and multilateral trade arrangements to increase exports. These should reduce the potential for conflict by stabilizing fiscal income, increasing social entitlements, and stabilizing income and employment, particularly in primary export sectors crucial to rural livelihoods.

ii) Focusing structural adjustment towards strengthening export capacity before import liberalization; and securing long-term credit to investment before reforming the financial sector, thus stabilizing incomes and jobs for vulnerable groups, while providing long-term benefits from integration into the world economy.

iii) Establishing external solvency by cancelling all outstanding official debt, with the condition that the resources released be used only for reducing monetized deficits and providing public health and education, thus improving long-term human development, especially for the poor, and giving greater content to the 'social contract' between the public sector and all social groups.

iv) Reorienting ODA towards reducing inter-group and inter-regional inequality, and towards strengthening the state's capacity to deliver health, education and security to all citizens. This implies adopting conflict reduction (and by extension, the reduction of vulnerability) as the priority in development cooperation with poor countries, rather than broader notions of 'economic development', which disguise social and regional redistribution of income and assets.

v)   Regulating international trade and investment in arms, oil, gems, timber and other 'sensitive' commodities to minimize the destabilization of LLDCs. This could be achieved within existing multilateral trade and investment agreements and by creating specific transitory conditions for poor countries.

At present, humanitarian relief is usually mobilized *after* conflict has broken out, with collapsed administrative, production and transport systems and population movements leading to health and nutrition emergencies. Intervention would be better used in preventing such emergencies from occurring in the first place. The arguments above suggest that appropriate international economic measures are essential for *all* vulnerable countries as we cannot forecast conflict in individual countries precisely enough to take corrective action. Indeed, 'early-warning' systems can only identify conflicts when conditions have almost deteriorated to irreversibility. These arguments also imply that humanitarian aid in response to conflict-related emergencies should consider the following:

i)   Closer donor coordination to ensure that import financing directly alleviates poverty and improves inter-group fairness.
ii) Economic incentives to conflict reduction in allocating aid to states and NGOs.
iii) Avoiding destabilizing effects (such as abetting drugs trade) of donor interventions that undermine the positive effect of humanitarian aid.

These tentative conclusions underline the need to reconsider aspects of international economic linkages that increase vulnerability or the risk of conflict.

Notes

1. Except perhaps for the last echoes of the Marxian tradition and Galtung's revisionist structural approach to imperialism, where the resistance of traditional social forms to the modernizing force of international capitalism is seen as a major source of conflict on the periphery of the world economy – an insight that might be worth revisiting. See Galtung (1971) and Nafziger and Richter (1976).
2. For a useful discussion of absolute and relative deprivation in explaining CHEs, see Nafziger and Auvinen (2000), who, however, emphasize *absolute* deprivation, compared to this chapter's greater weight to *relative* deprivation (a group's previous level of income or to that of another group) as triggers of conflict.
3. Afghanistan,** Angola,** Bangladesh,* Benin,* Bhutan, Burkina Faso, Burundi,** Cambodia,** Cape Verde, Central African Republic,* Chad,* Comoros,* Djibouti, Equatorial Guinea, Eritrea,** Ethiopia,** Gambia, Guinea, Guinea-Bissau, Haiti,** Kiribati, Lao PDR,* Lesotho, Liberia,** Madagascar, Malawi, Maldives, Mali, Mauritania, Mozambique,** Myanmar,* Nepal, Niger, Rwanda,** Samoa, São Tomé, Sierra Leone,** Solomons, Somalia,** Sudan,** Togo,** Tuvalu, Uganda,* Tanzania, Vanuatu, Yemen**, Zaire,** Zambia (UNCTAD 1996); asterisk (*) indicates serious conflict since 1970, double asterisk (**) since 1990.
4. Burundi,* Comoros,* Eritrea,* Ethiopia,* Kenya, Lesotho, Madagascar, Malawi, Mozambique,* Rwanda,* Somalia,* Sudan,* Tanzania, Uganda,* Zaire,* Zambia, and Zimbabwe* in East/Southern Africa; Benin,* Burkina Faso, Cameroon, Central African Republic,* Chad,* Congo,* Côte d'Ivoire, Equatorial Guinea, Gambia, Ghana, Guinea, Guinea-Bissau, Liberia,* Mali, Mauritania, Niger,

Nigeria,* São Tomé, Senegal, Sierra Leone* and Togo* in West Africa; Cambodia,* China, Lao PDR,* Mongolia, Myamar,* Vietnam,* Afghanistan,* Bangladesh,* Bhutan, India, Nepal, Pakistan,* Sri Lanka* in Asia; Albania, Armenia,* Azerbijan,* Bosnia,* Georgia, and the Kyrgyz and Tajikistan Republics in Eastern Europe and Central Asia; Yemen* and Egypt* in the Middle East; and Guyana, Haiti,* Honduras* and Nicaragua* in Latin America.

5. The slower growing countries' growth appears to be more volatile, which increases uncertainty.

6. However, even the explanatory power of their regression model is poor (explaining only 16 to 19 per cent of CHEs), while the coefficient linking income levels to conflict in the probit model is remarkably low: '...a 100% increase in GNP per capita reduces the probability of an emergency by 13%' (Auvinen and Nafziger 1999: 286).

7. For instance: 'Indeed, there seems to be a two-way causal relationship between GDP growth and CHEs, but the relationship is stronger from GDP growth to emergencies than vice versa' (Auvinen and Nafziger 1999: 280).

8. See Stewart *et al.* (1997).

9. Compared to US$260 for LDCs generally (UNCTAD 1996).

10. That is, export value deflated by the import price index; or the 'income terms of trade'.

11. UNCTAD's (1996) estimate of the trend in primary commodity prices for LDCs (excluding crude petroleum) is a 5.3 per cent annual decline (1980–90), and a 2.5 per cent annual increase (1990–95), a net fall of 35 per cent (1980–95).

12. Uncertainty leads to lower private investment due to the 'option value' of delaying investment until more information or stability becomes available (Dixit and Pindyck 1994).

13. These are often key sources of excise duty that can be collected by the national treasury directly from a few producers.

14. Of course the new entrepreneurs are often the old bureaucrats!

15. Indeed, grant aid from bilateral donors is often used to service multilateral debt, which cannot be rescheduled.

16. UNCTAD has no LLDC fiscal data; but the World Bank (1996b) gives an average level of government consumption (which excludes transfer payments such as debt service) of 10 per cent of GDP in 1994, compared to the LLDCs' debt service/GDP of approximately 5 per cent.

17. Existing OECD guidelines, however, do not support tying counterpart funds to specific projects (DAC 1997).

18. Presumably because they are constitutionally bound to be 'non-political'.

19. UNCTAD (1996) contains a comprehensive list of arrangements between LLDCs and IFIs since 1980; 36 countries have at least one, while Zaire has thirteen IMF interventions and Tanzania ten WB structural adjustment programmes (1980–95).

Part II
Domestic Economic Responses

4
State Legitimacy, Tax Reform and the Provision of Basic Services

John Toye

4.1 Introduction

This chapter argues that basic social services on an expanded scale, financed by increased domestic tax revenue, are important in preventing a civil conflict or CHE, or its recurrence. It first outlines a general framework to analyse civil conflicts in LDCs, indicating the role of fiscal policy in mitigating CHEs, and then examines Ethiopia since the fall of Haile Selassie, to see how it fits into the general framework. Finally, the chapter explores the broader implications of a relationship between provision of basic social services, financed by a reformed tax system, and the restoration of political legitimacy.

Apthorpe (1997) indicates that a CHE is a diplomatic euphemism for a chronic political emergency as distinct from a natural emergency. The existence of political and military conflict (and the killing and displacement of people) defines the complexity of a CHE. A CHE covers a multitude of political sins: the collapse of state authority (as in Liberia or Somalia), internal animosity (as in Rwanda and Burundi), or internal but exacerbated by two super-powers (as during the Cold War).

4.2 Fiscal aspects of the crisis of state legitimacy

The first step in the argument here is to link the degree of state legitimacy with a CHE. Legitimacy, despite its subjective and intangible character, is a critical dimension of state strength (Holsti 2000). The second step is the link between the state's material basis, including its capacity to tax and provide basic social services, and its ideational basis or capacity for legitimacy for its citizens. If these links are valid, fiscal policy should be positive in arresting and reversing the erosion of state legitimacy.

Nathanson (1998: 5) reasons in the following way:

> Many people have wondered whether government power is legitimate and whether we have a moral duty to obey the laws of the state.... If

justice requires, for example, substantial government activity to assist the poor or to provide all citizens with a good education or adequate health care, then a government that fails to do these things is treating its citizens unjustly. If this is a serious injustice, citizens who are not properly treated will feel less allegiance to the government....They will believe that their obligation to obey the law is diminished by the injustice of the government and its policies...

A further connection is that state legitimacy requires not only a just provision of basic services, but also a just pattern of taxation to finance them.

State legitimacy is rarely all or nothing, but a matter of degree, and subject to alteration. Government action can improve or erode legitimacy, thus changing the risk and intensity of a CHE.

What are the most important causes of the erosion of legitimacy? Many LDCs, which have suffered from colonialism established by conquest and maintained by repression, lack a history of legitimate governments. Moreover, many post-colonial states, particularly in SSA, lacking well-developed national independence movements and imitating the monopoly power of the colonialist, elicited no greater sense of popular allegiance than the governments that they replaced. Many of these states have created a patron-client system of corruption, in which a few 'big men' gain financially at the expense of the poor majority, polarizing wealth and preventing a vigorous middle class. With the exception of high-performing East Asian economies, LDC governments have failed in their development strategies, a situation made worse by difficult international economic conditions since 1980. Persistent economic failure has made it harder to sustain clientalistic corruption. Maintaining elite incomes requires increased corruption and more pronounced regional discrimination. To retain client loyalty, political elites may permit additional depredations of the poor and marginal community, resulting in consequences similar to those in Sudan (Keen 1994). Some governments have responded to economic failure by increasing income from foreign companies seeking natural-resource rents at rock-bottom prices, from foreign aid agencies with money to disburse for more projects, or for more promises of policy reforms. These tactics do not always succeed, as in the cases of Sierra Leone and Liberia (Reno 2000).

Once legitimacy has eroded, the risk of rebellion to oust the government is increased. Collier and Hoeffler (1998) have developed a simple economic model of the causes of civil war. This model has relevance to a situation in which the government can no longer rely on the loyalty of its citizens and the determinants of political action are reducible to the calculus of short-term interest. The model is expressed by

$$Uw = (p(D).T; M; C)$$

where

> Uw = the utility of war to the rebels
> p = the probability of a rebel victory
> D = government defence expenditure
> T = the gain to the rebels conditional on victory
> M = expected months of warfare
> C = the rebels' costs of coordinating their forces.

The model predicts that, when Uw exceeds zero, the rebels will launch a civil war.

Collier and Hoeffler (1998) use this model to identify four key characteristics of SSA countries that have been vulnerable to civil war. First, having a small number of distinct ethnic groups increases vulnerability, by lowering C. They show empirically that both an ethnically homogeneous population *and* a population consisting of a large number of ethnic groups both face significantly reduced risks of war.

Second, the share of GDP that a country derives from natural resources is neither unusually small (less of a prize for rebels to try to capture, so T is reduced), nor unusually large (a higher T will be more than offset because the existing government will have greater scope for funding its military expenditure from non-tax revenue, so permitting a higher D).

Third, low per capita income increases vulnerability, since this, together with the natural resources endowment, is a proxy for the country's tax base. The smaller the tax base, the smaller is the potential for funding military expenditure without destabilizing the economy. Thus the more likely it is that the rebels will fight the government forces on equal military terms, and the more likely that, if they do fight, they will win.

Loss of state legitimacy is necessary but not sufficient for civil conflict in the Collier-Hoeffler model. The model indicates that incentives to rebel are reduced by government's exploitation of a tax base, which enlarges resources and eases the trade-off between spending on military budgets to deter a rebel offensive and spending on social services to improve state legitimacy.

However, not all governments succeed or even try to restore legitimacy. Some may put their faith in repressing rebels with a pre-emptive strike that can be the 'tipping event' leading to a CHE (Holsti 2000: 255). If civil war breaks out, the tax base will almost certainly shrink, but the base remaining will be more vigorously exploited. The government's military spending may increase, probably at a faster rate than savings in other areas of public expenditure. It can be expected that total public expenditure will grow faster than tax revenues, giving rise to an expanding budget deficit. Stewart *et al.*'s (1997) empirical data not only reinforce these expectations but also indicate that total government spending increases as a share of GDP except where the capacity to collect tax revenue completely collapses.

It is important that, if governments fear vulnerability to CHEs, they do not increase repression or resort to unsustainable financing (printing money, excess foreign borrowing, or an inflation tax), thus continuing the downward spiral towards violent civil conflict. In the final analysis, collecting tax revenue, which requires some element of voluntary compliance by those who pay, is an important indicator of the legitimacy of the regime.

A government that seeks to restore its legitimacy should urgently seek ways to reverse the erosion of its tax base and any decline of tax revenues as a percentage of GDP. Tax reform and collection is dependent on keeping corruption within bounds. Section 4.5 recommends VAT, which has considerable potential both for raising revenue and restraining corruption.

It must be recognized that, before the outbreak of a CHE, the motivation of the ruling elite may not be consistent with the pursuit of policies to remove corruption and institute a just pattern of taxation and public spending. Tyrannical governments that systematically use public corruption to ensure their own survival and oppress particular groups will not be interested in improving the transparency or the accountability of their tax and spending systems. What appears as mismanagement should not, in such cases, be attributed to technical policy mistakes: it is a deliberate strategy of control (Nafziger 1993). These are regimes that think that they can rule without any concern for achieving legitimacy in the eyes of their own population. It is hard indeed to see how regimes of this kind can be deterred from courses of action that will lead them to provoke CHEs.

4.3   Preventing CHEs: the case of Ghana

We can illustrate how reforming the tax system and reducing corruption might reduce the risk of a CHE by examining Ghana. By the end of the 1970s, Ghana had been reduced by predatory military rulers to such economic distress and low legitimacy that it arguably could have collapsed into a CHE. Collier and Hoeffler's (1998) economic variables would have predicted conflict. Natural resource (gold and timber) endowment was substantial, output was steadily declining, and population was growing from 2.5 to 3 per cent yearly. Despite violent political conflict during the late 1970s and early 1980s, including the ousting of corrupt generals, the trials of rebels, elections and a coup, there was little political mobilization of the population. The Collier–Hoeffler model would indicate that the large number of small ethnic groups raised the costs of mobilization, so that overall the costs of rebellion probably exceeded the benefits.

Moreover, although it cannot be said that this was sufficient to avoid a CHE, in 1983 the government of Jerry Rawlings adopted the policy of increasing domestic tax revenue, raising the public expenditure to GDP ratio, and increasing the share of public expenditure going to social services. From 1980 to 1995, central government revenue rose as a percentage of GDP from 8.3 to 22.7, while total expenditure rose from 10.9 to 20.6. Over the same period, the share of central government spending on education, health, social security, welfare, housing and community amenities rose from 38.3 to 42.3 per cent (World Bank 1997b: 240–1). The legitimacy of the Rawlings government increased over the pre-1983 governments, as opponents made no coup attempts after 1985 and the government won a series of reasonably fair and free elections in the 1990s. Fiscal policy is probably not the sole factor in bolstering legitimacy compared to the 1970s, as there have also been liberalizing constitutional changes and a generally improving economic position.

4.4   The case of Ethiopia's post-CHE fiscal recovery

Ghana may exemplify the prevention of a potential CHE, while Ethiopia represents an effort to avoid a CHE repetition. In the aftermath of a CHE, the prospects for recovery will depend largely on the degree to which state legitimacy can be restored. What kind of regime can best do that?

It cannot be assumed that the best outcome is for government to deter potential rebels. Indeed, the government might be so tyrannical that its replacement by rebels might improve welfare. Humanitarian actors may be better employed in negotiating an early transfer of power by the government than in advising the government how to mobilize to bolster its dubious legitimacy.

The fact that the victorious new government in Ethiopia was recruited mainly from Tigray province was not enough to deprive it of legitimacy. What matters is whether governments can create an economic environment to manage ethnic conflicts over distribution, are sufficiently self-restrained to avoid antagonizing potential ethnic opponents, and can distribute income to diffuse resentment by the bottom half of the population. The Rwandan government, also dominated by one ethnic group, had satisfied none of the three criteria by 1993, and the result was genocide. Uvin (2000: 166) attributes this genocide to 'the failure of a state-building and development model that was based on ethnic, regional and social exclusion; that increased deprivation, humiliation, and vulnerability of the poor; that was top-down and authoritarian; that produced daily corruption, clientelism, and impunity; and that left the masses uninformed, uneducated, and unable to resist orders and slogans'. Ethnicity must be understood in its broader historical and political context (Alexander *et al.* 2000).

Ethiopia has a long history of recurrent famines. The 1972–74 famine, which killed from 50 000 to 200 000 people, an amount modest by historical standards, set off a long period of political turbulence, which included the overthrow of Emperor Haile Selassie, Mengistu's coup within the successor government (the Derg), the 'Red Terror' of 1977–78, the Ogaden war with Somalia, and the major famine of 1984–85, in which an estimated one million people died, and minor famines of 1987–88 and 1990–91. Throughout this period, the Derg was in continuing armed conflict with Eritrea, and from 1975 with the Tigrayan People's Liberation Front. IDS-IDR (1996) includes a narrative of events in Ethiopia suggesting a prolonged CHE.

The Derg pursued 'Ethiopian socialism', which involved the nationalization of all banks and insurance companies, all industrial and commercial enterprises, all urban and rural land and extra-urban houses. The attempt to socialize agriculture involved establishing agricultural producers' and service cooperatives. These changes resulted in a dramatic increase in public employment.

The economic cost of Ethiopia expelling the Somalis from the Ogaden in 1978 was substantial. Productive capacity declined, the money supply expansion accelerated inflation, severe foreign exchange rationing created a parallel market, and the budget deficit increased rapidly. Meanwhile, savings and investment dwindled and per capita income fell. But in addition, the 1978 treaty with the USSR effectively locked Mengistu's government into 'socialist' economic institutions, despite its economic failings, in return for Soviet external support.

The legitimacy of the Derg waned, with the toll of wars, and efforts at resettlement and 'villagization'. Peasants, with their psychological attachment to the home place, resisted resettlement, and commuted to their initial homeland. Although the regime changed its economic behaviour in 1988, after the USSR refused to resupply the Ethiopian armed forces, efforts at liberalization to attract Western external support came too late and the Mengistu regime collapsed in military defeat in 1991. The victorious Tigrayan-dominated Ethiopian Peoples' Revolutionary Democratic Front (EPRDF) established the Transitional Government of Ethiopia (TGE), which sought to expel the cycle of famines and civil strife.

In 1992, the TGE's fiscal peace dividend allowed defence spending to fall by more than half, saving about half a billion birr. The government reduced the budget deficit and increased agricultural and general public services, but social services were unchanged, except for a considerable squeezing of capital expenditure to maintain current expenditure. After 1992, the TGE ruled out a reallocation of public expenditure from defence to social services on the grounds that 'the transition to peace does not so much provide a fiscal dividend as avert a financial catastrophe' (Bevan 1992: 6). Moreover, after 1992, the government undertook a modest reallocation from defence to social services; the budget deficit continued to rise through the mid-1990s, but declined through 1997 from a boom in international coffee prices and the rise in revenue from tax reforms. The government abolished some taxes, reduced marginal tax rates, replaced excises with more income-elastic indirect taxes and improved tax administration. A border war with Eritrea after May 1998, though temporarily strengthening the ruling coalition, has hurt Ethiopia's fiscal position. As of 2000, increased competence in economic management, lower levels of corruption (by standards of neighbouring countries), and reduced rural poverty have contributed to increased state legitimacy.

4.5   Restoring legitimacy by fiscal reform

Ethiopia has broader implications for fiscal policy in LDCs prone to civil conflict. As a CHE declines in intensity, one immediate need is to create (or restore) adequate basic social services – education, health, clean water supply and social safety nets for the very poor. Why is this important? The CHE has damaged civilian communities and disrupted the delivery of services. Expanded services are essential for reintegrating and resettling IDPs and ex-combatants. Finally, providing basic social services is powerful in establishing the legitimacy of the successor state in the population.

Restoring normal levels of basic social services need not be daunting for an LIC, as the expenditure budget for a typical LDC is markedly smaller, even as a share of GDP, than in MICs and DCs. Second, the share for basic social services is less than one-eighth of the total in LICs compared to more than one-third in MICs and more than one-half in DCs. The resources required for normal levels of basic social services are much less than what the government spends on each of defence, economic services and administrative and other government services (IMF 1995).

If basic social service spending has fallen below normal levels during a CHE, a government should reallocate expenditure, especially away from defence. Still, to maintain peace the successor government may need to spend part of the peace dividend to demobilize and reintegrate former combatants, and to upgrade the quality of the armed forces responsible for future maintenance of peace and enforcement of tax collection. Nevertheless, this should be only temporary, so that resources can be mainstreamed into general social programmes in the medium term.

One limitation in reallocating expenditures to basic social services is the substantial variability in public spending, especially in SSA, and its close link to the variability in tax revenue (Bleaney *et al.* 1992). It seems causality in SSA runs from revenue to expenditure, rather than vice versa, for the following reasons:

i)   Revenue instability is exceptionally high in SSA, with the standard deviation of year-to-year revenue changes for 17 SSA countries 2.85, compared to 1.88 (Latin America) and 1.55 (Asia) (Bleaney *et al.* 1992, Table 1).

ii) SSA's exceptionally high revenue instability is related to the openness of the economy, presumably because of the revenue effects of primary commodity booms and slumps, and the level of inflation, presumably because of the revenue-reducing effects of high inflation mentioned earlier.

iii) SSA is unlikely to plan for such highly variable year-to-year changes in expenditure, because current expenditures represent continuing functions and policy commitments and very few capital projects can be completed efficiently within a year.

iv) Most SSA countries are struggling to reduce (or prevent increases in) budget deficits, some adopting cash budgeting rules to meet these objectives, a reverse of the 'first plan expenditure and then raise the required revenue' hypothesis.

The constraining of expenditure by revenue can have both short-term and medium-term impacts on reallocating spending to basic social services. In the short run, highly variable expenditures limit a planned reallocation between functions and make it impossible to deliver rational expenditure programmes. With fiscal distress, cash budgeting serves to preserve the macroeconomic balance, but at the expense of the ability to plan expenditure by sector and production unit.

In the medium term, improving basic social services is limited by inadequate domestic revenue, which requires fundamental tax reform. In reform, VAT, which is highly productive of revenue, should have a central place. A study of 50 countries that had adopted VAT by 1992 indicated that general government expenditure as a share of GDP was positively associated with the number of years that VAT had been in place (Becker and Mulligan 1998: 24). A smaller survey, citing the experiences of Argentina, Chile, Costa Rica, Korea and Indonesia, concluded that 'in developing nations the VAT *has* tended to be something of a money machine' (Gillis *et al.* 1990: 220–1). Broadening the scope of VAT over time gradually widens the tax base and establishes a collection system that is income elastic. Indeed, so efficient has VAT been in raising large revenues that it has become a target for attack by opponents of 'big government'. The revenue productivity of VAT in turn permits simplifying the tax system since other more complex, but less productive, taxes can be abolished. This kind of tax reform lowers the political resistance of taxpayers to the expansion of the size of the government budget. This may be bad news for enthusiasts of 'small government' in DCs, but not for poor, post-conflict countries facing a severe revenue constraint.

The potential advantages of the VAT are such that the number of countries that have adopted it has increased ninefold from a mere 10 in the 1960s to 90 in the 1990s, including by now many LDCs. While some of the current users of VAT have not made a great success of it, the fiscal tool is now available for governments seriously seeking to increase their legitimacy.

One way or another, the revenue constraint must be progressively eased, if the momentum of improving basic services is not to be lost. Doubtless LDCs are far from reproducing the grand bargain of a 'welfare state', in which government provides extensive social security services for a population that pays substantial personal direct taxation. Nevertheless, a more modest fiscal bargain between government and people in LDCs is feasible, that is basic health and education services financed through increased indirect domestic taxation. This is the goal towards which all developing societies that wish to avoid complex humanitarian emergencies must struggle, as best they can.

5
Agrarian Reform, Land Redistribution, and Small-Farm Policy[1]

R. A. Berry

5.1 Introduction

Most CHEs occur in poor countries. Many such emergencies involve land in some way. Famines are due to problems in the realm of production of and access to food often in combination with violent conflict. Rural violence often revolves around land disputes and/or landlessness. And an unequal distribution of land contributes to low incomes, poverty and maldistribution of income, all of which tend to go with poor infrastructure, poor health and educational services and other factors which may predispose towards emergencies. Accordingly, a system of land rights which provides broad access to the population, combined with policies strongly supportive of small-scale agriculture appears to be one of the best forms of insurance against CHEs, judging by their absence in countries or regions where equalizing agrarian reforms have been implemented. When the initial land distribution differs markedly from the desired one, this implies a need for agrarian reform. Ironically, though its potential for good is seldom tapped, those relatively few episodes where it has been have contributed positively to the welfare of tens of millions (perhaps hundreds of millions) of the most down-trodden people.

Inequality contributes to social tensions and land is in most societies by far the most important of the assets, which a considerable share of families either have or aspire to having. When the gap between those with much land and those with little corresponds to the difference between two ethnic groups and two classes, the recipe is in place for a very high level of dissatisfaction, jealousy, tension and – when the right spark is there and the state is either too weak to control the violence or in the hands of one side in the confrontation – violence.

Unfortunately, the data leave no doubts that millions of families in LDCs are landless or nearly so, that many of these live in very bad and precarious conditions and that, accordingly, the need for land reform remains great in many countries. FAO compilations indicate that the purely landless population rose from 171 million people in 1980 to 180 million in 1985 (Alamgir and Arora 1991: 97). In Asia and Africa as a whole, one-third to one-half of smallholders have to subsist on parcels of less than one hectare. Many are in marginal areas and have to support relatively large families.[2]

This chapter elaborates on the relationships between land access, land structure and certain types of emergencies. As background, Section 5.2 reviews the evidence on the impact of land structure on incomes, poverty and social structure. Section 5.3 looks at the record of famines, rural violence and other types of crises in order to clarify the causal links with land distribution. Section 5.4 summarizes the main conclusions on those links.

5.2 Land distribution and small-farm policy as determinants of income distribution, poverty and vulnerability to emergency

'Entitlement' sums up the problem of economic insecurity associated with lack of guaranteed access to income of some sort (Sen 1981). In poor societies, where the majority of the population is located in rural areas, the main direct source of income is land, so access to it and the income it could provide has always been a central theme of society.

The reasons for land reform and the pressures which occasionally lead to it are widespread across countries and over time. Whether long-past or quite recent, the record shows the large social gains which come from successful reforms, the frequent subsequent reversal of such social and economic gains, the possibility that gains will be concentrated among families who are not the poorest, and the frequent lack of complementary measures in support of reform beneficiaries.

A healthy agrarian structure provides its emergency-preventing effects through several channels. First, by both raising the level of agricultural output (including especially that of food)[3] and by improving the distribution of agricultural and overall income, a land reform decreases the level of poverty (defined either in terms of absolute or relative income).[4] The starting point for most positive conclusions on this has been the frequently observed inverse relationship between size of plot and land productivity (Berry and Cline 1979; Lipton 1993b; Binswanger *et al.* 1995). Factors contributing to that relationship include the greater labour use on small farms due to the lower opportunity cost of that factor and its higher productivity due to a less serious supervision problem and the greater incentive to earn on the small farm (especially relative to absentee-owned large farms of the sort often criticized in the literature on Latin America). Apart from the microeconomic evidence on the inverse relationship between farm size and land productivity,[5] the benefits of certain types of land reform receive confirmation from (or at least are not contradicted by) a record of output and income growth after their implementation, which suggests that reasonably well executed reforms do not lower the rate of output growth in agriculture and may raise it. This was true of the most famously successful reforms, those of Japan, Taiwan and Korea, all undertaken immediately after the Second World War, and under pressure and/or assistance from the US government. And though there was no serious attempt to complement the land reform begun in Iran in 1962 with better extension, credit services or distribution of water rights, it transformed a society of extremely wealthy landlords and virtual serfs into a more equitable system of small peasants, and its output effects seem to have been substantially positive (Aresvik 1976). The small- and medium-sized farms created in this reform had productivity levels over twice that of the large farms even though a smaller percentage of their land was irrigated.

A second benefit from wide access to land ownership and control which an egalitarian land system implies, is that it gives families more ways to smooth their incomes over the course of the year and thus reduces the frequency of seasonal food crises. Third, healthy agrarian systems in which small farmers play the principal role tend also to have flourishing non-agricultural activities, many carried out by these same farm families (Ranis and Stewart 1987). Finally, productive egalitarian communities are relatively free of violence, much of which has its origins in inequalities and the related poverty, dissatisfaction and jealousy. They tend to be socially efficient in that they are able to arrange more effectively for the provision of public goods (education, health, etc.), including crisis relief. Finally, the positive bonds that unite families in such communities raise their proclivity to provide direct assistance to each other in times of crisis, complementary with the public provision of such assistance. All of these advantages pay off best when the context includes also a healthy relationship with the rest of the economy, including the government, in which public investment in infrastructure and in R & D allows the sector to grow and where neither it nor the rest of the economy dominates policy in such a way that sectoral exploitation occurs.

5.2.1   Designing a good land reform

The experience of history, both ancient and more recent, provides clear hints on the sort of land reform that would be of greatest lasting benefit to the poorer members of an agrarian society and would, as part of those benefits, reduce the probability of CHEs. In the case of settled agrarian systems, its central features would include:

i)   Relatively low ceilings on parcel size, both to discourage the post-reform reconcentration of land and to assure a wide distribution of benefits among potential beneficiaries at the time of the reform. Generally the best arrangement is one that distributes all available land essentially equally among all families, since this produces the most egalitarian result and since it appears that the inverse relationship between size and land productivity generally continues to hold for very small parcels. A redistribution that leaves a substantial large farm sector or leaves open the possibility of development of such a sector (Bolivia, Mexico) runs the risk that government dedication to the reform sector will be weak and that the sector will not get the support it needs to be productive. One that does not impose ceilings on future size of holdings invites reconcentration. The main argument in favour of permitting some degree of concentration is that better entrepreneurs should be allowed to operate more land than less competent ones, if output is to be maximized. Significant economies of scale may come into play for a very few crops. Both these points are better seen as arguments for land rental rather than for ownership of more than a limited amount.

ii) Implicit in or related to the first requirement, the inclusion of landless workers as well as tenants among the beneficiaries, where they (the landless workers) have the skills to be successful farmers. Frequently this group is excluded, most often for political reasons (as in Peru and the Indian states of Kerala and West Bengal).

iii) A good package of complementary support measures in the areas of infrastructure, credit, technical assistance, etc. Its presence (as in Japan, Taiwan) or absence (as in Mexico, after the revolution) is a major determinant of the output effects of the reform and therefore of the degree of poverty alleviation which follows.

iv) Rapid and clean implementation of the land redistribution. It is widely accepted that the process must be executed efficiently if conflict is to be minimized; where there is a lack of clarity, credibility or dispatch, conflict is likely to persist. The East Asian reforms were efficient in this sense, while the Colombian attempts of the 1930s were not.

The main exception to the above guidelines pertains to those situations – now mainly in Africa – where some form of communal tenure appears to operate relatively well and where rigid application of the 'western' individualistic model runs the risk of both lowering output, worsening distribution and disturbing traditional practices with meaning and value in the context of the society. Reyna and Downs (1988) argue that the decline in the productivity of farmers in many African countries (or the slow growth of that productivity) is in part the result of central governments which have weakened or replaced traditional and highly effective systems of land allocation and social life by favouring the individualization and commercialization of land, by making concessions of fallow land to the new government elites (as in Kenya and Nigeria (Bruce 1988)) and, earlier, in many countries of Latin America), favouring the urban proletariat over the rural dwellers. The new local elites have transformed the traditional rules and conventions about land tenure to new ones which work to their benefit.[6] Though freehold tenure was supposed to afford the security needed to enable owners to make capital improvements and raise productivity, in fact access to land is less secure than under the indigenous systems which focused on such assurance; current insecurity is due in part to the continual and confusing overlapping of the systems (Hoben 1988).

What of the potential of a more market-friendly approach to improving the distribution of land? As with all such broad questions, one must wait for the record to unfold to be sure.[7] But there seems limited ground for optimism that such approaches, as they are likely to be used in practice, will have more than a marginal impact on agrarian structure. Without traditional confiscatory land reform, the new approaches appear unlikely to make much difference. When complemented by such traditional reform, they may have greater value, partly through the 'threat effect', which can make landlords more flexible in the face of expropriation. Removal of legal constraints on land subdivision is a minimal enabling device (Lipton 1993a).

Given the typically higher productivity on small than on large farming units, plus the successful growth records of agriculture after the implementation of redistributive reforms, one would also expect that such reforms would typically reduce peasant unrest and vulnerability to famines. As discussed in sections 5.3.1 and 5.3.2, famines and violence produce CHEs in countries that have high levels of rural inequality and have not benefited from significant reforms.

5.3 How a healthy small-farm system reduces the frequency of CHEs

What is the impact of reasonably successful land reforms on the subsequent outbreak of CHEs? Most important, the countries or regions with reforms creating small private farms have suffered no subsequent CHEs, even when support policy has been weak. The record in countries moving to some form of collective agriculture has not been good; China, Cambodia and, most recently, North Korea have all suffered such serious problems in the production and distribution of food as to cause or contribute to CHEs.

The existence of a healthy small farm system reduces the likelihood of both violence and famine, the two broad contributing factors to CHEs. Famine and political conflict tend to reinforce each other. Armed violence can exacerbate or even create famine conditions, and any situation of famine heightens conflicts for food and other assets and can weaken the social fabric and thereby contribute to violence. Since most violence (rural or urban) occurs in situations which, at least initially, did not involve famine or mass starvation, we look first at the phenomenon of violence and its relationship to an unhealthy land structure.

5.3.1 Healthy small agriculture as an antidote to violence

Rural violence is a major source of CHEs that arise in agricultural societies. Chronic, systemic violence can certainly be serious; however, the main concern here is the outbreaks that create major emergencies. These may take the form of guerrilla wars – pitting rebels against the state – some of which may turn into large enough affairs to be called revolutions. Sometimes the violence has ethnic, class or other aspects to it; often the class backdrop to violence overlaps with the ethnic component.

Clashes over wealth appear at or near the root of almost all major episodes of internal violence. Since land is the principal asset, it is the principal source of tensions and conflict in many situations, from outright agrarian revolutions to chronic but severe rural violence.[8] The great revolutions of the twentieth century were fundamentally peasant wars linked to agrarian inequality – the Mexican revolution of the early twentieth century (Katz 1988), the 'peasant wars' in China, Vietnam, Cuba, Nicaragua, El Salvador and others. Capitalism's advance undermined the peasants' access to the land, resources and sociopolitical mechanisms they needed to sustain their way of life.

This section argues that very few, if any, of the CHEs that have taken place wholly or partly in rural areas could have occurred in a context of healthy egalitarian small farming, and attempts to categorize settings that frequently produce high levels of violence. Conflict and violence can arise in settings of absolute scarcity (such as Rwanda currently) or of absolute plenty; most Latin American experiences support Fairhead's (2000) view that conflicts are less often generated by resource scarcity than by resource wealth.

Serious conflict often arises in settings of unequal land distribution which are complemented by a conscious sense of grievance on the part of those with little or no land that some of what the largeholders hold rightfully belongs to them. Whether and when conflict on a large-scale breaks out then depends on additional ingredients to the mix. When stagnating or declining incomes result from any combination of price falls, increasing population pressure, and failure of policy to assist in raising productivity, the mix may become explosive, especially if the landed class is perceived to have weakened. If the basic conflict over assets is compounded by any combination of class, ethnic or religious differences, the likelihood that it will escalate into full-scale warfare and lead to a CHE is heightened. Latent or actual suspicions, dislikes and hatreds can in that case be more easily mobilized by those pursuing the goal of asset acquisition; this both increases the likelihood that conflict will break out and that it will be hard to rein in. It also increases the cruelty likely to be displayed and decreases the humanitarian impulses that may alleviate some of the costs associated with the conflict. Sometimes the inter-group hostilities are complemented by intra-group tension, dislike and opportunistic behaviour. When there is little mutual support or cohesiveness even within the group, many weak individuals will be particularly at risk, the loss of control, civility and order will be marked and the likelihood of CHE the greatest.

Conflict over the control of land can arise when the powerful attempt to push out the weaker, at some later time when the weaker attempt to right this 'injustice', or when new frontier areas are being contested. Most of the uprisings, rebellions and revolutions from below which caused CHEs in the twentieth century began with an aggrieved group (or groups) and a sufficiently even balance of power between this group and its opponent (which may be the state, the land-owning elite, a combination of these two, or another aggrieved group) to make it worthwhile to follow the path of conflict. Whereas the sense of injustice was present among the indigenous groups of El Salvador from the time of their displacement over a century ago, its twentieth-century explosions relate not only to the severity of their situation but also to the weakened state of the oligarchy (in the early 1930s) and to the fact that a by-then-strong guerrilla movement in the 1980s felt it had a chance to defeat the traditional powers. Similarly, when the Mexican revolution broke out, the Diaz regime was already weakened by inefficiency and corruption (Brown 1971). A weak state also raises the likelihood that ethnic and other types of violence will fester. In many cases, however, the state is de facto on one side of the battle, and in other cases levels of government (e.g. national and local) are in conflict on land issues.

Uncertainty contributes to violence and to CHEs in various ways. Lack of clarity with respect to who has rights to land, or whether other parties will react firmly to any attempts to change the status quo constitutes an invitation to aggress or contest. Uncertainty and ambiguity are especially characteristic of property regimes either in transition or with competing and overlapping systems, true of much of the world where a traditional property rights system now co-exists with a particularly recent Western system of individual property rights.

A review of some of the more notorious CHEs provides useful insights into the nature of the links with land issues. In Latin America the subjugation of indigenous peoples and the very unequal allocation of land created a domestically focused latifundia-minifundia system and laid the foundations for a number of uprisings during the colonial period. After 1850 agricultural produce became a major source of export earnings, and the growth of production for export profoundly affected land tenure and social relations in the countryside. Both peasants and landlords responded to the new opportunities which were opened, leading to competition for land and labour. In some cases landlords were able to create a dependent labour force by pressuring the peasants off their land. In others overt conflicts occurred. One setting for conflict was the creation of large commercial estates in areas of already dense Indian settlements, e.g. the great sugar haciendas in Morelos, Mexico, the coffee *fincas* set up in Guatemala and El Salvador, and the sheep ranches in Peru and Bolivia (Legrand 1986). Despite sometimes strong resistance, the peasants usually lost these conflicts (Pearse 1975; Browning 1971). Often the major outbursts came later. In several Central American countries unequal access to land has been a continuing source of conflict, and the failure of agrarian reform has had tragic consequences. The derailing of the planned 1955 reform in Guatemala by CIA intervention contributed to decades of continuous violence in that country and to the armed conflict that claimed about 100 000 lives (Pastor and Boyce 2000: 381). El Salvador's recently ended 12–year civil war claimed about 75 000 lives. Although some countries, like El Salvador and Nicaragua, did wind up with a sort of reform, in no case was it early enough or complete enough to lay a healthy base for socioeconomic stability, and so these countries remained hotbeds of conflict until quite recently.

The experience of El Salvador illustrates one path to a CHE. After pushing the indigenous communities off their communal property in the nineteenth century, the coffee oligarchy often had to deploy military force to maintain rural law and order and to suppress intermittent peasant revolts, the most serious of which occurred in 1932 when the great depression reduced coffee prices and the employers cut wages and employment; between 10 000 and 30 000 people died in the massacre which followed (Pastor and Boyce 2000). Military governments kept the lid on brewing tensions until 1979. Then a modernizing military coup, undertaken partly with a view to fending off a revolution, combined progressive steps – including an agrarian reform law to nationalize the large estates – with some repression. When the revolutionaries became persuaded that only with a military victory could they achieve their goals, civil war was ensured (Pastor and Boyce 2000). As usual, this brought a serious erosion of law, order and security which, in turn, led to many deaths.

Mexico's early twentieth-century agrarian revolution bears many similarities to the Central American tragedies. It was preceded by a sweeping government-supported consolidation of rural holdings between 1880 and 1910 which 'detached an ever-increasing number of peasants from the land and created a new class of agricultural wage laborers' (Reynolds 1970: 136). Though the impact of this transformation on rural incomes was initially disguised by improving terms of trade for agricultural exports, when rural real incomes began to fall pressures mounted for a return of the communal and private holdings which had been taken over; this process culminated in the Mexican revolution. Deepening peasant unrest triggered the occupation of some lands; chaos and violence brought increasing desolation to the countryside. While some of the fighting involved real social and economic issues, some was little more than jousting among rival leaders (Cumberland 1968). As armies marauded and wasted, it became very difficult to produce food, shortages became extreme, prices skyrocketed and government and rebels both printed money. The crop failures, including a 'corn famine' in 1917, contributed to widespread malnutrition. The phenomenally heavy loss of life – as many as 2 million between 1910 and 1924 (ibid.: 241) – also owed much to poor medical facilities, so that the severely wounded seldom survived, and to the routine execution of prisoners. 'One of the major elements in the ferocity of the Revolution was a deep and passionate desire for land on the part of those whose very subsistence depended upon agriculture in one form or another' (ibid.: 246). The conflict wrecked the economy and left deep scars which debilitated the nation for another generation.

Twentieth-century Vietnam provides another example of violence traceable to the expulsion and exploitation of long-established peasant populations. Prior to the arrival of the French, the Sino-Vietnamese upper class had not disturbed the cultural patterns of the original inhabitants of the area, as long as these paid their dues (Wolf 1969). In the mid-nineteenth century, however, rice was turned into a major export commodity through the creation of a class of large landholders (French and Vietnamese) capable of producing substantial surpluses. Some of their land was newly colonized but some came from the displacement of peasants. With land increasingly scarce for the peasants and interest rates (from moneylenders) high, the burden of rural indebtedness prompted frequent pushes for reform, and led to the creation of nationalist and socialist parties. During the Second World War the Viet Minh guerrilla army was formed, leading ultimately to the defeat of the French, with massive death and suffering both in the north (won by the Viet Minh in 1954), and in the south. Ironically, the context of the suffering in the north was the land reform programme itself, the first phase of which – the simple redistribution of land – was carried out by party cadres with the utmost ferocity and often with great arbitrariness (Wolf 1969). Public denunciations to air grievances against landlords often damaged the innocent with the guilty. According to one estimate 50 000 were killed and 100 000 jailed at this time (Fall 1967: 156). While the French were dedicating most of their military efforts to the north, the Viet Minh in the south came into control of at least half of the villages. Their free distribution of land owned by both French and Vietnamese landlords to the peasantry bought popularity (Wolf 1969). When the newly installed Diem regime started its own land reform under less attractive terms than those of the earlier Viet Minh distribution, it was not warmly received. For this and other reasons the Viet Minh had the advantage in the battle, for the minds of the peasantry and the history of land inequality moved towards its particular denouement in the war of South Vietnam.

Inequality associated with past encroachment is, then, one important recipe for rural violence. A contrasting context is that of the *frontier* where control is still being disputed and where the state is not strong enough to settle the issue on its preferred terms.[9] Many Latin American settlements in previously thinly populated lowlands and jungle areas fit this mould. Expanding international demand has often provided the economic stimulus to quickly give what were often 'waste' lands an economic value, and to bring peasant settlers into conflict with land entrepreneurs. The sequence of events in Colombia illustrates both how elusive a healthy agrarian structure can be and how costly is the failure to achieve it – that country might have had little rural violence in the absence of the land struggle. But the combination of that struggle and the tensions to which it contributed with other factors frequently led to violence and CHEs. Close to half a million people have died in a series of outbursts, the most extreme of which, *La Violencia*, saw about 200 000 killed in the late 1940s and early 1950s. As in many countries, frontier expansion in Colombia typically occurred in two stages. First, peasant families without land titles moved into the new areas, cleared and planted the land. Then came land entrepreneurs intending to create large farms and turn these settlers into tenants by asserting property ownership. Growing conflicts over public land eventually compelled the government to intervene to clarify the legal definition of private property (Legrand 1986). Prior to 1874 the independent *colonos* (settlers) were not in a position to fight, so the creation of the great estates appears to have proceeded fairly peacefully. After that date they resisted with greater frequency due, according to Legrand (1986), to the passage of national legislation supportive of settlers' rights. The settlers took cases to court collectively and although the landlords tended to win these disputes, usually by conniving with local authorities, the settlers' sense and memory of injustices remained strong (Legrand 1986). They took the offensive in the late 1920s and 1930s, invading many of the great estates formed earlier, just as a growing demand for coffee brought large entrepreneurs once again onto the prowl for land. The moderately progressive Liberal government's acceptance of the view that the monopoly of land by the great latifundia lay at the root of the country's agricultural backwardness (López 1927) left its position vis-à-vis the largeholders ambiguous. The depression provided an added argument for support to the *colonos*, as well as a new source of tension. Once the squatter movements got under way, the squatters became mobilizable political capital. The squatters, while doing better than before, still could not force the landlords to give up their claims and the result was chronic conflict.

Various policy initiatives attempted to deal with the conflict and violence in the frontier areas and the related problem of inadequate agricultural production. A short-lived judicial approach was too radical to have a chance of success. Purchase and parcelization of large properties were too expensive. Finally, legislation in the form of Law 200 of 1936, although appearing to be favourable to the peasants, seems in fact to have reinforced the position of the large estate owners by taking away the argument that the land which the peasants claimed was in fact public (Legrand 1986). In failing to slow the continuing appropriation of public lands in the frontier regions, or to deal with the underlying tensions between settlers and large entrepreneurs over those lands, it no doubt contributed to the escalation of rural violence which broke out a decade later. *La Violencia* was neither simply a bloody war between the two political parties (as it has sometimes been described) nor simply a peasant war. Landlords and peasants used it to settle by force old and new land disputes. In addition, widespread banditry developed behind the partisan barriers, as more and more of the originally political gangs focused on private revenge and economic profit (Zamosc 1986). The areas of concentrated land disputes in the 1930s, with the exception of the Caribbean coast, became foci of violence in the 1950s. In some regions the violence signalled a new offensive of estate owners against peasants who had made inroads in the 1930s and 1940s (Legrand 1986). In some cases attacks by the army on the peasants may have been partly due to pressure by local landlords eager to monopolize the newly opened land (Gilhodes 1974). Intensification of large-scale usurpation of public lands heightened the conflicts. Legrand (1986: 170) concludes that although the squatters lost out in most cases, 'Colombian frontier expansion gave rise to an ideology of peasant protest centred on the reclamation of public lands that remains a vital tradition in the rural areas today'.

Although often (and often erroneously) characterized as having land surplus, Africa has already suffered land-related CHEs and may be destined to suffer many more, judging by the present trends of rapidly rising population, slow economic growth, ambiguity of rights to land as the new Western system comes into conflict with traditional systems, and weak and often rapacious governments. No recent CHEs are more tragic than those of Rwanda and Burundi. Combining with the terrible heritage of ethnic conflict between the Tutsi and the Hutu groups in Rwanda has been a high level of intra-group violence substantially related to land. André and Platteau's (1997) study of a densely populated area in the northwest of Rwanda (1988–93) revealed, in a context of slow growth of non-agricultural income opportunities, an acute competition for land, which resulted in an increasingly unequal land distribution and rapid processes of land dispossession through the operation of disequalizing transfers in the (illegal) land market, as well as the 'gradual erosion of customary social protections following the commoditization of land'. The pervasive incidence of land disputes led to rising tensions in social relations and even within the family, paving the way for more and more overt conflict. Increasingly, the indigenous tenure arrangements are drawn exclusively so that return migrants, divorced women, orphans, etc. are being kept out. The tradition of the youngest son taking care of the parents has largely fallen into disuse, so that the elderly increasingly feel neglected and abandoned.

Though the 1994 civil war was started by macropolitical forces cynically playing on ethnic divisions in order to retain power, the land-based conflicts went a long way to setting the stage for the violence and allowing it to spread so quickly and devastatingly. Those who died were disproportionately people with relatively large landholdings or people considered to be troublemakers (André and Platteau 1997) or who behaved opportunistically. Thus, the war provided an opportunity to settle scores or to reshuffle land properties. The erosion of the traditional system of land rights contributed greatly to dispute and conflict, directly through the way it deprived groups of their previous rights, and indirectly because of the uncertainty it bred.

Rwanda is unlikely to be the last African CHE in which land conflict plays a major role. Klugman, who discusses Kenya's history of violence and repression and growing land pressures in recent decades, indicates that:

> Unequal access by groups to land, employment, and state benefits has been exacerbated by rapid population growth and the economic stagnation to which Kenya has become prone since the early 1980s....Social and economic conditions combined with ethnic tensions have significantly increased the likelihood of a CHE in Kenya' (2000: 296).

Such an emergency would, in Klugman's view, follow an outbreak of large-scale group conflict in the country.

In Colombia and cases like it, the state was not directly involved in pushing settlers off their lands and, at times, even tried to provide some support to them. Often, however, governments are the source of the aggression against small farmers, either with a view to creating collective or state farms (as in Russia) or in collaboration with intended (large-scale) beneficiaries (as in nineteenth-century Mexico). Sudan's 'mechanized farming project' of 1968 pushed cultivators off the land and drove out pastoral nomads, then turned the land over to large-scale operations that created relatively few jobs and channelled the gains to a new agricultural elite. In the lower Jubaa valley of Somalia local farmers were forced off the land, first to make way for mechanized state farms and then, following the reform of land registration legislation in 1975, by urban elites. Both of these projects were funded by foreign donors and no productivity gains resulted. The political elites gained at the expense of the poor, and the ground was laid for future unrest and violence, fuelled by either or both the poverty of the expelled groups and their sense of injustice.

5.3.2   Agrarian reform/small-farm policy and famine

Although obviously related to a general shortage of food, famines and the associated suffering and death are also related to the distribution of purchasing power and the capacity to produce food for one's own needs (Sen 1981). Some degree of starvation and malnutrition in poor countries is a generally recognized phenomenon. When, instead of involving a small percentage of the population, inability to either produce or purchase for oneself extends to a significant proportion of the population, it constitutes a famine.

The likelihood of mass starvation is directly determined by four factors:

i)   The average level of income and productivity in the society (best defined in terms of staple foods).
ii) The typical level of inequality.

iii) The extent of fluctuation in purchasing power in the society as a whole and especially for the poorer part of it, which depends in part on fluctuations in local production and in part on the extent to which prior reserves or current borrowing can be used to smooth such fluctuations by buying from other countries or regions.

iv) The extent to which better-off members of the society are able and prepared to help those less well off, especially in situations of crisis like that of a famine. An absolute shortage of food contributes to famines by making it scarcer and raising its price (if markets are the sole arbiter of its distribution).[10]

Inequality accentuates the problems of the poor.

In many famines, some degree of absolute food shortage, of unequal distribution of income, fluctuations in degree of access by the poor, and weak social mechanisms to help the poor in this sort of crisis are present. As one might expect, 'The victims typically come from the bottom layers of society – landless agricultural labourers, poor peasants and sharecroppers, pastoral nomads, urban destitute, and so on. Contrary to statements that are sometimes made, there does not seem to have been a famine in which victims came from all classes of the society' (Drèze and Sen 1989). In the Indian subcontinent, the majority of famine victims in the nineteenth and twentieth centuries have come from the class of landless wage labourers (ibid.).

A strong small-farm agriculture is likely to be the best possible preventive of famines since it raises total agricultural output; it usually implies that a higher share of that output is of basic foods (as opposed, for example, to export crops); it often involves a mix of agricultural products and helps to generate a vibrant non-agricultural rural sector, which further increases the income-earning opportunities of the population and the diversity of income sources; and it tends to go with a strong social network, which improves the likelihood of mutual assistance. Although such assistance is by no means unknown or even uncommon in patron-client situations, it appears to be less pervasive and predictable than in smallholder societies.

Famines are often associated with conflict, both as cause and as effect, and their complicated dynamics are often important to the outcome. Social relations and access to assets change simply with the threat of famine. Therefore, even in cases where violence and conflict are not part of their direct cause, famines are divisive phenomena. Also noteworthy is the fact that though famines involve and are typically initiated by starvation, many of the deaths are from various epidemic diseases that breed on debilitation, the attempts to eat whatever looks edible, breakdown of sanitary arrangements and massive population movements in search of food (Drèze and Sen 1989). Prevention of famines is therefore intimately related to the prevention of epidemics.

The presence and severity of famines are very much affected by the actions and capacities of governments and by violence (in which the government is sometimes involved). Instead of helping to combat famines, states have often created or deepened them, as illustrated by the Soviet experience of the 1930s and by Kampuchea in the late 1970s. Duffield (1994a) and others see many famines as the result of a transfer of resources from the politically weak to the politically strong, in which case they are best seen as integrally linked to conflict itself. Marginalized groups in southern Somalia (Dinka) became destitute not only because of the drought but also because the state stripped them of cattle and other major assets. Ethiopia and Somalia have withheld famine relief from certain victims. Ake (1997) describes state-making as the equivalent of primitive accumulation but more violent, a matter of conquest and subjugation – revoking the autonomy of communities. Ruling elites look for local collaborators and allow these to exploit local populations in return (Nafziger and Auvinen 2000). Famine is often the result of the disruption of a way of life, in which government decisions usually play a role at one level or another. In contexts like these the distribution of access to land is part of a bigger picture of conflict, but it is at the centre of the struggle since land and cattle are the survival necessities.

At the other extreme from the aggressive 'state as source of famine' is the state that is effective in its prevention. There have been several threats of famines in India since independence but these have not materialized, largely due to public intervention, such as the impressive effort in the state of Maharashra in preventing the severe drought of 1972–73 from developing into famine through a massive public works programme employing almost 5 million people. In Africa, Botswana is one of a number of countries with good records of famine prevention (Drèze and Sen 1989). In the middle of the spectrum, in a sense, are those governments that do nothing, either through the belief that there is little that can be done, as in the case of British policy during the Irish famines of the nineteenth century,[11] or through the lack of competence to deal effectively with a famine crisis, as exemplified by Chinese experience in the great famine of 1958–61, estimated to have accounted for 23–30 million deaths (Drèze and Sen 1989: 8).

A brief review of salient aspects of a few major famines helps to clarify the causal factors, the groups victimized the most, and how land tenure may affect both the threat of famine, its likely results, and the best possible antidotes. Experience confirms that an adequate total availability of food is not a guarantee against famine, therefore the onset of the great famine of 1943 in Bengal, in which an estimated 3 million people died, preceded the decline in total food availability. Floods had already restricted the demand for labour, putting the landless wage workers at risk, and making them the main early victims (Drèze and Sen 1989). Other groups gained in purchasing power, in particular urban dwellers whose incomes were increased by the war economy. In short, much of the problem was due to unequal access to food. A more egalitarian distribution of land (and thus a smaller number of landless wage labourers) would have meant a more equal distribution of income and of direct access to food and would have greatly reduced levels of suffering and death.

The Bangladesh famine of 1974 was also related to floods, which reduced the food supply (after the event) but which diminished worker incomes immediately. It was aggravated by socially excessive hoarding. The floods raised rice prices due to expectations of higher future prices, expectations which, in fact, went far beyond what later took place (Ravallion 1987). When the government failed to institute a suitable stabilizing response (Alamgir 1980), the die was cast. In the four districts most widely hit, the ratio of wages for rice labour to the price of rice fell by 44–87 per cent (year to year) and the price of land to that of rice by 54–103 per cent (Ravallion 1987: 14). Because of the latter decline, distress sales of land, common under such extreme circumstances, brought less alleviation than they would have otherwise. Ravallion (1987) concludes that perhaps a third of mortality may have been the result of the high volatility of the rice price; people who have to rely on the current foodgrain market for current consumption needs are typically a high proportion of famine victims. Vulnerability to price fluctuations is clearly greatest for the poorest families, who are disproportionately the landless or near landless. In addition, however, it should be noted that in a healthy small-farm system, reliance on food markets for survival may be much less than in other systems. Even if the ratio of wages to staple grain price fell sharply, this fact would have much less impact on food availability. In short, relatively equal access to productive resources implies relatively equal direct entitlement (via production for own use) and correspondingly less dependence on the market.

In recent decades most famines have taken place in SSA. Conflict has played a major role. In 1983–85, though drought threatened a large number of African countries, only some of them – notably the war-torn ones – actually experienced large-scale famine (Drèze and Sen 1989). The disruption of both food trade and food aid by domestic political conflict has contributed to millions of deaths and to the continent's immense refugee problems. Droughts have been involved, but the centrality of their role is not clear. The contrasting quality of public action across the countries may have been the more important proximate factor, and historical experience has clearly had a heavy impact on these recent events. The deteriorating food position began before the Sahel droughts (1968–74) and can be traced back to colonial policy (Eicher and Baker 1982). The continuing crisis is due to African governments' neglect of agriculture. After independence, African political elites needed to secure the support of urban dwellers rather than smallholders. Within agriculture the payoff was perceived, as in the colonial period, to lie with large-scale commercial, export-oriented activities. In part, this reflected the potential thereby created for patronage in the form of access to large farms, cheap inputs, etc. It also reflected the limited understanding among African decision-makers (as elsewhere in the world) of the fact that smallholdings are often more efficient than larger ones, especially when the latter do not face true market prices for the inputs they use.

The weakening of traditional land tenure arrangements and the systems of mutual social responsibility of which they are a pivotal part removes another of the defences against famine. In many societies systems of inter-action (e.g. between pastoral activity and cultivation) and of mutual support have developed to protect against the impact of drought and the threat of famine (Drèze and Sen 1989). Main elements of the adjustment mechanisms include exchange arrangements, migration and intra-house-hold redistribution. There are clear limits to the protection provided by these systems in times of famine, when ordinary patterns of behaviour undergo severe strain, but it is better to have them than to not.

Ethiopia's struggles with famine date back at least to the ninth century, with at least one major struggle occurring each century since then and with the worst (the 'great famine' of 1888–92) killing a third of the population (Kumar 1990). Until the overthrow of Selassie in 1974 this highly agricul-tural country was mainly feudal. At that time, land was nationalized, there was a massive redistribution of usufructuary rights, and hired labour was banned. These changes in general proved beneficial to the peasantry, but levels of productivity in agriculture have remained very low, due to a com-bination of periodic violence and a weak support system for peasant agri-culture, related to an unfortunate and excessive focus on large mechanized state farms.

The famine of the early 1970s, estimated to have cost more than a million lives, was initiated by a drought in the northern district of Wollo (Kumar 1990), though the reports of the time do not suggest a countrywide short-age, nor did prices rise much. The subsequent famine of 1982–85, which paradoxically took place during a land reform instituted by the military gov-ernment by then in power, was even worse, with deaths certainly exceeding a million and perhaps 1.5 million (Kumar 1990: 203). Intermittent food crises were now accentuated by the effects of the Ogaden conflict of 1977–78, the social convulsions associated with the coming of the military regime, and the debilitating effects of the civil war against separatist forces in the north. In the face of each of these famines the state's response, the contribution of the international community, and the effectiveness of famine relief left much to be desired. In the early 1970s Selassie's unconcern aggravated the crisis; a decade later the new regime's plans for the upcom-ing tenth anniversary of its revolution played a similar role (Kumar 1990); international aid really got moving only in 1984, too late to save the major-ity of lives at risk. The 1980 famine was a classic case of failure to nip the problem in the bud. Large movements of people put a strain on the receiv-ing areas. Large sales of assets to survive the first couple of years left many families highly vulnerable to the pressures of later years. Kumar (1990: 185) believes that 'as the crisis operated to reduce crops and the arable grazing land, servants and dependants of farmers were evicted, and were amongst the first to move to look for work elsewhere. Tenants also suffered eviction, and these as well as the small-scale family land (rist) holders, were gradually forced to sell livestock, compounding the effects of losing them as part of the impact of the drought'. Pastoralists in both north and south lost through precipitous falls in the relative price of animals to grain.

Weather, violence and the near-subsistence condition of many families have all played a large part in Ethiopian famines; under such circumstances prevention would not be a simple matter. Still, it is arguable that had the land reform undertaken by the military government which replaced Selassie created a small-farm private agriculture, and had it been followed-up by reasonably effective support for those farms, the outcome would have been quite different.[12] Instead of this strategy, the government emphasized the establishment of large-scale mechanized farms on the East European model. A high dependency on imports of tractors and chemicals soaked up virtually all of the public investment in agriculture. Even before the drought of 1983 there was ample evidence that this policy had failed, but the government pushed even harder in this direction (Cheru 1989). Resources were extracted from the peasantry via low producer prices and a quota system whereby they had to sell to the (monopsonistic) agricultural marketing corporation. This helped to weaken the regular market for foods and to channel more of it into the black market. Had the government focused on the productivity of small-farm agriculture through the development and dissemination of improved technologies, investment in infrastructure, education, etc., the vulnerability to famine would have been significantly reduced. The need to move large amounts of food to desperate areas – a challenge in which both the Selassie government and its successor signally failed – would have been much less.

5.4   Overview and conclusions

Various empirical evidence points to the central conclusion of this chapter: that the best long-run preventive of CHEs in the rural areas of LDCs is a relatively equitable distribution of the rights to land and of the support provided by the state (credit, technical assistance, infrastructure, etc.). Hence, where the existing distribution is quite unequal, a reform to correct this defect would be good insurance against CHEs. An equalizing reform has the potential to raise output (because of the high productivity of which small farms are capable), to improve the distribution of income associated with agricultural production (and hence reduce absolute poverty) and to reduce the tensions and feelings of injustice, which, under certain circumstances, can fuel unrest and violence. Such reforms can thus diminish the threat both of famine, one major source of CHEs, and of rural violence, another major source.

The historical record of CHEs confirms the prominent role of agricultural inequality, which has contributed to low output and incomes, to peasant unrest, and to the associated loss of life in rebellions sparked by the sense of injustice it breeds. Some CHEs are fuelled by the poorer classes' feelings of injustice, as with the Mexican revolution and the Vietnam war. Others are associated with land aggression of putative largeholders (Colombia), or of the state (Sudan).

Though countries or societies with relatively egalitarian distributions of land have had CHEs, this has typically occurred only in LICs in ecologically vulnerable settings. The countries or states undertaking major land reforms in the twentieth century have thus far been free of CHEs in the years thereafter, except for those communist countries in which the social conflict that produced the reform also generated a CHE (Vietnam, Cambodia and Russia) or where the CHE was the result of government incompetence in dealing with a food crisis (China). Small private farms created by reforms have flourished in Taiwan and Korea, countries which backed up the reforms with strong policy support for small farms. In Egypt, Iran, Kerala, reform areas of Mexico and Bolivia, and elsewhere, the outcomes have also been generally satisfactory.

Although full-blown agrarian reform faces many obstacles of a political nature, its potential value is of such magnitude that any country at risk of a CHE deserves an analysis of how such reform, coupled with strong small-farm support policy, could help to reduce its likelihood. Part-way steps have proven quite valuable in a number of cases.

Notes

1. The term 'reform' is used for a wide range of changes, including some which increase the concentration of land. Here the discussion is limited to cases in which an increase in the number of families with access to enough land to help them avoid poverty is at least a reasonably likely result, since otherwise it would not be expected to contribute to prevention of agriculture-related emergencies.
2. Land is, of course, only one (albeit usually the main) possible source of income for rural families, so access to other jobs can take the sting out of landlessness. Unfortunately data reporting both family access to land and to other sources of income are rare. But life expectancy figures and other indicators of welfare leave no doubt that in today's world the main victims both of chronic poverty and of emergency crisis are those in rural areas. Whereas historically in DCs life expectancy was greater in rural areas (Easterlin and Campos 1997) than in urban ones, that situation is reversed in today LDCs.
3. Nafziger and Auvinen (2000: 117–24) find that a higher rate of growth of food production per capita reduces vulnerability to CHEs, albeit only modestly.
4. Logic suggests that absolute deprivation would contribute especially to famines and the famine-related component of CHEs, while relative deprivation might be as or more important in providing the fuel for conflict and its component of CHEs. Nafziger and Auvinen (2000) highlight the role of relative deprivation. As discussed in Section 5.3.1, many agrarian conflicts are fed by peasants' sense of injustice related to having been pushed off their land, even if this occurred long ago.
5. Land productivity is the most relevant measure of overall productivity when labour is in surplus and other factors of production are not important.

6. Individualization has gone much further in Kenya than elsewhere. In central Kenya the process was associated with a very successful period for smallholder agriculture, though it is unclear how much the process contributed to this outcome. On other counts the strategy has not played out as expected (Bruce 1988). Kenyan farmers have largely failed to comply with the legislation and where they have done so it is with objectives different from those anticipated by its architects (Green 1986). The massive programme of consolidation of land holdings, cadastre and registration of individual titles begun in the 1950s was expected by some to lead to a skewed distribution through sales, but few expected those in charge of the adjudication process to exploit it to appropriate land for themselves (Bruce 1988). The failure of the adjudication teams to recognize secondary rights in land was prejudicial to many, including major groups such as women. Sales have not contributed to efficient consolidation; plots purchased are often far from existing holdings and land is often bought as security for loans, for speculation, or to hold for children's eventual needs. Most purchases are financed by income from non-agricultural sources and do not create the hoped-for 'yeoman farmers'. The process has been leading to a new landlessness, some increase in tenancy and major rural-urban migration, partly due to the landlessness.

7. The limited historical evidence available does suggest some prospects for direct use of market and tax incentives to move land into the hands of smaller farmers, as in the case of Ecuador, but the effects have not been large (Zevallos 1989).

8. In their cross-country regression analysis, Auvinen and Nafziger (1999) find that CHEs are more likely in settings of high income inequality (as measured by the Gini coefficient). The same result is reported by Alesina and Perotti (1996).

9. Wolf (1969: 202) notes that in Russia, China, Mexico, Algeria and Cuba the revolutionary movements among the peasantry 'seem to start first among peasants who have some access to land, rather than among the poor peasants or those deprived of land altogether'. Mitchell (1967) concurs that the greater power of landlords and relative docility of peasants in the more 'feudal' areas account for the fact that government control is easier in such situations. Possession of some land gives the peasant a degree of independence and hence some leverage which he or she can translate into protest more easily.

10. The regressions of Auvinen and Nafziger show slow growth of per capita food production to be a source of humanitarian emergencies. And many individual cases reveal the importance of overall food production. The Irish famine of 1845–47, for example, was the result of a disastrous fall in total food availability brought about by a recurring failure of the pest-ridden potato crop (Woodham-Smith 1962; Mokyr 1983). Food availability declined considerably during the Sahel famine of the 1970s and the Ethiopian famine was preceded by a dramatic collapse in food availability.

11. Adam Smith was quite unequivocal in his condemnation of intervention in the form of famine relief. Referring to the eighteenth and the previous two centuries, he concluded that 'a dearth never has arisen from any other cause but a real scarcity, occasioned sometimes, perhaps, and in some particular places, by the waste of war, but in by far the greatest number of cases, by the fault of the seasons; and that a famine has never arisen from any other cause but the violence of government attempting, by improper means, to remedy the inconvenience of the dearth' (1961: 32–3).

12. Cheru (1989: 116) opines that 'the impact of the drought could have been minimized, if not avoided completely'.

6
Protecting Environmental Resources and Preventing Land Degradation

Gaim Kibreab

6.1   Introduction

This chapter explores the relationship between environmental degradation and CHEs, and how environmental protection can reduce vulnerability to political conflict and CHEs. CHEs result from a complex coalescence of inter-related political, social, economic, military and environmental forces. There are four types of CHEs: i) sudden onset emergencies caused by natural disasters such as volcanic eruptions, earthquakes, floods, hurricanes, forest fires and tornadoes, ii) sudden onset emergencies caused by man-made disasters such as chemical spills (Bhopal), dioxin release (Seveso), nuclear accidents (Chernobyl) and oil spills (Kuwait), iii) slow-onset emergencies caused by natural and man-made disasters, such as drought, pest infestation, deforestation, overgrazing, overcultivation, erosion, desertification, salinity, siltation, water-logging, aquifer depletion, etc, and iv) complex political emergencies associated with the widespread intra-state conflicts of the last decade and a half.

The focus of this chapter is the type of emergency stated in (iii) above in which the emergency develops more gradually as a result of crop failure or loss of livestock and other productive assets. This type of emergency is partly associated with land degradation reflected, among other things, in crop yield decline, deterioration of rangelands resulting in livestock morbidity and mortality, and deforestation which may not only lead to reduction of access to fuelwood, construction materials, herbal medicines, wildlife, wild fruits, etc., but also contributes to soil erosion. Forest products are collected not only for self-consumption but also for sale, and deforestation results in loss of major income, especially for the rural poor. This loss tends to weaken or undermine the traditional safety-net or coping strategies and without external intervention can contribute to drought or famine. For example, in countries experiencing recurrent CHEs in northeastern Africa, the problem of land degradation is linked with misguided policies pursued by governments. In agriculturally and pastorally based economies, land degradation affects incomes and consumption through its impact on wildlife and agricultural, livestock and forest production.

The chapter is limited to examining whether measures to counter slow-onset/natural and man-made environmental problems of land degradation reduce poor countries' vulnerability to CHEs. First, it defines the three key concepts used in the study – degradation, sustainability and vulnerability.

6.1.1   Land degradation

Land degradation is caused by a combination of natural, climatic and human processes. Degradation is linked with sustainability, and sustainable land use can continue indefinitely (Blaikie and Brookfield 1987; Kibreab 1996). A resource can be degradable depending on its resilience or sensitivity (Walker *et al.* 1981). Sensitivity refers to the degree of change from natural or human factors while resilience refers to ability to withstand pressure or recover to its previous condition after being subjected to conditions affecting its intrinsic properties. For example, savannahs are highly resilient with remarkable capability of recovery despite disturbance (Noy-Meir 1982).

Degradation is defined here as reduction in the productive capability of a resource under a given land-use practice and management regime without necessarily implying that the damage is irreversible. Blaikie and Brookfield (1987: 4) define degradation socially; degradation means a reduction in the capability of the land to satisfy a particular use or a social need.

The following equation is key to understanding the relationship between natural and human forces in degradation, and also for mitigating degradation and restoring productive capability:

Net degradation = (natural degrading processes + human interference) – (natural reproduction + restorative management) (Blaikie and Brookfield 1987: 7).

This definition indicates that loss of capability results from drought, other natural processes and human interference, and that restoration of capability ensues from natural processes and human conservation and renewal. Examples of human restoration include replenishment of soil nutrients during fallow periods, filling of gullies by new soils and vegetation growth, and conservation measures such as rotational cropping and grazing, fertilization, manuring, terracing, water harvesting, tree planting, etc. Degradation occurs when the degree of loss of capability is greater than the rate of regeneration. The key elements in degradation and sustainability are, therefore, the property of the resource and how humans utilize it.

6.1.2   Environmental sustainability

In agrarian economies, sustainable resource use is largely a function of appropriate land-use practices. The problem is not defining sustainability but determining how to achieve it. Sustainable land-use practice is one that lasts and, in agriculturally and pastorally based economies, it is inextricably linked with livelihood security. Environmental sustainability is *sine qua non* for sustainability of economic activities that directly utilize renewable resources (such as water, wildlife, fisheries, arable land, pasture and forests) as inputs to produce goods and services.

Appropriate land-use practices are absolutely indispensable. Land-use practices not appropriate to physical and climatic limitations contribute to natural resource depletion. An intensive land-use practice not accompanied by measures to limit resource use to sustainable levels or to maintain productivity at a higher level of intensity may cause 'irreversible' environmental damage. Nevertheless, knowledge about when irreversibility occurs is still rudimentary. Moreover, under proper management, irreversible damage in arid and semi-arid regions is rare.

For example, the ox-plough-based agricultural technology still dominant in the Eritrean highlands can be traced back as far as *c*. 500–1000 BCE (McCann 1995). Traditionally fallow periods, and rotational grazing, appropriate harvesting (cutting and trimming rather than stumping), and natural regeneration of forest resources were used to maintain soil fertility and prevent depletion of renewable resources (Kibreab 1996). However, these practices have become less common during recent decades, under pressure of human and livestock population growth, land shortage, a lack of technological progress, and policy disincentives.

6.1.3   Land degradation and vulnerability to humanitarian emergencies

Vulnerability refers to a person's general state of being unable to withstand, cope with, or recuperate from the effects of emergencies triggered by natural and man-made crises. Whether disasters occur is determined not only by the crises' severity and frequency but also by the household's and community's capability to withstand, cope with, or recuperate from crises. In food security, Downing (1991) defines vulnerability as 'an aggregate measure, for a given population or region, of the risk of exposure to food insecurity and the ability of the population to cope with the consequences of that insecurity'. According to UNDP (1994), 'disasters occur when a hazard interacts with vulnerability'.

A drought resulting in one or two seasons' crop yield decline or failure may not necessarily cause severe shortages in food and loss of livelihood, unless the coping strategies of the population have already been weakened from long and cumulative adverse circumstances that render it vulnerable to trigger events. In parts of countries such as Sudan, Ethiopia and Somalia, land degradation manifested in the progressive decline of productive capability constitutes a vulnerability factor. The people, depending on degraded environments for survival, live permanently on the edge of subsistence crisis. The crop yields from their degraded resources tend to hover near the subsistence or physiological minimum under normal weather conditions. A slight reduction, precipitated by a trigger event such as adverse weather in a single season, may lead to malnutrition and early death. In this sense, land degradation increases vulnerability.

6.2   Reducing vulnerability to complex humanitarian emergencies through environmental protection

The central question addressed here is whether we can reduce people's vulnerability to potential CHEs by protecting environmental resources. People are differentiated socially, politically and economically, and the impacts of disasters are mediated by a person's socioeconomic position. Thus, here, 'people' refers to a socioeconomic community instead of a country, for when a disaster occurs it is vulnerable members, and not the powerful or even society in general, that suffer the consequences. As Buchanan-Smith and Maxwell (1994: 4) argue, '[T]he central idea is that household vulnerability is defined by the capacity to manage shocks: some households may be unaffected by shocks, some may recover more quickly, and some may be pushed into irreversible decline. Some households, indeed, may even profit from the misfortunes of others'.

In what way can the protection of environmental resources reduce people's vulnerability to CHEs? In most LDCs, the environment constitutes the single most essential source of livelihood. The vast majority of rural people meet their basic needs directly or indirectly from the environment. As Durning (1989: 40) states:

> [I]n the rural developing countries, human reliance on ecosystems goes unmeditated by the long chains of commerce, industry, and civil infrastructure that shape life in the rich countries. For the have-nots, food comes from the soil, water from the stream, fuel from the woods, traction from the ox, fodder from the pasture, reeds to make mats from the stream bank, fruit from the trees around the hut.

This means that the welfare of millions of the rural poor is inextricably linked to the well-being of the environment. Slow-onset natural and man-made environmental problems such as crop yield declines, depleted forest and rangelands, and the loss of palatable and nutritious perennial plants, do not cause famines and other CHEs but make a person or a group vulnerable to stressful events.

By the same token, non-degraded productive environmental resources constitute protection or bulwark against stressful events such as CHEs that might be partly caused by adverse weather conditions, pest infestation or livestock diseases. Protected environmental resources do not prevent periodic natural or man-made disasters from occurring, but they reinforce and foster the ecological resilience of resource users, manifested in the capability to resist, cope with, and recuperate from their consequences with dignity and integrity.

A degraded environment, by itself, does not cause famine and other CHEs, but also depends on other factors such as the lack of availability of assets, social support networks, off-farm income-generating opportunities, migration outlets and alternative or supplementary sources of livelihood derived, say, from common property resources (CPRs). A famine can also be mitigated before reaching crisis proportions either through importing grains from surplus areas or through emergency relief. Indeed land degradation manifested in reduced resource productivity can, in the presence of drought or conflict as a trigger and the absence of timely outside intervention, deteriorate into a disaster causing immense human suffering. 'Famine generally occurs when poor crop yields lead to severe shortages in food in a particular area, and market mechanisms or government interventions are insufficient to balance these shortages with supplies from elsewhere in the country or from overseas...' (Grainger 1990: 117).

Although land degradation is not the cause of famine, it is a vulnerability factor whose removal through environmental regeneration and conservation programmes may substantially fortify the ecological resilience of those who live on the brink of subsistence. A non-degraded environment or an environment with bolstered productive capability serves as a bulwark against the consequences of natural or man-made hazards.

A major objective of environmental regeneration or conservation programmes is to maintain or augment the productive capability of the basic resource – land and the associated renewable resources. For owners or workers of renewable resources, expanded productivity means enhancement of capability in terms of increased access to food crops, forest produce, pasture and woodlands. A community that produces surplus food crops and goods can provide a buffer against future misfortunes. This reduces the vulnerability of people to drought and other environmental hazards that may otherwise predispose them to famine and a subsequent CHE.

This presupposes that the environmental or conservation programmes respond to locally felt needs and build on indigenous environmental knowledge and traditional resource management systems. Otherwise peasants, pastoralists and others who derive their livelihoods directly from the environment may be worse off, being more vulnerable to disasters by losing crucial sources of livelihood. Whether a programme reduces the risk of a CHE depends on removing the causes of land degradation.

Why do people adopt land-use practices that threaten the sustainability of the resources on which their livelihoods depend? And why do they not take remedial measures to mitigate or offset the effects of degradation? These questions focus not only on physical processes but also institutional and structural factors that determine incentives for resource holders to conserve and invest.

In agrarian economies, constraints to be overcome are overcultivation, deforestation, overgrazing, siltation and water-logging. These problems are the proximate rather than root causes of degradation. A programme that addresses proximate causes, such as inappropriate land-use practices, is not likely to reduce vulnerability to CHEs unless implemented in conjunction with measures that tackle root causes. These proximate causes result from complex and interlinked sociopolitical, economic and environmental factors, the ultimate causes.

Most of the literature attributes the primary cause of land degradation in LDCs to high population density (Eckholm 1982). Malthus (1798) hypothesized a negative relationship between demographic pressure and the environment. He stated that the potential increase in food supply could not keep pace with that of the population and theorized that, if humans did not exercise preventive checks (moral restraint and responsible attitudes to marriage), population growth would be brought to a halt by welfare checks (poverty, disease, famine and war). Boserup (1965) postulated the reverse, considering population pressure to be an essential precondition for technological innovation in agriculture. The thrust of her model was that the risk of collapse in livelihood security from diminishing agricultural returns, amid rising population densities, provides an opportunity for socioeconomic progress rather than a threat to subsistence.

The inverse relationship between natural resource depletion and population pressure is still often invoked without supporting evidence. Not only do recent empirical studies in LDCs show that population pressure per se does not necessarily cause natural resource depletion, but high population pressure can also provide an opportunity for undertaking labour-intensive reafforestation and soil and water conservation activities which improve the productive capability of renewable resources (Kibreab 1996; Tiffen *et al.* 1994). Population pressure contributes to land degradation in the presence of other underlying causes.

Resource users' decisions concerning land-use practices are shaped by an interplay of diverse factors. However, in Ethiopia, Sudan, Somalia, and Afro-Asian and Latin American countries experiencing CHEs, the major cause of unsustainable resource use has been the lack of socially sanctionable and legally enforceable property rights regimes or secure rights of usufruct. A corollary is that programmes to regenerate or conserve natural resources are unlikely to succeed unless they are implemented in conjunction with reforms which provide communal or individual security of tenure. Secure property and usufruct rights not only provide an institutional framework for devising sustainable land-use practices, but also provide resource users incentives to invest in agricultural intensification and labour intensive conservation.

6.2.1   Property rights and conservation

People who live on the edge of survival are rational because they are resource insecure. Resource-insecure people are prudent about allocating scarce resources, as a slight mistake in decision-making can have distressing consequences on their subsistence security. Before they commit scarce resources – land and labour – to an environmental regeneration or conservation programme, they will ask questions about short- and long-term benefits and costs, including ownership and use rights of the resources. In agriculturally and pastorally based economies, experience shows that environmental resource protection is unachievable unless preceded or accompanied by institutional changes that provide communal or individual security of tenure. Available evidence suggests that poor farmers 'with secure rights to a piece of land tend to care for it meticulously, taking a long-term view and forgoing current benefits for dependable future gains' (Durning 1989: 41).

Property and secure usufruct rights are critical not only for sustainable livelihood and natural resource management, but also in environmental regeneration or conservation programmes. Property rights regimes or secure rights of usufruct provide i) security or immunities against the encroachment of others in the form of socially recognized and sanctioned privileges expressed in formal laws, customs, mores and conventions, ii) opportunities for systematic allocation of access to and regulation of use of natural resources among collective owners or joint users, and iii) incentives for investment in conservation activities. Property rights do not represent rights over material objects but rather rights with respect to people (Gluckman 1955). A person's rights in property represent 'the power to limit the ability of other persons to enjoy the benefits to be secured from the use and enjoyment of a material good' (Bates 1989: 28). Where resources are scarce, the power of property and usufruct rights holders to limit outsiders from gaining entry, or the power to stipulate the conditions of entry as well as the ability to enforce these rights are *sine qua non* for peasants' and pastoralists' positive responses towards environmental regeneration or conservation programmes.

Renewable resources can be held under three forms of property rights regimes, namely communal, state and private property. The nature of the property rights regime is not inherent in the resource, each of which is capable of being nationalized, privatized or managed collectively (Gibbs and Bromley 1989). Each resource can also be held as de jure or de facto open access resource (*res nullius*) whether or not formal or informal institutions regulate access and regardless under which one of the three property rights regimes it is held.

The Western concept of property refers to either private or state property. Any resource outside these two property rights regimes is considered a 'common property' resource that is not owned by anyone. Among mainstream scholars, resources held in common are said to be insecure and subject to over-exploitation – the 'tragedy of the commons' (Hardin 1968). This view has been rigorously criticised (e.g. see Cox 1985; Ciriacy-Wantrup and Bishop 1975; Runge 1983; Kibreab 2000) as ahistorical and misconceived because 'common property' is not the same as an open access resource. 'Common property' refers to communally owned resources where institutions are designed to regulate allocation among co-owners and exclude non-members.

In northeast African countries with recurrent CHEs, state ownership of land and the other renewable resources has been an ultimate cause of land degradation. The problems of state ownership of renewable resources are twofold:

i) In many LICs, governments view themselves as the sole source of services and economic development, thus striving to attain revenue maximization, spurring them to over-exploit natural resources and disregard long-term sustainability. A number of studies of the Sahel show that the causes of famines were linked to government policies that encouraged cultivation of cash crops and neglected subsistence crops (Grainger 1990).

ii) State ownership of natural resources abrogates the ownership and usership rights of traditional resource users as well as their resource management systems without creating viable substitutes for what existed before because of inability of governments to enforce the new institutional arrangements (Bromley and Chapagain 1989; Kibreab 1996). The consequence of this is that resources that were previously managed sustainably by local resource users become de facto open access resources where access is unlimited and use is unregulated, resulting in depletion of resources.

Does state ownership of renewable resources contribute to vulnerability to environmental hazards and consequently to CHEs? A first caveat is to limit discussion to situations where weak states exercise ownership and control of natural resources without regard to their administrative and financial capability. States with capability to enforce such arrangements could also be managed by corrupt elites and may use the power of the state in their interest at the expense of the rest (North 1990).

Whether state ownership of natural resources is commensurate with equity and sustainability depends on whether the state concerned is i) amenable to public accountability, ii) free from corruption and prebendalism,[1] iii) capable of formulating and implementing an overall land-use policy, iv) capable of establishing a legal framework for adjudication in rights to land and other renewable resources, and v) capable of protecting the rights established through a process of settlement.

Where CHEs have recurred, these five conditions have been lacking and consequently transfer of control of natural resources from local communities to the state has created vulnerability to environmental-born CHEs from inappropriate land-use practices.

A second caveat is that nationalization of natural resources and the usurpation of the power by governments do not affect a country's population uniformly. The impact of these acts depends on the socioeconomic status and relationship to the 'state class' of those affected.

In countries suffering recurrent CHEs, the consequence of the incapability of enforcing institutional arrangements has been eventual de facto open-access to renewable resources. State ownership has set in motion exploitative and chaotic land use not subject to traditional or formal regulation, as well as encroachment on the livelihoods of peasants and pastoralists. In countries experiencing CHEs, state ownership of resources combined with a lack of capacity of implementation have been the major causes of land degradation and of subsistence producers' exposure to slow-onset man-made or natural emergencies.

Thus, whether environmental programmes can reduce vulnerability to CHEs depends both on the institutional framework and the approach for designing and implementing programmes. An effective programme requires building on principles of secure ownership and usufruct rights, and utilising existing local knowledge and organizations. Evidence from many LDCs suggests that environmental protection programmes that are implemented at the expense of the rights of indigenous and local populations to access to renewable resources increase the vulnerability of these populations (for India see Jodha 1986; for Indonesia see Colchester 1989; for the Philippines see Colchester 1992; for Latin America see Dorner and Theisenhusen 1992; for Kenya see Waller 1988; for Ethiopia see Turton 1989). Afro-Asian history is replete with environmental projects such as forests, national parks and wildlife, which undermined long-standing coping strategies, reducing the capacity of local resource users to withstand, cope with, or recover from slow-onset emergencies triggered by man-made or natural disasters such as drought.

Historically, the assumptions that underpinned most environmental programmes were that i) rural people were the major causes of resource depletion, ii) they would not take remedial action without outside intervention, and iii) they lacked indigenous techniques for managing their environment. Consequently, governments used draconian interventions to exclude rural people from their traditional sources of livelihood, increasing their vulnerability to CHEs. Even after independence, environmental conservation has been based on the principle of exclusion of rural people. The following illustrates the error of the three assumptions.

On 6 April 1997, *The Observer* published an article on the Mkomazi Game Reserve, which was established in 1988 by forcibly evicting 8000 Maasai pastoralists and their 75 000 herd of cattle from 1400 square miles in northern Tanzania. The reserve has had disastrous consequences for the Maasai and the environment. The Maasai were displaced from their ancestral land, and confined to smaller and marginal areas degraded by animal and human concentration. The result was a disruption of traditional migration routes, a dramatic decline of livestock productivity, increased livestock and human morbidity and mortality, a fierce conflict between the Maasai and surrounding farmers over dwindling resources, and animal theft prompted by lack of alternative means of survival. Paradoxically a project initiated to protect 'environmental resources' created increased vulnerability to CHEs. The Maasai are accustomed to living on the razor-edge of survival. Their productive practices were premised on the inevitability of recurrent crises. When they lost their familiar environment and basis of livelihood to the wildlife project, their capacity to withstand and cope with familiar crises was diminished dramatically.

The establishment of animal and plant kingdoms by excluding rural societies has been common in many African countries such as Kenya, Zimbabwe, South Africa, Uganda and Sudan, and indeed almost universal in LDCs. Establishing large parks and reserves undermines rural peoples' ability to withstand, cope with, and recover from seasonal crop failures or animal losses from slow-onset emergencies triggered by natural disasters. This approach to environmental protection breaks down the long-standing coping strategies rural people have developed in response to the harsh conditions inherent in arid and semi-arid regions.

Nevertheless, if properly conceived, programmes of environmental protection can still play critical roles in reducing vulnerability to CHEs, provided these programmes overcome the constraints that cause land degradation. Designers of environmental programmes need to understand indigenous farming and resource management systems and why local people are forced to adopt unsustainable land-use practices and are discouraged from taking actions to offset or mitigate land degradation. These issues are critical, focusing attention beyond physical processes and the 'blame game', and helping to broaden analysis to structural and institutional constraints which influence land-use practices and also land users' incentives to invest in agricultural intensification and labour-intensive conservation (Hoben 1995).

Once institutional constraints are addressed, the next step is to identify environmental risks that predispose people to CHEs, and devise interventions that prevent the risk scenario from unfolding and that reinforce the ability of the population to become resilient to such risks by improving the productivity of their resources. However, the problem of reduction of productive capability (degradation) is perceptual and consequently, the constraints such programmes aim to overcome should be defined either by the affected population or at least together with them. Following is a discussion of the importance of participation and the types of environmental resources protection that can contribute to reducing the risk of CHEs.

6.2.2   Participation

Environmental programmes can achieve their potential only through the motivation and participation of people previously excluded from decision-making and implementation. People's participation is necessary in the conceptualization, design, implementation, monitoring and evaluation of resource conservation, agricultural extension, forestry and water development programmes. The rationale is simple. If the purpose of environmental protection is to remove or minimize the constraints that spur inappropriate land-use practices and their consequent increase in CHE risk, then to be successful, the programme must understand the nature of the problem and how the community perceives it. The most effective way to understand community perception is in a participatory process. Successful programmes are those whose objectives match the priorities of local resource users and which elicit their continuous commitment and participation.

6.2.3 Measures for environmental resource protection

In countries experiencing CHEs, the main environmental problems are adverse weather conditions, pest infestation, animal and human diseases, soil erosion, loss of soil fertility and weed infestation, deforestation, and changes in grass species composition reflected in the loss of palatable and nutritious grasses and increase in unpalatable and less nutritious species, siltation and water-logging. The environment in Africa, especially in the northeast and south, has always been prone to hazards so that people have lived on the razor-edge of survival (Kibreab 1996). The relationship between man and nature has never been that of balanced harmony (Mesfin 1991). The environment has always been in disequilibrium. Lonsdale, for example, declares that '[E]nvironmental crisis and demographic collapse are scarcely new to Africa. They are as old as the continent's ascertainable history' (1989: 271). Most traditional resource management systems and productive activities that evolved were, therefore, devised to avoid, overcome or minimize environmental hazards. However, in recent decades these traditional coping strategies have been weakened so that the rural poor have become more vulnerable to slow-onset emergencies.

There can be no standardized approaches to overcoming inappropriate land-use practices, because the necessary measures vary depending on local agro-ecological conditions. Following are a few environmental protective measures that can reduce the vulnerability of rural peoples to CHEs or reinforce their resilience.

Countering soil erosion

The rate of erosion is generally a function of four main physical factors: erosivity of rainfall, the erodibility of the soil, the topography and the amount of vegetation cover. The extent of soil erosion on a given site, therefore, varies with landform, surrounding landform, slope, soil type, vegetation cover and agricultural practices. Erosion is a function of natural processes and the intensity of human interference, which varies with the ability of particular landforms to absorb intensified changes in land use. Soils with low resilience and high sensitivity are easily degraded and do not readily respond to land management once degradation occurs (Kibreab 1996).

Thus, the best remedial action is to avoid bringing such sites into a production process. Soil erosion can also be minimized by implementing soil and water conservation programmes based on participation and self-help. Some communities afflicted by recurrent CHEs have a long tradition of soil and water conservation techniques such as construction of stone-walled terraces, earth bunds, stone-walled diversions, structures across slopes, and ridging along contours. For example, after visiting the Eritrean highlands in the 1890s Wylde stated, '[N]o expensive European engineers are required for this work, as the natives...thoroughly understand terrace cultivation and irrigation, and hardly waste a drop of water' (1901: 25). In the 1940s, Nadel also observed, '[T]he Eritrean cultivator makes extensive use of terracing where his farms lie on sloping ground; the terraces are well built and are kept up with much care' (1946: 4). During the last decades these conservation methods had almost become obsolete because of political, institutional and economic disincentives. With favourable incentives, people can build on indigenous knowledge to overcome soil erosion and improve soil productivity.

Countering loss of soil fertility

Agricultural productivity is influenced by a myriad of variables so that it is difficult to measure the role of specific factors in productivity change, such as how much the change results from the degradation of soil nutrients and how much from low and erratic rainfall.

Generally, in countries with CHEs, the major causes of crop yield decline in order of priority are depletion of soil nutrients, weed infestation, inadequate rainfall, insect pest infestation and soil erosion (Simpson and Khalifa 1976). Although these are the most important factors, crop yield decline is also a function of other interacting factors, such as poor management manifested in inappropriate seed-spacing, untimely sowing, improper cultivation methods, inefficient weed control, poor varieties and poor seed quality, reduced moisture availability because of increased run-off, scarcity or high cost of labour which delays agricultural operations, lack of extension services, and fluctuation in producer prices (Kibreab 1996).

A major cause of depletion of soil nutrients is continuous cropping without fallow periods or fertilizer. Inequitable distribution and shortage of arable land amid a growing population have rendered traditional methods of replenishing soil nutrients obsolete. The increasing pressure on smallholder agriculture from the expansion of commercial agriculture has forced smallholders to bring degradation-prone marginal areas under cultivation and to adopt unsustainable land use which depletes soil nutrients.

A return to traditional methods of countering soil exhaustion is unrealistic because of land shortage. The only realistic approach to productivity improvement is through adopting improved farming practices and more intensive production technologies reflected in increased inputs of capital, labour and skills on constant land. Intensification increases output without reducing (degrading) the productive capability of the environment (Brookfield 1972: 31).

Countering deforestation

Deforestation can result from i) clearance of land for agricultural production, ii) fuelwood consumption for cooking, heating and lighting, and iii) wood consumption for construction materials. Depending on the sensitivity and resilience of the land, removal of vegetation cover can harm the environment. Woodlands also play a key role in local economies as sources of building materials, fuelwood and fodder. Tree leaves, seeds and pods constitute important sources of fodder. Other products such as fruit, gum, honey and medicines are also gathered from woodlands. However, not every form of land clearance for agriculture, and tapping of woodland produce for fuelwood and for construction, causes deforestation.

If harvesting of forest produce is matched with the rate of biomass regeneration, yields can remain sustainable indefinitely. Woodland resource users have been able to plan for sustainability by understanding the dynamic behaviour of trees, that is, by knowing how certain trees grow over time. It is only when forest resources are exploited without taking their sustainability into account that deforestation may occur.

The most effective way to counter deforestation is by reducing demand, for example through alternative energy sources, energy efficient stoves, or implementing supply enhancement such as i) improved management of woodlands, including rotational use of sites, ii) appropriate harvesting techniques, and iii) community tree planting or agroforestry for building materials and fuelwood (provided that questions of land and tree tenure have been addressed).

Tree planting is also an effective way of combating the problems of salination and water-logging. Tree cover reduces salination by pumping moisture to the surface, thus lowering the level of ground water. Tree roots also help to open up soil particles leading to increased water infiltration.

Countering the problem of overgrazing

Overgrazing occurs when livestock density becomes excessive and too many animals are grazed on the same area of rangelands, leading to changes in plant species composition, compaction and soil erosion, increases in unpalatable and non-nutritious plant species, reduction in perennial grasses, and increases in annuals with the consequent decline in livestock productivity and increased mortality. The social consequence of these changes is that the livelihoods of those who depend on livestock deteriorate.

In the mainstream literature, rangeland degradation from overstocking is overstated, and factors engendering unsustainable rangeland use are often misconceived. For example, in northeastern African countries experiencing recurrent CHEs, the expansion of commercial agriculture and the burning of grazing and browsing resources by charcoal producers have been major causes of livestock concentration. Pastoral and agro-pastoral groups also keep large animals as security against adversity.

Thus, the most effective way to overcome overgrazing is by devolving control of rangelands to pastoralists and by addressing the insecurity that forces pastoral groups to keep large numbers of animals.

6.3   Environmental degradation and political conflicts

This chapter also addresses whether 'protection of environmental resources' can reduce LICs' vulnerability to political conflicts. If the problem of environmental degradation is addressed, can the occurrence of political conflicts be prevented?

Most recent conflicts are intrastate, but they have no single cause. The explanation for why and when conflicts occur is difficult. Two countries with seemingly similar volatile situations may unfold in very different ways. One country may face deadly political violence while another may avoid violent conflict. Although many recent conflicts escalating to CHEs have been fought between communities with different ethnic, religious, clan and language identities, the economic, social and political roots of this deadly violence are complex. Nafziger's introduction, in this volume, outlines some of the roots of CHEs found in Nafziger *et al.* (2000). Can environmental variables be added to the sources of CHEs?

Some researchers see a link between conflicts and droughts. Timberlake argues that during the 1980s every African nation 'suffering from civil war also suffered from drought' (1985: 186). However, these drought-stricken countries were exceptions rather than the rule because most countries suffering from drought did not experience war. During the 1980s there were major droughts in Africa, India, China, Indonesia and Brazil, yet only a few African countries were afflicted by war. In SSA, 31 countries suffered from drought, but only 5 of them, namely Mozambique, Angola, Chad, Ethiopia and Sudan, were plagued with internal wars (Glantz 1987).

Since the mid-1980s there has been a growing interest in the relationship between environmental degradation, war, conflict and forced migration (Kibreab 1997). However, opinions vary widely as to whether environmental degradation is a cause of conflict and CHEs. An important assumption underlying the burgeoning literature is that war and conflicts and consequently population displacements are due to environmental degradation (Homer-Dixon 1995). Timberlake (1985: 185), for example, points out that in the 1980s, 'environmental degradation...fuelled conflict and instability across Africa...The environmental degradation of much of Africa threatened to stir conflict in the continent for generations to come'.

The Horn of Africa is often cited as a region where environmental scarcity from degradation of resources has given rise to violent conflicts forcing millions of people to flee in search of succour and safe haven (Molvaer 1991). Nevertheless, what this region has been experiencing is not environmental change engendering political conflict and insecurity. Rather, the escalating levels of insecurity, conflicts and violence have compelled people to concentrate in safer zones, intensifying the process of degradation of the available local resources, while the unsafe areas remained under-used (Kibreab 1997: 22). People in the region have lived since time immemorial on the razor-edge of survival. They had multiple coping strategies and responses that involved substitutions in production, income, assets and consumption. Their productive practices aimed at minimizing problems stemming from variable rainfall patterns, soil fertility, river systems and vegetation cover and quality. The underlining principle of such production systems was mobility designed to take advantage of environmental variability in different ecological niches.

The escalating levels of violence, conflicts, insecurity and the misguided policies of the various governments in the region led to the breakdown, on the one hand, of long-standing traditional resource management systems and strategies for coping with and recovering from the consequences of environmental hazards and, on the other, the resilience of the physical environment. When degradation of the natural resources in the safer areas became life-threatening, people were left with no alternative but to become internally or externally displaced. To see these population displacements as being primarily caused by environmental degradation is to mistake correlation with causation. In war-torn societies, conflicts, insecurity and violence are primary causes of environmental change, breakdown of coping strategies, food insecurity and consequently of population displacement and not the other way around. Scholars increasingly realize that 'violence plays a decisive role in the breakdown of coping strategies...' (Hendricksen *et al.* 1996: 17).

The direct impact of military action on the environment is not properly documented in Africa; evidence from elsewhere, however, clearly suggests that war, by causing environmental change, can be a major cause of population displacement. According to Shaw (1989), the Vietnam War (1950–75) produced more than 25 million craters (6 to 30 metres wide), destroyed 1 million hectares of forest and rendered more than 2 million hectares of land unproductive due to the use of the pesticide 'Agent Orange' and other toxic chemicals. Populations in the affected areas had no choice but to be displaced internally or externally in search of new sources of livelihoods.

The available evidence suggests that in the countries experiencing CHEs, political conflicts and wars have been some of the causes or contributors to environmental degradation rather than the other way around. If environmental degradation is a consequence rather than a cause of political conflicts, then arguably the protection of environmental resources may not reduce vulnerability to political conflicts. To be sure, as noted before, in countries fighting intra-state wars, we cannot attribute the source of the conflict to a single factor. Competition over scarce resources, in combination with other factors, fuels conflict. Protection of environmental resources, by augmenting the productive capability of the basic resource – land – may ease local tensions that, in the absence of this appropriate remedial action, would have kindled the flame of a humanitarian emergency.

The protection of environmental resources that manifest in improved productivity of available resources may also have an indirect impact in easing social tension by increasing the absorptive capacity of the local, regional and national economies of the countries. Two dramatic and far-reaching impacts of economic stagnation in most war-torn societies during the last fifteen years have been the immense population shift from rural areas to cities and the presence of millions of disenchanted young people in rural areas without any prospect for absorption in rural or urban economies and societies. These population shifts have been taking place in the absence of structural transformation in the economies concerned. Structural transformation here refers to increases in labour productivity, declining shares of agriculture in total output, technological progress and industrialization. The consequence of this lack of transformation has been that neither people who emigrate to the cities nor those who stay put in their areas of origin are able to become part of the productive sections of society. These people have no stake in their societies and often constitute the 'reserve army' of the forces, for example of warlords who use ethnic, religious and clan differences as a basis of division and mobilization for promoting their sectarian interests. Well-conceived and participatory environmental protection and regeneration programmes may, by increasing the productive capacity of available resources, absorb the 'surplus' rural labour force and consequently turn the same into a 'reserve army' of production rather than destruction. Where there is a proliferation of small weapons, the presence of a large number of disenchanted people without a stake in the status quo constitutes dynamite that can explode violently. It is in this context that environmental protection and regeneration programmes can be seen as reducing the risk of humanitarian emergencies.

Note

1. Prebendal refers to 'patterns of political behaviour which rest on the justifying principle that such offices should be competed for and then utilized for the personal benefit of officeholders as well as their reference or support group' (Joseph 1987: 8). Prebendalism connotes an intense struggle among communities for control of the state. Corruption is endemic to political life at all levels (ibid.).

Part III

Governmental and Non-Governmental Strategies

7
Preventing Humanitarian Emergencies: Human Security and Strategic Action

Raimo Väyrynen

7.1   The promises and limits of preventive action

Complex humanitarian emergencies are deep, multidimensional crises triggered by the large-scale use of violence. In such emergencies people are killed, or suffer from violence, displacement, hunger and disease. Humanitarian crises are almost always associated with civil wars, but not all such wars result in emergencies as their intensity and scope may remain limited. To qualify as a humanitarian disaster, the crisis must exceed a certain threshold of severity measured by the amount of death and suffering. One can also make a distinction between sudden and protracted humanitarian emergencies; the former is manifested in an outburst of violence and death, while the latter is embedded in the structure of society.

Focusing on the structural factors that increase the vulnerability of society leads us to make a distinction between background conditions and processes of escalation. As a rule, background factors are a necessary but not sufficient condition for the outbreak of an emergency, while escalation processes are sufficient and sometimes even necessary conditions. Thus, an analysis of the escalation processes is of vital importance. One possibility is to consider the causes of emergencies to be primarily structural, while escalation processes are fuelled by risky actions by the parties. This approach is followed by Gurr and Harff (1996) who regard group capacity and incentives for political action, and the state capacity of coercion, as 'risk factors'. In addition, they list eight 'accelerators', such as external involvement and new discriminatory policies by a regime that aggravate the problems. Together these background factors and processes define the risk of an emergency or genocide. A similar approach has been adopted by Wallensteen (1998a) who makes a distinction between structural and direct prevention, the former addressing background conditions and the latter proximate causes.

The essence of escalation is qualitative change. It is captured well by Smoke (1977: 34) who defines it as 'the crossing of saliencies, which are taken as defining the limits of conflict. As a war escalates, it moves upward and outward through a pattern of saliencies that are provided situationally'. He suggests that strategic steps taken by parties to cross salient limits are the defining characteristics of the escalation process (Smoke 1977; on strategic action, see Väyrynen 2000c). These limits can be either legal, such as the ban on chemical weapons, or physical, such as the inviolability of national territories. One way to tap saliencies is to consider the severity of conflicts which, according to Kriesberg (1997), can be either isolated, extensive or protracted destructive acts. Of these, the two latter are more likely to lead to escalation.

Escalation can be either vertical or horizontal. Vertical escalation means an increase in the magnitude or intensity of dispute; its prevention aims to limit human and physical destruction from the use of military force. Horizontal escalation expands, in turn, the geographical and social domains of conflict and draws into the sphere of violence new groups or states. In the prevention of escalation, timing is important as its continuation makes constructive and effective responses increasingly difficult (Scherrer 1999).

The escalation process is the critical link between the background factors and the outbreak of violence. This view suggests that the key requirement of effective prevention is to stop the processes of vertical and horizontal escalation. On that score, Nikolaïdis (1996: 34) is right in observing that 'the challenge to early-warning systems is not so much in identifying societies at risk in general, but in recognizing the patterns of change that will lead to the acceleration of conflicts'. Therefore, the escalation process should be in the centre of the analysis. Similarly, Lund (1998) queries, 'After warning, what?' and stresses the need for systematic 'rolling prevention' to stop escalation.

A different approach has been advocated by Hansen (1996), who criticizes the tendency to divorce complex emergencies from their societal context and to treat them primarily as decision problems. He suggests that emergencies have not been precipitated by the erosion of Cold War structures and new risks of war, but by the 'intensifying effects of population growth, environmental degradation, and economic disequilibrium, both nationally and internationally'. In other words, a complex emergency is not an aberrant phenomenon, but an aspect of the deepening crisis in developing societies, which calls for a 'radical social adjustment' rather than the delivery of additional relief.

It is important to note that preventive action should focus on forestalling major violence, not conflict in general (Jaberg 1997). The focus on the imminent risk of major violence has been called 'operational prevention' (Lund 1997: 39). However, due to the complexity and severity of humanitarian emergencies, the analysis has to go beyond operational aspects and also tackle the structural causes. Political, and especially military instruments are less appropriate because the cure needs genuine social and economic reforms, and a comprehensive overhaul of political and legal institutions to provide justice and stability in society. Economic and institutional strategies of prevention are costly and require earlier action, but they are also potentially more effective. In the end, an effective long-term prevention of emergencies has to be supported by a 'culture of prevention', which, in addition to governments and international organizations, also involves media and various voluntary organizations (ibid.: 151–5).

In summary, effective preventive action requires a concerted long-term strategy by the international community to reduce economic and social vulnerabilities and maintain political stability in peripheral societies. At present, no such strategy exists; the international community does not have appropriate lead institutions and resources for continued and focused action to prevent emergencies. There are signs of such strategies, however. The WB has started to pay systematic attention to post-conflict peace-building and prevention, stressing in particular the need to harness social capital to prevent violent conflict (Colletta and Cullen 2000). It has been rightly pointed out that the 'warning-response gap' in preventive action is rarely caused by the lack of timely and accurate warning, or even by the inability of decision-makers to take this information seriously, but is due to the absence of appropriate instruments and political commitments (George and Holl 1997; George 1999).

Obstacles also include the inertial nature of international relations; governments avoid local involvement until risks become big enough to demand action. Delays in preventive action are due to fears that intervention in a crisis creates an unpredictable, open-ended commitment, which leads to a 'mission creep' and, ultimately, entraps the government. Thus, failure to act is often due to a national assessment that unilateral risks in crisis intervention are bigger than collective benefits. Even if the inertia of international relations can be overcome, effective preventive action faces other hurdles. The objectives and interests of governments differ, making it difficult to mount concerted action by international institutions even when its need is recognized. These institutions themselves may also be at fault. The UN failed badly in preventing the Srebrenica massacre. It took four years to produce a detailed and candid report on the reasons for this major humanitarian failure (UN 1999).

In many crises, the multiplicity of governmental and non-governmental organizations means that the division of labour is often unclear, making the coordination of preventive actions difficult. They may even compete with each other for political attention and funding. The failure to forestall war in Yugoslavia in 1991–92 was, in part, due to a lack of institutional capacity and inadequate coordination, which together led to inconsistent and inefficient responses. The limits on international capacity are reflected in the fact that the dissolution of the Soviet Union received most of the attention and Yugoslavia remained a sideshow (Väyrynen 1996).

Some of these problems appeared also in Burundi where UN plans to create a multinational force in 1996 to prevent the potential massacre failed. Over 200 non-governmental and governmental organizations were involved in the provision of humanitarian relief, democracy assistance and mediation services because such involvement needed only modest political commitment and material resources. External actors gave up efforts to contain the internal violence as it would have required riskier and costlier commitments (Lund *et al.* 1998; Hara 1999). The Burundi case also suggests that the reluctance of governments to engage in robust collective action easily puts the onus on NGO operations

Humanitarian assistance is, in a way, an easy option for governments, but it is not enough to solve major problems. As a result, differences emerge on whether to rely on peaceful diplomatic means or resort to coercive economic and military measures. Many are sceptical about the effectiveness of penalties and advocate incentives, or a combination of both. On the other hand, as experience in Bosnia in 1995 and Kosovo in 1999 shows, the use of force may be needed to signal the seriousness of intent of the international community to terminate a crisis. Finally, humanitarian disasters are genuinely difficult and often impossible to manage. The core problem may be that the material and political capacity of international organizations is simply too limited to deal with multiple complex crises (Esman 1996).

Faced with these hurdles, preventive efforts may be a non-starter even when there is recognition of the need for action and adequate resources for it. These complexities have led advocates of preventive action to stress that instead of 'late' prevention, the international community needs 'early' prevention of crises. Then, contentious issues are still specific, attitudes of the parties are still pliable, the number of actors is limited, costs of the action are smaller, and reliance on resolution rather than containment is more likely to yield positive results (Evans 1993).

7.2   Types of preventive actions

The concept of preventive action has at least three different meanings: i) short-term concentrated diplomatic or military operation by international actors to avoid an outbreak of violence, ii) defusion of tensions in society with medium-term arrangements to share power and enhance the legitimacy of governance, and iii) long-term policy to reduce structural vulnerabilities and inequities. The last approach has been criticized, though, for defining the prevention of violence in too broad terms and thus reducing the clarity of the concept. A better alternative would be a narrower definition that focuses on the prevention of violence outbreaks (Jaberg 1997).[1]

Short-term action to prevent the outbreak of war is reactive by nature, while long-term efforts to reshape structures in advance of violence are proactive. A proactive approach tries to alter, before violence breaks, the conflict environment to reduce human suffering (Reychler 1997).

Consistent with proactive thinking, redefining the military approach to complex emergencies has to be called for. The military, instead of focusing on short-term security, should become involved in all phases of the crisis cycle, including humanitarian relief, conflict resolution and social reconciliation (Mackinlay and Kent 1997).

Comprehensive, proactive approaches are embraced by the Commission on Global Governance (CGG), which emphasizes that 'a comprehensive preventive strategy must focus on the underlying political, social, economic, and environmental causes of conflict' (1995: 93–8). However, with a comprehensive approach, one has to maintain focus, as it can degenerate into a list of all good things needed in society. The purpose of preventive action is not to create a perfect society, but to address those particular causes and processes that are likely to lead to a breakdown of the economy and public order, and thus increase the people's vulnerability. Therefore, preventive action must be well targeted and strategically defined to make sure that there is both domestic capacity and international commitment to carry out the action.

A similar concern is echoed by Lund (1996: 35–6) who questions the 'wisdom of equating preventive diplomacy with the job of correcting often pervasive and deeply rooted social ills'. Not all detrimental socioeconomic and cultural conditions lead to violence, while well-meaning but casual reforms may exacerbate rather than mitigate conflicts. The relationship between action, goals and outcomes is necessarily vexed in preventive diplomacy, which tries to eliminate an undesirable future option, i.e. either the outbreak or escalation of violence. The task, then, is to produce a desirable social reality, an alternative to the disaster scenario. Preventive action has the task of creating corrective feedback to forestall escalation. Due to the complex links between actors, processes and issues, the effects of preventive action are often delayed, mediated and indirect. Thus, there is no direct causality between action and its outcomes which, as a result, can also be unintended or even perverse (Jervis 1997; see also Smith 1999).

From a strategic perspective, the key issue with preventive action is whether it aims to preserve the status quo or change the underlying structure of the crisis. This strategic difference is tapped by the conceptual distinction between crisis management, dispute resolution and conflict transformation. Conflict management aims to de-escalate conflict, and dispute resolution to settle the issue, thus restoring the status quo ante, while its transformation seeks to create a new structure or situation in which the reasons for the use of violence are reduced (Auvinen and Kivimäki 1997). Thus, conflict transformation should be the main form of strategic action in efforts to avert a humanitarian crisis. As conflicts can seldom be resolved in any lasting manner, the best that one can do is to make them less destructive and more manageable. This requires a modification of the underlying social reality to defuse the escalation potential. Thus, conflict transformation relies on the redefinition and reordering of relevant actors, issues, rules and interests. Compared with standard models of conflict resolution, it makes an effort to recognize the complexity of conflict situations (Väyrynen 1991 and 1999).

Constructive conflict transformation can rely both on structural (reconstruction) and non-structural (reconciliation) measures to move society from instability to dynamic stability (Reychler 1997). This conceptualization of conflict transformation covers both the manipulation of root causes and the containment of escalation as methods of conflict prevention. Reconciliation can be effective in alleviating violence in limited conflicts where divisive issues are malleable, but if the confrontation is complex, the society's foundation has to be reconstructed before reconciliation produces results. Conflict prevention often stresses external actions to maintain peace or stop escalation. Such actions are needed due to the intractability of the conflict; relations between parties may be so polarized that only external pressure and incentives can break the stalemate. However, as Bosnia and Kosovo suggest, external action alone is not enough; effective conflict transformation requires the participation of civil-society actors (Ropers 1997).

7.3   Strategies of preventive action

By combining goals and means, operational preventive action is strategic in nature. The specification of this strategy defines, in turn, the intrusiveness and duration of intervention. The means of preventive action are often conveniently divided into diplomatic, institutional, economic and military instruments. Such functional classifications, however, are inadequate as they mask, for instance, the distinction between coercive and non-coercive measures.

Coercion involves the use of punishment, or its threat, to deter the target from committing a certain act or compel it to carry out another act. Threats are time-limited ultimatums to communicate to the target a set of requirements with which it is expected to comply. To avoid escalation of a crisis, threats should be specific and credible in case the target fails to heed the signals. Coercive measures may be objected both on normative and policy grounds, but their relevance in conflict prevention cannot be denied (Jentleson 2000).

The policy of the Contact Group in the former Yugoslavia is an example of the graduated nature of coercive action (Boidevaix 1997). For instance, in March 1998 the Group threatened to impose credit, travel, visa and arms sanctions on Belgrade unless it withdrew the special police units from Kosovo and ended the violence there. When this did not happen, the United Nations Security Council (UNSC) imposed sanctions, while the North Atlantic Treaty Organization (NATO) continued to pursue a two-track policy of diplomatic contacts and military pressure. Neither approach stopped Belgrade's repression in Kosovo, and the failure of preventive action led NATO to launch an air war against Serbia. The Contact Group had a critical role also in balancing the NATO advocacy of, and the Soviet objections to, the use of coercive measures against Serbia in the Kosovo crisis of 1998–99.

The use of pure military coercion for preventive purposes is unlikely. Although economic sanctions are often ineffective (Pape 1997), one should not reject their use for preventive purposes too lightly. It is clear that the economic sanctions imposed on the apartheid regime in South Africa had a constraining effect on its repressive policies. In highlighting the long-term implications of apartheid, sanctions seem to have convinced the white minority that reconciliation with the majority was, after all, the safest way to the future. One can also claim that the imposition of economic sanctions in July 1996 by the Organization for African Unity (OAU) on Burundi after a military coup helped to prevent repetition of the Rwandan tragedy (Evans 1997). Thus, while economic sanctions in the first instance are unable to avert an outbreak of violence, they may, in conjunction with other instruments, accomplish reasonable goals.

Non-coercive measures normally contain promises and rewards to secure and maintain compliance. Economic instruments can be used to 'purchase' compliance, while political means may confer legitimacy as a reward (Rothchild 1997). More broadly, incentives can be defined as the 'granting of a political or economic benefit in exchange for a specified policy adjustment by the recipient nation' (Cortright 1997: 6). These types of incentives can be called specific in contrast to diffuse ones in which benefits do not presuppose any particular response, but rather good behaviour in general.

There is some evidence that non-coercive incentives are more likely to succeed than coercion. On the other hand, they are criticized for potentially rewarding non-compliance, leading thus to appeasement and 'moral hazard'. US support to Iraq during its war with Iran in the 1980s is an example of a policy that backfired badly; instead of convincing Saddam Hussein that an attack on Kuwait was futile, these incentives encouraged him to try his luck. The incentives produced aggression instead of its prevention. This experience underlines the fact that to achieve the desired results, incentives must be carefully calibrated and timed, and integrated with the potential use of threats and penalties (Cortright 1997). Case studies suggest that success in preventing or stopping aggression requires effective communication and, in the case of non-compliance, implementation of threats (Jakobsen 1998).

To be able to assess the effectiveness of different means of prevention, one has to take note of the character of contemporary crises, which are more complex today than during the Cold War. Not only is the international structure more decentralized, but also the changing nature and number of actors and issues have added new elements. Furthermore, lack of clarity regarding rules of behaviour has contributed to the increasing complexity of crises (also linked closely with the underlying socioeconomic conditions than before). All this has made decisions and the implementation of international responses more demanding.

As shown by the evolution of peacekeeping operations, the nature of responses has changed. Simple operations to separate warring parties have been converted into multidimensional actions for implementing peace agreements and democratic transitions. As these operations face opposition from local parties (Bosnia and Somalia), the international community has tried to enforce agreements even against their will. These efforts backfired and taught the sober lesson that the UN suffers from 'multiple strategic incapacity'; it may be able to facilitate, but not enforce, agreements. Therefore, it has to rely on non-coercive rather than coercive instruments. Mere facilitation, however, is seldom enough, which is why the UN should be able to 'enhance' consensus with a combination of incentives and pressures. Moreover, successful escalation prevention and peace maintenance require transforming the original confrontation into a less explosive one (Doyle 1996). Consequently, there is perception that Chapter VI is too little and Chapter VII is too much; therefore, the middle ground of 'Chapter VI $\frac{1}{2}$' is thought to provide the best direction for future action.

Although coercive measures sometimes offer the only option for preventing or stopping violence, their use may, on the other hand, produce undesirable consequences. Such measures may harden the situation and elicit punitive counter-reactions, leading to an escalation of violence. Therefore, coercive threats can be inefficient and even counterproductive. An exception to this may be a stalemate in which the parties have already started to move towards a solution. In this situation, threats can be 'useful in tightening the jaws of a deadlock, making the stalemate more painful and future alternatives more attractive'. The deadlock can be alleviated with a mixture of coercion and positive incentives (Aurik and Zartman 1991). In fact, the mixed strategy of promises and threats is considered the most effective policy to wield influence in a conflict situation (Rothchild 1997; Cortright 1997).

The simple functional classification of preventive instruments masks also the difference between 'remote' and 'proximate' strategies of influence. Remote strategies avoid direct involvement in the conflict zone (hands off), while proximate strategies require a hands-on approach. By also introducing a distinction between ad hoc and systemic preventive actions, Nikolaïdis (1996) specifies four main types of instrumental preventive actions. These action categories are distinguished by their time perspective and degree of intrusiveness, but they do not make an explicit difference between compelling and inductive strategies. Remote strategies, such as deterrence, avoid local engagements and either try to keep the third parties out of the conflict or to deter local parties from escalating the crisis. During the Cold War, the great-power presence in conflict zones often had incendiary influence. In fact, opposition to the intrusive and escalatory great-power policies was originally the chief reason for preventive diplomacy; the idea Hammarskjöld tried to realize in Lebanon in 1958.

A ban on arms deliveries to a conflict region is one method of remote prevention to reduce the destruction of war. On the other hand, an embargo can also freeze military power relations and favour the strongest party to the conflict. The UN arms embargo on the former Yugoslavia favoured Serbia without protecting the international peacekeepers, and prompted the Sarajevo government to conclude political deals with Muslim countries (Cigar 1995; cf. de Rossanet 1996).

Hands-on strategies aim higher than remote deterrence. External parties, through local engagement, make an effort to steer the conflict toward a more peaceful solution. This engagement may vary from diplomatic mediation to a sustained long-term commitment to conflict transformation. Such commitments can, however, lead to accusations that alien liberal economic and political models are imposed on historically and culturally different societies. Preventive deployment is an in-between strategy that attempts to hinder the horizontal escalation of crises. The non-escalation of the Yugoslavian crisis to Macedonia has been often attributed to the containing effect of the preventive UN deployment (UNPREDEP) (Archer 1994; de Rossanet 1996). In reality, preventive action in Macedonia also aimed to contain domestic tensions between the Albanian minority and the Macedonian majority, i.e. UNPREDEP also had a conflict resolution function (Clément 1997; Leatherman *et al.* 1999). Moreover, due to the participation of US forces, UNPREDEP became a tripwire to great-power policies and capabilities.

The standard approach to the early warning and prevention of violence relies on a phase model of conflicts (Miall 1992; Evans 1993; Nikolaïdis 1996; Lund 1996). The underlying assumption behind these models is that the management of each stage requires different instruments and institutions; i.e., the intensity and urgency of the crisis affect the choice of methods during various phases of the conflict cycle. Obviously, the assumption that conflicts follow a smooth and predictable cycle of outbreak, escalation and abatement is an oversimplification. Instead, conflict trajectories are often characterized by long periods of simmering tensions and sudden outbursts of violence, as well as discontinuities and reversals of the process. Remedies, therefore, must be contingent, conditional, and contextual.

Building on the cyclical model, one can distinguish between three separate but interrelated approaches to preventive action: i) *conflict prevention*, i.e. preventing violent conflicts from arising between the parties, ii) *escalation prevention*, i.e. preventing both vertical and horizontal escalation of hostilities, and iii) *post-conflict prevention*, i.e. preventing the re-emergence of disputes (Väyrynen 1996). This conceptual framework differs from the standard approach in which preventive diplomacy consists only of pre-conflict actions.

According to this typology, one can define conflict prevention as

actions, policies, procedures, or institutions undertaken in particularly vulnerable places and times in order to avoid the threat or use of armed forces and related forms of coercion by states or groups as the way to settle the political disputes that can arise from the destabilizing effects of economic, social, political, and international change. Conflict prevention can also include action taken after a violent conflict to avoid its recurrence (Lund *et al* 1997: 2–3).

This definition is compatible with the contingency model of conflict resolution, i.e., the choice of means must be contingent on the nature and stage of the crisis. Therefore, intervention is tailored to each stage of escalation and is expected to produce, through a sequence of commitments, a series of specific outcomes (Fisher 1997). Albeit simplified, the cyclical model is useful, as it distinguishes preventive action from other forms of diplomacy. Lund (1996) makes a distinction between peacetime diplomacy and crisis diplomacy, and places preventive diplomacy in-between the two. He suggests that preventive diplomacy is needed when peacetime diplomacy has failed, but the situation has not yet deteriorated into a crisis. The key to success in preventive action is the correct timing and effective utilization of political opportunities.

The complexity of conflicts means that operational prevention must simultaneously consider several dimensions of the conflict. The conflict cycle can be dichotomized by using the outbreak of major violence as the dividing line ('before' versus 'after'). The preventive instruments can be classified by two criteria; their distance from the object ('remote' versus 'proximate') and the amount of force involved ('coercive' versus 'non-coercive'). The use of these conceptual devices yields the classification of the operational strategies of prevention as shown in Table 7.1.

The table implies that the major difference between remote and proximate strategies is that the former rely on commitments to punish or to reward depending on compliance by the target. This is true especially in the pre-conflict strategies of prevention. In a deterrence situation, non-compliance with the norm leads to its enforcement by punitive measures. The alternative is compellence, in which the target actor is pushed by coercive measures to behave in a particular way. In an inducement situation,

Table 7.1   Political and military strategies of preventive action

		Coercive	Non-coercive
Remote	Before	1. Deterrence, punishment	2. Inducement, rewards
	After	3. Isolation, enforcement	4. Legitimation, recognition
Proximate	Before	5. Inspections, disarmament	6. Engagement, support
	After	7. Coercive diplomacy, limited military force	8. Mediation, negotiation

compliance with the norm is rewarded by material or political support. One can also mix these two strategies, which happens when non-compliance is addressed by incentives rather than punishments. In such a case, the enforcer tries to reassure the target with manoeuvres that stress the anticipated future gains of cooperation.

Proximate pre-conflict prevention requires presence in the target country to prevent deterioration of a conflict into violent crisis. Coercive presence, for instance, may aim to identify and dismantle arm caches and to reduce, in general, military capabilities. Had this been permitted to the UN forces in Rwanda in early 1994, many lives would have been saved (Melvern 1997). Non-coercive intervention makes an effort to engage local actors in cooperation to strengthen the local capacity to defuse the potential for violence. Obviously, coercive presence poses a bigger challenge to sovereignty than non-coercive engagement. On the other hand, some non-coercive strategies, such as the establishment of mass media to disseminate peace-supportive information, can also be problematic from the standpoint of sovereignty.

A non-coercive policy tries to induce the local parties to stop or limit the fighting with conditional promises of international legitimation. This can be realized, for example, by recognizing statehood or granting membership in an important international organization, such as the EU (Nikolaïdis 1996). Recognition of Slovenia and Croatia by the EU, and particularly by Germany, in 1991 was an effort at remote inducement to halt a war that had already started. This case also highlights the pitfalls of the recognition policy, as it may have adverse spillover effects in other countries. Croatia's international recognition may have helped to stop its war with Serbia, but it also greatly impaired the position of Bosnia-Herzegovina and prepared the ground for atrocities there.

7.4   Transforming a violent society

A more viable international security system would require the establishment of a normative international order, institutions capable of mounting collective actions, and the mutual commitment and cooperation of the major powers to the enforcement of norms. In other words, collective ability to reshape and steer domestic conflicts is possible only in a 'new world order'. Defined in such an ambitious way, the establishment of an international preventive regime is an illusion. As pointedly stated by George Soros (1996), there is no general desire to prevent conflict. The international community does not have a clear, collective understanding of what the main problems are in peace operations and humanitarian interventions. Therefore, in most cases, international interventions are dictated by the interests of the participating states.

The failure of an early international response to the Rwandan genocide in 1994 is a stark reminder of how the paucity of UN leadership and the reluctance of major powers, especially the US, to launch an effective protective operation can fail an entire nation (Adelman and Suhrke 1996). Another pertinent example concerns Boutros-Ghali's efforts to launch a preventive military operation, first in Burundi and then in Zaire, to stop the crisis escalation (Evans 1997; Lund *et al.* 1998).

The failure of the international community in Rwanda has been amply documented. The commander of the minuscule UN force in Rwanda, General Romeo Dallaire, witnessed in 1998 how the international troops were too small and hamstrung by the rules of engagement to stop the genocide. Despite his appeals, and supporting evidence produced by the US Central Intelligence Agency (CIA), the UNSC and the Secretariat dragged their feet and stymied the preventive operation. In particular it was blocked by Washington, which considered it too risky to send troops into harm's way without a clear-cut exit option. It is somewhat hypocritical that the main culprit of inaction, President Clinton, finally admitted in March 1998 that 'never again must we be shy in the face of evidence'. To compensate for the 1994 ban on the use of the word 'genocide', thus avoiding legally mandated action, he used it in his Rwandan speech 11 times (*New York Times* 1998).

External intervention does not always help to prevent the outbreak of a crisis or its escalation. Recalcitrant governments can, to a surprising degree, divert the impact of external coercive measures. Often, to be successful, international intervention should lead to an intrusive and enduring foreign presence in the target country. The post-Dayton experience in Bosnia shows that such an intervention is possible, but it requires a strong, long-term commitment to the maintenance of peace in a war-torn country. It is clear that the international community is ready for only a few such commitments at any given time. With obligations undertaken since 1999 in Kosovo, East Timor and Sierra Leone, it can be assume that the limit of such commitments is close.

The costs of intervention are significantly reduced by the consent of the target country because consent deprives the target of the argument that external actors are violating its sovereignty. Consensual conflict prevention requires that international forces behave in an impartial manner, and convince the local actors by persuasion rather than punishment to avoid violations of the peace agreement. Consent is easier to procure and maintain if the intervening agent uses incentives as the main means of influence. However, consent is a slippery concept: it may work if there is a viable government in the target country to make commitments on its behalf, but reality is often different, as the country in crisis has either an authoritarian regime, whose legitimacy is in doubt, or a government so fragmented that its commitments would have very little credibility. Furthermore, international actors have to operate in an environment characterized by the conflicting demands of the local parties suggesting difficult choices and compromises. International actors may also have conflicting objectives and means (Rothchild 1997).

Indeed, internal political polarization and fragmentation pose major challenges to preventive action. A simple solution is to support the 'good guys' and oppose the 'bad guys'; the former are included and rewarded, while the latter are excluded and punished. Western policy vis-à-vis Republika Srpska in 1997–98 provides evidence on the differentiated use of rewards and punishment. In 1999, a similar policy was pursued in Serbia where cities controlled by the opposition were rewarded with EU oil deliveries, while the strongholds of the Milosevic government were subjected to punitive sanctions. During the presidential elections of fall 2000 a similar approach was pursued. However, such a differentiated strategy does not necessarily work. Those rewarded may consider aid as their 'birth right' when its influence wanes over time; for example, the impact of US economic aid on Israeli policies appears to be quite limited. On the other hand, differentiation tends to fuel resentment among the excluded and thus polarizes the situation. The situation may deteriorate further if the favourite party is not strong enough to prevail despite external support.

In brief, short-term preventive measures seldom produce long-term results. They can be achieved only if there is an enduring commitment to reduce the vulnerability of a country to political and humanitarian disasters. However, vulnerability as such does not need to lead to an emergency, but must be linked with a particular pattern of crisis escalation (path dependence). The risk of escalation increases significantly if a country is ruled by an authoritarian, or even worse a predatory, regime. Such a regime does not respond to the predicament of the society, but considers its own power position and enrichment to be the primary goal.

A common approach to address the identities in conflict resolution argues that multi-ethnic societies can never be restored by intermingling different groups. Therefore, 'stable resolutions to ethnic civil wars are possible, but only when the opposing groups are demographically separated into defensible enclaves...true national homelands' (Kaufmann 1996: 137). However, it is clear that partitioning calls for a continuation of the demographic relocation that started during the war. This view is based on the assumption that war itself has hardened ethnic identities to such an extent that they cannot be reconciled by building trust between the parties. This is why post-conflict settlement cannot be achieved by a return to conditions prevailing before the war; 'solutions to ethnic wars do not depend on their causes' (Kaufmann 1996: 137). Thus, the separation of ethnic communities cannot work as a preventive strategy; it takes a war and its ensuing toll to create the preconditions for ethnic separation. This has been acknowledged by Kaufmann (1999), who accepts that partitioning should be attempted only after violence has passed a certain threshold and when communities are already largely separate.

Political realists consider efforts to prevent the root causes of humanitarian emergencies futile. They also regard power-sharing between competing groups as inefficient; it is too voluntaristic and does not assure a 'hard' minority veto that would always be respected by the majority. Such a veto can be achieved only by providing the minority with adequate military forces to defend itself (Kaufmann 1996). This view suggests that the failing state resembles international 'anarchy'. Therefore, one should draw from the lessons of international balance of power and deterrence politics to create stability in a divided society (Posen 1993; cf. Roe 1999). However, the emphasis on partitioning and the criticism of power-sharing overlook the complexity of power-sharing policies. An integrative policy of institution-building alone may not succeed after a divisive war. One may need a conso-ciational approach that undertakes to assure group autonomy, proportional representation and minority veto in a confederal structure (Sisk 1996; Rittberger and Kittel 1996). Obviously, in many cases, integration and power-sharing are difficult to realize, while in others the dividing lines are not so deep as to exclude reconciliation. In a comparative perspective, Kosovo may exemplify the former and Macedonia the latter category (Burg 1998).

The difficulty of the political and institutional reconstruction of war-torn societies suggests that power-sharing should be tried as an early preventive strategy. There is much evidence to show that efforts to impose a central-ized state over ethnically and politically divided societies do not necessar-ily fail. Therefore, the power-sharing mechanism should be strengthened at an early stage when attitudes and institutions have not hardened, and vio-lence has not yet broken out nor escalated into a deadly confrontation. Democracy is not the cure for all diseases, but is better able to defuse the potential for violence or even to agree on autonomy or secession (Levine 1996). If internal power-sharing and institutional designs fail because of societal divisions, it should be queried whether international intervention could convince the parties otherwise. The first answer is obviously no, as 'there are limits to what international institutions can do to turn despotic nationalists into liberal democrats...as they have only "limited leverage"' (Levine 1996: 338). International institutions may try to promote power-sharing and democratization, but it is too much to ask them to guarantee a particular political regime in a crisis-ridden society.

The enforcement policy may try to separate the parties into exclusive ter-ritorial compartments. To succeed, it requires either a balance of power on the ground or continuing international intervention to maintain that balance. This intervention aims both to support the weaker party materi-ally and to come to its rescue if the internal balance or deterrence fails (Kaufmann 1996). Today, international actors have established intrusive intervention regimes for nation-building in Bosnia, Kosovo, East Timor and Sierra Leone, but it is doubtful whether they can accommodate many more new cases to this regime.

In general, international institutions prefer advice and mediation to costly enforcement actions. Ultimately, the local parties themselves have to take the final responsibility for peace. As postwar power-sharing is difficult, more emphasis should be placed on its early promotion (Sisk 1996). The transition of the Baltic countries to democracy and market economy in the early 1990s shows that a positive engagement, spiced with a combination of pressures and incentives, by international institutions can help to avert instability. In these countries, a stable transition took place despite the heavy Soviet legacy and the controversial position of the Russian minorities there.

South Africa is an intriguing case of preventive action. Clearly, the brutality of apartheid and the mobilization of the black population contained seeds of a violent upheaval. The prospects of escalating violence and non-governability of the society were the main reasons for the apartheid regime to open talks with Nelson Mandela and the African National Congress (ANC) (Sparks 1995). This decision was further motivated by the squeeze of international economic sanctions that showed no signs of relenting. Thus, the combination of internal and external pressures had a preventive effect as it convinced the government of the need to conclude a political pact with the ANC on the transition to democracy; the 'shadow of the future' overwhelmed the white minority.

In conclusion, the most viable approach to long-term institutional conflict prevention is to promote power-sharing arrangements by political and constitutional means, including international protection of minority rights. In recent years, international law on minority rights has gained a more operational dimension. In particular, the Organization for Security and Cooperation in Europe (OSCE) High Commissioner on National Minorities is mandated to monitor the implementation of minority rights and become involved if these appear to be threatened. This involvement has a dual function: to try to de-escalate tensions involving national minorities and alert the OSCE to act to protect these rights if threatened. It is a widely shared impression that the OSCE Commissioner has been an active and successful actor in the prevention of conflict of nationalities (Foundation on Inter-Ethnic Relations 1997).

7.5 Economic and humanitarian strategies

In addition to political means, one can distinguish at least two other strategies – humanitarian aid and economic instruments – to reduce the vulnerability of countries and people to disasters. These means can be used in all three phases of preventive action before, during and after the conflicts (Väyrynen 1996; see also Hansen 1996). In the pre-conflict phase, both humanitarian assistance and development aid can rectify existing problems by making available social, health and educational services and encouraging participation in joint decision-making. The use of external resources for compensatory purposes, i.e. to promote distributional justice and prevent violence, runs counter to the traditional justifications of humanitarian and development aid. They are expected to impartially help everyone in need and increase economic efficiency and growth, as well as serve social and educational purposes.

It has become increasingly clear, though, that a single-minded commitment to impartiality or efficiency can have adverse distributional consequences that undermine the original objectives of humanitarian and development assistance. Due to unintended consequences, external resources may exacerbate existing imbalances; not least for the reason that the use of these resources is largely decided by the recipient government which, in turn, may reflect a particular ethnic or political configuration of power. Such consequences of development and humanitarian assistance have gradually alerted the aid agencies to take the multiple effects of their own actions more seriously. For this purpose, it is suggested, external assistance should incorporate some basic 'extra-developmental' and 'extra-humanitarian' goals, especially to avoid conflict, promote distributional justice and not to harm any ethnic community (Esman 1997: 9–10).

In fact, a Norwegian report (Norwegian Institute of International Relations 1998) recognizes that it is 'legitimate to use development aid as a "carrot" or "stick" to get parties to accept third-party mediation and, also, to change policies that are increasing the risk of conflict'. One possibility involves partnerships and contracting, in which donor and recipient countries agree on some policy objectives that decrease the vulnerability of society to various threats. The report has developed a comprehensive programme on how development aid can be used to support preventive action. It stresses that there is no single preventive strategy but several partial strategies, which can be targeted, tailored and conditioned differently depending on donor objectives and conditions in the recipient country (Norwegian Institute for International Affairs 1998).

International actions can either try to avoid indirectly the harm done inadvertently or deliberately aim to prevent and defuse violence and repression. Indirect strategies are, as a rule, negative in the sense that they make an effort to prevent the disintegration of the target society and thus reduce the ensuing human suffering. Positive strategies purport to promote constructive goals, such as reconciliation of tensions and social integration. In assessing the possibilities of IFIs to pursue these strategies, Reinecke (1996) observes that their role is least important in indirect negative strategies, while they have greater relevance in direct negative strategies by providing economic backing for peace agreements or power-sharing schemes. Potentially, the IFIs can play a major role in conflict prevention. Thus, the IMF has tried since the early 1990s to reduce excessive military spending as a precondition of its assistance and, in that way, reduce the risk of war and the trade-off between guns and butter (Stevenson 2000).

In indirect positive strategies, IFIs should make sure that they do not worsen the situation by inadvertently escalating ethnic and other conflicts in the target society. Following the model of environmental impact assessment, they should integrate in the analysis of individual projects and their regional and social consequences and ethno-national assessment (Reinecke 1996; see also Esman 1997). Finally, direct positive action targets aid and other financial transfers at the structural and/or dynamic causes of violent conflicts.

Political conditionality of economic transfers is an indirect prevention strategy. It makes an effort to enhance compliance with international norms on human rights, democracy and peace. If a country engages in a gross violation of these norms, its access to international trade, aid and investment can be denied. Japan and Germany have used political conditionality to enhance civility in among its partners of cooperation (Uvin and Biagiotti 1996). In a preventive perspective, political conditionality can, ideally, ensure the compliance of the recipient to minimum standards of civility, which would, in turn, forestall deterioration of the situation (Lund 1997). On the other hand, it is a controversial political approach; governments in the South blame those in the North for efforts to undermine their political consolidation and economic growth by imposing selfish external conditions.

The choice of strategies in intranational crises is difficult, as is shown by models indicating that donors have difficulties in reducing political repression with aid, even when reducing repression is a condition for grants. Despite the political dilemmas, perhaps cooperation with a repressive government may be a good alternative if the objective is effective delivery of aid rather than political change (Palda 1993). Especially aid policies of the major powers mix security and development objectives, which gives the rent-seeking elite the opportunity to benefit from this ambiguity. It is possible that ultimately neither objective – i.e., political gain and local welfare – was achieved, as happened with the extensive US economic and military aid to Somalia. It obviously reduced starvation and open violence, but this limited success came at a high financial and political cost. In fact, economic and institutional recovery has progressed better in Somaliland, where no major intervention took place, than in Somalia proper (Rawson 1994; Ahmed and Green 1999). Recently however, efforts to create a national political compromise have made some progress.

These observations are not, of course, an argument against more proactive international policies to target the causes of humanitarian emergencies. Modesty and caution, however, would be appropriate. Economic instruments may be useful in conflict prevention, but their causal links to successful prevention 'are often diffuse and unclear' (Lund 1997: 12–13).

7.6   Conclusion

The prevention of violent conflicts and humanitarian emergencies calls for strategic action in which available means are related to attainable goals. The goal can be either 'late' prevention of an outbreak or escalation of a violent conflict, or 'early' prevention of an emergency by tackling its root causes. The strategic nature of prevention means that it should be targeted to save human lives in a vulnerable situation that threatens to become out of control. The emphasis on strategy also means that the response has to be graduated; i.e. it has to proceed by steps from one subgoal to another. Successful prevention of humanitarian crises requires patience, commitment and engagement.

Except for a brief interlude in the early 1990s, national governments have been reluctant to become involved in systematic conflict prevention. In addition to the inertia of decision-making in decentralized international relations, governments are unwilling to take risks unless national stakes or public pressure in particular crises are very high. Therefore, the onus of prevention falls primarily either on domestic actors in crisis-ridden countries or international organizations. In fact, local actors should primarily be responsible for averting deterioration of a situation. In reality, ground-up strategies are not always able to forestall deterioration. There are, however, examples of successful efforts to stabilize the situation, such as traditional peace-making in Africa (Ahmed and Green 1999; Prendergast 1996a).

The paucity of local success stories means that international preventive strategies are badly needed. The time perspective of these can range from short-term emergency actions to halt the outbreak of a civil war, through medium-term constitutional reforms to long-term economic and ecological strategies to reduce vulnerability of the society. National governments and international organizations have usually favoured a 'remote' approach in which prevention is based on military deterrence, economic sanctions, political recognition or other actions in which the third parties do not need to become concretely engaged in local controversies. Practical experience indicates, however, that none of these 'remote' strategies have been very effective in preventing massive death toll if a society is at the edge of a humanitarian abyss. This conclusion underlines the need to develop new strategies, especially conflict transformation to replace standard conflict-resolution approaches. Conflict transformation requires that the interests and stakes of the parties are redefined with a combination of incentives and punishments, the emergence of new actors is encouraged, and key actors are legitimated, so that new avenues, such as mutual power-sharing, can be opened.

Economic sanctions are post hoc measures that are seldom effective in the early prevention of conflicts. However, bilateral and multilateral development cooperation can provide more relevant tools for early prevention. There is an interesting new emphasis both in OECD and individual donor governments to make sure that such cooperation does not lead to undesirable political consequences and that it can be used even as an instrument to prevent ethnic conflicts and human-rights violations. The IFIs have also become more active in promoting peace-building as a preventive goal, though their full potential in this task has not yet been utilized. Perhaps the best way to reduce the risk of future humanitarian emergencies is to integrate that goal more closely in both public and private economic transactions in the globalizing world.

Note

1. For various types of preventive action, see Lund (1996: 37–49).

8
Democratization and Institutional Reform

Richard Sandbrook

8.1 Introduction

Democratization is a gamble in plural societies. On the one hand, democratization, in conjunction with low levels of socioeconomic development and ethnic fragmentation has often enhanced the likelihood of civil war (Jakobsen 1996). On the other hand, some new democracies in ethnically heterogeneous societies have proven adept at fostering peace and prosperity, as in Mauritius, Botswana and post-apartheid South Africa. Table 8.1 indicates that, in Africa, new democracies and semi-democracies have been associated with high and medium intensities of internal war, as well as with peaceful politics.

Although democracy is not a panacea for deadly conflict, particular circumstances make it a gamble worth taking. The Churchillian adage remains true: democracy is the worst form of government, except for all the rest. Under certain conditions and on the basis of certain institutional strategies, democratization can play a positive role in conflict management. This chapter identifies these efficacious conditions and institutional strategies.

Africa is the focus of this investigation. No region has been as afflicted by CHEs since 1980 as this continent. Bosnia, Kosovo and Tadzjikistan in Europe, Sri Lanka, Cambodia and Afghanistan in Asia, and Haiti, El Salvador, Colombia and Peru in South and Central America have all borne the extensive human costs of prolonged, violent conflict. In Africa, however, the list of political emergencies is even more extensive.

More than half of SSA's 48 countries have been buffeted by countrywide or regional civil wars or wars with neighbours since 1980 – often a combination of both (see Table 8.1). In West Africa, deadly conflicts in Liberia, Sierra Leone, Equatorial Guinea, Guinea-Bissau and Senegal (Casamance) have interacted in a mutually destabilizing pattern. The devastating internal wars in Liberia and Sierra Leone drew in peacekeeping forces from several members of the Economic Community of West African States, principally Nigeria. Similarly, civil wars have linked together in Central and Southern Africa. Eight contiguous states endured rebellions or civil wars in the middle

Table 8.1   Conflict in African countries, 1990–97

	Type of regime[*]	
Level of conflict	*Authoritarian*	*Democratic/semi-democratic*
High (Country-wide insurrections, civil wars and genocides)	Algeria (1992–) Angola[**] (1975–96) Burundi[**] (periodic) Chad[**] (periodic) Ethiopia[**] (1974–91) Liberia[**] (1989–) Mozambique[**] (1976–92) Sierra Leone[**] (1991–) Somalia[**] (1977–) South Africa (1984–94) Sudan[**](periodic since 1955) Togo (1991) Zaire/Congo[**] (1996–)	Central African Republic (1996–97) Congo (Brazzaville 1993–97) Rwanda[**] (1994–)
Medium (Regional or periodic insurrections and civil wars that do not threaten the centre)	Djibouti (1991–) Egypt (1992–) Mali (1990–95) Niger (1985–) Nigeria (periodic since end of civil war in 1970) Uganda (1986–)	Ghana (1994–95) Kenya (1991–92; 1997) Senegal (1990–)
Low (Absence of organized political violence)	Burkina Faso Cameron Gabon Guinea Guinea-Bissau Lesotho Mauritania Morocco Tunisia	Benin Botswana Côte d'Ivoire Madagascar Malawi Mauritius Namibia Tanzania Zambia Zimbabwe

Notes
[*]   at time when violent conflict began
[**]   complex humanitarian emergencies
Source: Author's files and PRIO (1997)

and late 1990s. Armed interventions by neighbouring states intensified the turmoil: Uganda supported the Rwandan Tutsi forces in 1990–94; Uganda along with Rwanda, Burundi and Angola assisted Laurent Kabila in his over-throw of Zaire's Mobutu in 1996–97; Rwanda and Uganda then backed rebel forces against Kabila in 1998–99 while Angola, Zimbabwe, Namibia and Chad buttressed Kabila's army; and war-torn Angola intervened in Congo-Brazzaville against President Lissouba and his forces in 1997 and 1998. And the defeated combatants of three decades of civil wars, scattered in exile throughout this region, heightened insecurity by hiring out as mercenaries. Central African conflicts have, in turn, spilled over to exacerbate civil wars and insurrections in the Horn and East Africa, mainly in Sudan, Uganda and Somalia. In 1998–99 a bloody border war pitted two erstwhile allies in the Sudanese conflict, Ethiopia and Eritrea, against each other. Many other countries – notably Nigeria, Kenya and Côte d'Ivoire – though avoiding state collapse, civil war or interstate conflicts, are nonetheless threatened by isolated rebellions and sporadic political violence.

Because most African states have undergone political liberalization since 1990, this continent provides fertile ground for exploring the links between violent conflict and democratization. The latter term is used in two senses. First, in the formal sense, this process involves two phases. An *electoral transition* begins with a crack in, or breakdown of, an authoritarian regime. This phase ends with the holding of a fair election and the installation of a new government. To be free and fair, an electoral system must reflect certain core civil and political liberties: freedoms of movement, association and expression and the right of all adult citizens to vote and hold office. The second, lengthier phase concerns the *consolidation of democracy:* the development of a widespread commitment to the formal institutions of democratic contestation and rule. In Africa, perhaps only Mauritius and Botswana are consolidated democracies, though some opposition leaders in these countries would demur. There is, as well, a second, informal sense of democratization: the activities of grassroots movements to empower groups of citizens by asserting their rights or enhancing their control over their livelihoods in oppressive circumstances. This chapter uses democratization to refer to both the formal and informal processes.

How can democratic institutions serve as an antidote to complex humanitarian emergencies in Africa? The nature and causes of this pathology must first be reviewed before discussing preventive or palliative care.

8.2 A pathology of complex humanitarian emergencies

'Complex humanitarian emergencies', 'complex political emergencies', or just plain 'complex emergencies' – the term varies but the nub of the malady is deadly conflict that rips a society asunder. Civil wars, insurrections and state collapse exact an enormous human toll (Nafziger, this volume; Cliffe and Luckham 1999). In 1990–95, major armed conflicts left 5.5 million people dead and displaced 40 million people (PRIO 1997). Warfare also feeds upon, and further magnifies, mutual fear and distrust along ethnic, religious or racial lines. It accelerates economic decline through the destruction of social and economic infrastructure, the exodus of skilled refugees, capital flight and disinvestment, and the channelling of government revenues toward the war effort. Warfare, compounded by drought and environmental scarcity, leads to famines and accompanying epidemics which the weakened state is either unwilling or unable to counteract.

Because of this multidimensionality, a single pathology of this vaguely delineated malady cannot be isolated. Complex emergencies share only a family resemblance, though they all feature civil wars or state collapse. There are, to extend the medical metaphor, several strains of this disease, as with hepatitis with its 'A', 'B' and 'C' variants. This chapter addresses the strain of political emergency found widely in Africa. Its syndrome manifests four mutually reinforcing processes: growing ethnic/communal tensions in a plural society; an increasingly predatory and incapacitated state; a stagnant and declining economy with a concomitant increase in absolute poverty; and a deteriorating environment which heightens scarcities and threatens livelihoods. A downward spiral involving these four interconnected processes fosters a pervasive sense of insecurity, fear and mistrust which the government is unwilling or unable to assuage, or actively aggravates through its discriminatory, oppressive and corrupt practices. To regain a sense of security and power, people, therefore, identify with their primary community (tribe, clan, race, religion). A dramatic event – a political assassination, a severe famine, the violent suppression of a demonstration, a military mutiny, a collapse of living standards – eventually precipitates violence that escalates into civil war or state collapse.

Each of these symptoms is considered in turn below.

8.2.1   Rising ethnic tensions

Ethnic tensions endure in many countries *without* leading to armed conflict. Ethnicity, defined broadly as encompassing tribes, races and nationalities, refers to an inclusive group identity 'based on some notion of common origin, recruited primarily through kinship, and typically manifesting some measure of cultural distinctiveness' (Diamond and Plattner 1994: xvii). Ethnic tensions arise neither from this cultural distinctiveness per se, nor generally from a primordial hostility. In many of Africa's polyethnic societies that artificial colonial borders produced, ethnicity manifests only a moderate political saliency, as in Ghana; cross-cutting or narrower identities stemming from class, religion, gender, clan and patron-clientship also shape political behaviour. In other societies (e.g., Rwanda and Burundi), however, ethnic cleavages are rigid, persistent and decisive in determining political allegiances.

Differential ethnic access to state power, public goods and/or economic opportunities sharpens ethnic hostilities (see Holsti 2000). When, in this context, a state's authority withers to the point that it cannot guarantee law, order and basic services, or a regime openly exploits ethnic differences, the stage is set for ethnic tensions to escalate into armed combat. Ethnic bosses are tempted to manipulate the prevailing insecurity, fear and alienation to mobilize support among their communities by offering protection and other services. Civil wars develop as regional/ethnic movements, and are emboldened by state decay to challenge the central authorities or a perceived ethnic enemy.

8.2.2 An increasingly predatory and incapacitated state

A predatory state is one in which office-holders and their clients prey upon society by extracting wealth, through legal and illegal means, without offering any useful services. Such a state is the most degraded form of neo-patrimonialism. Governments may even resemble an organized crime syndicate, in that office-holders engage in drug-running, money-laundering, fraud and other scams (Hibou 1999). State capacity erodes as rent-seeking, corruption and arbitrary governance eviscerate political authority, public revenues and the integrity of the civil service. Nonetheless, a decaying state, in retaining a capacity to act repressively, remains a threat to its own people.

'Warlord politics' (Reno 1998), in countries such as Liberia, Sierra Leone, Chad, Congo/Zaire and Somalia, has followed such a process of political decay. Warlords abandon their allegiance to central authorities in order to freelance. They build their power on the grievances of clans, ethnic groups or regions, and the distribution to followers of booty and the revenue obtained from foreign firms who export local natural resources – diamonds, gold, rubber or tropical timber. Civil society weakens, as professionals emigrate, associational membership dwindles and repression grows. As the government increasingly resembles a criminal gang, new warlords emerge, demanding their share of the national wealth (Reno 1998). The resultant economic collapse alienates the large cohort of semi-employed and unemployed young men – creating a fertile soil for warlords to recruit warriors to their private militias.

8.2.3 Declining economy and growing absolute poverty

The causes of Africa's economic decline, which began in the 1970s or even earlier in some countries, are complex and disputed. On the one hand, the WB and the IMF, both highly influential, have attributed the decline largely to domestic failings in Africa – poor policies and governance that distorted market signals and raised the risks of investment. On the other hand, many other experts, including in the 1980s the Ethiopia-based UN Economic Commission for Africa (ECA), have rejected this 'internalist' explanation in favour of one that stresses onerous external constraints – terms of trade, technological gaps, commercial rules favouring advanced-country interests and so on. Undoubtedly, the timing of Africa's economic crisis (beginning in the early 1980s), owed much to international trends. A deep recession in the West, two increases in the price of oil (1973 and 1979), and exceptionally high interest rates damaged poor, oil-importing, and commodity exporting African economies. In fact, both external and domestic constraints are important.

Regardless of the precise causes, economic well-being deteriorated markedly in many countries in the 1980s. Already abysmal per capita incomes dropped to an average $US330 in 1987–88. A modest growth of 1.4 per cent in the 1960s plummeted to 0.2 per cent in the 1970s, and to –2.8 per cent in the 1980s. More than half of the African population has subsisted in absolute poverty since the early 1980s. The populace of Nigeria, Liberia, Niger and others suffered a decline in real incomes of 25–50 per cent (World Bank 1990). Even in the unlikely event that the region has attained an annual increase in output of 4 per cent in the 1990s, SSA's poor will still have grown by 85 million. While Asia's share of the world's absolute poor has declined, Africa's has steadily expanded, according to WB statistics.

Drastic reductions in social expenditures since 1980 have accentuated the crisis. In the 1960s and 1970s, basic health indicators, including life expectancy and infant mortality rates, markedly improved. During this period, school enrolments grew faster than in any other region – the primary school population nearly doubled. But budgetary cutbacks and declining incomes lowered rates of primary school enrolment, caused life expectancy and infant mortality rates to stagnate, and worsened nutritional levels.

The record, however, was not uniformly bleak. Consistently high economic performers include Botswana and Mauritius, and Côte d'Ivoire, Gabon, Kenya, Malawi, Mali, Senegal, Tanzania, Lesotho and Zimbabwe experienced either high growth in the early years or long stretches of modest growth. Ghana, Tanzania and Uganda have achieved periods of high growth under structural adjustment. Also, some of the poorer countries, such as Tanzania, rank higher on the human development scale than many other countries with higher per capita incomes (UNDP 1998). Nonetheless, most Africans in the early 1990s were as poor or poorer than at independence.

Economic decline, state decay and ethnic antagonisms may become locked in a mutually reinforcing, vicious circle, often aggravated by environmental scarcities.

8.2.4   Environmental degradation and scarcities

Whether environmental degradation is a cause or an effect of deadly conflicts is debatable. Most accurately, this trend is both a cause and an effect (see Chapter 6). Internal wars have certainly contributed to environmental decline and resource scarcities in many cases, including notably in Sudan that has suffered Africa's longest-running and most deadly civil war. But the obverse is also true. Competition over scarce resources combines with ethnic, political and economic processes to fuel violent conflicts.

Consider famine, the most striking manifestation of environmental deterioration and scarcity in Africa, with 27 countries 'at risk' (Watts 1991: 13). Civil war is often associated with the emergence of famines. In addition, national and international development patterns play a significant role in fostering droughts that then lead to famines: greenhouse gas emissions in industrial countries produce climatic change of which the now-frequent African droughts are a likely byproduct; transnational logging companies engage in unrestricted logging with negative impacts on soil erosion and micro-climates; and mega-projects (as again in Sudan) displace people on to marginal land where fragile soils swiftly deteriorate. Also, concentrated land ownership, as in countries of South-Central and Eastern Africa, squeeze poor peasants on to small landholdings which they may overexploit in order to survive. Finally, increasing populations in the countryside lead to growing scarcity of land, which in turn can generate farming and grazing practices that degrade the soil – as strikingly in strife-torn Rwanda and Burundi.

Famine, moreover, combines with the other processes in a mutually destructive manner. Economic decline raises the risk of famine in several ways. It lowers public revenues and, hence, expenditures on infrastructure, health services and measures to prevent further ecological destruction and restore degraded areas. It reduces employment and purchasing power, thus rendering households more vulnerable when drought strikes. And economic decay undercuts a country's import capacity as falling export revenues limit the government's ability to import food during periods of drought. Drought and famine, in turn, reinforce economic decline by lowering agricultural productivity, cutting export revenues, and draining scarce resources on food imports and relief.

Environmental scarcities also contribute to the growing ineffectiveness of the state by eroding a regime's legitimacy and revenues (Homer-Dixon 1994). Droughts and famines – or even the impoverishment attendant upon growing populations on decreasingly productive land – heighten demands upon government at the same time as export receipts and revenues are probably falling. The inability of the state to respond adequately to the hardships of citizens aggravates popular grievances, while shrinking revenues and demoralization erode administrative capacity.

Finally, famine will probably heighten civil strife, especially civil wars. Growing economic hardships and weakening central authority will encourage aggrieved groups or warlords to challenge the government or settle scores with ethnic rivals. Also, drought and the associated deforestation and desertification spur population movements, as people leave their homes in search of refuge in the cities, other regions, or other countries. Such migration often engenders ethnic conflict. Migrants place burdens on the people of the host area: food prices rise, excess labour depresses wages, and increasingly scarce common property resources engenders competition over water, forests and grazing areas. Insecurity in both migrant and host communities can solidify group identities and provoke violent conflict (Swain 1996; Homer-Dixon 1994). Conversely, civil wars make populations vastly more vulnerable to famine. They displace farmers, destroy crops, impair roads, railways and health facilities, and lead combatants to manipulate famine relief for partisan advantage (Watts 1991).

So how can this pernicious downward spiral of political, economic and environmental decay be forestalled or, if underway, halted and reversed?

8.3   Democratization as antidote

Democratization, at best, constitutes only one component of an effective preventive strategy. Neither forestalling deadly conflict nor 'peace-building' in war-torn societies can succeed without a long-term and developmental approach (see Bush 1996). The root causes of humanitarian emergencies are political and economic; therefore, '[t]he efforts to prevent humanitarian emergencies are part and parcel of the strategies of sound economic and political development' (Nafziger and Väyrynen 1998).

Democratization is therapeutic insofar as it widens opportunities to reform a society's dysfunctional institutions. *Institution* is a word open to many interpretations: the term is used here to refer to 'a regularized pattern of interaction that is known, practised, and accepted (if not necessarily approved) by actors who expect to continue interacting under the rules sanctioned and backed by that pattern' (O'Donnell 1996: 36). Political institutions are, thus, the formal and informal rules of the game that shape the behaviour of people when they contest and exercise power, as well as their, and the general public's, expectations regarding the actions of others. It is characteristic of the neo-patrimonial political systems – such as those found widely in Africa – that the institutions that count are largely *informal* rather than *formal*. Formal institutions, whether elections, legislatures, parties, judiciaries, civil services, the separation of powers, local government, civil associations or independent media, embody the formal or normative rules of gaining and exercising power. They are publicly honoured and often privately circumvented. The informal institutions, on the other hand, structure political behaviour and expectations, even though they are publicly unacknowledged or even condemned.

The essence of neo-patrimonialism is the private appropriation of the state's powers. The prime stratagems (informal rules) by which rulers gain, hold and exercise political power are numerous, including: presidential supremacy over all organizations; the distribution of state-generated rents, sinecures and benefits to political followers; the reliance upon personal and ethnic loyalties; and the ultimate resort to a personally loyal armed force. These institutions serve the short-term interests of the strongman and his followers; but some of them are dysfunctional in the sense that they create uncertainty, stifle an independent business class, waste scarce resources on unproductive activities, and foster ethnic or regional hostilities.

Whether democratization can spur institutional reform and rebuilding is questionable. The problem is that institutions, particularly the unacknowledged informal ones, are notoriously resistant to change. They are rooted in the history and political culture of a society and the material interests of powerful social forces. Many experts are therefore sceptical, arguing that old neo-patrimonial traditions will quickly corrupt and even overwhelm fragile democratic institutions. Not only do the new democracies confront hostile socioeconomic conditions and non-democratic historical legacies, but they also must cope with the social costs to key constituencies inherent in their structural adjustment programmes. These circumstances, the sceptics argue, impel elected governments to centralize power and resort to populist rhetoric, clientelistic politics, and the cultivation of particularistic loyalties. Corruption, closely associated with pervasive clientelism, will also probably resurface (see for example O'Donnell 1994; Kohli 1993). The 'governance' perspective is more hopeful, though it is focused specifically on promoting market-oriented reform. Democratization, it is hoped, will empower domestic social forces which have a vested interest in defending a new order of limited and market-friendly government, accountable and honest officials, transparent decision-making, effective and predictable administration, and a rule of law that protects human rights, private property and the sanctity of contracts (see for example Leftwich 1993; van de Walle 1995).

Under certain conditions, democratization can be instrumental to institutional building and reform. It can play a positive role *directly*, through the design of well-adapted constitutional and legal rules governing the contestation for, and exercise of, power. The process can also play an important *indirect role* by opening up the political space for constituencies to mobilize behind their new formal institutions. Without the development of associations, movements and independent media to fight for institutional reform, the experiment will quickly fail, allowing the old ways to re-emerge. The danger, of course, is that political mobilization will occur along divisive, ethnic lines; constitutional reform and political practices will need to counteract this tendency.

The nature of institutional rebuilding needed to prevent deadly conflict is complex. Democratization must surmount three institutional challenges in countries threatened by a vicious downward spiral of political, economic and environmental decline. First, to build order and stability, democracy must restore political institutions capable of managing the conflicts and competition arising from ethnic/communal cleavages and the political tensions associated with the growth process. Second, to build prosperity and legitimacy, democracy must forge the institutional preconditions for functioning markets and poverty alleviation.[1] This challenge encompasses the first, because investors are unlikely to invest in fixed assets in the absence of stability and mutual confidence. Markets, however, also require the development of a compatible set of more narrowly economic and social institutions. And third, to reduce environmental degradation and environmental scarcities, democracy must, at the least, empower local communities and ordinary citizens to become defenders of their local resource base. However, while these three challenges are generic, *there is not a single set of appropriate institutional responses to these challenges*. Institutions will need to be tailored to fit the traditions, socioeconomic conditions, political problems and segmental divisions of individual countries. The social pathologist can therefore aspire only to formulating general guidelines on institutional change.

8.4   Challenge: developing conflict-management institutions

Conventional wisdom in Africa's early post-colonial period held that multiparty democracy inevitably aggravated ethnic divisions, and that one-party states were therefore advisable in plural societies. Democracy, few would deny, has often degenerated into a zero-sum game, in which one ethnic group or coalition wins and others lose. And the losers have legitimately feared that their exclusion from power and public goods might be permanent. Hence, democratic contestation has quite frequently heightened inter-ethnic mistrust, animosity and polarization. One-party and military governments, however, have also not been adept at avoiding ethnic conflict (see Table 8.1): they, too, have based themselves on a particular region or ethnic coalition at the expense of out-groups. Some of the continent's bloodiest civil wars have had little or nothing to do with democratization, as in Nigeria (1967–70), Somalia, Sudan (since 1983), Liberia, Sierra Leone, Chad, Ethiopia and Zaire/Congo. Today, one thus finds a more nuanced appreciation of the potential strengths, as well as weaknesses, of particular democratic arrangements.

Democracy can manage ethnic divisions – but only if its institutions foster compromise, inclusion and cooperation across cleavages. This rather self-evident proposition seems to sum up the current consensus (Gunther and Mughan 1993). Lijphart did much to popularize the notion that 'majoritarianism',[2] not democratic contestation per se, was the real problem (1977: 28). Majoritarian or 'winner-take-all' approaches were destructive because they raised ethnic tensions by excluding some groups from power and resources, sometimes indefinitely. Instead, institutions should encourage 'consensual' governance that builds mutual trust by including all groups in sharing power and public goods. This notion led Lijphart (1977) to advocate 'consociational democracy' in which every political institution would promote cooperation and proportionality in the allocation of resources. While the European-derived model is probably too restrictive to apply *holus bolus* to African cases, the essential idea is germane. Similarly, Donald Horowitz advocates democratic institutions that align the self-interest of dominant political actors with policies of accommodating ethnic/religious groups other than their own. The aim is to create, before elections, 'multi-ethnic coalitions of commitment' whose participants agree on the rules of the game (Horowitz 1991). Although no single set of institutions can achieve this benign situation in all societies, Horowitz and others propose constitutional arrangements that appear better suited to the task than others.

8.4.1 Electoral systems

The debate among constitutional engineers has centred around whether proportional representation (PR) is more conducive to political harmony than the 'first-past-the-post' plurality system. Few will deny that poorly designed electoral rules will aggravate pre-existing ethnic conflicts, whereas appropriate ones will enhance cooperation. Most experts contend that PR is superior to plurality election within single-member constituencies because the former, unlike the latter, encourages coalition-building and consensual governance (Lijphart 1991; Reynolds 1995; Gunther and Mughan 1993). PR, at the least, ensures that even minor ethnic interests receive a voice in the legislature. The plurality system, on the other hand, poses the danger that elections will produce an ethnically exclusive government – quite conceivably on the basis of a minority of the popular vote – which will use its mandate to discriminate in favour of its ethnic supporters. Groups excluded from power will probably refuse to accept such a situation, especially if they perceive that their exclusion may be permanent. Democratic rules will be unlikely to contain the resulting frustration and anger. But proportional representation also poses risks: it encourages the proliferation of political parties along personal or ethnic lines, rendering parliament a cacophony of particularistic voices.

African cases illustrate the drawbacks of both systems. In Kenya in 1992 and 1997, for example, the 'first-past-the-post' system allowed the minority-tribes-based governing party (KANU) to prevail in both the presidential and parliamentary contests, because a splintered opposition split the majority opposition vote. This outcome further embittered the excluded Kikuyu, Luo and Luhyia and diminished the utility of democracy as a mechanism for reconciliation. Ethnic violence accelerated as each of the competitive elections approached. In Niger and Madagascar, on the other hand, PR created a proliferation of parties and a succession of unstable governmental coalitions after the 1992 and subsequent elections.

Fortunately, however, hybrid electoral systems promise gaining some of the benefits of each system while minimizing the costs (see Lijphart and Waisman 1996). Two-round voting in multi-member constituencies, with the second round a race between the top two parties, is a method of encouraging coalition-building in many districts. Another option is PR that operates not on a national list but on the basis of territorial districts with limited numbers of representatives and a high minimum threshold of votes to win a seat. This option should minimize the proliferation of parties that PR otherwise generates. Other complex but efficacious alternatives exist that mix the two polar systems. Consider the case of Mali. The National

Conference that drafted the electoral code in 1991 wrought a compromise between, on the one hand, the many delegates who feared that PR would fragment parties and foster unstable coalitions, and, on the other, the representatives of minor parties who feared a plurality system would exclude them from power. The code mandated PR in the 19 urban commune councils, and, at the national level, 55 multi-member districts in which the party winning a majority in the first or second round took all the district seats (from one to six, depending on the population of the district). This system, while not preventing a frequent turnover in prime ministers (in a presidential system), nonetheless limited the fragmentation of parties, allowing several large parties to emerge.

8.4.2   Presidential *vs* parliamentary systems

There is also a long-standing debate over which of these constitutional arrangements is superior in managing conflict. Some argue that parliamentary systems tend to exacerbate ethnic divisions by concentrating power in a single, regionally based party or coalition, while excluding others (Gunther and Mughan 1993). Others contend, to the contrary, that presidential systems relying on direct elections are more antithetical to ethnic harmony (Linz 1990; Reynolds 1995). The high stakes involved in contests where the president bestrides the political system, the adversarial, winner-take-all nature of the election, and the long wait between contests (four or five years) – all these factors can poison interethnic relations in deeply divided societies. Because the prime minister will need to compromise and bargain with other parties, a parliamentary system is judged more conducive to reconciliation, especially with a PR electoral system.

This inconclusive debate indicates that either system can promote a winner-take-all, exclusionary mentality that deepens ethnic conflicts. Neither arrangement is, therefore, inherently superior to the other; circumstances and astute constitutional engineering determine which serves better to mitigate ethnic divisions (Horowitz 1992). Parliamentary systems may foster reconciliation under certain conditions: no majority ethnic group exists; several parties emerge; and retaining power then requires the building of coalitions across ethnic divides. Presidential systems may also mitigate social divisions, if the electoral code stipulates that the successful candidate must win a certain proportion of the vote in most regions, as well as an overall plurality (Horowitz 1992).

Sudan is an example of what can happen if an unsuitable institutional model is adopted. All three parliamentary regimes (1956–58, 1965–69, 1986–89) committed the same constitutional errors, and all three paid the same price – a coup d'état and inflamed ethnic/religious divisions. The two main sectarian parties, the Umma and the Democratic Unionists, could expect together to win a majority of seats on the votes of their loyal Ansar and Khatmiyya followers. This fact encouraged their leaders to champion a majoritarian, winner-take-all parliamentary system. But this system inevitably alienated those in the south, west and east who were generally excluded from power (Salih 1991). Parliamentary regimes therefore became just another face of northern, Muslim domination (Ali and Matthews 1998). Perhaps, if Sudan's united rebel forces prevail, the next constitution will avoid falling into the same trap.

Not that ingenious, well-balanced constitutional requirements will necessarily succeed – reality is too complex for that degree of certainty. For instance, Nigeria's constitution in the Second Republic (1979–83) shrewdly endeavoured to build in mechanisms to promote cooperation and inclusiveness. These mechanisms included the separation of powers between the president and the assembly and the requirement that the president must win a plurality, plus 25 per cent of the vote in no fewer than two-thirds of the 19 states. Although the Second Republic succumbed to a coup, this failure did not arise from an ethnic/regional conflict. Rather, the governing elite's mammoth corruption, culminating in the rigging of the 1983 elections, undermined the legitimacy of democracy, paving the way for a military takeover (Joseph 1987). Similarly, Kenya's constitutional requirement that the president obtain a plurality plus at least 25 per cent of the vote in five of eight provinces appears well designed to enhance inter-ethnic coalition building. But this requirement has been subverted by ethnic cleansing of provinces, divide-and-rule tactics in dealing with the opposition, and (according to many observers) election-rigging, all of which further inflame ethnic hostilities.

However, in Botswana, Mauritius, Ghana and Madagascar, constitutional arrangements have succeeded in muting cleavages. Key to their success is an inclusionary governing party or coalition, and an inclusionary opposition, too, in the cases of Mauritius, Ghana and Madagascar. Since the governing party or coalition has a broad but shifting base and/or the opposition remains potent, no group is permanently excluded from power. In this case, democratic contestation has aided integration.

8.4.3   Unitary government *vs* the devolution of powers

Studies of democracy in divided societies often advocate federalism as a way of reducing ethnic conflict. Lijphart's celebrated model of 'consociational democracy' included federalism (a special case of 'segmental autonomy') as one of its four features (1977: 41–2). Federalism, it is contended, can reduce ethnic conflict by removing some divisive issues from the central government's jurisdiction; by fostering intra-ethnic disputes over resource allocation within ethnically homogeneous regions; and by lessening disparities among regions by redistributing revenues from the centre to the regions (Horowitz 1994). On the other hand, federalism may buttress parochial loyalties and the regional power of an assertive ethnic group, as appears to be true of the Zulu in South Africa's KwaZulu-Natal Province today. But federalism, in any case, has rarely long survived in Africa, succumbing to centralized control by insecure national governments or to secession (Katanga, Biafra).

Secession rather than federalism may be the only answer in some countries. No amount of constitutional tinkering or decentralization will succeed unless communal leaders want the arrangements to work. Recently, several commentators have argued in favour of secession in 'dysfunctional' nation-states, especially if the development of EU-type supranational associations accompanies separation (Herbst 1996/97: 136–9; Chirot 1995). Eritrea's peaceful separation from Ethiopia in 1994, following a referendum the previous year, reassured those who feared that secession in any African country would open a Pandora's box of violence and fragmentation. Such reassurance, however, was short-lived: the two countries went to war in 1998–99 over a disputed boundary.

Enhancing the prospect that democratization will moderate or channel ethnic tensions hinges on two conditions: astute constitutional design, as just discussed, and the likelihood that fearful elites and people will give democratic institutions a chance. The latter condition is more likely in some historical and structural circumstances than others.

If an ethnic minority dominated the previous authoritarian regime, democracy's prospects will be bleak. Resentments and hatred will likely vitiate whatever institutional mechanisms are instituted (Welsh 1993). In Africa, political and economic domination by an ethnic minority has usually spawned violent explosions, as seen in the settler colonies: Algeria, Kenya, Rhodesia and South Africa. Only the last has managed a conciliatory democratization in the post-colonial era. Post-colonial ethnic oligarchies also have provided hostile terrain for democratic processes: Burundi and Rwanda (Tutsis), Zanzibar (Arabs), Liberia (Americo-Liberians) and Kenya (Kalenjin and allies under Moi).

More generally, a history of intense ethnic conflict and ethnic stereotyping will obviously militate against reconciliation via democratization. The prospects for muting these communal divisions improve if i) the pro-democracy movement includes leaders of all ethnic origins, and ii) these leaders are able to negotiate institutional arrangements that foster power-sharing and compromise *before* the electoral transition takes place (de Nevers 1993). Mali, with the exception of the Tuareg, satisfied these positive conditions, workable compromises being expedited in 1991 through the mechanisms of a provisional government and a representative National Conference. Overarching loyalties engendered by Islam and the Bambara language fortified national integration in this case.

Certain structural conditions also impinge on the likelihood that democratization will promote ethnic harmony. First, if one communal group forms a majority, leaders of this group will be encouraged to strive for control rather than cooperation across cleavages, as has been Sudan's unfortunate fate. Conversely, if ethnic groups are all small or similar in size and power, then political leaders may see little gain in making appeals to ethnic identity. Their interest will instead lie in forging coalitions; consequently, people will feel less threatened by ethnic domination under such conditions (Lijphart 1977; de Nevers 1993). Yet even these benign circum-stances do not guarantee that democratization will not stoke communal tensions. Tanzania, as a one-party state since independence, had an envi-able reputation for social harmony in the context of many small ethnic groups and no dominant religion. But the combination of market-oriented reform and transition to multi-party democracy in the 1990s has deepened ethnic/racial and religious (Christian/Muslim) tensions. Both processes, by creating winners and losers, have raised fears that certain regional/religious coalitions will dominate government to the detriment of out-groups (Kaiser 1996). The issue is whether well-designed democratic institutions will, in time, channel and moderate these inevitable stresses.

Second, if socioeconomic levels are not widely divergent along ethnic/regional/religious lines in a plural society, then the chances of rec-onciliation are enhanced. Conversely, marked inequalities along communal lines, as in Rwanda and Burundi, arouse suspicions and lower the prospect that democratization will enhance power-sharing and reconciliation.

Finally, the importance of leadership should not be discounted. Leaders are not merely the agents of historical and structural forces beyond their control. Leaders and movements, though constrained by social, economic and political conditions, generally exercise some degree of choice on matters of war and peace. Astute strategy and tactics vastly enhance the prospects that democratization will support rather than undermine ethnic harmony. Leaders who avoid inflammatory speeches restrain the tempers of ethnic followers, and compromise can overcome difficult circumstances (de Nevers 1993). Nelson Mandela's key role in negotiating a peaceful end to apartheid in South Africa illustrates the significance of statesmanship. While outside observers were predicting a race war, Mandela, from his prison cell, shrewdly engaged his captors in talks that established the prin-ciples for a transition to majority rule. Mandela was even willing to make commitments unsanctioned by the ANC to advance the process. In his words: '[t]here are times when a leader must move out ahead of the flock, go off in a new direction, confident that he is leading his people the right way' (Mandela 1995: 627). Following the democratic transition, President Mandela used his personal authority to build a non-racial South Africa under very difficult conditions.

8.5   Challenge: building the institutional foundations of growth

A drastic decline in living standards and a concomitant rise in poverty is another dimension of the complex-emergency syndrome. If democratiza-tion manages ethnic conflict via inclusionary institutions and an equitable regional/ethnic distribution of resources, this enhanced stability will facili-tate economic recovery (Easterly and Levine 1997). Conversely, economic development will itself be conducive to the survival of democracy by providing the resources for ethnic reconciliation and heightened prosperity. A virtuous circle of democratization, ethnic harmony and development will then counteract any slide towards state dissolution. Whether democratization will contribute to this synergy by promoting economic recovery is a key question.

Although there is no one-to-one relationship between democratization (or democracy) and economic growth, democratization may have an indirect effect on economic well-being by promoting the institutional reforms that are a necessary condition for market development. What are these needed institutional reforms, and how might democratization foster them?

Institutional change is central to Africa's recovery. Sustained growth and prosperity are rare in Africa for many reasons: external terms of trade shocks, heavy external debts, natural and man-made disasters, poor initial conditions, political instability, predatory political institutions and policy errors. With respect to the last three factors, the negative impact of weak and arbitrary neo-patrimonial governance is critical in many countries. Neo-patrimonial elites, faced with governing weakly integrated and poor peasant societies, use the state to distribute economic resources in order to maintain their support and combat fissiparous tendencies. Weber provides a key to understanding the logic and consequences of this system. He analysed the historical development of 'patrimonial' rule and 'political' or 'booty' or 'patrimonial' capitalism in early-modern Europe, Asia and Africa. Weber's main point is that patrimonial rule, though compatible with the expansion of trade, hinders 'production-oriented modern capitalism, based on the rational enterprise, the division of labour and fixed capital' (1968: 1091, and, more generally, 1091–99). This result occurs for various reasons, but principally owing to this system's arbitrariness and exploitation by political insiders of state-supported monopolies and sinecures, which discourage long-term investments.[3] If neo-patrimonial rule subordinates economic production to political considerations, then political-institutional reforms are required that circumscribe clientelism and personalism, establish a new basis for legitimate authority, rebuild the rule of law, construct a disciplined, efficient and expert civil service, and institute accountability at all levels (Aron 1996). This institutional agenda adds up to a daunting challenge.

How, if at all, will democratization help meet this challenge? The current 'governance' approach, as articulated by the World Bank (1992b) and the donors, pins its hopes on democratization, primarily because the alternative paths to institutional renewal appear so unpromising. Democratization, it is hoped, will empower domestic social forces which have a vested interest in defending a new order of limited and market-friendly government, accountable and honest officials, transparent decision-making, effective and predictable administration, and a rule of law that protects human rights, private property and the sanctity of contracts.

In practice, however, as with ethnic tensions, democratization may actually worsen economic problems. Consider systemic corruption, which constitutes a major drag on productivity and growth (Mauro 1997). A return to democracy may encourage corruption by providing both an opportunity and a motive for corrupt behaviour (see Harris-White and White 1996). The former arises, ironically, from the economic liberalization that invariably accompanies democratic transitions in contemporary Africa. Adjustment programmes increase inflows of external grants and loans while requiring the privatization of many public assets. By thus augmenting the resources in the hands of politicians, these programmes provide new temptations to power-holders. A new motive arises from the high cost of mounting national election campaigns, since serious contenders must often distribute patronage to potential supporters. These expenses inspire government leaders to demand kickbacks on government contracts and to employ state resources (vehicles, personnel, media) for partisan purposes. As well, political uncertainty and the spectre of personal poverty motivate insecure politicians to build up their private fortunes by any means available. The weakness of procedural norms in fledgling democracies makes these pressures on officials all the more telling.

But this, again, is only half the story. Democratization also unleashes powerful reformist impulses. First, the constitution lays out the new formal rules of the game, together with agencies charged with overseeing and enforcing these rules, including independent auditors, courts and commissions. Second, the newly entrenched civil and political rights stimulate the organization and assertiveness of civil associations (Gyimah-Boadi 1996). Independent newspapers and opposition parties publicize the transgressions of political leaders and bureaucrats. Constituencies mobilize to defend new institutions – for example, law societies take the lead in championing the independence of the judiciary. Coalitions involving professional organizations, church bodies, students, human-rights associations and NGOs form to press forward the goal of constitutional government. In Kenya, for instance, the National Convention Assembly united 600 members in 1996–98 behind a demand that the Moi government permit public participation in constitutional reform.

Democratization, in short, does not guarantee the political-institutional reforms that might underpin a productive economy. Such reform involves a series of struggles over many years. But emergent democracy probably does provide a more propitious context for needed socioeconomic change than conceivable alternatives.

8.6   Challenge: empowering local institutions of environmental defence

Environmental crisis is another key element of the multidimensional crisis we term a complex humanitarian emergency. Environmental degradation and growing scarcity of natural resources can form an interlocking circle with deepening rural poverty, predatory politics, ethnic tensions, and violent conflict between countries and/or communities. Protection of the local resource base, especially land, may therefore ease tensions that might otherwise escalate into complex emergencies. Can democratization help address environmental degradation and scarcities?

The answer, at first glance, is apparently no. Third-world democracies have generally failed to curb two critical local vectors of degradation: rapacious corporations and the desperate rural poverty that drives herders and cultivators to unsustainable husbandry.

Yet there are two indirect ways in which democratization can mitigate environmental shortages. First, popularly elected governments have proven to be adept at quickly and effectively responding to famines – the most devastating manifestation of natural-resource scarcity in poor countries with large rural sectors. India has justly received praise for instituting a famine-relief system that has prevented famines since independence, despite periodic droughts. Although Indian democracy has many shortcomings, the electoral weight of the countryside has nonetheless motivated national governments to respond quickly to regional food shortages. In Africa, too, democracies have effectively distributed emergency food supplies in drought-stricken regions. Haile Selassie's autocratic government in Ethiopia was overthrown in 1974 owing partly to the public outrage evoked by its refusal even to acknowledge the drought and famine which had ravaged the countryside. In Zambia, by contrast, the government of Frederick Chiluba earned accolades for moving speedily to prevent a local drought from evolving into a famine, following a democratic transition in late 1991.

Similarly, Botswana, democratic since independence, has earned a fine reputation for drought relief. Politicians of the governing party have found that attention to this important programme translates into popularity in their rural constituencies. 'Drought relief is coming to assume a role in Botswana politics comparable to education and welfare in industrialized countries' (Holm and Morgan 1985: 477). Hence, government leaders have resisted advice to reduce government expenditures by cuts in this area.

Second, democratization can empower local communities and NGOs to promote and defend locally based strategies of resource conservation. The celebrated Brundtland report (World Commission on Environment and Development 1987) held that poverty was a prime cause of environmental deterioration, in that poor people had no option but to overwork or overgraze the land and overexploit the forests in order to survive. A contrary view was soon articulated: that poverty was not a prime *cause* but a prime *symptom* of a condition that produced local-level environmental degeneration, namely the disempowerment of rural communities (Vivian 1992; Watts 1991; Ghai 1994; Broad 1994). This disempowerment manifested itself as outside agents abrogated the traditional rights of people to use local resources, and curtailed their ability to manage them. Insofar as, traditionally, local communities had developed sustainable patterns of managing resources, this disempowerment often had negative environmental repercussions. Vast logging concessions, new mines, the establishment of plantations and ranches, the building of dams, irrigation schemes, roads and railways – all these have frequently devastated local livelihoods, cultures and eco-systems. More socially and environmentally sustainable development, according to the 'empowerment' perspective, requires the participation of the local communities in resource management.

The organization of the poor and indigenous groups is what empowers them to act effectively as managers and 'environmental activists' (Broad 1994). Localized community organization is crucial; this organization, however, needs the expertise, funds and protection that environmental and human-rights NGOs and mass-based peasant or labour unions can provide. '[A] densely webbed civil society...creates a culture of popular resistance' (Broad 1994: 817). This culture makes it more likely that local groups will defend their natural resources against threats from governments, businesses and landowners. Political liberalization, by instituting civil and political rights, expands the political space for such organizations and networks to form and resist environmentally destructive development. Local activists may confront commercial loggers or commercial fishing fleets, protest environmental pollution by mining and oil companies, resist enclosures of the commons by landowners and corporations, replant trees and assert their right to manage community resources.[4]

The 'empowerment' view of environmental sustainability gains support from abundant evidence of the capacity of local communities to manage their eco-systems in a sustainable manner (for example, Ghai and Vivian 1992; Friedmann and Rangan 1993). A striking confirmation of this view is found in a study of a transitional forest-savannah region in northern Guinea (Fairhead and Leach 1996). The study contradicts the conventional scientific view that this region had formerly been forested, and that the people had degraded the forest into savannah. Instead, it finds the precise opposite to hold true – that the inhabitants and their ancestors had, despite population increase, fostered forest growth in the savannah wherever they had settled, cultivated and raised animals. Rather, outsiders have threatened the environment. Government agencies and donor organizations, supposing the local communities to be incapable of conservation, have imposed master plans and regulations that declare time-tested farming practices illegal (Fairhead and Leach 1996).

A quite different instance of environmental renewal at the grassroots is that of the Green-Belt Movement (GBM) in Kenya (Ekins 1992). Founded in 1977 as a project of Kenya's National Council of Women, it aimed to organize rural women around the project of reforestation. The GBM started tree nurseries, replanted public green-belts, and encouraged private farmers to plant trees on their landholdings. These activities not only have combated soil erosion, but have also created jobs for rural women and enhanced their solidarity and power. In the first decade, between 2000 and 3000 women participated in the cultivation and planting of trees, with about 2000 new green-belts and 15 000 replanted farms to show for their effort (Ekins 1992). Nonetheless, the authoritarian Moi regime soon perceived the GBM and its leader Wangari Maathai as political threats. Its harassment of Maathai did not deter her, however. She played an important role in Kenya's democracy movement in the 1990s, thereby illustrating the close connection between environmental activism and political liberalization.

With qualifications, the empowerment viewpoint provides a practical way of confronting environmental decline. One flaw is the tendency to romanticize the relationship of poor and indigenous people to their environment. Local communities will not, under certain conditions, prudently manage the local resources on which they depend (Leach *et al.* 1997). Traditional ways of living in harmony with nature often do not survive the commercialization of natural resources which accompanies the extension of market relations. And local communities rarely have a common interest: more often, such communities are neither undifferentiated nor democratic. An elite based on class, caste or ethnicity often dominates local power structures, and determines how local resources will be allocated. Local management, under these conditions, will certainly not reflect empowerment of the poor/local communities.[5] Nonetheless, the poor have often acted as environmental activists – when their resource base is threatened by degradation, when they have a sense of permanence in an area, and when political conditions permit them to organize and engage in collective action (Broad 1994). Democratization at the national level, while not guaranteeing decentralization and democratization at the local level, does widen the political space for national and international NGOs to organize so as to confront local oligarchies and press an agenda of resource conservation.

Thus, insofar as democratization attunes the central government to the food-security needs of rural people and furnishes a facilitative framework for environmental activism at the local level, it indirectly responds to the destructive tendency of environmental degradation.

8.7   From vicious to virtuous circles

Whether human ingenuity can avert complex political emergencies in countries undergoing or at risk of a slide into deadly conflict is a question that has assumed growing importance as political upheavals have proliferated. In Central Africa alone, insurrections and civil wars wreaked havoc in eight contiguous countries, and armed interventions into these internal wars by nearby states magnified the upheavals. The Horn of Africa and West Africa also sustained a series of interrelated political catastrophes. Nor were these upheavals peculiar to Africa. One journalist, in a much-cited article, claimed that Sierra Leone in 1994 was a 'microcosm' of what was occurring, 'albeit in a more tempered and gradual manner', throughout much of the third world: '[t]he withering away of central governments, the rise of tribal and regional domains, the unchecked spread of disease, and the growing pervasiveness of war' (Kaplan 1994: 48). Although this scenario was unduly pessimistic, it did reflect widespread anxieties as each headline brought further bad news.

In light of these dire circumstances, democratization can be an important component of a broad strategy to forestall deadly conflict. Since an effective remedy depends on a sound diagnosis, a syndrome of four symptoms – ethnic polarization, weak and predatory governance, economic collapse, and environmental degradation – was explored, the interlocking of which creates a vicious circle leading ultimately to civil war or state collapse. Democracy does not offer a 'quick-fix' to these problems: indeed, democratization is a risky strategy as it unleashes tensions that may aggravate the underlying crises.

However, democratization's long-term promise is, under certain conditions, to replace this vicious circle with a 'virtuous' circle of peaceful, prosperous and ecologically sustainable development.[6] Political liberalization can advance this goal both directly and indirectly. Its direct effect is felt in the constitutional-legal institutions that manage conflicts in deeply divided societies, lay a foundation for economic prosperity and recognize the traditional tenure rights of ecologically sensitive local communities. As these changes occur, the democratic state also enhances its capacity. Peace, governmental responsiveness, and growth generate the legitimacy, revenues and legality on which a stronger state hinges. Indirectly, civil and political rights, independent media and courts, opposition movements and grassroots associations generate the political space for constituencies to organize in support of valued institutions.

What then is the prognosis for instituting such a virtuous circle? Obviously, the earlier in a downward spiral that a democratic transition is attempted, the greater the prospect of success. A breakdown into civil war will severely limit democratic prospects, owing to the heightened enmities, fears and insecurities that such conflict breeds. It is also better if constitutions arise from negotiations, such as by means of a national conference; these negotiations generate compromises mitigating actual or potential cleavages. In addition, the international community can play an important role. Although external interventions often exacerbate conflicts, they can also be positive. Mozambique's success to date in sustaining democracy and building peace can, in part, be explained by the continuing oversight provided by the UN and the donor countries. Moreover, democratic polities, to become consolidated, must deliver a better life to citizens. Such economic progress may require reform of the global economy, not just an increase in foreign aid (Sandbrook 2000). Finally, African governments' growing willingness to intervene militarily in neighbouring countries further destabilizes countries by encouraging local insurgents. But there are ongoing negotiations to replace unilateral military interventions by regional peacekeeping forces.

Democracy movements confront enormous challenges. They search for suitable political, social and economic arrangements in the face of multiple crises, recalcitrant domestic governments and impatient and niggardly donors. But no longer should their quest be dismissed as wrongheaded, on the grounds that only authoritarian regimes can create order. Although democratization often fails, it nonetheless provides a better opportunity for needed institutional reforms than the earlier, discredited autocracies.

Notes

1. For White (1995) these first two challenges constitute the agenda of a 'democratic development state'.
2. That is, the principle that only a plurality or majority vote of the relevant constituency is required to elect governors and pass legislation.
3. For further elaboration, see Sandbrook (1993).
4. For an excellent study of how grassroots organizations have mobilized to resist environmental plundering, see Broad and Cavanagh (1993).
5. For a case study of how factional relations undermine astute local environmental management, see Woodhouse's (1997) analysis of a collectively owned Maasai ranch in southern Kenya.
6. For an elaboration of this theme, see Sandbrook (2000).

9
Donor Governments

Helge Hveem

9.1   The issues

Donor governments' response, or failed response, to CHEs was the subject of intense debate and severe criticism during several crises in the 1990s.[1] But donor governments and their critics appear to apply different standards of judgement. For some, *efficacy* is the main criterion, and emergency operations are judged on the basis of the speed and adequacy of the response. For others, *justice* or *impartiality* is a main criterion. These critics ask whether assistance is being provided to all the people in all CHEs in an egalitarian manner. For yet another group, *legitimacy,* or the issue of societal acceptance of aid by recipient and donor populations alike, is of primary importance.

The issue of legitimacy applies not only to the source, but even to the channel for emergency assistance. Donors and recipients thus often disagree on what constitutes an acceptable channel for emergency relief. Some are satisfied with patron-client type of channels, while others prefer channels based on kinship. Others still accept only non-discriminatory aid offered on the basis of equality between donor and recipient.[2] These controversies account for much heat in the debate on the success or failure of the national response. But none of the abovementioned criteria are straight-forward.[3] Does efficacy mean cost efficiency in the provision of rescue resources to save taxpayers' money, or effectiveness as measured by the lives saved regardless of the costs? The humanitarian dictum clearly favours the latter interpretation and suggests a 'Hippocratic oath to aid' (Anderson 1999).

In practice, the three criteria identified here are correlated. Advocates of global integrity argue that justice is a precondition for legitimacy and consider only UN-led operations as legitimate. But many analysts, questioning UN-led operations, see a trade-off between legitimacy and efficacy. Those promoting justice agree over what the criterion implies in practice, and in criticizing donors for their failure to respond, they talk of discrimination of the victims of CHEs. If the resources applied to emergency operations are a measure of discriminatory behaviour, they have a point. But those who emphasize efficacy argue that, given the lack of resources for all emergencies, it is better to save as many lives as possible efficiently in a few places rather than spread resources thinly in many with only marginal effects in each.

Three questions are addressed here. First, why is there a failure to respond adequately? Why and how both intervention and a 'no-action' decision are taken needs to be understood. Second, why do responses differ? These two questions are answered by looking at a few donor governments: the EU and France, Norway, Japan and the US. The main criterion for the selection is that these countries are major contributors to funding or influencing decisions regarding emergency operations. The countries respond differently in major respects. Information on the organization and performance of emergency handling varies greatly, and this makes strict comparison impossible. Still, we can learn and draw policy implications from these cases. Third, do donor countries learn from experience, and is feed-back available to guide subsequent decisions? Democratic countries are not unitary actors. The outcome of policy-making cannot be predetermined, but results from exchanging diverging views on the urgency and nature of intervention are needed.

9.2   Profiling and explaining donor country contributions

Differences in human, material and organizational endowment influence responses to CHEs. If GNP per capita is a proxy for endowment, it is found that countries differ widely in their potential for responding to emergencies. Thus, capability may be more important in defining the type of response than diverging policy views.

9.2.1   Comparing financial contributions

In the mid-1990s, approximately 85 per cent of total assistance for CHEs was donated by EU members and the US. Table 9.1 shows that when members' bilateral aid and donations from EU institutions are included, the EU in 1993–98 contributed more than half of all humanitarian aid. Moreover, global humanitarian aid has peaked and is declining.[4] Also, military involvement in relief is becoming more common (Minear and Weiss 1995; Weiss, this volume), adding significantly to cost. However, peacekeeping operations are generally excluded from emergency assistance statistics. In Somalia, where the cost of the six-month operation was US$4 billion, there was a huge mismatch between resources for military protection and relief operations. Indeed, political discourse and the media have highlighted the share of military operations to aid recipients, suggesting that considerable military backup is necessary to render humanitarian assistance.

Another tendency is the shortfall in donor country contributions compared to capability. Per capita contribution measures responsiveness to

Table 9.1 Distribution of total humanitarian aid by major donors, 1993–98 (in million US$ and as % of total)

	European Union		*United States*		*All others**		*Total*	
	US$	*%*	*US$*	*%*	*US$*	*%*	*US$*	*%*
1993**	2.316	*52.2*	1.513	*34.1*	605	*13.7*	4.433	*100*
1994	2.612	*58.4*	1.250	*27.9*	615	*13.7*	4.476	*100*
1995	1.397	*51.8*	762	*28.3*	536	*19.9*	2.695	*100*
1996	2.042	*54.7*	1.220	*32.7*	467	*12.6*	3.730	*100*
1997	1.170	*52.8*	549	*24.8*	498	*23.4*	2.217	*100*
1998	1.289	*49.2*	861	*32.8*	471	*18.0*	2.621	*100*

Notes
* Japan's total commitments were reported at only US$37 million in 1997, but increased to US$113 million in 1998. For Norway, the corresponding figures are US$200 and 187 million, respectively.
** Austria, Finland and Sweden are included in the total for EU starting from 1993 even though these countries did not become members until 1 January 1995.
Sources: European Commission Humanitarian Office (ECHO) 1993, 1994 and 1996; UNDHA (1996) for 1995 and 1997; Office of Complex Humanitarian Affairs (OCHA) of UNDHA for 1998 (these figures may reflect underreporting)

exogenous crises. This measure indicates that several small DCs contributed considerably more than the major powers. Nordic countries, the Netherlands and Switzerland surpassed the US as per capita donors. If total assistance is used as a yardstick, Norway and the Netherlands ranked among the five major donors of assistance to CHEs in the mid-1990s, surpassing, for example, Japan. This ranking, however, does not consider contributions to military operations or all assistance to refugees. Small countries, nevertheless, are more sensitive to CHEs than the great powers. Why?

9.2.2 Explaining behaviour

Explanations may be classified by whether outcomes result from competitive values, interests and actors (Allison 1971), including the interaction of decision-making at different levels (Rosenau 1967; Putnam 1988).[5] Domestic politics and the nature of the political system are among the most relevant factors. The small countries mentioned above are democracies with strong civil societies, and they are not likely to be swayed by the geopolitics of an emergency. Another factor is the relationship between the emergency setting and the actors responding to it. Finally, these factors cannot be explained until the international context of the emergency is explored.

A decision to intervene is affected by factors at several levels. Three categories of factors that trigger government response to emergencies abroad can be indentified:

i) Particular interests, which lead a government to defend its 'national interest'; or religion or ethnicity that influences government action.

The neo-realist explanation is straightforward: intervention is justified if (and only if) national interest is affected. Substantial evidence supports this explanation. The US and EU were both reluctant to intervene in Bosnia rapidly with force to avoid risking NATO unity, offending Russia, and destabilizing post-Cold War stability in Europe (Freedman 1994–95). Russia's intervention was not motivated by humanitarian concerns, but almost exclusively by geopolitical and military factors (Baev 1994; McNeill 1997). US intervention in Somalia, large-scale and rapid once the decision was taken, was mainly spurred by long-term strategic interests in the sub-region. So probably was French intervention in Rwanda through 'Operation Turquoise', while US intervention in Haiti had mixed motives (Maguire *et al.* 1996);

ii) An overriding humanitarian ideology, or universally accepted obligations that call for action to prevent casualties, provided that objective factors indicating the emergency's gravity are present. This ideology purportedly became prominent in France after the 1987 proclamation of 'the right to humanitarian assistance and the obligation of states to contribute to it' (Pellet 1995). Other scholars argue that the 'statist' view, assuming that sovereign states act on humanitarian values, is wrong and that action must be based on transnational coalitions (de Waal and Omaar 1995; Wheeler 1997);

iii) Institutional factors that compel governments to respond to a crisis. Such factors could, for instance, be commitment by governments to respond to UNHCR or other multilateral agencies, or strict procedures by national institutions to limit self-interested or misguided responses.

These three categories are the national interest, the ideological-humanitarianist, and the institutionalist respectively. They represent 'necessary primary conditions' that motivate government to respond to a CHE abroad. They are not, however, mutually exclusive. Often international and national factors interact to promote or deter action. The analysis should thus use a multi-level model to represent this interaction for a more general theoretical approach (Putnam 1988; Hveem 1994, 1997). Similarly theoretical modelling should analyse interaction between government, civil society and transnational NGOs. Civil society appears, also beyond Western polities, to interact with state institutions and exercise considerable weight (Risse-Kappen 1995).[6] While civil society can exert pressure on governments and thus influence policy, governments may also influence civil society to promote state interests (DeMars, this volume). Perhaps a coalition of domestic pressure groups and transnational NGOs constitutes the strongest possible lobby for 'truly' humanitarian action.

Consensus indicates that institutional early warning is crucial. Famine warning improved in places during the 1990s (Buchanan-Smith and Davies 1995). Yet the major problem may not be early-warning systems, but to find ways for warnings to penetrate the ignorance barrier and to initiate action. Several factors must be present to trigger a definite response. One trigger, or secondary (process) cause, may be pressure by important domestic groups, or mass media coverage. Adelman and Suhrke (1996) refer to the mechanism as the 'messenger', and the EU refers to it as 'advocacy'. The mechanism is often set in motion by 'humanitarian concern' or normative predisposition to respond. This predisposition can be either ethical or altruistic, sometimes arising from the concern of civil society. But involvement often rests solely on strategic or economic interest in the crisis. Also, if the lives of citizens of the donor country are threatened, media coverage can usually be expected (Jakobsen 1996). The following case studies support the assumption that advocacy is decisive.

Finally, necessary resources must be available. Large endowment does not mean that resources are necessarily available. In the EU and most donor countries, resources are constrained by budgetary procedure. Raising funds through semi- or non-governmental institutions is not usually practical. In 1995, the International Committee of the Red Cross network and NGOs contributed less than 0.1 per cent of all humanitarian emergency assistance (UNDHA 1996). Given that only governments tax individuals and firms, substantial resources must come from a state agency. Furthermore, a donor government can mobilize extra-budgetary resources only in exceptional circumstances. NGOs, however, are of importance as pressure groups on governments and as operators in the field.

Research has identified a dozen CHEs, and supports UNDHA information.[7] If emergency assistance was pledged according to global 'objective criteria', then the magnitude and speed of the response would always match the emergency's intensity (indicated, among other things, by casualties, internally displaced persons (IDPs), etc.). A preliminary look at data indicates that this correlation is weak, at best. For instance, in 1995, former Yugoslavia received ten times the amount of aid given to Chechnya, and twenty times that pledged to Sierra Leone.[8]

According to UN data, more than half of all 1995 aid was channelled through multilateral (mainly UN) agencies, the largest being UNHCR, the World Food Programme (WFP) and UNICEF. Only funds channelled through UNHCR have remained fairly stable since 1992. Five per cent of assistance is transferred as bilateral aid. NGOs, with more than two dozen large organizations operating in humanitarian emergency assistance, accounted for 27 per cent and the ICRC for 15 per cent. NGOs were the most important channel for assistance to half of the 12 CHEs (the Caucasus, Haiti, Liberia, Sierra Leone, Sudan and Tajikistan), whereas the ICRC network was the major source for Chechnya. Multilateral efforts dominated in the remaining five emergencies, including the former Yugoslavia and the Great Lakes of Africa, where aid was by far the greatest. Table 9.2 shows the geographical distribution of assistance from the four donor countries reviewed.

Aid concentration to former Yugoslavia and the Great Lakes can be attributed to some of the three primary causes discussed above. The major

Table 9.2   Geographical distribution of humanitarian emergency assistance: major powers and Norway, percentages (1995)

Emergency location	Donor			
	United States	*European Union**	*Japan*	*Norway*
Angola	11.7	10.7	5.3	12.1
Caucasus	4.0	10.6	1.6	4.4
Chechnya	2.6	3.5	0.5	1.7
Former Yugoslavia	27.1	27.4	42.8	48.6
Great Lakes of Africa	37.5	27.4	28.3	15.3
Haiti	0.1	1.6	4.7	0.7
Iraq (Kurds)	4.0	5.5	2.6	2.5
Liberia	3.2	1.7	7.3	1.6
Sierra Leone	2.1	1.4	2.2	1.2
Somalia	3.0	2.0	1.2	2.6
Sudan	3.0	5.8	2.6	8.0
Tajikistan	1.3	2.4	0.6	1.2
Total volume (million US$)	761.9	1.396.8	140.2	143.7
Share of donor in total volume (%)	29.8	54.6	5.6	5.5

Note
* Includes assistance from both bilateral pledges and from common institutions: ECHO and the Commission DG 8.
Source: UNDHA Complex Emergency Support Unit, Financial Tracking Sub–Unit (1996)

powers want to maintain stability in Europe for political and religious-cultural reasons, and in Central Africa for European-African political relations. Accordingly, the slow response to these two emergencies was not caused by lack of interest or of humanitarian inclination, but procedure. Japan's (and Norway's) relative emphasis on the former Yugoslavia could, on the other hand, point to idiosyncratic factors (such as the roles played by Yasushi Akashi and Thorvald Stoltenberg as crisis mediators).

The factors not given priority should also be discussed. The relatively modest assistance to Chechnya may be explained by reluctance to intervene in what the Russian government argued was an internal affair. Somalia, Sudan and Sierra Leone are obvious cases of a mismatch between the objective depth of emergency and the volume of assistance. Samatar (2000) indicates that this illustrates the lack of appreciation by US decision-makers of the true causes of the Somali crisis. To say that Somalia lost its importance as soon as Cable Network News (CNN) left, is too simple as its effect in general may not be decisive (Jakobsen 1996). The US, concentrating some attention on Liberia for historical reasons, had limited interest in Angola and virtually none in Sierra Leone. The most important factor that kept Sudan in the spotlight was religious-cultural. In fact, 'Operation Lifeline Sudan' was a relatively successful UN-led international emergency operation from 1989 onward (Minear *et al.* 1991).

9.3 Explaining donor response: the five cases reviewed

Even with disaggregated and longitudinal statistics, examining a CHE is incomplete without qualitative analysis of policy-making. We attempt, as a beginning, to rectify this situation.[9]

This section focuses on policies and institutions adopted by key actors to support participation in CHE operations, reviews countries in which donors attempt to determine whether a pattern of decision-making can be identified, and tries to explain decisions on emergencies. The survey examines policies and institutions in emergency assistance, the resources allocated, the channels used to disseminate aid, and how donor countries address preparedness and early warning. The analysis concludes with recommendations for improving policies and institutions for humanitarian aid, which imply more resources, improved organization and better donor coordination.

9.3.1 Japan: the reluctant latecomer

Japan has been the largest single contributor of ODA since 1989, contributing small but increasing funds to UNHCR and other multilateral agencies since the mid-1990s. Japan uniquely channels most emergency assistance through multilateral organizations (90 per cent in 1995) rather than bilaterally or through NGOs. However, Japan's ODA budget fell while funds for CHEs, after falling in 1997, increased again in 1998.

Japan's policy, while difficult to characterize, has been explicit in differentiating between peacekeeping and international emergency relief. According to the Peace Cooperation Law of 1992, emergency relief operations are intended for victims of natural disasters only and not for refugees or other victims of man-made conflicts. Japan, a relative newcomer to the field, lacks tradition and personnel, and faces cultural and linguistic barriers. Many civil society-oriented pressure groups want Japan to focus on domestic or regional issues. Moreover, Japanese political and bureaucratic elites have been and are still reluctant to be involved abroad in CHEs and complex politics (Inoguchi 1993), a situation that has hardly changed. Japan concentrates primarily on East Asia, which needs relatively less emergency assistance than Central Asia. Table 9.2 indicates, however, that Japan has put as much priority on African crises as the two other major powers.

The Prime Minister's Office and Defence Agency are in charge of peacekeeping operations, while the Ministry of Foreign Affairs is responsible for humanitarian emergency relief. Personnel for relief are recruited mostly on an ad hoc basis from various institutions and professions. For instance, the Association of Medical Doctors in Asia (AMDA), with some 1500 members (1200 Japanese) ready for relief efforts, is among the most active in emergency operations since 1991. Only a few Japanese operations[10] have been outside Asia.

Japan's policies and institutions are developing incrementally. Its reluctance may be explained by the limitations imposed on its military and foreign role after the Second World War. Yet, as a result of international and domestic changes, conditions are now suitable for a more active and permanent role. Japan's inaction may result from a lack of urgency. Japan is not a member of the UNSC, but membership may necessitate a more active role in peacekeeping and crisis management (Shinn 1996), and the government may already be preparing for this.[11] Sadako Ogata, as UN High Commissioner for Refugees, indicated that Japan's quest for an eventual UNSC seat will require a 'global vision [that] would apply to domestic matters of other countries' (*Nikkei Weekly*, 3 February 1997).

9.3.2   The US: a weakened hegemon

The US, with its long tradition and well-established institutions in humanitarian emergency assistance, continues to draw on its vast capabilities for initiating and executing international operations. Despite a distinction between humanitarian emergency action and peacekeeping operations, the decision-making process leading to involvement in the two is not very different. On several occasions the US demonstrated its ability to establish working coalitions. The consent of the US, a hegemonic power that has paid so far roughly one-third of the UN's peacekeeping budget, is essential for a viable collective operation.

The US demonstrates perhaps the greatest potential for conflict between national interests and humanitarian-institutional incentives within the country itself. While institutional capability to handle situations is relatively strong, political friction among the institutions responsible for policy and implementation, and resource limitations of recent years have reduced the country's capacity to act. The US lifts budget constraints to humanitarian operations only when its national interests are clearly affected.

Humanitarian emergency action is carried out by five different institutions:

- USAID's Office for Foreign Disaster Assistance (OFDA) within the Bureau of Humanitarian Response;
- USAID's Food for Peace Office (in the same bureau);
- the State Department where several sections are involved, including the Bureau of Refugee Programs;
- the Department of Defence, particularly its Office of Refugee and Humanitarian Affairs; and
- a special unit for humanitarian efforts at the National Security Council.

US federal budget allocations during the late 1990s reduced ODA and increased humanitarian (primarily disaster and refugee) and military aid. Public support is greater for humanitarian and military aid than for economic aid (Randel and German 1996; Crocker 1996). However, US humanitarian action has become less flexible because of budgetary and political constraints imposed by Congress (Shiras 1996).

Clinton's Presidential Decision Directive 25 (PDD 25) of May 1994 primarily concerns peacekeeping, but is also relevant for humanitarian emergency action. Under PDD 25, policy-making principles and procedures have become more hierarchically structured and more transparent, and budget allocation more straightforward. PDD 25, which outlines criteria for guiding US policies, calls for a more selective and effective approach to peacemaking. While national security interests remain foremost, US authorities will seek:

> collective rather than unilateral solutions to regional and intrastate conflicts that do not touch our core national interests. And we will choose between unilateral and collective approaches, between the UN and other coalitions depending on what works best and what best serves American interests (Lake 1994).

PDD 25 affects the administration's decision on whether to focus US support on UN-sponsored or regional operations. In crises, the eruption of 'urgent humanitarian disaster coupled with violence' and 'the political, economic and humanitarian consequences of inaction by the international community have been weighed and are considered unacceptable'. Decisions will be based on the 'cumulative weight of the above factors, with no single factor necessarily being an absolute determinant'. The new policy document also defines the conditions applied to new UN operations to increase time and cost efficacy, and establish hierarchical lines of command. A follow-up statement by the State Department stresses the crucial role of peacekeeping forces in providing the context for humanitarian relief.[12] Finally, the UN Department of Peacekeeping Operations is provided with information on the US personnel and equipment, but this notification 'in no way implies a commitment to provide those capabilities, if asked by the UN' (National Security Council 1994).

In the decision-making process in policy formulation, emphasis is on the multivariate, inter-sectoral character of operations that consist 'of military, political, humanitarian and developmental elements in varying degrees'. The organizational implication is that no single agency can manage effectively all facets of an operation. Therefore, designated lead agencies are to engage in full and regular interagency consultation. In all cases, however, the State Department remains responsible for the conduct of diplomacy and instructions to embassies and the UN mission in New York, the Department of Defence for military assessment and activities, and the National Security Council for facilitating interagency coordination.

According to the Foreign Assistance Act, the USAID Administrator is the President's Special Coordinator for Disaster Assistance. USAID is said to have a round-the-clock logistical and organizational readiness that enables it to respond within 24 to 72 hours after a disaster breaks out. USAID is thus the chief agency for implementing US operations dealing directly with humanitarian assistance; these operations, however, have been affected by a general decline in resources. At the same time, USAID became involved during the early 1990s in the increasing number of CHEs. USAID's emergency relief programmes were traditionally devoted to natural disasters, but by 1995, 90 per cent of international disaster assistance was earmarked for victims of CHEs. In 1995, USAID responded to 57 recognized disaster situations in 51 countries, 19 of which were complex emergencies. The agency is said to have compensated for the decline in resources with a more selective approach in terms of the scope of assistance, focus on the root causes of crises, and promoting early warning, preparedness and mitigation. The Famine Early-Warning System in Africa is one such mechanism (USAID 1996).

To assess whether the US delivered on its promises, we need to examine its past record and new conditions for participation. How has the US responded to complex emergencies since the late 1980s, and why? And how well does the rational decision-making model outlined by US authorities stand up to reality? Our observations can be summarized in four points with supporting illustrations from some emergencies, including Bosnia, the Great Lakes, Somalia and Haiti.

The importance of national interests, which US authorities articulate more clearly and candidly than other donors, is evident. In the Great Lakes, the Pentagon dominated the decision not to intervene (Adelman and Suhrke 1996). Operations in Somalia had been widely considered a costly disaster. No action, or perhaps the wrong measures, were taken to address the root causes of the domestic humanitarian crisis – a political system dominated by rivalling clans. The disastrous results seemed to be due to the US authorities' perceptions of the nature of the crisis and their handling of it (Samatar 2000).

During the crisis in the Great Lakes region, there was adequate early warning, issued in January 1994 by the CIA. Adelman and Suhrke (1996: 67) describe this warning

> as a worst-case projection of the course of current events which included deaths in the order of half a million casualties....Covering a country of marginal concern to the US, the report was not distributed widely, nor did it reach the higher decision-making echelons.

A key element in Washington's deliberations up to 1997 was its interest in protecting the Mobutu regime and its reluctance to take action that could distance it from the US. The Pentagon's view had considerable weight in the decision not to intervene in Rwanda and Eastern Zaire. In addition, there was widespread assumption that Rwanda would follow the trend of other collapsing African states. Kaplan's (1994) popularizing view on the 'coming anarchy' was rapidly disseminated through the media and, coinciding with the failure in Somalia, contributed to Washington's scepticism towards intervention. Hoffmann's (1995/96) more analytical approach classified the African cases as either 'failed', 'troubled' and 'murderous' states. While images of 'collapsed' or 'failed' states may be misplaced or exaggerated (Bayart *et al.* 1992; Prunier 1995a), they supported the belief that African societies were incapable of governing themselves, and that the US should stay out of African 'quagmires'. In fact, the belief that the collapse of states in Africa is a frequent and central cause of humanitarian crises may have also acted as a post hoc rationalization for non-intervention.

9.3.3   The EU: complex actor, aspiring hegemon

Whereas roughly half of total humanitarian emergency assistance from EU governments is delivered through common EU channels, only about 15 per cent of its total ODA is handled through the corresponding institution, the European Development Fund (EDF). EU decision-makers claim that this arrangement gives them greater influence over policy in CHEs.

Humanitarian operations grew sevenfold over 1990–96, with the peak year in 1994 after which donations fell in absolute terms. But because of the general decrease in donations, the EU maintained its global share at roughly 50 per cent. The absolute drop reflects the radical cut in Lomé IV budget financing under the special agreement with ACP countries. Budgets are based on allotments made in the preceding fiscal year and additional funds are designated as emergencies occur, thus making it impossible to know how much the EU funding is changing until the financial year is over. The need to ask member governments for additional financial contributions is a serious concern for the Commission.

Responsibility for humanitarian operations is lodged with the EU Commission's Directorate General VIII. The main operational arm, the European Community Humanitarian Office (ECHO), established in 1992–93, almost immediately multiplied funding levels and introduced emergency assistance as a policy issue for the Council of Ministers. A Council regulation, adopted in 1996, defines the scope of humanitarian aid and the EU arrangements with international organizations, NGOs and government agencies. A special committee of member states, chaired by the Commission, was set up to assist its policy-making under Council regulation. The Committee on Humanitarian Aid gives advice on long-term global projects, while the Commission is responsible for urgent operations. The Committee on Foreign Relations in the European Parliament has an interest in and often emphasizes humanitarian aid.[13] At the initiative of the former French prime minister and now MEP, Michel Rocard, the Parliament also instigated *Observatoire Humanitaire*, a special unit to improve the EU's monitoring and early action on CHEs.

It is often pointed out that the EU programmes of humanitarian assistance have been too slow to respond to emergencies.[14] One reason is the cumbersome procedure for appropriating EU reserve budget funds and the requirement that 80 per cent of initial funds must be earmarked before new appropriations. The EU relies on intergovernmental consultation, but can still act more readily than most other regional organizations. Funds for collective EU operations are allocated ex-post, and national authorities have the de facto power to veto them. Thus, by March 1997, only 34.6 million ecu, a little over 5 per cent of ECHO expenditures for 1996, had been allocated for the year 1997 (European Commission Humanitarian Office 1997). The question arises whether there is a trade-off between intergovernmentalism and efficacy and preparedness; if a common EU position is impossible for political reasons, would unilateral national action be more efficacious?

Second, the Commission, particularly ECHO, faces a difficult task in harmonizing and coordinating policies. Foreign policy and security matters are organized in the Emergency Preparedness System (EPS), the second 'pillar' formally separate from the Commission. Member countries are obliged under the Maastricht Treaty to 'ensure the defence of the positions and the interests of the Union, without prejudice to their responsibilities under the provision of the United Nations Charter' (Art J.5). In reality, member countries have pursued their own policies, for instance in Bosnia and Rwanda, and friction has developed between the Commission and the EPS, as in the Great Lakes where EU response was slow and insufficient compared to the need for aid. Germany and France were reluctant to intervene for political reasons (Freedman 1994–95). As governments put priority on security and foreign policy, the probability of unilateral action or action by only a few states increases. 'Operation Turquoise' is a case in point (Lanxade 1995).

Third, the potential for controversy and lack of coordination increase when multiple actors implement aid decisions. In 1998, under the EU's framework partnership agreement, about 170 NGOs distributed humanitarian assistance. The allocation of funds for NGOs is based on the tender principle, which leads to an unequal national distribution of funds. France contributes little to the overall budget, yet the aid contracts with French NGOs accounted for around one-third of 1996 allocations. ECHO also runs a 'disaster preparedness' programme, which focuses on natural disasters and ascertains that resources are available in several locations throughout the EU. In addition, the programme is responsible for training local personnel in countries particularly vulnerable to CHEs. The disaster preparedness programme, however, accounts for only a small percentage of ECHO budgets, with the bulk going to emergencies caused by socio-political conflict.

As donors gain experience, their operations improve. To promote efficacy, ECHO has produced a manual for evaluating humanitarian aid. One informant states:

> We are trying to assess whether a transport operation gets item x from place A to place B at acceptable costs; we do not look into what happens

to x at place B. This situation has created some pressure to push evaluation towards a more extensive system, one which looks into whether aid is in fact resulting in improvement of the conditions of the target group. Efforts to link relief, rehabilitation and development go in the same direction.

ECHO staff turned to Commissioner Emma Bonino with optimism after her appointment in 1995. Frequently outspoken, she criticized the UN and the great powers for inaction and outlined an independent profile for the humanitarian concerns of the EU. ECHO's activities received a blow, however, when an expert group's 'fraud report' in 1999 singled out the unit for alleged mismanagement of funds (Committee of Independent Experts 1999). Several projects in Yugoslavia in 1993–94 were said to be fictitious and the former director of ECHO and some consultancy firms were implicated. In 1998–99 legal procedure was initiated against the former director. Despite criticism that investigation of these allegations was slow and non-transparent, the events did not seriously damage the reputation of ECHO or its Commissioner. In 1999 Bonino left for the Santer Commission, to be replaced by a Dane, Poul Nielson.

9.3.4   France: the ambitious loner

France is the second leading donor both in the volume of aid and political weight (Stern 1997; McLeod 1995; Côt 1996), and the donor-country that has most radically changed its policy over the years. Strongly opposed to UN peacekeeping operations (PKO) in the 1960s, France became one of the UN's firmest supporters in the 1990s. The country's PKO doctrine has remained consistent over time, insisting that the centre of UN decision-making should be in the UNSC (Smouts 1997).[15] But during the 1990s, to put more emphasis on humanitarian concerns France softened its insistence of geopolitics and national interest as the only policy rationale.

France prides itself on being the country able to provide the fastest and most determined response to peacekeeping and emergency relief needs (Keller 1992). In France, the private sector is the dominant channel for humanitarian relief. During the late 1990s, Médecins Sans Frontières (MSF) and other organizations have had a strong profile in medical action. Due to NGO and media pressures, the government has acknowledged the need to combine military and humanitarian action (Pellet 1995; cf. Torelli 1993). Recently, also civilian and military leaders have pushed for integrated operations. In Bosnia, humanitarian concerns convinced Paris to send a strong military contingent, as General Morillon's (1997) personal account indicates. The decision was further underpinned by the failure of the 'safe areas' there (Torelli 1995).

Institutional considerations are important in examining France's decisions. Among the countries reviewed, France has the most hierarchical decision-making structure, extensive presidential powers, and a long tradition of coordination among state agencies responsible for external affairs. Francois Mitterand, as president, established a top-level council, comprising the prime minister, the foreign minister, and the chiefs of staff, to make decisions and provide support for the quest for political influence and rapid reaction (Smouts 1997; Keller 1992). The president has the dominant role in decision making, with the National Assembly having only limited influence (even the financing of operations is ex-post – Daudet 1997). The French have a clear-cut doctrine, comparable with PDD 25 (Smouts 1997), which is so hierarchical that parliamentarians have questioned its legitimacy (Fondation pour les Études de Défense 1995).

External and internal reactions to 'Operation Turquoise' led to a turning point in French humanitarian operations. According to the official French perception, the mission was a great success that saved many lives (Connaughton 1994, quoted in Adelman and Suhrke 1996; Morillon 1997). However, critics argued that the operation, while saving lives, may have exposed those involved in the Hutu-Tutsi conflict to fatal danger (Destexhe 1994–95). Others criticize the operation as coming too late, which the French counter by pointing out that they tried to mobilize a collective UN operation much earlier, but without results. Moreover, Adelman and Suhrke (1996: 54) contend that the operation's 'overall effect was to further undermine the institution of collective international intervention as delegated to the UN', despite the UNSC's endorsement of the operation as 'strictly humanitarian'. Other critics maintain that the operation intervened in Rwanda's political process to promote French geopolitical interests in the region.

France's future role is uncertain. One can argue that France in the 1990s chose peacekeeping and humanitarian operations to promote itself as a major power. If the US reduces its role, there is more space for the French, but its government also faces financial constraints. These showed up in budget negotiations in the French parliament during the late 1990s, although cuts were smaller than in the US.

9.3.5   Norway: small and beautiful?

Norway is the largest per capita donor of humanitarian aid. According to UNDHA statistics, its 1997 assistance was US$45 per capita compared to less than US$3 for the US. Five internationally active Norwegian NGOs act as pressure groups in relatively transparent and non-hierarchical policy-making, which is facilitated by consensus on policy priorities. Except for immigration policy (Brochmann 1996), Norway's polity is the most united, both on ODA and relief aid, among the countries discussed. In fact, there is almost a 'corporatist' relationship between the Ministry of Foreign Affairs, responsible for budgets and macro-political decisions, and the major NGOs.

The government claims a proactive approach to CHEs.[16] Parliament allocates part of the budget ex-ante, but reserves additional budgetary funding for unforeseen emergencies. While a foreign ministry unit had considerable power to extend assistance,[17] this controversial system was amended in 1997.

In the mid-1990s, some 70 per cent of its humanitarian emergency assistance was channelled through Norwegian NGOs and the ICRC. Norway has, together with other donors, demanded better coordination of emergency assistance within the UN system, and between it and the NGOs. To focus international actions and facilitate multilateral operations, the then prime minister, Gro Harlem Brundtland, proposed in 1996 to the UN General Assembly that the international community establish a 'fund for preventive action' to mobilize resources prior to actual emergencies.

Another illustration of the Norwegian government's claim of a proactive strategy is the Norwegian Emergency Preparedness System (NOREPS). It stockpiles, both in Norway and in disaster-prone areas, relief items such as high-nutrition foods, lifesaving equipment and vital infrastructure. The aim is to have these supplies airborne within 24 hours after an aid decision is made. Stocks are mostly, if not entirely drawn from Norwegian producers, and some management tasks are left to the Norwegian Trade Council, a semi-private agency for export promotion. The official response is that there is no political bias in access to stocks and that other governments have taken a serious interest in the NOREPS model. Table 9.2, however, indicates that facts cannot completely vindicate allegations of discriminatory behaviour. The Norwegian preparedness system also includes teams of relief workers, currently totalling some 400 individuals, who are prepared to join relief operations within 72 hours.

Although a major donor in both absolute and relative terms, Norway's political influence is limited. As a small country, its main contribution could be to innovate ideas and models that could be duplicated in other countries, or to take part in multilateral institution-building. In this respect Norway is often involved in a Nordic, or a Nordic-Canadian network that promotes these aims at the international level. The humanitarian proposals by these 'like-minded' countries are in line with similar efforts to establish permanent UN institutions to manage peacekeeping operations.[18] The Canadian government may have duplicated Norway's policy when Canada in 1997 set up a fund to direct financial resources instantly to the sites of international crises (*Toronto Globe and Mail* 1997).

9.4 Conclusions

9.4.1 Explaining the cases

Japan's role as a latecomer that lacks international experience and has weak civil support for international action may explain its modest participation in CHEs. Civil society pressures for public awareness, preparation for intervention, and ideological-humanitarian motives pertaining to CHEs are stronger in other countries. The strength of civil society may partly explain why, for instance, humanitarian aid in the US has been spared the cuts in ODA. In France, humanitarian engagement became a major element of foreign policy in the late 1980s, but later lost some strength. Perhaps in both the US and France, national interests have a stronger impact on state behaviour than humanitarian factors when intervention may become more reminiscent of imperialistic motivations (Nafziger 1996). Institutional factors play a role, although not as much as national interest. If decision-making is concentrated, then subsequent action can be rapid (as in Norway) and massive (as with the major powers). Once top-level political consensus was achieved under President Mitterand, France responded with speed and decisiveness. The failure of the US and Europe to intervene in Rwanda and the former Zaire should be attributed more to geopolitical than institutional factors (Emizet 2000).

Donor intervention is most likely to occur where it is motivated by a combination of national interest and humanitarian concerns. Still, such a combination can be uneasy and contentious (DeMars, this volume). Sometimes institutional factors may drive intervention to such an extent that it may be questionable whether it should be referred to as humanitarian at all. Compromises or mixed motives are not unusual, and may even become an obstacle if diverging interests are involved in policy-making. If intervention is seen as relief aid, Somalia, Rwanda and Haiti can be considered a relative success, but a failure if the aim was to end 'the physical suffering caused by the disintegration or the gross misuse of the authority of the state, and helping create conditions in which a viable structure of civil authority can emerge' (Parekh 1997: 55; Samatar 2000).

9.4.2   From an 'ideal model' of intervention to policy proposals

What actually happens is far removed from what observers consider ideal. Action may be slow, inadequate and perhaps partisan if impartiality means treating CHEs and victims equally. What can and should be done?

Voluntarism: modelling an ideal response

Before answering that question, we need agreement on a universal baseline model of international humanitarian intervention. Proposals already exist, varying between i) a moderate humanitarianist-normative view (Minear and Weiss 1995), ii) a more radical, maybe constructivist view (Wheeler 1997), and iii) 'humanitarian realism' (Adelman and Suhrke 1996). While these proposals agree on fundamentals, they also differ in important respects.

One issue being debated is whether state sovereignty is the basic structuring element. Scholars often differentiate between the international system, based on state sovereignty, and international society, whose proponents maintain that also non-state actors have the right to intervene when fundamental principles are at stake. The 'radical' view by the French MSF, championing a *droit d'ingerence*, is a case in point.[19]

The universal ideal code calls for an intervention that is immediate; sufficient, and in proportion to the problem; non-partisan regarding recipients; independent of particular donor interests; and accountable to the public (for a more elaborate proposal, see Minear and Weiss 1995). In such an ideal system, governments would respond i) whenever an emergency has occurred, according to objective criteria, ii) after action is requested by a competent agency, iii) when adequate planning has been carried out, and iv) if necessary to help multilateral institutions to coordinate action. Funds, in an ideal world, are available before operations start, and resources have been collected according to donor capacity.

In reality, mobilization of funds is inconceivable without participation of the state, the only entity that has the privilege to collect taxes and sanction tax evaders. While NGOs can channel (civilian) humanitarian assistance, they cannot operate without state support. A report issued by the ICRC criticizes NGOs for poor-quality assistance and for a lack of accountability to 'clients' or donors. The ICRC (1997) has subsequently introduced a ten-point code of ethical conduct for its national societies and other agencies.

9.4.3   Coping with reality: some policy proposals

To mobilize support, advocacy needs political and material support for intervention. Second, a workable compromise between efficacy and legitimacy on the one hand, and impartiality and self-interest by the donor on the other, is necessary. The nature of this compromise may vary among emergencies, but none of the four components can be neglected if intervention is to be successful. The Madrid Declaration signed at the Humanitarian Summit in December 1995 appears to accept these premises.[20]

Intervention is perhaps optimal under the following conditions: i) a strong humanitarianist-ideological incentive for action supported by strong domestic lobbies and transnational coalitions, ii) an institutional predisposition for action based on contractual obligation or commitment to a certain procedure, and iii) some self-interest by major donors. But a problem can arise if donor self-interest or standard operating procedure outweighs legitimate interests in the target country. Moreover, non-governmental actors cannot always be relied on to represent the 'ideal' model. These actors may pursue their own interests either to support specific clients or to promote their own status and growth.

Some studies have focused on the UN's failure to act or its mal-action.[21] Nevertheless, the UN should remain the focal point for policy coordination and legitimatization. If 'multilateral' implies that governments operate through preset, impartial and coordinated procedures, then few examples of the UN functioning in this way can be cited. In fact, the gap between the ideal and reality is highlighted by the fate of the proposal at the UN General Assembly (UNGA) in September 1996 to establish a permanent body under UN auspices to coordinate humanitarian emergency operations. The proposal received some verbal support from the EU and the US, but both finally preferred to handle CHEs bilaterally.[22]

What can be done to bridge the gap? Detailed proposals have been offered,[23] and the following points are based on findings from our sample survey of donor countries:

- *Learning from experience.* One needs more systematic assessment of past emergency experiences, insight into cultural and socio-political settings, and improvement of decision-making procedures in complex situations. Changes such as the introduction of PDD 25 appear to be motivated by ad hoc and conjectural factors, such as the experience in Somalia, rather than genuine learning.

- *Increased preparedness.* There is room for improved insights into the nature of man-made emergencies and their better dissemination, including national and multilateral warning systems. If early-warning information is treated as proprietary or if the information is not disseminated early or widely enough, then existing warning systems are not optimal.

- *Facilitating rapid deployment.* An organization for rapid delivery of relief exists in all five countries. The EU, Japan and the US concentrate mostly on natural disasters rather than man-made catastrophes. This bias must be corrected and a wider range of a priori measures needs to be undertaken, such as prior commitment of funds and personnel, the pre-positioning of relief items and equipment, the advance placement of resources and infrastructure prior to emergencies.

- *International coordination.* While virtually all emergency actions are taken under the UN Charter, the prominence of national motives results in a lack of operative coordination. This issue, raised in the Nordic UN Project (1990), contributed, under the UNSG, to improved coordination at the country level. The need for multilateralism in solving the collaboration problem was also emphasized by the Independent Commission on International Humanitarian Issues (1988).

- *Delegating responsibility.* There are several reasons why donors should continue to delegate operational responsibility to NGOs. However, reliance on NGOs illustrates some serious gaps, as their activities are often badly coordinated, and they may even compete fiercely with each other. Instead of favouring NGOs from their own country, governments need to delegate operational responsibility and the creation of preparedness systems to reliable parties in the areas most likely to be affected by crises.

- *Getting the intervention right.* Donor countries and 'radical' interventionists in particular may not agree on the mode and aims of intervention; *is* there a universal definition, is the concept culturally relative, or does it vary across regions? Donor governments should work together to achieve a consensus not only on the rhetoric but also the practice of intervention.

- *Contextual and post-emergency factors: getting development policy right.* In addition to getting intervention right, the prevention of the re-emergence of the crisis calls also for an appropriate approach to development. When donations for emergency relief are compared to the distribution of development aid, there is little linkage of the two in bilateral aid patterns, for instance in Japanese aid.[24] Several donors have been working to link emergency relief to ODA policy. This is true for the US, but also increasingly evident in the EU; several of its members have started to merge emergency operations with development aid programmes (CEC 1996b: iii and annex). In Norway, the issue has been studied (Norwegian Institute for International Affairs 1998), and efforts have been made to coordinate the two streams of assistance in countries such as Angola and Mozambique.

The Norwegian report classifies measures as 'preventive efforts in normal times and preventive measures when dangerous signs of tension emerge' (Chopra *et al.* 1995: i). The report proposes the establishment of a joint UN-based early-warning system; the identification of an informal list of 'countries in special situations' to assess whether ODA should be specifically targeted to these countries; the establishment of a 'triage' procedure whereby a smaller number of countries on this list are selected for special attention; and the design of a strategy to address six concrete objectives: prioritize security ('security first'); disarmament, demobilization and reintegration of combatants; repatriation and reintegration of refugees; rule of law and respect for human rights; democratization; and socioeconomic development.

The rationale for linking emergency relief with ODA is straightforward, but is partly based on weak or erroneous assumptions. Underdevelopment, poverty and increasing socioeconomic gaps in a society increase the probability of an emergency (Nafziger and Auvinen 2000; CEC 1996a), yet economic development does not automatically safeguard against crises. Most emergencies are caused by the political struggle for power, territory, identity and distributive issues. Moreover, Uvin (2000) indicates that ODA may be a cause of human distress, not a remedy against it. Hence, the questions whether to link development policy and humanitarian action – and how to do it – are controversial, warranting considerable research and debate. The seven proposals above could make a difference.

Notes

1. We refer here to the responses of the main donor governments, actors whose position of influence, financial resources and/or organizational capacity make them a priori major sources of emergency action.
2. See Médard (1982) for a classification.
3. For a more thorough discussion of the problems of setting such criteria, see Weiss, this volume.

4. The most recent information on ODA trends confirms this, particularly in Africa, which in 1999 received less economic assistance than Israel alone.
5. Hveem (1994) outlines a model, applied to Norway's foreign economic policy-making, that integrates these two broad approaches.
6. Jetschke *et al.* (1996) use a similar approach in comparing the introduction of human rights in Uganda and the Philippines.
7. UNDHA (1996) specifically mentions Angola, Caucasus, Chechnya, former Yugoslavia (mainly Bosnia), Great Lakes Region (mainly Rwanda), Haiti, Iraq (Kurds), Liberia, Sierra Leone, Somalia, Sudan and Tadjikistan.
8. Systematic reporting of CHEs to UNDHA, not initiated until 1992, has reliability problems; hence diachronic analysis is difficult.
9. Adelman and Suhrke (1996), an exception, put together a good beginning.
10. Ethiopia 1992, Somalia 1993, Mozambique 1993 and Rwanda 1994.
11. Reference is made to the setting up in 1996 of a commission to advise the government on Japan's future global policy (based on private communications from Japanese sources).
12. 'UN Peacekeeping Supports US Interests', released on the Internet by the Bureau of International Organizations, 22 February 1996.
13. The Committee was particularly active during the chairmanship of the then MEP Bernard Kouchner, co-founder of Médecins Sans Frontières and, in 1999–2000, UN representative in Kosovo.
14. See Winn (1996) on the EU's handling of CHEs in the 1980s.
15. Criticism suggests that France's stand has been shaped by geopolitical and national interests. France did not participate in the Congo operation in 1961 because of an interest in Katangan secession and it joined the UN Interim Force in Lebanon (UNIFIL) at Lebanon's request because this was consistent with France's own political and cultural interests.
16. Former Deputy Minister Jan Egeland (1988), responsible for humanitarian emergencies, has referred to Norway as a 'potent small power'.
17. This procedure may be unique to Norway, a country known for relatively tight governmental control over public resources. The unit also contrasts with the more complex bureaucracy for ODA.
18. See Government of Canada (1995).
19. Hoffmann (1995–96: 38) may adopt this view when justifying intervention with such criteria as 'massive violations of human rights, which encompass genocide, ethnic cleansing, brutal and large-scale repression to force a population into submission, including deliberate policies of barbarism, as well as famine, breakdown of law and order, epidemics and flights of refugees that occur when a "failed state" collapses'.
20. The declaration was signed by the USAID Administrator, EU Commissioner, UN Under-Secretary General for Humanitarian Affairs, heads of several UN agencies involved in humanitarian relief, and the presidents of the ICRC, MSF and EU and US networks of NGOs.
21. Adelman and Suhrke (1996) on Rwanda; Amer (1993) on Cambodia, and Chopra *et al.* (1995) on Somalia are representative.
22. See Summary of Conclusions EC-US Consultations Humanitarian Working Group on 24–25 October 1996.
23. See, for instance, Adelman and Suhrke (1996); PRIO/NUPI (1997); Rotberg and Weiss (1996); and Hanisch and Mossmann (1996).
24. The source is the Ministry of Foreign Affairs, Tokyo.

10
Transnational Non-Governmental Organizations: the Edge of Innocence

William E. DeMars

10.1 Introduction

Complex humanitarian emergencies are arenas of plunder by the 'four modern horsemen' of war, famine, disease, and displacement (Natsios 1997; Green 1994). Since 1945, the first of these has usually appeared in the shape of internal war rather than interstate conflict. The link between civil war and humanitarian catastrophe was a common factor in Biafra, Cambodia, Ethiopia and Afghanistan during the Cold War, and the correlation persisted through the 1990s, as exemplified by Somalia, Bosnia, Rwanda and Kosovo.

The foreign policy community in the West has been surprised and unprepared for the persistence of internal war since 1989. It was widely expected that these wars would simply die out after the withdrawal of superpower sponsorship for proxy warriors. The next experiment was muscular military humanitarianism through the UN to squelch internal wars. After one spectacular success in 1991 in northern Iraq, this policy stumbled in Somalia and former Yugoslavia, and went awry in the 1994 genocide in Rwanda. 'Early warning and conflict prevention' are the rationale for sustaining global engagement after disillusionment with the high cost and low success rate of military intervention in internal wars.[1]

The imperative of early action for conflict prevention rests on an apparent fusion of humanitarian and political agendas. The humanitarian goal to limit suffering would be better served by preventing famine, genocide or refugee movement than by any amount of ex-post palliative response. This goal appeared to be within reach, now that Cold War adversaries no longer fuel civil wars. Since major powers inevitably step in to manage the destabilizing consequences of CHEs, the reasoning goes, early action would stave off the worst consequences at lower cost in blood, treasure and political capital. This marriage of political and humanitarian agendas, while harmonious in theory, is troubled and contentious in practice.

The policy practice of early warning and conflict prevention straddles a contradiction, due to its links to the battle against budget-cutting isolationists. On the one hand, the imperative of conflict prevention is invoked to justify truly early responses, such as 'preventive development' advocated by the UNDP, that would require a substantial increase in non-military foreign policy expenditures. On the other hand, the same discourse of preventive action is used to justify substantial reductions of aid budgets, on the promise to do more with less.

This contradiction in the policy project of conflict prevention leaves scholars with several alternative strategies for justifying research. One option is to use the contradiction as a lever to lift policy practice so that it more closely matches the high ideals of policy discourse. Accordingly, some scholars analyse the economic and political 'root causes' of conflicts at a very early stage, and design policy tools that could be used to address these in a comprehensive system of conflict prevention. Another research approach is concerned with designing policy tools, and evaluating success and failure, for what might be called 'just in time' conflict prevention in crisis hot spots.[2] Both of these approaches evince an explicit, normative commitment to promote more effective conflict prevention.

A third alternative, and the author's preference, is to analyse the changing patterns of political interaction among the several sets of international and indigenous actors attempting to influence the course of contemporary internal conflicts. Major donor governments, operational UN agencies, and a plethora of diverse international NGOs together constitute a decentralized, global humanitarian network (Minear and Weiss 1995; Macrae and Zwi 1994). The members of this network are active in most of the same conflict-prone countries, and it is they who will do early warning and conflict prevention, if it is to be done at all. The analytical approach here is to focus on the political process of interaction among these actors, and to examine the inadvertent consequences of their actions as well as the intended effects. Such an approach clarifies the tensions within the political coalition for prevention, and may lead to setting more realistic operational goals for the enterprise.

Following this approach, we can pose the question: Do international NGOs contribute to early warning and conflict prevention? The short answer can be 'yes', 'no', or 'it depends'. The following three sections of this chapter unpack this paradoxical response. The first section argues that NGOs are integral to the conflict prevention agenda, and presents the innocent case for preventive action. The second identifies several structural limitations on NGO effectiveness. The third section summarizes the challenges for overcoming the limitations and achieving effective conflict prevention. The conclusion highlights the dilemmas of conflict prevention by 'throwing NGOs at the problem'.

10.2   An innocent case for NGO preventive action

NGOs are private organizations that pursue public purposes. They neither seek political office (like political parties), nor use or advocate violence (like terrorists and insurgents), nor pursue profit (like business firms). NGOs occupy a 'non-profit sector' that takes divergent configurations in different societies (Salamon and Anheier 1994). NGOs fashion their mandates from universal principles of human needs and human rights, and claim on the basis of these principles that their operations are above politics. They press this apolitical claim even (or perhaps especially) when acting in the politically contested international realm. We are concerned primarily with NGOs that operate on a North–South axis. Their headquarters, funding, leadership and social base are located mostly in the DC democracies, while their activities are designed to influence LDCs and the former communist world. Local partner organizations in the South may exercise considerable tactical independence, but usually they are linked closely to the funding sources, normative mandates and organizational styles of their Northern partners.[3]

NGOs that work in internal conflicts, as well as in pre-conflict and post-conflict conditions, have evolved in five relatively distinct sectors: relief and development, human rights, refugees and migration, victims of war (ICRC) and conflict resolution.[4] In recent years, several new NGO sectors relevant to conflict prevention have sprung up to promote democratization and build civil society (Diamond 1995); to demobilize soldiers after peace agreements in civil wars (Refugee Policy Group 1994a), and to specialize in early warning and conflict prevention (Rubin 1996). A few NGOs are exploring forms of closer cooperation with elements of the US national security bureaucracy for purposes of pooling information for conflict early warning (DeMars 2001).

This list of NGO sectors follows the conventional approach of categorizing NGOs according to distinct 'issue areas'. However, the conventional approach fails to illuminate the fluid dynamism of the NGO world. Many organizations strain the limits of non-governmental identity. Quasi non-governmental organizations (QUANGOs) rely on a government for nearly all of their funding, but maintain significant independence in operations and governance. The National Endowment for Democracy, for example, is funded by the US Congress but governed by an independent, bipartisan board. It can channel funding to pro-democracy movements, human rights organizations and mass media development initiatives with greater operational and political flexibility than an agency of the US government (Diamond 1995). In another variation, it is not uncommon for USAID to contract with one of many for-profit consultant and service organizations based in the Washington area (known as 'beltway bandits') for services to be delivered in a developing country. These may be identical to services provided by some non-profit NGOs, or may be new services (such as demobilizing soldiers in the early 1990s) to which non-profits are slow to respond. These ambiguities notwithstanding, QUANGOs and beltway bandits fall within a broad definition of NGOs as private actors that pursue public purposes.

If the standard issue-area categorization fails to capture the organizational ambiguity of some NGOs, it also fosters the misleading assumption that NGOs are slaves to the international principles in their mandates, which they passively 'implement'. In reality, while each NGO is guided by principles in a broad sense, its executive staff retains an enormous scope of tactical freedom, if only because its financial and normative supporters live in one country while its beneficiaries live in another. Hence, as much as they are guided by norms, NGOs also adapt and shape their principles 'on the fly' in response to the tactical demands of maintaining an operational niche in each country or situation.

These tensions in organizational funding and norms point to a larger reality – international NGOs are chameleons living on the edge of political innocence.[5] To understand how they are adjusting to the new mission of early warning and conflict prevention requires exploring both sides of NGO innocence.

The innocent case for effective NGO conflict prevention rests on an idealist assumption – that principled international action can succeed with good intentions, energy, and a little money. This is an assumption of innocence in a double sense. It affirms that NGOs are not guilty of the evils they seek to repair, and also that they are not aware of the tragic potential of their own good intentions. The assumption of innocence (in the first sense) is probably a prerequisite for initiating NGO action in a situation of great violence and deprivation, and it is often sufficiently close to reality to allow NGO innocence (in the second sense) to remain undisturbed.

The innocent case for NGO effectiveness in conflict prevention can be articulated in three straightforward propositions. First, NGOs are integral to conflict prevention as a policy project. Second, NGOs are there on the ground in countries undergoing or vulnerable to conflict and humanitarian crisis. Third, at least under certain restrictive assumptions, all NGO action contributes to conflict prevention. For many practitioners, the first and third propositions are self-evident and rarely remarked upon, while the second is official policy doctrine and rarely questioned. Spelling out these assumptions and analysing their implications can serve to clarify both the power and the limits of NGO innocence.

10.2.1 Essential partners

NGOs are integral to conflict prevention as a policy project, which is itself part of a larger process of restructuring major power foreign policy in a world without a communist threat. Borrowing themes from the corporate lexicon, the large, civilian bureaucracies of Cold War internationalism located in major power governments and the UN are downsizing and restructuring. The US foreign relations budget declined 51 per cent in real terms between 1984 and 1996 (Eagleburger and Barry 1996). Since the late 1980s, donor funding of UNHCR has not kept up with the increasing numbers of refugees and displaced persons that the agency is expected to serve (Loescher 1994). Secretary-General Kofi Annan proposed a 10 per cent reduction of Secretariat staff and budget as a first step in a thoroughgoing UN restructuring.

Downsizing has been accompanied by a trend toward forming operational partnerships with NGOs. The US and EC have channelled a growing proportion of their foreign aid budgets through NGOs during the 1980s and early 1990s (Borton 1993). Today more official development assistance flows through NGOs than through the entire UN system, excluding multilateral lending agencies (Mathews 1997). Indeed, much of the aid that does pass through the UN is also handled by NGOs. Independent UN agencies with humanitarian field operations (including UNHCR, UNDP and the WFP) routinely distribute emergency assistance through NGOs that have direct contact that recipients (Duffield 1994b).

Delivering foreign aid is not the only foreign policy function performed by emerging NGO-government alliances. For example, in Eastern Europe and the former Soviet Union, the US State Department often takes a back seat to George Soros' Open Society Fund in timing and targeting aid to favour progressive (or cooperative) actors and governments (Bruck 1995).

Internationalist bureaucracies that are shrinking or threatened with cuts – including USAID, CIA and UNHCR – are increasing NGO partnerships to serve four broad purposes. First, they need to cut administrative and operational expenses. NGOs are attractive for their efficient use of funds and the budget flexibility of temporary project contracts. Second, in order to limit the extent of budget slashing, internationalist bureaucracies turn to NGOs to mobilize public and elite support for new missions. Secretary-General Boutros-Ghali (1996: 10) declared his dependence on NGOs to help persuade member nations to support UN activities: 'I wish to state as clearly as possible – I need the mobilizing power of NGOs'. By forming alliances with NGOs, executives of these bureaucracies seek to control the downsizing process and prevent draconian cuts. NGO alliances not only allow them to claim greater efficiency, but also amplify the case for funding new bureaucratic missions.

Third, NGOs are useful to internationalist bureaucracies that seek to maintain a global scope of operations embracing every continent and region, if not every country. Funding an NGO operation provides a representative presence and source of information in a particular country, but is cheaper than staffing a field office. Finally, the 'new world order' presents the international community with a host of new tasks such as demobilizing soldiers after peace agreements, and old tasks in new environments such as food aid to genocidal refugees, for which effective methods and techniques are not known. Hence, internationalist bureaucracies need to empower tactical experimentation. NGOs are ideal for this role, not only because their independence and diversity encourage innovation, but also because the sponsoring or funding agency can distance itself from failed NGO experiments.

All four purposes are well served under the rubric of early warning and conflict prevention. J. Brian Atwood, director of the USAID in the Clinton administration, championed conflict prevention as a new aid rationale (Atwood and Rogers 1997), and advocated government-NGO partnerships as an efficient method for achieving it. Conflict prevention offers a weak argument for budget expansion, but a stronger justification for avoiding excessive cuts that would cripple the international capacity for 'managing chaos' in failed states and humanitarian crises (Crocker *et al.* 1996). In a study for the CSIS, Natsios (1997) specifies the budget and bureaucratic requirements of creating a US capacity to respond to complex humanitarian emergencies. He argues that budget cuts that would close large numbers of USAID missions around the world would have a 'disastrous impact on both the early warning and emergency response capacity of the international system' (Rosenfeld 1997).

The early-warning imperative demands continued global engagement even in regions, such as Africa, that are peripheral to the dominant economic interpretation of national interest. Hence, the early-warning rationale for maintaining global bureaucratic scope is attractive not only among humanitarians in Geneva, but also among national security and intelligence analysts at Foggy Bottom and Langley.

Effective conflict prevention requires an enormous amount of tactical experimentation, because no one really knows how to prevent or resolve particular internal conflicts. Early-warning proponents argue (often implicitly, if they do not acknowledge the experimental nature of the enterprise) that this experimentation should be conducted by NGO personnel, mid-level state department officials, and UN civil servants. Based upon observation of emerging policy practice, Lund (1996) advocates constructing a regime of preventive diplomacy that is decentralized, multilateral and layered. This structure would empower middle and lower levels of the State Department, other foreign ministries, the UN and regional organizations, all working with NGOs, to conduct conflict resolution and prevention without necessarily raising the issue at higher political levels.

Boutros-Ghali advocated increasing partnerships between NGOs and UN organizations in terms that echo these objectives. While giving little credence to the objective of using NGO partnerships to downsize the UN, he did acknowledge the prominent role of NGOs in delivering assistance, often 'under perilous and difficult conditions' (1996: 9). He also called for NGO help to mobilize member state support for UN peacebuilding missions, to act on every continent to promote democracy and warn of nascent crises, and to test new ideas and approaches.

In summary, NGOs are integral to the policy project of preventive diplomacy. In internationalist bureaucracies the discourse of 'early warning and conflict prevention' is linked closely to the practice of forming NGO alliances to serve objectives of cutting costs, mobilizing support, maintaining global operational scope and innovating new techniques.

10.2.2 There on the ground

If they are essential partners for conflict prevention, part of the reason is that NGOs are there on the ground (or can get there quickly) in countries undergoing or vulnerable to conflict and humanitarian crisis. The presence of NGOs from a variety of normative sectors in countries prone to civil war was taken for granted in the mid-1990s. In fact, this is a comparatively recent development. Each of five well-established sectors of humanitarian NGOs was originally designed with a mandate that excluded civil wars, and each sector passed through a complex historical process to alter its mandate and standard practice in order to operate in the midst of internal conflicts. As a consequence, although NGOs are there on the ground in internal conflicts, they are often pulling in different directions.

Space limitations prohibit a detailed analysis here. Briefly, relief and development NGOs were designed to favour governments, but now work rather indiscriminately with any insurgent, warlord or predatory government that controls access to population (DeMars 1997). Human rights NGOs have consistently monitored violations in civil wars only since 1991, and they provide an analysis that can clash with the relief and development agenda (Amnesty International 1994; Human Rights Watch 1993). Refugee NGOs are in a position to influence major power government policy toward civil wars because the interpretation of displacement issues is central to generating the political will for humanitarian action. The ICRC cooperates with other operational organizations active on the ground, but the Red Cross notion of neutrality is at odds with the growing assumption that humanitarian action always influences the course of wars (Ignatieff 1997). Finally, conflict resolution NGOs seek to influence a society's definition of citizenship, which controls the bounds of its political community, while claiming neutrality in the conflict between rival ethnic groups (Leatherman *et al.* 1999). The dynamism and diversity of the NGO community can be expected to continue to evolve.

10.2.3 All good things

The working assumption of much NGO policy in conflict arenas is that all NGO action contributes to conflict prevention and conflict resolution. To some extent, this is a necessary premise for NGO involvement because projects are designed to be modular, portable and replicable. Whatever the mandate, NGOs market their services in universal terms that minimize the importance of differences between contexts of action.

At stake is whether there is any generic preventive action that can be expected to dampen conflict regardless of the effects of intervening variables. The innocent case for NGO conflict prevention holds that there is reliable, generic preventive action. This has been called 'blind prevention' whose effectiveness is independent of the particular conditions within which it is applied (Nicolaïdis 1996: 26). In general, NGO action would contribute to conflict resolution if three subsidiary assumptions hold:

i) NGO actions generally produce their intended effects, ii) successful NGO action in any mandate encourages conflict prevention (or 'all good things go together'), and iii) the inadvertent consequences of NGO actions are either benign or less significant than the intended consequences.

To spell out these assumptions invites an analysis of the conditions under which they hold, or how they can be made to hold. Indeed, much of the emerging policy literature on conflict prevention explores just those questions. Without reviewing the entire literature, it is possible to identify several of the obstacles that interfere with the causal link from NGO action to effective conflict prevention.

10.3 The end of innocence: barriers to NGO conflict prevention

This section calls into question the three assumptions above, which underlie the belief that NGO action in any field automatically serves conflict prevention.

10.3.1 Hidden failure

The first assumption, that NGO actions generally produce their intended effects, would seem the most solid of the three. Indeed it is, as a first approximation. Relief NGOs deliver food that is eaten by hungry people; human rights NGOs report accurate information on violations; refugee NGOs call attention to situations with real potential for generating migration, or actual displaced populations; conflict resolution NGOs get people talking across ethnic barriers. The extent of outright fraud and dissembling is relatively unimportant, and uninteresting in this context.

At the same time, to scratch below the surface of NGO operations is to discover missing links in the causal chain from action to effectiveness. Among seasoned professionals, relief NGOs are notorious for neglecting to evaluate the effectiveness of their operations in the last emergency, in favour of moving on to the next big famine (Kent 1987; Cuny 1983). De Waal (1990) has presented substantial evidence that Africans die from famine at much lower rates than predicted by international organizations, and that famine survivors in Africa owe less to international food aid, and much more to indigenous famine survival strategies, than international relief providers are willing to acknowledge. NGO predictions of famine mortality are often less scientific assessments of reality than political statements designed to bludgeon lethargic aid bureaucracies into action. Tactical exaggeration is a well-established practice in the relief field, and the numbers are rarely corrected in retrospect. This selective inattention is an element of the relief culture, 'Those in the relief business are familiar with such exaggeration, but it has always been considered bad taste to draw attention to it, for fear of sounding callous' (de Waal and Omaar 1994a: 7).

For human rights NGOs, the problem is not accuracy of information, but focus and priority. Many humanitarian and political observers want to know, not necessarily the details of particular violations, but instead the relative scale and seriousness of human rights problems for comparative analysis of different countries or the same country over time. Some human rights NGOs have actively thwarted researchers who sought to quantify NGO data on human rights abuses for comparison across cases and over time (Lopez and Stohl 1991). NGOs worry that such quantification would lend violators an excuse that they were not as bad as other violators, and would lead the public to lose the sense that each violation is unacceptable and the rights of each victim are precious.

Another problem is that the mandate that serves as a lens for seeing part of reality also acts as a filter to exclude other dimensions. Human rights NGOs may highlight a relatively minor violation and ignore larger ones due to a mismatch between NGO mandates and the nature of violence in a particular conflict. Today this problem is reduced, because the increasing number of NGOs in the global human rights movement has made it more difficult to perpetrate large-scale violence undetected. And there have been spectacular examples of effective and timely monitoring, such as the Human Rights Watch reporting on the genocide in Rwanda during mid-1994 (Des Forges 1996).

In the refugee field, to predict a refugee flow requires making assumptions about the causal linkages between violence or malnutrition and people's decision to migrate. These are often little more than guesswork. The Horn of Africa during the late 1980s developed a bevy of 'systems' for early warning of famine and migration, run by NGOs, UN agencies, donor governments and ministries of regional governments. They collected large quantities of data on indicators such as rainfall, crop yields, food reserves, nutritional status, local food prices, death rates and eating 'famine foods'. All this effort yielded no agreement on the causal relationships of the various indicators to each other, as some practitioners candidly admitted (USAID 1989; Kent 1989). Predicting and preventing mass migrations is guesswork – albeit morally and politically necessary – that gains a veneer of scientific authority from early-warning systems.

Research on peace processes in Africa yields a mixed conclusion on the efficacy of international NGO peacemaking initiatives. In a recent set of studies, only one externally initiated project was reported to have unambiguously positive outcomes. International projects were often thwarted while local initiatives succeeded. One study of the 1994 resolution of intra-ethnic conflict in southern Sudan concluded: 'The involvement of international organizations or governmental agencies needs to be kept to a minimum and strategically employed to address specific gaps in the process and not as a substitute for indigenous leadership' (Smock 1997: 19). This conclusion appears to call into question part of the mission of the emerging sector of conflict resolution NGOs.[6]

In summary, NGOs feed large numbers of people but may not save many from dying of starvation; NGOs report human rights violations but do not reliably highlight the greatest sources of violence; NGOs predict refugee flows on the basis of questionable assumptions of their causation; and NGOs bring conflict resolution techniques into local situations often without resolving conflicts. In addition, for the relatively new NGO sector of democracy promotion, recent evidence suggests that the tangible results are quite thin (Wedel 1998; Carothers 1996). Hence, it is questionable to what degree international NGOs actually produce their intended effects. The reality probably falls well short of the image.

It is important to recognize that these conclusions are derived from analysis conducted within the humanitarian community, which is, thus, capable of self-evaluation and learning. This capacity to collect and analyse information, though largely a side-effect of the intended purposes of NGO work, is one of its most important and useful consequences.

10.3.2   Unintended consequences

'All good things go together' is the second assumption behind the idea that principled NGO action contributes automatically to conflict prevention.[7] According to this assumption, the political, economic and social contexts of humanitarian action can be ignored with the confidence that effective action in one sector such as human rights or relief aid will redound positively to dampen conflict, or will at least do no harm.

This assumption may have been sustainable during the Cold War, when the context for humanitarian action was relatively stable if less than benign, but it is called into question as the obscure outlines of new patterns of world politics come into view. Two new elements of the global context that influence the consequences of humanitarian action are the new threshold for political salience of humanitarianism in the North, and the changing nature of the state in the South. These are tentative explorations of emerging realities, so are as much hypotheses about where we are going as descriptions of where we are.

There is a significant gap between the discourse of early warning and conflict prevention and the actual policy practice. How this gap is rooted in the utility of the prevention agenda for downsizing internationalist bureaucracies was discussed earlier. Here the concern is to spell out the implications of the gap for policy practice. The 'early' in early warning takes on a bitterly ironic meaning for the victims of internal conflict, and a hidden meaning for the major power governments that design the responses to conflict. Observing the practice of the international community since 1993 supports a view that conflict prevention is considered early enough if it meets three priorities of cost containment. In descending order of importance, the first priority is to contain internal conflict from escalating to interstate war, the second is to contain the outflow of refugees (at least to DCs), and the third is to contain the financial and political cost of humanitarian programmes.

By these criteria, conflict prevention has been successful in both the Great Lakes region of Africa and the former Yugoslavia. To a humanitarian sensibility it is astonishing and offensive to attribute success in conflict prevention to international policies that have allowed genocidal killing, the displacement of millions and innovative forms of ethnic warfare. Nevertheless, neither crisis has escalated to open interstate war (covert, proxy wars between neighbouring states follow well-established practice in LDCs), and refugees and displaced persons have been successfully contained within each region. And while the financial costs have been substantial, the political costs to major power presidents and prime ministers have remained well below those of the Somalia debacle.

These two regions have been the focus of considerable innovation in the policy practice of early warning, and allow an empirical analysis of the operational meaning of 'early'. Countless delegations of NGOs, diplomats and journalists have visited Burundi in the years since 1994, earnestly seeking to 'prevent another Rwanda', generally understood to be an escalation of violence to a scale approaching a million deaths. As part of the effort to contain the conflict and prevent escalation, humanitarian NGOs and UN agencies provided relief assistance for up to one million 'dispersed and displaced' persons within Burundi and just outside its borders (Sollom and Kew 1996). At the same time, calling this 'prevention' signalled the international community's tolerance of the ongoing killing of several hundred people per week in Burundi, with a cumulative death toll of more than 10 000 a year. Lemarchand (1998: 5) observed that 'no other country in the continent has received more assiduous attention from so many conflict-resolution experts than Burundi over the last three years – and with so few results'.

A strange puzzle is how to explain the deterioration of relatively effective conflict prevention in Kosovo. While violence flared in Bosnia and Croatia from 1991 to 1995, Kosovo seemed immune. It was fully revealed only in 1999 that US Secretary of State Lawrence Eagleburger, in the closing days of the Bush administration in December 1992, sent a cable directly to Yugoslav President Milosevic stating, 'In the event of conflict in Kosovo caused by Serbian action, the US will be prepared to employ military force against Serbs in Kosovo and in Serbia proper' (quoted in Gellman 1999). The threat was reiterated twice in the first year of the Clinton administration and then allowed to dissipate. If the warning had been sustained with credibility, perhaps the NATO military action against Serbia in 1999 could have been avoided.

The three priorities of cost containment do not include humanitarian values. In other words, according to the patterns of major power action, neither relief assistance nor human rights protection in their own right constitutes criteria for successful conflict prevention. Humanitarian values may be proclaimed as the official objectives of multilateral operations, but they are pursued selectively – only when they overlap with at least one of the three goals of cost containment. There are two ways to view this reality from the point of view of human values. The pessimist despairs that humanitarianism in its many expressions is used opportunistically to support political ends. The optimist is grateful that there still exists some political basis to empower humanitarian action, and seeks creative ways to extend its reach.

One clear implication of this analysis is that the proposal to use conflict prevention as a rationale for a serious increase in ODA to LDCs is unlikely to be taken up by wealthy states. The rhetoric of 'early' prevention notwithstanding, foreign assistance on a scale sufficient to stabilize national economies and governments is not the wave of the future. The Westerners who allowed genocide to rage uncontrolled in Europe during the fiftieth anniversary of the victory over the Nazis are not about to have an attack of conscience about LDC development. More to the point, the premise that development in the South can be generated by aid from the North is based on an image of the third-world state that no longer reflects reality.

10.3.3   State of the state

The third-world state is changing.[8] With few exceptions, the authoritarian welfare state is being replaced by either the democratic privatizing state or the collapsing state. International NGOs have played significant roles in all three forms of state, under conditions of both peace and war. The impact of NGO action in LDCs depends crucially on the kind of state within which it is acting.

The mainstays of the authoritarian welfare state were superpower military assistance and both bilateral and multilateral economic aid. This is a broad state form that embraces a wide range of regime types including military juntas, personal rule, various Marxist models and a spectrum from populist to predatory. In all variations of the authoritarian state, international development NGOs patched the holes in the state welfare blanket by sustaining the poorest populations. By supplementing the state's welfare functions, and legitimizing its promises of upward mobility, development NGOs acted as auxiliaries of an expanding state (Murphy 1994).

This form of third-world state sowed the seeds of its own demise because dependency on external aid encouraged internal corruption, heavy handed repression and counterproductive economic policy – all of which made the state more vulnerable to challenge by armed rebels (DeMars 2000). In short, nostalgia for blind conflict prevention through NGO development programmes is misplaced, not only because the authoritarian state within which such prevention could work is now all but dead, but also because that form of the state generated self-destructive internal contradictions.

The third-world state is shrinking in size and economic capacity due to the highly competitive environment of international trade and investment, decreases in foreign aid from the North, and structural adjustment policies of the IFIs (Sood 1995). With the single exception of Egypt, the international aid-supported authoritarian welfare state is no longer sustainable, even in the short term. One emergent model appears to be the democratic privatizing state, a form now hegemonic in Latin America and perhaps gaining ground in Asia and Central Europe. In this form, governments shed both welfare and productive functions in order to compete for foreign investment. Popular sectors in Latin America give up welfare in return for minimal human rights protections and democratic citizenship. In this context, international development NGOs both legitimize and mitigate the retrenchment of government welfare functions providing incomplete replacements for a shrinking state (Reilly 1995).

The Chiapas rebellion may represent the characteristic form of civil war in the democratic privatizing state. Its crucial battles are fought in the arena of international media (including the computer Internet) rather than on the ground, and rebels 'target' international investors and NGO audiences as much as government installations. Cross-border coalitions of NGOs become central actors in such conflicts (Ronfeldt and Thorup 1995). Conflict prevention in an environment of state democratization and economic privatization involves NGOs in growing numbers and diversification of mandates. Conflict prevention is a secondary agenda for many NGOs addressing human rights, population control, women's issues, environment, indigenous peoples, and democratization. The case for blind conflict prevention through supporting these diverse NGO mandates rests on their common role in expanding democratic space. However, there is evidence that such activities, and even the process of democratization itself, sometimes spawn violent conflict instead of stanching it.

Another successor for the authoritarian welfare state is the collapsing state. In this form, not only welfare and production, but also state security functions are 'privatized' into the hands of warlords, mercenaries, transnational criminal organizations and privateers (Reno 1998; Keen 1994; Rondos 1994). The phenomenon of ethnic conflict, particularly in Africa, is often little more than an ideological veneer for violence that serves private economic gain. In other cases, including the least successful transitions from communism in Central Europe and the former USSR, ethnic conflict may represent an intermediate form of authoritarian welfare state in the process of collapse.[9]

In summary, the innocent assumption that all good things go together for NGO action in conflict settings is challenged by the existence of two new elements in world politics – the cost containment criteria for international political support for conflict prevention, and the prevalence of the collapsing state. These two global elements work together to put NGOs in unsustainable positions: governments thrust NGOs into lead roles in CHEs without doing the necessary political spadework to facilitate humanitarian action; and the nature of conflict in collapsing states is such that any external input is easily distorted into serving anti-humanitarian ends.

10.3.4   Inadvertent power

This brings us to the third assumption of innocence: that the inadvertent consequences of NGO actions are either benign or less significant than the intended consequences. A growing body of evidence suggests that the inadvertent power of NGOs in collapsing states may be as important, or more important, than either success or failure in achieving desired outcomes. In other words, the side-effects of humanitarian action may be more important that the intended effects. While few practitioners might agree with this bold assertion, most would acknowledge that the post-Cold War environment for humanitarian action makes it much more difficult for NGOs to ignore the political context, and political impact, of their actions.

The inadvertent power of NGOs in civil wars and humanitarian crises takes several distinct forms. First, NGOs provide material and political resources to warring parties. This is the most familiar form, and has a long history. The accusation that international relief aid is 'prolonging a war' goes back at least to the Nigerian civil war, as does the policy of some NGOs providing humanitarian assistance on one side of a war out of solidarity with the people and a perceived just cause (Jacobs 1987). It has been known for long that relief food, even when it is not diverted for direct military or economic gain, can free up resources by feeding a civilian population, can deter enemy attack on the locations of relief activities, and can provide other benefits through port fees, enhancing roads and logistics, and stimulating the local economy. However, the nature of civil war has changed in ways that make the consequences of supporting today's adversaries more alarming (Anderson 1999).

Not only has the nature of internal war changed; the international humanitarian network has altered as well. Today, NGOs of some stripe will work with almost any adversary no matter how predatory its treatment of the population under its control. In the absence of large-scale external assistance from major powers, and with impoverished local economies unable to sustain taxation, many of today's adversaries in civil wars survive on the margin. In such an environment of scarcity, the relatively modest economic spillover from the operations of an international relief NGO can bolster local warlords.

Aside from material benefits, NGOs can promote the political prominence of an adversary in the international arena by negotiating with them for humanitarian access to victims of the conflict. For example, the name Laurent Kabila first appeared in the *International Herald Tribune* in a story that quoted the head of a refugee advocacy NGO who had just returned from seeing Kabila in the bush (Buckley 1996). Public reports of human rights violations can also reinforce conflict dynamics by fuelling the identity of righteous victimization on the part of the groups that suffer the violence (Anderson 1999).

The second form of NGO inadvertent power in civil wars and humanitarian crises is less familiar. In collapsing states, NGOs and UN agencies find themselves creating or sustaining state-like structures in order to establish the necessary preconditions for humanitarian action. At various stages of the Somali emergency, each agency hired a separate contingent of armed guards in order to protect individual aid operations from looting by the fighters of various factions. The political economy of violence was such that fighters were not paid by their respective warlords, but supported themselves by looting both the population and the international aid agencies. Protection for the relief operation itself required hiring some of the fighters to give them an alternate source of support. This practice has been generalized to other emergencies, and some NGOs employ, in effect, small private armies to protect relief operations (Slim 1995).

Aid agencies create another form of state-like structure when they establish elements of local government representation or administration as part of relief operations. 'Operation Lifeline Sudan' has been the scene of innovative experimentation in recent years.[10] However, such external social engineering can be hazardous. In camps for Rwandan refugees in eastern Zaire in 1994–95, many agencies attempted to build alternative representative structures to limit the power of the former government and militias of Rwanda who were present in the camps. A prominent international NGO hired groups of young refugee men as 'scouts' to lead the food distribution. Some scouts clashed with the militia, which responded by driving out the NGO and killing all the scouts.

It seems reasonable to conclude that local governmental structures created by international NGO or UN relief agencies in collapsing states must either fade away, merge with local warlords or other power centres, or be crushed by them. This is a dangerous game for NGOs to play without support by major powers behind the scenes pressuring warring parties to respect the prerogatives of humanitarian action.

The inadvertent power of NGO action in collapsing states is a mixture of desirable and undesirable consequences, depending on one's normative position. The benefits that a warring party may gain from humanitarian aid or human rights reporting are undesirable from the perspectives of Red Cross neutrality and conflict prevention, but perhaps desirable if one thinks that victory by a particular party would bring greater justice or stability. The consequences of NGO action for creating state-like structures of local representation are desirable if stable peace can come only from reconstructing the territorial state system. Alternatives to the sovereign state are under serious consideration in some quarters, particularly for Africa (Herbst 1996/97).

The three assumptions underlying a belief in the automaticity of NGO contributions to conflict prevention – that NGO action generally produces its intended effect, that all good things go together, and that inadvertent consequences are benign or insignificant – are all called into serious question by the scrutiny the prevention agenda itself has engendered. The conclusion is clear: there is no generic preventive action; there is no blind prevention. To deliver relief aid, or establish a development project, or report human rights violations, or predict displacement, or engender relationships across ethnic groups, or promote democratic practices does not necessarily strengthen conflict prevention. Any action can be hijacked by the entrepreneurs of conflict. The context must be attended to, and operations must be adjusted and adapted to particular circumstances as they evolve. There is no generic preventive action for governments and the UN, either. Neither military deployment nor personal diplomacy will succeed without being harmonized to the particular realities of the conflict. In Somalia, both methods were bungled, and both succeeded when in competent hands (Sahnoun 1994; Crocker 1995). If international actors must tailor their actions to particular circumstances, they need detailed information on which to base the adjustments. For information on CHEs and the conflicts from which they emerge, governments and the UN turn to NGOs. Despite all their weaknesses, this is one way that NGOs are indispensable to continued international engagement.

The paradox that is central to the role of NGOs in conflict prevention, and to the project of conflict prevention itself, has now been reached. On the one hand, the assumptions of innocence that underpin faith in the efficacy of generic NGO prevention have been shown to be deeply problematic. Whether NGO action is early or late, it is often unable to accomplish its mandated goals, and success in this does not translate reliably to effective conflict prevention. Moreover, the inadvertent consequences of NGO action are as likely to foment conflict as to dampen it. In short, of the good intentions that NGOs bring to CHEs, many are not achieved, and many others do not go together. On the other hand, if generic conflict prevention cannot succeed, a tailored and fine-tuned approach might. But it turns out that NGOs, with their flaws and contradictions intact, are indispensable for acquiring the detailed information on which the fine-tuning must be based.

10.4   The edge of innocence: a chastened case for NGO conflict prevention

NGOs will continue to be recruited for lead roles in early warning and conflict prevention, despite their particular failures and weaknesses. Facing the high potential for conflict in peripheral regions, the new reflex of US policymakers and the international community – strapped for funds and lacking either political will from above or popular support from below for stronger measures – is to 'throw NGOs at the problem'. In practice this will mean stretching shrunken aid budgets by channelling them through NGOs (either directly or through a UN intermediary), encouraging experimental NGO tactics, relying on NGO advocacy to build popular support for government engagement, and drawing upon NGO information on the evolving situation.

Throwing NGOs at the problem accomplishes much less than a naive faith in the promises and goals of NGO mandates would lead one to expect, and may be counterproductive in some respects. Nevertheless, this response is a reasonable one given a general lack of information, and the uncertain effectiveness and much greater cost of other policy options. Swarming a country with NGOs may or may not be effective from the point of view of immediate conflict prevention, but it serves policy-makers in several ways. First, it buys time with low-risk operations by independent actors whose misadventures can be disavowed by governments, while avoiding premature commitment to a costly policy that may be unsustainable politically or operationally. Second, NGOs can break the monopoly on information held by authoritarian governments or opposition groups by gathering information across a broad range of issues, geographic areas and demographic groups and conveying that information to world capitals. Third, operational NGOs bypass the central state structures of LDCs' governments, thereby serving the broad US strategy of shrinking the local state. Finally, NGOs generate and legitimize an array of future policy options for governments, ranging from a minimal agenda of conflict containment through a maximal agenda of military intervention. NGOs accomplish this by their analysis and advocacy of particular policies, and even more so by their very presence and engagement with actors in the conflict.

NGO advocacy can generate public support for government action and provide allies for bureaucratic policy battles. NGO presence offers conduits for resources and channels for communication with indigenous political elites. Best of all from the point of view of the government policy-maker, NGOs are so diverse and contentious among themselves, and so individually weak, that they present a broad menu for selective coalition with government sectors. A government can selectively empower one sector or NGO and shape its policies, or can select an NGO normative discourse to legitimize either inaction or action.

So, NGOs rarely provide solutions for emerging or raging conflicts, but they do provide engagement that enhances government policy-maker options for informed future action. The realistic alternative in particular situations is not multilateral, principled, decisive action. The more likely alternative is disengagement and ignorance of the real situation.

In several respects the conflict prevention agenda is bad news for NGOs. Governments with little political will and few resources thrust NGOs forward as a substitute for an effective response to humanitarian crises. NGOs are besieged by the hazards of operating in collapsing states, and their normative principles are compromised by the donor priority of cost containment. As a consequence, warning and action are chronically late, wearing thin the 'early' in the policy formula. At the same time that NGOs are put in these impossible situations, their operations are subject to unprecedented levels of scrutiny by other NGOs, academics, intelligence agencies and foreign ministries. While in public NGO personnel continue to celebrate the new mandate as a source of funds and policy access, they may increasingly lament the intractable political tangles they are asked to finesse in the name of prevention.

International NGOs have managed to function in environments of contradictory political agendas before. During the Cold War these agendas were relatively familiar and stable, and navigating their hazards became second nature to relief and human rights NGOs. Today, as political realities shift under their feet, NGOs of various stripes are forced to pay more attention to politics in order to stay out of it, or at least to pick the right partner. If the analysis here is correct, NGOs may not be so out of place in such settings. Working on the edge of political innocence may be precisely what international NGOs do best.

Notes

1. For the theory and policy of early warning and conflict prevention, see Leatherman *et al.* (1999); Carnegie Commission (1997); Crocker *et al.* (1996); Rotberg (1996); and DeMars (1995).
2. Leading examples include Rubin (1998); Lund (1996); Rotberg (1996); and Prendergast (1996b).
3. For recent analyses of NGOs in world politics from a variety of perspectives, see Korey (1998); Keck and Sikkink (1998); Smith *et al.* (1997); Hulme and Edwards (1997); Weiss and Gordenker (1996); and Willetts (1996).
4. For introductions to these sectors, see Henkin (1995); Best (1994); Loescher (1993); and Forsythe (1991).
5. Smith (1990) and Slim (1995) have characterized relief and development NGOs as 'chameleons' that operate between politics and neutrality.
6. For an alternate view, see IPA (1996).
7. Packenham (1973) identified the assumption that 'All good things go together' as a liberal premise embedded in theories of political development and modernization influential during the 1950s and 1960s.
8. On the changing LDC state, see Reno (1998); Ayoob (1995); Wendt and Barnett (1993); and Jackson (1991).
9. Snyder (1993: 12) has called ethnic nationalism the 'default option' of failed states. Lake and Rothchild (1996) argue that ethnic conflict is rooted in state weakness and the fear that it generates.
10. The following material is from interviews in Washington, DC by the author during October 1995.

11
Multilateral Military Responses
Thomas G. Weiss

11.1   Introduction

Experimentation with humanitarian delivery and protection continues as a dominant characteristic of world politics. The collective inability to act early highlights that 'prevention' has penetrated international discourse but not practice. The most striking Western reaction to humanitarian crises in the last half decade has been unleashing the humanitarian impulse, with outside military forces in the avant-garde.[1]

That almost 1 per cent of the world's population is displaced by war, and probably an equal number have remained behind with totally disrupted lives (Hampton 1998; ICRC 2000; UNHCR 1997), is one motivation to improve third-party military responses in war zones. Another is the oft-cited switch from military toward civilian war fatalities, which now constitute 95 rather than the 5–10 per cent of total war fatalities earlier in this century. This chapter asks whether the military could be used earlier to prevent crises.

However, the actual politics and risks of pro-action are in many ways more complex than those of reaction. Military prevention of CHEs is highly problematic because of the decentralized and anarchic nature of international relations, the relative weakness in multilateral capacities, and the lack of perceived vital interests by most major powers in CHEs. Prevention is cost-effective in the long run but cost-intensive in the short run and has a similar fundamental problem as collective security (Downs 1994; Lepgold and Weiss 1998). Key domestic constituencies must be per-suaded to pay substantial immediate costs in order to gain uncertain future benefits. Counterfactuals with high price-tags and political risks are hard sells. The focus here is thus on multilateral military interventions after massive tragedies. Whether the objective is prevention or reaction, the essential first step is to understand the costs and benefits of previous military interventions, rather than function in what Roberts (1996: 8) has called a 'policy vacuum'.

211

Euphoria at the end of the Cold War was short-lived. The seeming backlash (Ramsbotham and Woodhouse 1996; Harriss 1995) against 'military-civilian humanitarianism' overlooks varying costs and benefits of such efforts since 1991 (Jackson 1993; Weiss 1997, 1999a). Humanitarian interventions may become less prevalent than earlier in the 1990s, but 1999 interventions in East Timor and Kosovo provide evidence that this policy option remains relevant.

11.2   The contribution by armed forces to humanitarian action

The more routine involvement by third-party military forces in humanitarian efforts in war zones is a phenomenon of the post-Cold War era, but the use of military forces for such purposes is not new (Cuny 1991). In fact, often there is an almost automatic association in the Western public's mind between the military and disaster relief, with the expectation that the armed forces will assist civilian populations after emergency strikes.

In the last half century, military assistance in natural disasters has become a routine extension of civil defence. Armed forces often possess an abundance of precisely those resources that are in the shortest supply when disaster strikes: transport, fuel, communications, commodities, building equipment, medicines and large stockpiles of off-the-shelf provisions. In addition, the military's vaunted 'can-do' mentality, self-supporting character, and rapid response capabilities as well as its hierarchical discipline are useful within the turmoil of acute tragedies.

But the military actually performs two functions in the humanitarian arena: logistics (relief activities and support for civilian relief agencies) *and* security. It is not easy to distinguish the two components of humanitarian 'action', delivery and protection, because they are so linked (Weiss and Collins 2000). Also, it is easier to quantify delivery than protection, which is why so much attention is paid to goods and personnel devoted to the delivery of food, medicines and shelter in war zones. 'Protection' amounts to more than human-rights monitors or legal protection officers in the employ of UNHCR, but is harder to measure (Cohen and Cuenod 1993; Henkin 1995).

The discussions of using the armed forces in war zones often conflate the two functions. The first benefit is the logistics cornucopia through the provision of direct assistance to people in need and also to support the work of civilian organizations. The second benefit results from the military's direct exercise of security capacities, related to its primary function of war-fighting and using superior force to overwhelm an enemy. The military can gain access to suffering civilians, when insecurity makes it impossible or highly dangerous, and foster a secure environment to permit succour and protection for civilians. The security function has come under severe commentary from sympathizers and critics alike, with 'humanitarian intervention' and 'humanitarian war' often viewed as oxymorons (Roberts 1993). Moreover, in the absence of leadership from the major powers, the potential political costs of body bags or of involvement in a quagmire have led to something akin to a zero-casualty foreign policy, an obvious constraint for the exercise of the protection function.

The end of the Cold War meant the evaporation of the *raison d'être* for the bulk of military spending in the West. The much-vaunted peace dividend did not materialize, but the availability of military help for humanitarian tasks seemed to be a 'dividend'. The successful allied mobilization for the Gulf War and the subsequent use of the armed forces in support of humanitarianism in northern Iraq along with substantial if sometimes less popular versions in Somalia, Bosnia, Rwanda and Haiti have provided a means for militaries to fend off pressures to reduce their infrastructure and personnel. A quip about the US military seems to have more general applicability: 'For the near future our military is more likely to participate in humanitarian interventions and in peacekeeping than it is to participate in war or in peace enforcement' (Seiple 1996: v–vi).

11.3 Five post-Cold War cases of military–civilian humanitarianism

The dramatic acceleration in the number and variety of UN military missions has been accompanied by proliferation of analyses about multilateral military operations.[2] Aware of the usual problems in comparing incomparable cases, here we will hazard some general policy lessons across disparate cases in the post-Cold War era, after first considering methodological issues.

11.3.1 Some methodological issues

First, the armed forces and humanitarian agencies are not forthcoming about data. Reliable data about the actual costs of delivery (of goods and alternative modes) are sketchy and usually not comparable among sources (Brown and Rosencrance 1999; Wallensteen 1998b). There is no standard methodology for reporting, even among OECD Development Assistance Committee (DAC) members.

Second, the emphasis on costs and benefits entails ambiguities, biasing analyses in favour of delivery over protection although both are essential and mutually reinforcing components of humanitarian action. Effective action in war relieves life-threatening suffering by providing emergency assistance and protecting human rights, both difficult to measure except by their absence or presence; relief, however, can be better quantified.

It is fair to criticize the military's unwillingness to undertake tasks that they could have, but did not, or to lambaste political authorities who refused to agree to appropriate mandates (for example, for demining territory, disarming belligerents or arresting war criminals). However, it is unfair to condemn the military for refusing to perform functions that go beyond their mandates (for example, reconciliation or addressing the roots of a conflict). It is unreasonable to judge the military in acute emergencies by standards against which even development and civilian humanitarian agencies measure up poorly (Uvin 1998), for example empowerment of local communities, avoiding dependence or fostering reconciliation.

This criticism of military help failing to address the 'roots' of hurricanes or earthquakes would appear ridiculous during natural disasters, but somehow such arguments receive more credibility in war. External military intervention can improve access and help move relief goods, contributing to an environment where human-rights abuses become less frequent. Intervention can also provide time for belligerents and outside mediators to launch activities. But the presence of outside military forces alone cannot resolve an armed conflict. The decision to use military forces should be seen as a temporary respite, not a solution.

Moreover, qualifying a 'success' or a 'failure' is problematic. Perceptions in troop-contributing countries about a particular humanitarian intervention are critical for future actions. External impact can be measured by determining the willingness of states to mount other diplomatic and military efforts and for publics and parliaments to support subsequent humanitarian undertakings – for example the contrast between bullish and skittish US discourse after northern Iraq and Somalia, respectively. Attempting to measure impacts within affected areas necessitates attaching a value to human life, which poses uncomfortable moral challenges.

Inevitably, value judgements, timing and objectives of actors and analysts, and the hidden agendas of UN politics and deliberations enter into the military decision. As an example, were military efforts in northern Iraq a success because 1.5 million Kurds were saved, or a failure because almost a decade later Saddam Hussein was still ensconced in Baghdad scoffing at international decisions? Were military operations in Somalia successful because death rates dropped in 1993, or a long-term failure because billions were spent to stop the clock temporarily?

Third, of cases of military operations and humanitarian action after the Cold War, five examples were selected because of their political prominence in the mid-1990s and because of modest historical distance from 2000. They undoubtedly affected calculations in the ministries of defence of the major powers concerning East Timor and Kosovo. Moreover, all were subject to scrutiny by the UNSC before outside military forces intervened under Chapter VII authorization.

These cases illustrate military–civilian humanitarianism without the pretence of neutrality, a less naive but more controversial approach than that championed by the ICRC and other humanitarian organizations as well (Wiener 1998; Weiss 1999b). The crises of the post-Cold War era are inspiring a growing literature about the politics of rescue (de Waal and Omaar

1995), including Betts' (1994) indication of 'the delusion of impartial intervention'.

There are varying circumstances and purposes for using force and myriad differences in UN involvement within and among the five case studies (Goulding 1996). Although in every case US participation has been crucial, the most significant change in the 1990s is that 'the emphasis has shifted from unilateral interventions' (Hoffmann 1995/96: 30). Moreover, for the US, multilateral military intervention is to be used in the future rather than the more unilateral forms of the past.

Meanwhile, there are case studies with data about costs and benefits that can be used: northern Iraq from 1991 to 1996; Somalia from 1992 to 1995; Bosnia from 1992 to 1995; Rwanda from 1994 to 1995; and Haiti from 1995 to 1996. This analysis complements work by Brown and Rosencrance (1999) to identify the costs of responding to versus preventing deadly conflicts.

In short, the five cases were all CHEs in which the UNSC authorized Chapter VII coercion, overriding the sovereignty of the political authorities in the targeted country. The cases thus can illustrate both the logistics and security capacities of the armed forces acting in a post-Cold War world in which multilateral support for humanitarian intervention is preferable to more unilateral procedures of the past.

11.3.2   Northern Iraq

In the aftermath of the Gulf War and the first Chapter VII enforcement since Korea, international public opinion was sensitized and could not then ignore 1.5 million Kurds whose desperate plight constituted a huge humanitarian challenge that appeared virtually overnight. Hard and fast distinctions between domestic jurisdiction and international responsibilities were set aside.

The extent, strength and rapidity of the allied coalition's 'Operation Provide Comfort' were impressive from April to July 1991. Over 12 000 US and allied troops (the main other players were France, the UK and the Netherlands, but another dozen countries were also involved) were deployed on the basis of an authorization from the UNSC. They delivered more than 25 million pounds of food, water, medical supplies, clothing and shelter. Soldiers escorted Kurdish refugees from their mountain hideouts back to the safe havens created in northern Iraq.

After humanitarian aid was gradually handed back to UN agencies and NGOs, the security function remained central in saving the lives of the refugees who returned home and in maintaining Kurdish autonomy. Civilian personnel were able to function because they were backed by a NATO security guarantee. As one group of observers close to the US effort accurately summarized: 'The military was clearly most effective in the early stages than in the intermediate- and long-term activities. By coincidence, the NGOs tended to be less effective in the earlier stages and more effective in the later period' (Brilliant *et al.* 1992: 34).

The costs of these efforts from April 1991 to June 1992 were about US$800 million for 'Operation Provide Comfort', almost US$900 million for other military operations, and some US$1 billion for humanitarian assistance (Minear *et al.* 1992: 44). There were serious problems: airdrops into minefields, meals-ready-to-eat (MREs) spurned by Muslims on religious grounds, and disagreements with NGOs. However, the benefits were also impressive: 1.5 million refugees were saved and repatriated; and violence, famine, repression, chemical warfare and disease previously pursued as policy by Baghdad were reduced. This is perhaps the clearest case to date of what even such a thoughtful critic as Sadako Ogata (1994: 4) calls 'a rare example of successful humanitarian intervention'. US protection and assistance have cost an average US$130 million per year since the original withdrawal.

The longer-term benefits of the intervention are ambiguous. The political situation is uncertain, for the Saddam Hussein regime and for Kurdistan. Lives have undoubtedly been saved, but northern Iraq is hardly a pleasant place to live. Nor has rehabilitation and reconstruction, let alone reconciliation, begun.

11.3.3   Somalia

Three separate military operations should be distinguished regarding humanitarian delivery in the Horn of Africa. The first UN Operation in Somalia (UNOSOM I) began with the arrival of 500 Pakistani soldiers in September 1992 who were unable to deploy effectively. Another 2500 soldiers never arrived because their actual presence was contingent upon the consent of the warring parties. The Unified Task Force (UNITAF), or 'Operation Restore Hope' according to the Pentagon's terminology, took over in December 1992 on the basis of UNSC Resolution 794. The 37 000 soldiers (from 24 countries, with 26 000 from the US) remained until April 1993 with a unanimous Council mandate to use force to ensure the delivery of humanitarian relief. The second UN phase, UNOSOM II, took over and lasted until March 1995. UNSC Resolution 814 spelled out the mandate of this first enforcement action under the direct command and control of the Secretary-General, an action which was more ambitious than UNITAF's and was not only to ensure access but also to improve overall security by using whatever force was necessary to disarm Somali warlords.

The clumsy shift from Chapter VI (with consent) to Chapter VII (without consent), and from UN to US and then back to UN control but with an autonomous US rapid reaction capability during the last phase along with the lack of an overall political strategy, constituted one set of problems. The absence of commitment and staying power was another set. In Washington, the approval of Presidential Decision Directive 25 (PDD 25) in May 1994 marked the official end to the Clinton administration's pro-multilateral attitude and foreshadowed the ongoing political debate about purported US subservience to the UN (Daalder 1996; Luck 1999). Given the virtual necessity for Washington's participation in major multilateral military operations, the unseemly images of 18 dead marines in October 1993 were considerably more costly than the tragic loss of these individuals – military multilateralism was put in abeyance. Total fatalities during the UNOSOM I period were negligible (eight military personnel) and during UNOSOM II far higher (143 military personnel), though less politically damaging and less publicized than the US-led phase.

Among the criticisms of the military's involvement in the Horn of Africa are the high costs of military air transport and the unwillingness to make better use of professional armed convoys. Sommer (1994: 71) wrote: 'Road transport was extremely difficult due to insecurity and looting. However, one could have continued to use this means, as ICRC and others did for some 80 per cent of the commodities delivered. They did so by negotiating security agreements with local elders, paying for protection, and/or consciously agreeing to accept high delivery losses'. Even cost-benefit analyses, however, run into complicating factors. Airlifts had been used prior to the intervention to 'jump start' the relief effort because the media portrayed such action as possible even during the period between August and November. Since the Pentagon and other Western donors had absorbed most of the cost, such airlifts were not as 'costly' as the statistics indicated.

However, the disequilibrium between the military and humanitarian components was striking. The US-led 'Operation Restore Hope' alone cost US$1 billion (the net cost was probably half this amount), which was about three times Washington's total aid contributions to Somalia since independence. The cost of UNOSOM II was about US$1.6 billion. The estimate for humanitarian aid ranged from 0.7 to 0.10 per cent of the non-incremental total costs (Sapir and Deconnick 1995: 168).

The relative weight of humanitarian assistance as part of total expenditures seems disproportionate. Yet determining whether military expenditures were justified depends on the perspective of the evaluator. In 1992 some 4.5 million people were in dire need of assistance, and 1.5 million risked starvation. These figures fell substantially as a result of a combination of factors: better access and security combined with market forces, improved weather and renewed agriculture. Andrew Natsios, who headed Washington's Office of Foreign Disaster Assistance (OFDA) at the time, argued that food prices were the most critical element and believed that 'while the airlift actually substituted for other means of delivery, rather than adding net new food into the country, the psychological effect on traders who had been hoarding stocks was such as to cause them to release the stocks, thus causing the price decline' (Sommer 1994: 56; Natsios 1996). The harshest critics of Washington's intervention have claimed that the obstacles to food delivery were not as bad as commonly assumed (African

Rights 1993). However, UNITAF hardly hurt Somalia and was effective in opening up roads and providing security for humanitarian relief so that those who had not already died could leave camps and plant crops, and those without resources could receive food aid (Farrell 1995).

The degree of suffering lessened dramatically as 2 million displaced people at the height of the crisis had decreased two years later, in December 1994, to about 465 000 refugees and 300 000 IDPs (Natsios 1996: 90). The estimated 400 000 to 500 000 deaths in the two years preceding December 1992 resulted directly from inter-clan warfare, internal power struggles and repression, or indirectly from famine. This high level of vulnerability was halted and emergency delivery finally took place on a large scale (Refugee Policy Group 1994b).

When the last UN soldiers pulled out in March 1995, however, the ultimate result of military help and humanitarian delivery was unclear. It was a 'non-event,' wrote Prunier, and 'life went on pretty much the same way as it had gone on during the late UNOSOM 2 period' (1995b). Three years and some US$3–4 billion had left the warring parties better armed, rested and poised to resume civil war. The country remains without a central government or state services although clans appeared close to selecting a president in late 2000. Lives were saved and subsistence agriculture and pastoral life had been renewed. Gains from humanitarian intervention in the short term cannot hide the stark reality that a commitment to longer-term nation-building is an absolute requirement.

11.3.4   Bosnia

The soldiers of the UN Protection Force (UNPROFOR) in the former Yugoslavia were an essential part of the landscape circumscribing humanitarian action beginning in February 1992 until after the Dayton Accord authorized NATO's Implementation Force (IFOR). The discussion here will not deal with UN blue helmets playing a preventive role in Macedonia or supposedly acting as a buffer between Croats and Serbs in the Krajina and western Slavonia. The latter component of UNPROFOR clearly had substantial and negative humanitarian impacts because their inability to achieve objectives (collecting weapons and facilitating the return of refugees) ultimately led to an offensive in Western Slavonia in May 1995 and especially to the 36-hour 'Operation Storm' beginning late in August 1995. This latter and largely Croatian offensive resulted in the displacement of approximately 200 000 civilians and soldiers, the largest refugee flows in Europe since the Soviet crushing of the Hungarian revolt in 1956.

The focus is only on the UNPROFOR soldiers in Bosnia because the 2.7 million needy victims in Bosnia-Herzegovina were the main motivation for the largely Western military response under UN auspices – and later in Bosnia under NATO auspices[3] as they were in 1999 when Belgrade refused to sign an agreement with the Kosovars. The suffering that accompanied displacement and war has been well documented (Burke and Macdonald 1994; Meron 1997).

The emphasis on Bosnia is apt because for UNPROFOR there was a Chapter VII operation albeit only for the protection of humanitarian personnel at first but with a more comprehensive mandate afterwards for civilians in the so-called safe areas (Goulding 1996). The numbers reached some 22 000 soldiers, reinforced by an additional 12 500-strong NATO Rapid Reaction Force, before Dayton. UNPROFOR's total annual costs in 1994 and in 1995 reached US$1.5 billion, about 70 per cent for the humanitarian-motivated efforts in Bosnia. NATO's supporting costs are not available.

The task of fostering a secure environment was a dismal failure. Despite over 167 fatalities (most in Bosnia, although UN figures do not provide this breakdown) and almost 1500 casualties among the UN's soldiers (US General Accounting Office 1995: 15), 'force protection' rather than security for Bosnians was the order of the day. Some of the least safe territories in the Balkans were under UN protection in six 'safe areas'. The unwillingness by the West to put military teeth in what *The Economist* caricatured as 'the confetti of paper resolutions' caused those with gallows humour to describe the UN's soldiers as 'eunuchs at the orgy'. UNPROFOR is a depressing illustration of 'collective spinelessness' (Weiss 1996) despite of substantial expenditures (some US$4.6 billion from February 1992 to December 1995) and even greater investments in rhetoric. The UN is arguably incapable of exercising command and control over combat military operations for humanitarian or any other purposes. The capacity to plan, support and command peacekeeping, let alone peace-enforcement missions, is scarcely greater now than during the Cold War.

Unlike other CHEs under review here, in Bosnia the percentage of humanitarian assistance provided by the military was relatively insignificant in relation to total military costs. The most spectacular performance was the 18-month airlift to Sarajevo which surpassed even the Berlin blockade in its duration. As Durch and Schear (1996: 50–1) wrote:

> The airlift into Sarajevo was the longest-running effort of its kind in history. From July 1992 until April 1995, when Bosnian Serb threats shut it down, the airlift brought roughly 175 000 tons of food and other relief items into the city. Road convoys over the same period brought in another 90 000 tons. At the same time, UN efforts to halt Serb artillery and sniping attacks on the city produced mixed results.

Also unlike most cases under review, the overall resources available for humanitarian assistance by civilian agencies in the Balkans were adequate. The former Yugoslavia received more than 100 per cent of requirements as it had in previous years, which contrasted with such other countries as Angola, Sudan, Somalia, Afghanistan, Iraq, Haiti and Sierra Leone with less than 50 per cent (US Mission to the UN 1996: 24).[4] The global sufficiency of resources did not, however, guarantee perfect satisfaction of needs. In 1994, for example, 85 per cent of the estimated food requirements of all Bosnians were met; but the residents of Bihac only received 33 per cent of their needs and those of the eastern enclaves of Gorazde, Zepa and Srebrenica only 65 per cent (US General Accounting Office 1995: 31).

Were the benefits commensurate with the costs? On the one hand it could be argued that the UN military presence in Bosnia facilitated succour to 2.7 million victims from 1992 to 1995. UNHCR was the world organization's 'lead agency' with about US$500 million, or half of its annual budget, devoted to the former Yugoslavia, while the International Rescue Committee (IRC) was in the forefront of NGO efforts. On the other hand continued violence may have killed a couple of hundred thousand persons (although this number is highly disputed with lower estimates ranging from 20 000–70 000), and 'ethnic cleansing' entered into the list of horrors as did rape as a war crime. There should be no illusion that the laudable humanitarian response orchestrated by UNHCR was an adequate substitute for more responsible international political engagement in the former Yugoslavia (Weiss and Pasic 1997).

UNPROFOR's machinations in Bosnia constituted the most expensive, dangerous failure of any military operation to facilitate humanitarian action that has been undertaken to date. Cedric Thornberry, who headed UN civil affairs from 1992 to 1994, wrote (1996: 75) that international 'attempts were the equivalent of trying to hold back the tide with a spoon'. Until the brutal shelling of Sarajevo in August 1995 and the Croatian-Bosnian offensive shortly thereafter goaded the West to act, the international military and humanitarian decisions in the former Yugoslavia had added up to intervention, but one in favour of Bosnian and Croatian Serbs and their patrons in Belgrade and against victims.

11.3.5   Rwanda

Military forces were integral parts of the international response to the suffering that emanated from the 1994 genocide. The UN Assistance Mission for Rwanda (UNAMIR) had been present in Kigali for about eight months when the genocide commenced on 6 April 1994. The UNSC reduced these UN military forces a few days later after the murder and mutilation of ten Belgian soldiers, almost half the fatalities for the entire period under analysis. The decision to reverse this tragic decision and increase troops took place after at least half a million people had lost their lives and 4 million others (about half the country's population) had been displaced. There were two stand-alone military initiatives: a two-month French security effort, 'Opération Turquoise', from June to August in order to stabilize the southwestern part of the country on the basis of Chapter VII; and the massive two-month US logistics effort, 'Operation Support Hope', from July to August in order to provide relief to the Goma region in Zaire. There were also a number of small national contingents that helped efforts by the UNHCR.

Fostering a secure environment, the military's clear comparative advantage for which there is no substitute, was dwarfed by their logistics efforts. With no outside military responses for two months, as many as 10 per cent of Rwanda's population were murdered and at least an estimated 250 000 women were raped (United Nations 1996). It can be argued, however, that 'Opération Turquoise' probably prevented another refugee crisis of the record-setting magnitude of the one in Goma, Zaire, in May; almost a million refugees appeared virtually overnight (14–18 July) accompanied by a cholera epidemic and widespread dysentery that killed an estimated 50 000 to 80 000 people.

The military were more successful in doing what civilians normally do better, namely providing direct assistance to some 4 million people in need. They delivered massive amounts of food (270 metric tons in 1994 alone), clothing, medicine, shelter and water (JEEAR 1995). Outside armed forces thus made essential contributions by using their logistical and organizational resources, but only *after* the genocide had occurred.

Once again, costs were staggering. UNAMIR's expenditures have averaged about US$15 million per month, with military fatalities of 26. The figures for the French two-month effort are officially some US$250 million and the US incremental costs for the same period 'totalled at least US$650 million, although they may have exceeded that amount by a factor of two or three' (Minear and Guillot 1996: 15). There were thus total military and humanitarian expenditures probably approaching US$2 billion in 1994 alone. Humanitarian assistance 'accounted for over 20 per cent of all official emergency assistance, which in turn has accounted for an increasing share, reaching over 10 per cent in 1994, of overall international aid' (JEEAR 1995: i). The vast bulk was channelled to the maintenance of refugees in asylum countries rather than their repatriation or assistance to the new government (ibid.).

Rapid military action in April proved totally unfeasible, but the costs of the genocide, massive displacement and a ruined economy (including decades of wasted development assistance and outside investment) were borne almost immediately afterwards by the same governments that had refused to respond militarily a few weeks earlier.

11.3.6   Haiti

Haiti has not really endured a civil war. However, it is included as part of the analysis for several reasons. The existence of massive migration and human-rights abuse likens it to countries that have suffered from violent armed conflicts. It has also been the target of international coercive action – that is, economic and military sanctions under Chapter VII of the UN Charter that resemble those in the other war-torn countries analysed earlier. Moreover, the basis for outside intervention was the restoration of a democratically elected government, a precedent with far-reaching humanitarian implications.

Multilateral military forces were essential to the solution that ultimately resulted in late 1994. First, however, came the embarrassing performance of the UN Observer Mission in Haiti (UNMIH I). Apparently, as a result of a rowdy demonstration on the docks in Port-au-Prince the order was given for the ignominious retreat in September 1993 of the *USS Harlan County* with unarmed US and Canadian military observers aboard. A year later in September 1994, the first soldiers of the UN-authorized and US-led MNF landed in Haiti. What Pentagon wordsmiths labelled 'Operation Uphold Democracy' grew quickly to 21 000 troops – almost all US except for 1000 police and soldiers from 29 countries, dominated by those from the Eastern Caribbean. This operation ensured the departure of the illegal military regime headed by Raul Cédras and the restoration of Jean-Bertrand Aristide's elected government.

Although 'consent' of sorts emerged from the last-minute agreement negotiated between the de facto military authorities and the US delegation headed by former President Jimmy Carter, the willingness to authorize and use force was an essential part of military and diplomatic calculations and tactics with important lessons for the future. The actual use of force proved unnecessary, but deterrence requires credibility and a demonstrated willingness to make good on Chapter VII threats.

A single military person was killed in action, the local population was almost universally supportive, and two important tasks with clear humanitarian impacts were accomplished. First and most immediately, the MNF brought an end to the punishing economic sanctions that had crippled the local economy and penalized Haiti's most vulnerable groups as the work of humanitarian and development agencies had virtually stopped. Second, the MNF established a secure and stable environment, which stemmed the tide of refugees, facilitated the rather expeditious repatriation of some 370 000 refugees, and immediately stopped human-rights abuses that had reached distressing levels even by Haitian standards.

Washington expended about US$1 billion for troops, of which only one-fifth was over and above what normal DoD expenditures would have been had the troops been at their home base in the US, and another US$325 million on assistance in the first half-year, only a small part of which was administered by American soldiers directly. Once the MNF achieved its goals, the international military and police presence was entrusted at the end of March 1995 to the UN Mission in Haiti (UNMIH II). The 6000 soldiers from over a dozen countries had an annual budget of over US$350 million. The continued involvement of a substantial number of US Special Forces (2500) and a US force commander for the initial UN follow-on operation demonstrated concretely Washington's commitment through the end of February 1996. Subsequently UNMIH was extended for four months at about half its former size before it was replaced by yet a smaller UN Support Mission in Haiti (UNSMIH) in July under Canadian financial, political and military leadership.

Haiti's balance sheet provides a relatively straightforward argument for multilateral military operations to benefit human values. There were few complications and only six total military fatalities. The perceived success helped resuscitate the image, at least temporarily, of outside intervention in a region that had traditionally resisted outside pressures. The most severe shortcomings, with implications for future conflict management, resulted from doing too little to improve the police, penal and judiciary systems. Moreover, fundamental economic relations remained unchanged in one of the world's most inegalitarian societies. Ironically, a key humanitarian impact of the Chapter VII military intervention was ending Chapter VII economic sanctions (Zaidi 1997).

The perception that vital interests of key states were threatened eventually spurred leadership and risk-taking. The geography of the crisis brought into prominence not just Washington but also Ottawa and several Caribbean countries. The rapid and painless attainment of security was dramatic, especially because the Chapter VII military operation set the precedent of being authorized to restore democracy. The effective projection of military force and the resulting humanitarian benefits have led some observers to question the UN Charter's logic of non-forcible economic sanctions *before* forcible military coercion (Maguire *et al.* 1996). A swifter military intervention undoubtedly would have proved more humanitarian than 'tightening-of-the-screws' through economic sanctions.

11.4   Toward a framework for assessing a bottom line

Table 11.1 contains the elements of a framework to compare the military costs for donor countries and the benefits for civilians in a targeted country resulting from humanitarian intervention. To paint as accurate a picture as

Table 11.1   Estimating military costs (for troop-contributing countries) and civilian benefits (for targeted country) from intervention

Military costs of intervention for troop-contributing countries	*$ Value*	*Casualties/ fatalities*	*Political impact*
	A	B	C
Civilian benefits of intervention for targeted countries	Displacement	Suffering	State of the state
• Humanitarian challenge before intervention	D	E	F
• Civilian benefits after intervention	D'	E'	F'

possible for each case, it is crucial to establish military costs for intervening countries. These should be broken down into three components:

A: There should be three indicators of costs, two military and one civilian. The dollar values of the military presence for security purposes should be those officially reported by troop contributors as well as any well-regarded estimates that are different (usually multiples higher). When possible, the value of purely military security should be distinguished from military humanitarian aid, and net figures (or incremental costs) should be given to indicate the 'true' cost over and above what finances would have been expended by troop-contributing countries to support troops at home bases. UN budgetary figures should be reported although these understate the financial costs for industrialized troop-contributors and do not take into account the concern surfacing about the loss of purely war-fighting skills resulting from humanitarian intervention (Lehman and Sicherman 1997). There should be an indication of the changing volume and value of civilian humanitarian aid, the assumption being that such assistance is facilitated by the military's presence. While crude, figures should take into account the total population of an affected area as everyone within it, not simply persons officially at risk, who benefit or are penalized by the military's presence.

B: Accidental and battle casualties, especially fatalities should be reported. The size, scope and duration of an operation should be taken into account, but an absolute number of deaths is probably the most relevant statistic in light of what is normally a low tolerance for deaths in troop-contributing countries.

C: There should be an appreciation of conventional wisdom regarding the overall weight of political and parliamentary reactions to a particular effort. They could be considered a 'net political benefit' influencing a population's or a particular administration's subsequent willingness to support multilateral military operations.

The nature of the humanitarian challenge (or crisis for civilians) on the eve of the military intervention in a targeted country should be reflected for three criteria. These same criteria should be examined for the period after the outside humanitarian intervention as a way to measure key possible benefits for civilians.[5]

D: Involuntary migration is probably the best reflection of the magnitude of a CHE and should be captured by UNHCR figures about refugees and IDPs. In some cases, the latter category of 'internal refugees' should be accompanied by indications of war victims who have not moved but are living in 'refugee-like situations'. A rapid improvement in these numbers (D') measured, for instance, by an increase in repatriation of refugees or a return by IDPs in a relatively brief interval after an outside intervention, would provide an important gauge of enhanced security, protection and confidence in the future.

E: Suffering should be measured by hunger, disease and human-rights abuse. The first measurement reflects those whose lives are at risk from a lack of calories, a variable number that comes from many agencies. The second measurement should indicate through WHO or UNICEF statistics the status of women and children, the most vulnerable members of a society who are also the most numerous among those involuntarily displaced. Finally, human-rights abuses are probably the most contested and unreliable of statistics within and across cases; and even essential measurements can change from case to case (for example, rape is much more of a factor, however contested the figures, in some conflicts than others). Nonetheless, a reflection of human rights is essential to capture accurately the nature of some suffering in war zones. Again, improvements in these three criteria (E') after an intervention would capture important pay-offs from intervention in the targeted country.

F: There should be a reflection of widespread judgements regarding the ability of governmental authorities in the country in crisis to exert effective control over territory, exercise effective administrative authority over its inhabitants, and provide security for them. The extent to which traditional attributes of statehood are present should provide an indication of the severity of a crisis or even a collapse of state sovereignty. Although a healthy civil society would be a useful indicator, the improvement in local governmental authority (F') would be more readily visible and also suggest possible benefits from intervention. Meanwhile, the reconstitution of 'failed states' is a challenge beyond the capacities of outside military forces (Herbst 1996/97). In any event, it is important to get beyond what King (1997: 12) has aptly dubbed 'narcissistic' intervention in which 'questions about the long-term effects of external involvement [are] pushed to the back of the queue'. It is also essential to understand better the implications of local economies fuelled by civil wars (Jean and Rufin 1996; Keen 1998; Duffield 1994b, 1997, 1998).

The preceding discussion of variables indicates a lack of clarity, specificity and objectivity that statistics are supposed to convey. Hence, it is more feasible and useful to suggest visually and qualitatively the value-laden judgements that emanate from a comparison of suggestive data across cases. In this way, the reader can identify immediately whether and why his or her bottom-line differs from the one here. As such, Table 11.2 is a crude and subjective attempt to capture my comparative interpretation of data across cases (rows) and across criteria (columns). The legend indicates that the more darkened circles, the more successful a particular case in comparison with others in this sample; and the more whitened circles, the more unsuccessful.

Table 11.2   Depicting military costs and benefits across cases

			Northern Iraq (1991–96)	Somalia (1992–95)	Bosnia (1992–95)	Rwanda (1994–95)	Haiti (1993–96)
Military costs							
		$ value:					
Least costly	●	– Military security	●	○	○	○	●
Costly	◉	– Military logistics	●	○	◉	○	●
Most costly	○	– Civilian humanitarian aid	◉	◉	◉	◉	●
		Casualties/fatalities	●	○	○	◉	●
		Political impact	●	○	○	◉	◉
Civilian crisis (before intervention)							
		Displacement	◉	◉	●	●	○
		Suffering:					
Most critical	●	– Hunger	●	◉	◉	●	○
Critical	◉	– Health	◉	●	◉	●	○
Least critical	○	– Human rights	◉	○	●	●	◉
		State of the state	○	●	◉	●	◉
Civilian benefit (after intervention)							
		Displacement	●	◉	○	○	●
		Suffering:					
Most beneficial	●	– Hunger	●	●	◉	◉	●
Beneficial	◉	– Health	◉	◉	◉	◉	◉
Least beneficial	○	– Human rights	◉	○	○	●	●
		State of the state	○	○	◉	◉	●

Perhaps the most subjective part of this evaluation stems from the necessity to reflect an adequate appreciation of the challenge on the ground at the time of an intervention. As with Olympic diving, the degree of difficulty in the assignment should be combined with the degree of execution to determine an overall assessment. This appreciation reflects three judgements: how dangerous and chaotic a particular humanitarian situation; how physically challenging a specific terrain; and how ambitious the operation's mandate. The MNF in Haiti, for example, would undoubtedly receive high marks for execution on the first two but with a relatively low degree of difficulty in comparison with far more dangerous and challenging operations in the other four cases. Meanwhile, even the partial pursuit of a mandate to enhance local police, judiciary and penal systems was considerably more ambitious than for the other cases, and this too should be factored into a composite judgement.

Although it is beyond the temporal scope of this initial cost-benefit framework, it would be useful to revisit targeted countries a decade after an intervention to determine whether the outside intrusion had a positive or negative impact on the containment, mitigation and potential resolution of a conflict that had led to the humanitarian crisis and military response in the first place. Policy analysts and decision-makers will be obliged to ask whether a humanitarian intervention has prevented, slowed down or exacerbated subsequent violence. This line of inquiry might lead toward a greater emphasis on either those tasks (for example, disarmament or revitalization of combatants) that the military can do but chooses not to, or where decision-makers have not approved a mandate; or on countries where an outside military presence remains until some semblance of local order and legitimacy are restored (for example, through improvements in police and the judiciary and through elections).

Despite uncertainties, Iraq and Haiti are placed here at one end of an analytical spectrum with civilian benefits (in terms of lives saved, improved access to alleviate famine and disease, and fewer human-rights violations) worth the military costs. Bosnia (prior to Dayton) is at the opposite end as a case because economic and political costs were high and not commensurate with civilian benefits. In between, Rwanda falls closer to the successful end of the spectrum (after July 1994), and Somalia closer to failure (particularly in terms of the political backlash against multilateralism in the US). However, a shift in subjective appreciation of particular data could push Rwanda and Somalia toward one end of the spectrum or the other.

The impact of forceful multilateral military operations on humanitarian action in war zones is neither as harmful as many detractors think nor as helpful as proponents argue. The downside to military logistics consists largely of looking at a particular military operation and asking, What is it worth? Every case demonstrates that the military is the most costly option. The best data, from Rwanda, indicate that military aircraft are four to eight times as expensive as commercial ones, and the latter mode already is twenty to forty times as expensive as normal road transport, which, in turn, is more expensive than bulk shipments by rail (JEEAR 1995). But in certain situations, military options may be the only ones available. Certainly northern Iraq in spring 1991 was such a case. And even the unilateral and multilateral efforts in Goma in mid-1994 demonstrated that an effective humanitarian response can sometimes require the human resources, logistics and rapid deployment capacity available only to the military.

Moreover, expenditures by defence departments are sometimes add-ons, and then high costs are not directly deducted from allocations for efforts by civilian agencies. Being clear about the sources and alternative uses for public funds is essential. Assuming that a sum approaching the resources disbursed by or attributed to the military within a particular crisis somehow could be handed over to civilian humanitarians, even in the medium to long run, would be simplistic.

It is more pertinent to ask questions about the relative costs of different militaries. For example, according to back-of-the-envelope calculations, US soldiers in NATO's Stabilization Force (SFOR) in Bosnia were reputed to cost some US$2 billion in the late 1990s. Questions should be asked about how much of this bill reflects what other militaries, especially European ones who mix more freely with local populations, regard as an excessive concern with self-protection and how much is a legitimate concern resulting from the US position as pre-eminent power, and pre-eminent target. It is impossible to determine how much civilian relief, let alone military humanitarianism is being deducted from development resources, although this is the usual implication when juxtaposing decreases in ODA and increases in emergency aid.

Interviews over the years suggest that a potential disadvantage of resorting to military logistics and support discourages undertaking tougher, security-related tasks. In light of the pressures on governments 'to do something', there is a seductive appeal of sending the military to furnish emergency goods and logistics rather than security. In fact, the preoccupation with having a clear 'exit strategy' and avoiding 'mission creep', in Washington and elsewhere, makes it appear easier and more attractive to provide clean water than to challenge genocide or even to embark on demining.

A central and stark finding emerges from the successes in northern Iraq and Haiti, the successful elements of the French presence in Rwanda, and even from the least successful moments in Somalia and Bosnia. The emphasis should be on the direct provision of security by armed forces in war zones. Roberts concludes: 'If the practice of the 1990s has proved anything it is that humanitarian assistance cannot realistically be considered in isolation from security...Protection is properly seen not as an occasional add-on to humanitarian relief supplies, but as a key aspect of the international community's response to wars and crises' (1996: 84–6). Yet, the West lacks leadership and a willingness to stay the course. Impartiality and neutrality are destroyed when enforcement begins. But there simply is no substitute for the armed forces to foster a secure environment.

11.5   Conclusions and further research

The fact that intervention is so costly and has such mixed results does not mean that states will agree to move earlier to save resources, or lives. A 'stitch in time' resonates nicely in such multilateral ears as those of the Carnegie Commission on Preventing Deadly Conflict (1997). But such a desirable framework usually also provides the least plausible rationale for states using UN military operations, a kind of 'alchemy' or 'pipe-dream' (Stedman 1995; Weiss 1997). The tone of discussions on prevention approaches a homily: the way to avoid civil wars is to eradicate their political and economic roots through the introduction of wise government and civil society, of rationality, of prosperity with distribution. The results from substantial aid and investment in the former Yugoslavia and Rwanda are hardly encouraging for those like the former Secretary-General wishing to make a case for 'preventive development' (Boutros-Ghali 1995: 99).

A new element in forestalling massive displacement and suffering would be both better information and a military capacity to respond. The former, consisting essentially of various aspects of early warning occurs in peace-time, is feasible and could be improved, although an independent UN intelligence-gathering capacity is unlikely. But the second and essential preventive capacity for times of crisis is non-existent. Although it has been heralded by many as a first success, the symbolic deployment of a detach-ment of UN blue helmets to Macedonia worked only because the interna-tional bluff was not called before the withdrawal in 1999 and a Chinese veto over Macedonia's diplomatic recognition of Taiwan.

Preventive soldiers must be backed not by hope but by contingency plans and reserve fire-power for immediate retaliation against aggressors. This amounts to an advance and genuine authorization for Chapter VII in the event that a preventive force is challenged. Although it is tempting to argue that something is better than nothing, UN credibility can ill-afford addi-tional black eyes. If there is no response when the UN's bluff is called, the currency of preventive UN military action will be devalued to such an extent that preventive action should not have been attempted in the first place.

A growing preoccupation with saving public resources could alter such myopia (Brown and Rosencrance 1999; Wallensteen 1998b). However, the political risks from sustaining fatalities or getting bogged down in a quag-mire are usually high enough to outweigh any purported economic savings from acting sooner rather than later. Despite the potential economic and military advantages (Callahan 1997; Carter and Perry 1999), allocating and disbursing billions of dollars of humanitarian aid is easier for risk-averse politicians and policy-makers than moving precipitously to commit armed forces. There is a low domestic political cost of such aid coupled with a minimal loss of credibility in case of failure, the opposite of potential mili-tary failures.

The contested 'CNN effect' can foster the humanitarian urge to come to the rescue but not to override risks for politicians if national interests are not at stake (Girardet 1995; Gowing 1994; Rotberg and Weiss 1996). As one former senior US military officer has noted, 'Few leaders are willing to invest their political capital in risky, controversial international interven-tions with uncertain outcomes' (Goodpaster 1996: 1).

It is not germane to ask whether military action, even when deemed suc-cessful, slows down coming to grips with such longer-term issues as reha-bilitation, reconstruction and conflict management. The military clearly is not a substitute for longer-term nation-building efforts or a sensible means to address the oxymoron of a 'protracted' emergency; but it can be a helpful ally. The existence of a political vacuum about conflict resolution, however, is not the fault of soldiers but of the governments that send them. Moreover, criticizing the military for a failure to consult more with local authorities and to address the socioeconomic roots of the conflict and begin reconciliation is to set up criteria that will never be met.

The logic of visceral responses to these questions should lead to more fundamental research about the complexities faced in international responses to sustain humane values in times of war. Whether the sum of the total experience in the five cases falls definitively on the plus or minus side of the ledger is an open question. However, adding to the terrible toll of Liberia and Sierra Leone, the continuation of the war in Chechnya, the Congo and Burundi, and the plight of left-over humanitarian problems in East Timor and Kosovo shatters any pretence of omniscient humanitarianism.

Yet in defining a future research agenda, analysts should be wary of dramatic pronouncements that are too closely tied to contemporary events. Many of us are learning not to extrapolate from the most recent experience. For instance, in April 1991 the dominant mood in policy and analytical circles after the Gulf War and 'Operation Provide Comfort' was 'we could do anything'. And barely three years later, almost to the day in April 1994, the same groups had a different mood, 'we could do nothing' to halt the genocide in Rwanda.

Although humanitarian intervention had supposedly fallen on hard times, NATO's response to Kosovo and the Australian-led intervention in East Timor were largely justified in terms of humanitarian and human-rights disasters. The last year of the twentieth century was either the *annus mirabilis* or *horribilis*, depending on one's views, for intervention. There are bound to be instances in which traditional peacekeeping, peace-enforcement and everything militarily messy in between will be relevant policy options in the next decade. Modesty and humility, both analytical and political, should guide our pursuit of multilateral military operations and humanitarian action. Understanding better the limitations of military coercion and of charity is a wise point of departure for the complex emergencies of the post post-Cold War era.

Notes

1. This chapter draws on Weiss (1997, 1999a), published with permission. The two sources provide a more detailed bibliography.
2. There are over 2000 entries in the English-language database, about a quarter relating to use in CHEs (Collins and Weiss 1997).
3. These and other statistics, unless otherwise noted, are drawn from UNHCR's annual (since 1993) *Populations of Concern to UNHCR: A Statistical Overview*. Donors seek better data about what we call the 'casualties of war' refugees, internally displaced persons, returnees and war victims for analysis as well as for planning, budgeting, fund-raising and programming. Yet conceptual and practical problems abound. In the view of UNHCR (1995: 244), despite 'the constant demands on UNHCR for facts and figures...[it is] difficult to answer such queries

with any real degree of accuracy'. In April 1995, the UNSC altered the mandates and names for what had been the three separate parts of UNPROFOR for the Krajina and Slavonia, for Macedonia and for Bosnia. The troops in Bosnia retained the 'UNPROFOR' label, which for the sake of simplicity is what is employed here throughout the analysis.

4. The Rwandan region at the end of the initial crisis was also an exception at about 90 per cent, a figure that has since diminished. The periods vary slightly, and there may be some needs and some disbursements not reflected in the data. The accuracy of the broad comparative data, and of the privileged position of the former Yugoslavia, are clear.

5. Eventually it would be useful to establish a base-line of the five cases before the humanitarian crises: that is, northern Iraq before the Gulf War, Bosnia before the break-up of the former Yugoslavia, Somalia prior to the famine and anarchy, Rwanda before the genocide, and Haiti prior to Aristide. This base-line would employ the same approach as in Cranna (1994).

12
Human Rights[1]

Andrew Clapham

12.1 Introduction

An analysis of human rights is important in understanding any humanitarian emergency. This chapter suggests that human-rights norms can aid understanding and suggest solutions to the tensions that underlie conflict. In fact, the chapter argues that the political problems that produce CHEs can only be resolved if the solutions incorporate respect for human rights as a cornerstone of the rebuilding programme. Without respect for these principles, paper peace agreements will never be translated into solid structures. The edifice of peace will crumble unless the foundations are fashioned out of the human-rights laws that have emerged through recognition of the need to create legal institutions to protect the identity and dignity of groups and individuals. This chapter shows how human-rights work needs to be built into the international community's responses to emergencies. Unless the human-rights issues are tackled at their root cause, this year's CHE could be next year's human catastrophe.

The approach here is to look at how human-rights law and monitoring can be useful in two specific phases. First human-rights information warns of an impending CHE. Second, human-rights instruments can be used in part to resolve the crisis. Too often people assume that human-rights issues should drop out of the humanitarian picture. This chapter shows *why* human rights are downgraded as imperatives at certain stages of the discussion, and *how* using human-rights principles and reports can assist in tackling CHEs effectively. It is suggested that the human-rights movement is a crucial underutilized resource in tackling CHEs. The movement is simply waiting to be tapped.

Clearly, human-rights violations are important indicators of a CHE. It is a truism that human-rights reports can provide excellent early warning of impending conflict. It is commonplace to recall that to prevent conflict one needs to tackle the causes of tension, in other words, human-rights violations. But although these assertions are obvious, the spheres of human rights and humanitarian assistance remain worlds apart. To analyse the causes and problems related to this schism, it is necesssary to enter into the UN's complex institutional landscape to discover points of tension, competition and divergence of interests. An examination of this terrain will enable us to make concrete proposals for better use of human-rights information, mechanisms, experts and law.

12.2 Failing to consider the human-rights dimension of CHEs

Before examining the use of human-rights information in preventing CHEs, this section looks at how human-rights issues are perceived by those concerned with the construction of global early-warning facilities. The UN Secretariat charged with early warning and peacekeeping has remained compartmentalized in its approach.

Reports on the human-rights situation in countries around the world are issued nearly every day. These reports are produced by international NGOs and national human-rights groups and journalists. The volume of these reports has led to some 'attention deficit' from states and intergovernmental bodies. Surprisingly, while intergovernmental bodies have created their own reporting mechanisms to keep them informed of the human-rights situation in a country, the same governments dedicate hardly any time to reading, debating and acting on such reports. One example highlights the tragic consequences of this attitude.

The UN High Commissioner for Human Rights (UNHCHR) has, over the years, created 'thematic mechanisms' and 'country rapporteurs' which receive information, undertake missions, and write analytical reports with recommendations.[2] One of these mechanisms, the UN Special Rapporteur on extrajudicial, summary or arbitrary executions (Bacre Waly Ndiaye), visited Rwanda in April 1993. The danger of the impending genocide was already apparent. In a report dated August 1993 the Special Rapporteur urged the member states of the UN to act to protect civilians from massacres. The first of a series of 12 recommendations reads as follows:

> A mechanism for the protection of civilian populations against massacres should immediately be set up, in terms of both prevention...and monitoring and intervention in cases of violence...To this end, international teams of human-rights observers and a civilian police force might be established, particularly in the high-risk areas; with the agreement of the Rwandese authorities, they would be placed under international supervision. The teams would enjoy the immunities and guarantees necessary in order to perform their function and would be stationed in the country until a national system could effectively take over.[3]

In February 1994 his report, before the UNHCHR, read in part, lessons should be drawn from the past, and the vicious cycle of ethnic violence, which has drenched both Burundi and Rwanda in blood must be broken. To this end, the impunity of the perpetrators of the massacres must be definitively brought to an end and preventive measures to avoid the recurrence of such tragedies must be designed.[4]

The UN member states did nothing concrete to respond to these warnings, either at that six-week session of the UNHCHR in February-March 1994, or through any other mechanism. Hundreds of thousands of Rwandans were then brutally killed in the political and ethnic violence, which erupted following the plane crash that killed the Presidents of Burundi and Rwanda on 6 April 1994. The tragedy is that some of this carnage might have been avoided, had government representatives cared to read and act on the Special Rapporteur's report. Diplomatic representatives get consumed with side issues at UN meetings while reports such as these go unread. The list of priorities for these intergovernmental meetings is established months beforehand. As is frequently pointed out, the problem is not the lack of early warnings but that when warnings are dressed as human-rights reports, decision-makers capable of mobilizing preventive action remain impervious to a 'human-rights analysis'.

The issue is not that decision-makers are deaf to early warnings. According to Gurr, 'Information networks that provide early warning of ecological disasters are better developed than the conflict early-warning programs...The international community also is predisposed to respond to them' (1996: 130). In this way, according to Gurr, 'Early warning of drought in Southern Africa in spring 1992 prompted a concerted international program of relief and rehabilitation that forestalled significant loss of life'. But human-rights information has rarely triggered early action. Stavropoulou (1996) chronicles the attempts by the UNSG to provide an early-warning facility in the Secretariat for mass exoduses and gross human-rights violations. From 1980 onwards efforts at processing early-warning information were thwarted by lack of cooperation between UN agencies and the failure of political bodies to take any action on the few warnings that were issued (Stavropoulou 1996: 424). Two issues remain constant throughout the last 17 years of the UN's work on early warning. Human-rights information is usually excluded from the frameworks, which are designed to coordinate early-warning information. And secondly, any information gathered through the UN's agencies may, in theory, be analysed for the purposes of predicting mass exoduses, but not to secure UN emergency operations.

At the early stages of an impending CHE two sectors will usually be attempting to address the issues and the parties. The political arm may be attempting to mediate or negotiate a peace plan or cease-fire; the humanitarian arm may be negotiating access and assistance. Both arms are wary of embracing human-rights issues for fear of alienating their interlocutors and upsetting their chances of securing their respective goals: peace and relief.

In some instances, hidden geopolitical motives of the governments involved will simply override the normative character of human rights and international law (Falk 1993). In other cases, a utilitarian philosophy dominates the thinking. The rhetorical response to the advocates of a human-rights solution is typically, 'What should one do if the quest for justice and retribution hampers the search for peace, thereby prolonging a war and increasing the number of deaths, the amount of destruction, and the extent of human suffering?' (Anonymous 1996: 250). It is not only the question of justice that gets excluded. Individuals with expertise regarding the international legality of certain agreements and compromises are also locked out. In the context of Bosnia and Herzegovina one negotiator writes:

> Two things emerged clearly during the negotiations: lawyers should give their opinions but should not dominate the negotiating process. The purpose of peace negotiations is to achieve peace. Lawyers are there to assist in that objective, not make it more difficult. Legal perfectionism can lead to disaster in negotiations. Another important lesson learnt during the negotiations is that a short text that the parties can agree on and that can be fleshed out later might make agreement possible, whereas a detailed blueprint can make agreement impossible. This is another instance where legal perfectionism can mean the death of negotiations (Ramcharan 1996: 21)

The answer must surely be that a peace, which respects the quest for justice and human rights will be a lasting peace and the best sort of preventive diplomacy. Short-sighted geopolitical fixes will start to lose their attractiveness once it becomes clear that public opinion will not support suffering and injustice, and that the problems are going to continue to surface as long as the causes are not properly dealt with. The human-rights community has started to hit out and reassert its role on the moral high ground urging that negotiators are jeopardizing the credibility of their governments and the international organizations they represent (Gaer 1997). Negotiators are being urged to work with human-rights organizations to 'develop new strategies to protect human rights, resolving the causes of conflict rather than merely containing them' (Gaer 1997: 5).

12.3 The potential use of human-rights information for early warning

Väyrynen has used four factors to define a humanitarian emergency: warfare, disease, hunger and displacement. He considers the human-rights dimension relevant, 'but embedded in the four other factors [rather] than an independent defining characteristic' (Väyrynen 2000a). In order to understand the potential of human-rights information as indicators of these factors developing, or for resolving the causes of each of these factors, each factor can be looked at in turn.

One UN human-rights body has made a start in listing which criteria might be considered as relevant for early warning of tension turning into armed conflict (warfare). The Committee on the Elimination of All Forms of Racial Discrimination lists the following criteria:

i)   the lack of adequate legislative basis for defining and criminalizing all forms of racial discrimination, as provided for in the Convention;
ii) inadequate implementation or enforcement mechanisms, including the lack of recourse procedures;
iii) the presence of a pattern of escalating racial hatred and violence, or racist propaganda or appeals to racial intolerance by persons, groups or organizations, notably by elected or other officials;
iv) significant patterns of racial discrimination evidenced in social and economic indicators;
v)   significant flows of refugees or displaced persons resulting from a pattern of racial discrimination or encroachment on the lands of minority communities.[5]

These criteria were developed as a response to Secretary-General Boutros-Ghali's suggestion in 1992 that the UN needed to 'consider ways to empower the Secretary-General and the expert human-rights bodies to bring massive violations of human rights to the Security Council together with recommendations for action'.[6] At the time there was considerable optimism that the human-rights treaty bodies could fulfil this role.[7] Moreover it was considered that the UNSC would play a major role in addressing and resolving conflicts at the early stages. The Committee on the Elimination of Racial Discrimination did issue decisions under its 'early-warning and urgent procedures' but it remains unclear whether any part of the UN took any further action on them (Stavropoulou 1996). Efforts at early action by other treaty bodies such as the Committee on the Rights of the Child and the Committee on Economic, Social and Cultural Rights have also been disappointing. By 1996 doubts were being raised about the effectiveness of the urgent action procedures being developed by the human-rights treaty bodies. The treaty bodies had recognized their inability to analyse such criteria for the purposes of early warning and early action and were suggesting that this function be carried out by the 'thematic mechanisms' of the Commission.[8] (The role of one such mechanism was discussed above in the context of Rwanda.) The reality is that the elaborate system of human-rights treaty monitoring established by the UN cannot yet be harnessed to provide the sort of analysis that would reliably predict the outbreak of armed conflict or warfare. Nevertheless, it is suggested that these same human-rights treaties can be essential in attempts to head off armed conflict. Rather than indicators for the international community, they can provide the tools of conflict resolution. The following paragraphs explain how.

Over the past few years, human rights have been used as part of peace agreements in a number of ways. First, human-rights norms may be the common denominator on which both sides can agree even in the absence of a ceasefire. This is what happened in the El Salvador peace agreements where the San José human-rights agreement was the first agreement to be signed by the parties and the human-rights monitors started work even before the ceasefire. In this case, human rights proved the common ground, which enabled the UN mediators to keep the parties talking and to commit them to 'avoid any act which constitutes an attempt upon the life, integrity, security or freedom of the individual', as well as to take steps 'to eliminate any practice involving forced disappearances and abductions'.[9] The parties also agreed to allow the UN to establish a verification mission and 'clarify any situation which appears to reveal the systematic practice of human-rights violations and, in such cases, to recommend appropriate measures for the elimination of the practice to the party concerned'.

As a result of this diplomatic breakthrough and the deployment of the UN Observer Mission in El Salvador (ONUSAL), the internal human-rights situation is considered to have improved to an extent, which opened the way for the signing of the final New York peace accords and the end of the war (García-Sayán 1995; Lawyers Committee for Human Rights 1995). The deployment of civilian human-rights monitors to a war zone was a gamble, which saved a good many lives and demonstrated the ease with which human rights can constitute common ground in a situation of entrenched antagonism. Subsequent agreements added to the original mandate of the Mission so that it later tackled issues such as judicial reform, the creation of a national civilian police force, and retraining the military. In fact, part of the proof of the success of this approach is that the parties to the conflict in Guatemala asked for a similar verification mission to be deployed in Guatemala 'even before the signature of the agreement on a firm and lasting peace'.[10]

Second, stressing human rights at the time of the political negotiations can remind the main actors of the international community's resolve to remove the causes of conflict rather than simply eradicating the symptoms from the world's news broadcasts. Unfortunately, few political negotiators are familiar with the logic and obligations of international human-rights law. Where human rights represent a point of controversy, rather than something which all sides consider mutually beneficial, the temptation is to eschew human-rights talk in favour of retaining the confidence of the negotiators. For example, in the case of Haiti, the UN and US were dealing with the military regime to engineer their withdrawal from power. The constitutional president (Aristide) was not a party to these discussions and negotiators saw little to be gained by insisting that the military agree to respect the role of the international human-rights monitors. It has been suggested that the failure to consider the human-rights reports and demonstrate a serious commitment to ending the violations during this sort of political negotiations encouraged the military in Haiti in their repression and cut the negotiators off from their 'best source on the local political reality' (Martin 1994: 87; O'Neill 1995: 119). Downplaying the UN's own human-rights reports also highlighted for the military government the splits among the international community and the preference on the part of the negotiators for a solution to the problem rather than determination to tackle the causes of the conflict (Martin 1997: 16).

Third, peace negotiations represent a special opportunity to get agreement on new national institutions, which may be able to resolve some of the conflicts that lie at the heart of the complex emergency. In Guatemala, the Agreement on Identity and Rights of Indigenous Peoples (1995) was signed soon after the first human-rights reports were published by the UN Human-rights Verification Mission (MINUGUA) and the human-rights approach focuses on discrimination and verification while ensuring that indigenous peoples participate in the creation and design of the new institutional mechanisms of protection (Baranyi 1995: 21).

As more and more crises revolve around the antagonism of factions and groups rather than nation-states, a case can be made for greater reflection regarding the current tools available at the international level for the peaceful resolution of disputes. Liberia, Afghanistan, Burundi and Sudan all present humanitarian agencies with the problem of how to prevent an escalation of the fighting and how to protect the delivery of humanitarian assistance. Familiarization with international standards such as those agreed to in the Sudanese context (Convention on the Rights of the Child, Geneva Conventions of 1949 and their 1977 Additional Protocols) is an important step. If these and other international standards can be used as part of negotiated solutions that are anchored in the social and economic context of the emergency, there may be interesting prospects for preventing armed conflict.

One last example of the use of international human rights and humanitarian law to resolve and prevent warfare has been the threat of war crimes tribunals. Let us take just one example of a threatened tribunal. In July 1996 the OAU adopted a resolution in which it warned the Liberian warring faction leaders that a negative assessment of the peace process would lead to a UNSC resolution that would include sanctions and the possibility 'of the setting up of a war crime tribunal to try the leadership of the Liberian warring factions on the gross violation of the human rights of Liberians'. This threat had some resonance in Liberia among the former faction leaders and demonstrates how the concrete nature of international humanitarian law can be used to prevent warfare and the consequent humanitarian emergency that often follows. Even though it is well known that the international community has failed to bring to justice all those leaders it has indicted for war crimes in the former Yugoslavia and Rwanda, the fact of their indictment and the international ignominy this brings can have important effects:

> In terms of pursuing justice within the former Yugoslavia and Rwanda, those indicted by the tribunal are now branded with a mark of Cain that serves as some measure of retribution, preventing them from travelling abroad and instilling in them the fear of arrest by an adversary or foreign government (Meron 1997: 7).

Disease and hunger are factors that can be directly correlated to work done on the rights to health and food. In Väyrynen's typology of CHEs, disease and hunger are assessed using statistics relating to the mortality rate of children under five and underweight children under five (Väyrynen 2000a). The result of combining these factors together with the other two aspects (war and displacement) leads to a classification of five 'strong' CHEs: Afghanistan, Mozambique, Angola, Somalia and Rwanda.

It may be worth considering what sort of contribution the world of human rights can make to tackling disease and hunger in the context of preventing humanitarian emergencies. We can take as a starting point the International Covenant on Economic Social and Cultural Rights of 1966. All five states mentioned above are parties to this Covenant and so have concrete legal duties as well as reporting obligations under the Covenant. In addition, there are a further 130 states party to the Covenant who also are obliged under Article 2(1) to:

> undertake to take steps, individually and through international assistance and cooperation, especially economic and technical, to the maximum of its available resources, with a view to achieving progressively the full realization of the rights recognized in the present Covenant by all appropriate means, including particularly the adoption of legislative measures.

The Committee charged with supervision of the Covenant has stated clearly that, in its view:

> a minimum core obligation to ensure the satisfaction of, at the very least, minimum essential levels of each of the rights is incumbent upon every state party. Thus, for example, a state party in which any significant number of individuals is deprived of essential foodstuffs, of essential primary health care, of basic shelter and housing, or of the most basic forms of education is, *prima facie*, failing to discharge its obligations under the Covenant.[11]

By shaping the discussion in terms of rights and the international legal obligations of states, we can elevate discussion about tackling hunger and disease to the level of legal imperatives rather than desirable policies.[12] This may be important for the determination of how states prioritize spending and how other states and financial institutions condition their assistance. This may be especially important for countries in crisis such as Somalia and Afghanistan or war-torn societies emerging from conflict such as Rwanda, Angola and Mozambique. But perhaps the biggest effect of reordering discussion around international legal obligations is the empowering effect it can have on grassroots groups and local organizations. By pointing to health and food as internationally protected rights rather than privileges or paper policies, the authorities can be coaxed into allowing for proper participation in the decision-making process. In countries such as Somalia and Mozambique the importance of the rights discourse is not that it provides a stick with which to beat the government – this makes little sense in such situations. The importance is that national authorities and international actors are bound to adjust their policies in order to realize certain key rights. What the human-rights regime has so far failed to do is to 'turn its guns' on those international actors whose policies exacerbate the denial of the rights to health or food in countries experiencing a humanitarian emergency. The challenge is how to hold foreign owners of, say, banana or coffee plantations to account for the fact that their policies are contributing to a denial of basic economic and social rights (Jungk 1999). Furthermore, where DCs are forcing local authorities to forego action on basic economic and social rights, DCs are in violation of their obligations under the Covenant but are mostly escaping scot-free.

There are attempts to transform the world of economic and social rights into something that more closely reassembles the world of civil- and political-rights monitoring (Chapman 1996; Eide 1989; Maastricht Guidelines 1997). Although the UN's human-rights bodies, such as UNHCHR, are supposed to tackle economic and social-rights questions, their thematic mechanisms remain skewed in favour of civil and political rights. For many years the Commission had no special rapporteur specifically assigned to economic and social rights (Alston 1997). The situation has now changed with rapporteurs on extreme poverty, education, food and housing. These rapporteurs could become important early warning.

Similarly the complaints mechanisms in the field of economic and social rights have lagged behind what has been developed for civil and political rights, and it was only in the 1990s that we began to see moves to create international avenues for complaint. It will be a long time before the nascent complaints mechanisms now being developed at the regional and international levels produce the sort of results from which meaningful conclusions could be drawn about impending crises. In fact the use of the international complaints procedures will probably reflect ease of access to procedures rather than useful comparative information on violations of economic or social rights and the prospects of a CHE. Nevertheless, the perceived problems regarding the quantification of violations of the rights to food and health should not blind us to the utility of using a rights-based approach and the existing human-rights procedures to tackling causes of emergencies such as disease and hunger. There could be a number of advantages to reorganizing discussions on the prevention of starvation and disease around demands for rights, and for refocusing attention on all economic actors and states to abide by their relevant international legal obligations in this field.[13]

With regard to displacement, the UN Secretariat has in the past attempted to gather information to warn the political bodies of forthcoming mass exoduses (Ramcharan 1991). Although this sort of work is less sensitive than the investigation of human-rights violations, the project was abandoned, and the Office for Research and the Collection of Information was dissolved in 1992. Work had started on a set of 'early-warning indicators' but constraints on resources prevented the project from developing into a working early-warning mechanism (Stavropoulou 1996). The role of developing early-warning indicators of refugee flight has been taken on by the UNHCR Centre for Documentation and Research and through projects based in various universities (Gurr 1996). Again, the problem for the UN goes beyond methodology. There is some apprehension that over-concentration on prevention by the Office of the High Commissioner for Refugees (UNHCR) will detract from its mandate to assist refugees, and that the Office will become embroiled in preventing people from exercising their right to flee and their right to seek asylum. However, there are signs that the UNHCHR may now start to complement the work of the other High Commissioner so that the human-rights dimension becomes more apparent in attempts to tackle displacement. In the words of Mary Robinson, the High Commissioner for Human Rights:

> Let me reiterate that human rights are indeed deeply connected to the problem of refugees for two main reasons: a) their violation is almost always the root cause of refugee flows and b) the problem of refugees, in the long term, can only be properly addressed and resolved through an improvement in the standards of protection of human rights.[14]

To summarize, human-rights law and programmes do cut across the causes of CHEs suggested by Väyrynen (2000a). But the causes he lists – war, disease, famine and displacement – are not easily analysed in terms of comparative human-rights violations in the same way that economists can compare country data (for the indicators used for the econometric investigation into the sources of CHEs, see Auvinen and Nafziger 1999).[15] However, rather than looking to human-rights law to give us indicators of disasters, we can utilize the law and monitoring procedures to constrain actors whose actions clearly contribute to war, hunger, disease and displacement.

Even if there are some factors relating to humanitarian emergencies, which seem to fall outside the scope of human-rights action, new links are now being made. Corruption and financial scandals are now seen as critical factors can destabilize the population or even trigger a humanitarian crisis (consider Albania and Zaire in 1997). Foreign commercial interests may fragment society and throw up new power bases outside the influence of the state authority (consider Liberia, Sierra Leone and Angola in 1997) (Reno 2000). There are few human-rights standards that have been drafted so as to relate directly to these fields, and human-rights monitors have not really concentrated on these 'extraneous' forces, yet corruption may become one of the key issues for understanding the potential of countries to dissolve into crisis. Corruption may become a key indicator for the possible pre-emption of a CHE. However, even if issues such as corruption and human-rights law are sometimes seen as separate issues, human-rights work on the independence of the judiciary and lawyers is increasingly seen as instrumental in the fight against corruption. On 28 July 1997, Secretary-General Kofi Annan put it in the following way:

> Our human-rights field operations are helping build national as well as non-governmental institutions for the promotion and protection of human rights. I am pleased and proud to say that we now have more staff working on human-rights issues in the field than at Headquarters. All these efforts yield another important dividend: they help to combat crime and corruption, which thrive where laws and civic institutions are weak.[16]

But perhaps the key to better early-warning systems is understanding the nexus between early warning and early action, and building better systems (Gurr 1996). Gurr has stressed the difference between 'risk assessment' and 'early warning'. For him, 'Risk assessments are based on the systematic analysis of remote and indeterminate conditions. Early warning requires near-real-time assessment of events that, in a high-risk environment, are likely to accelerate or trigger the rapid escalation of conflict' (Gurr 1996: 137). Gurr has developed four 'risk factors' that are to be used to place minority groups on a high priority 'watch list'. He suggests highlighting those who are i) politically mobilized, ii) targeted by public policies of discrimination, iii) living in an autocratic state, and iv) subjected to government repression. These high-risk factors may help to restrict the early-warning watching brief but the human-rights indicators, which would enable one to make this distinction, have still not been developed.

Human-rights information about violations in this area is abundant but difficult to use in a comparative way. The problem is that the worst governments will often restrict access to monitors and information. Therefore, comparing data on violations is pretty meaningless. But the problem is not that there is no system for the scientific comparison of emerging human-rights developments; the real problem is that the international community does not have the will or the capacity to react even when the warning bells have finished ringing and the writing is clearly on the wall. Where the causes of future emergencies are economic and social, the myopia is especially pronounced. There is a valid case to be made that presenting hunger and disease as 'flagrant violations of human rights' may help to focus the attention of the international community and NGOs.

12.4   Emergency humanitarian assistance and the human-rights dilemmas

Further problems arise if we look at the actual delivery of humanitarian assistance from the perspective of the relief workers rather than the human-rights actors. There is a 'central dilemma' that haunts organizations involved in the delivery of humanitarian assistance. 'The central dilemma is whether it is possible to supply humanitarian assistance, under the auspices of a governing authority that abuses human rights, without also giving undue assistance to that authority, and hence doing a disservice to the people one is aiming to help' (African Rights 1994b: 4). The side-effects of humanitarian assistance are obviously problematic. The humanitarian urge will continue wherever people are suffering and relief is feasible. The challenge is to try to alleviate the undesirable effects of this relief. Relief cannot only offer succour to a party abusing human rights; it can bind international actors into a relationship where they have to abandon their stated commitment to human rights and accountability as 'cooperation with the authorities' and 'maintaining field presence' become the guiding principles.

Bringing relief to besieged towns and offering medical attention and compassion to victims from all sides can be painted as a human-rights response. The issue arises whether some of the human-rights/humanitarian responses in a situation such as that in the former Yugoslavia were mere window-dressing designed to disguise Western unwillingness to resolve the conflict and help the victims of aggression. To let the UN take the strain can arguably delay resolution of the conflict and leaves UN personnel risking their lives to bring relief to the civilian populations. Over 150 UN military personnel were killed in the former Yugoslavia. It also left the UN hostage to demands and threats made by the warring parties.

12.5   Reporting

It is becoming increasingly clear to all those involved in reporting on human rights in the prelude to, and during humanitarian emergencies that the rumour mill can grind down people's tolerance and good judgement. Tension mounts and eventually the conflict is exacerbated. In some cases, new outbreaks of violence can be simply traced to false rumours. Often the propaganda is of the type which paints the enemy as sub-human with no regard for the 'other', thus exacerbating the hostility and destroying any last vestiges of humanity between the fighting factions.

The reporting dilemma is closely limited to the 'central dilemma' outlined above: how to report human rights without either losing the chance to provide assistance, or becoming complicit in human-rights abuses. The current practice is that humanitarian agencies often remain silent over the violations that they witness for fear of jeopardizing their programmes. While the imperative of confidentiality is mandatory for organizations such as the ICRC, other organizations have no such restrictions. However, even if silence can become complicity and reinforce the international credibility of the parties, careless reporting can be just as dangerous. There is a real risk that inexperienced humanitarian workers become pawns in the propaganda war and end up serving as the unwitting harbingers of stories designed to escalate the fighting.

Nevertheless, humanitarian relief organizations have become impatient with the consequences of interpreting neutrality to mean silence in the face of human-rights abuses. Although there are few formal channels for reporting on human-rights violations, international humanitarian organizations have sometimes organized themselves in the field to complement their relief work with advocacy. In some cases, this advocacy has included human-rights education for political and civic organizations and 'exposing human-rights abuses'.[17] Although not all relief organizations share this approach, there are signs that humanitarian relief organizations are complementing their assistance work with advocacy strategies based on respect for human rights (Darcy 1997). This advocacy is not merely designed to assuage a sense of discomfort over some of the unintended consequences of relief. It may also be part of a commitment to encourage polities, which respect the rights of civil society organizations and of individuals.

So far, hardly any resources have been dedicated to developing a trained cadre of expert human-rights investigators who could operate under UN or other authority in the field during emergencies. The Rwanda Human Rights Field Operation represented a first step in this direction and the experience has been a salutary one. It has highlighted the need for proper planning and thinking before the establishment of field operations. It has also thrown into sharp relief the fact that the planning of repatriation, reintegration and the return of displaced persons cannot take place oblivious to the indications of the projected human-rights conditions that these returnees are expected to encounter. In the case of IDPs, the gap in the legal and organizational landscape means that there is considerable potential for confusion (Kleine-Ahlbrandt 1996). In the case of the April 1995 Kibeho massacre in Rwanda, this failure to consider the issue of the internally displaced as a human-rights issue may have contributed to the failure by the international organizations on the ground to prevent the massacre of hundreds (perhaps thousands) of internally displaced persons as the army closed the camp. There is a good case to be made for better use of information from human-rights monitors and for monitors to be used more strategically to assess the prospects of a safe and voluntary return. This is because human-rights monitors bring a different perspective in a number of contexts. First, refugee or assistance agencies may have conflicting priorities and mandates when it comes to assessing the viability of return or even recommending a return. They could, therefore, be ill-equipped to determine the timing and conditions for a safe return. Second, the perception of impartiality may be a vital factor in persuading people to return. Independent human-rights monitors may be in a privileged position in this regard.

At this point we might state some interim guiding principles which are gaining some acceptance by those operating in the field. First, humanitarian agencies share the concern of human-rights groups to enhance respect for human rights and humanitarian law (MSF 1996). Second, lasting solutions have to be built on the principle that violators of human rights will be made accountable. Third, to remain a silent witness in the face of human-rights abuses can amount to encouragement and endorsement. Fourth, that 'speaking out' or 'going public' are not the only options for humanitarian agencies; other forms of protest may be similarly effective. The dilemma need not be terms of 'publicity' versus 'silence'. Fifth, for humanitarian workers to be seen and known to be engaging in human-rights research or publicity can endanger the safety of the workers, the safety of their locally recruited staff, and the safety of their interlocutors. Sixth, partnerships between the humanitarian field workers and the human-rights investigators should be developed so that information can be carefully processed and acted on in ways which reduce the risk to people in the field and enhance the accuracy and credibility of the reporting.

There remain many obstacles to reporting on human-rights violations and sharing information in the context of humanitarian emergencies. Despite the arguments outlined above, some humanitarian agencies will want to retain a humanitarian mandate, which is deliberately differentiated from human-rights work. For the ICRC, cooperation with 'warriors and warlords' is essential to the way of working to encourage respect for the laws of war (Ignatieff 1997: 66). Reporting publicly on violations or demanding compliance with human-rights norms can confuse the role. In some situations humanitarian workers will be threatened with death should they reveal human-rights violations they have witnessed (Minear and Weiss 1993). Nevertheless, the fundamental objectives of the laws of war aim to reach out and ensure humanitarian protection of individuals and groups (Abi-Saab 1986: 269). Human-rights law is similarly predicated on the need to protect individual dignity and many human-rights norms have now achieved the sort of universal acceptance enjoyed by humanitarian law. As human-rights law becomes less ideologically loaded, we can expect to see greater reporting on human-rights violations in the context of humanitarian emergencies. Done properly this can only help to prevent conflict and provide indicators for how to achieve a lasting peace.

12.6   Ending impunity

A theme throughout this chapter has been the necessity to tackle openly accountability for human-rights violations as part of the overall plan to build a lasting peace. In the case of the former Yugoslavia, an international criminal tribunal was set up to try to dissuade the perpetrators of human-rights violations even as the fighting continued. More usually there have been attempts to ensure accountability at the end of a crisis. In the last twenty years, a number of different types of truth commission have emerged to address this issue in different cultural and political contexts (Hayner 1994).

In the post-conflict situations of Bosnia and Herzegovina, Croatia, Liberia, Rwanda and Burundi, the balance of power is rather different from that which existed at the end of Latin American crises such as those seen in Chile, Uruguay or Brazil. The politics of reconciliation are absent and the demands for justice often drown appeals for forgiveness. In fact, it is often suggested that before victims can consider forgiveness, they need to see evidence of remorse or contrition. Where the perpetrators consider these were not inhuman acts – because they see the victims as less than human – then simply 'telling the truth' will not suffice. In the cases of the former Yugoslavia and Rwanda, the UNSC established international criminal tribunals. This represents a radical departure in terms of the international response to humanitarian emergencies. Both tribunals were set up to deal with international crimes and with a view to preventing future violations. The slow pace of the tribunals has led to some scepticism as to whether internationally dispensed justice can ever work. The problem has been the lack of cooperation from the authorities where the indicted criminals reside and the fact that there is again a vacuum at the international level. There is no international detective agency to investigate the crimes and collate the evidence, there were no agreed rules and procedures for prosecuting individuals at the international level, and in the context of the negotiated Dayton General Peace Agreement and the deployment of NATO, the big powers decided not to round up the key leaders indicted by the Yugoslav Tribunal for fear of taking NATO casualties.

But it would be churlish to suggest that the tribunals had no effect on the resolution of the humanitarian emergency. The terms of the international indictments and arrest warrants issued against the Yugoslav leaders prevented them from travelling, and paved the way for their exclusion from campaigning or standing in the national elections. These restrictions, coupled with the international opprobrium, may have eventually weakened their support and resulted in the emergence of leaders who will start to build a comprehensive peace. In Rwanda the delays associated with the tribunal's investigations gave many Rwandans reason to believe that the international community had decided to pass over their problems. However, the prospect of trials, testimony and punishment has reminded those who may be planning another round of violence that the international community has obligations to pursue the perpetrators of genocide and crimes against humanity. More abstractly, the work of these two tribunals has reinforced the idea that the laws of war and human rights are enforceable, and that actions in violations of these laws have consequences, even if one is part of an army or following government orders. The proposals for tribunals in Cambodia and Sierra Leone suggest that new models for international criminal justice are emerging. Clearly the international community continues to place considerable faith in tribunals as an essential element in ensuring international peace and security.

The adoption of the statute of the international criminal court in July 1998 means that when this new court is established, it will be able to try individuals for violations of human rights that constitute crimes against humanity, genocide or war crimes. One of the reasons for the establishment of such a court is that it will be able to try individuals in situations where the state has completely broken down or is, for some reason, unable to try the accused. The statute provides for the possibility of the UNSC to act under Chapter VII of the UN Charter and refer to the prosecutor a situation in which one or more of the international crimes in the statute appears to have been committed. The prosecutor may initiate an investigation in respect of a crime where the conduct occurred on the territory of a state-party or the accused person is a national of a state party. As of 1 November 2000, there were over 20 states party to the statute. The statute requires 60 states to be party before it enters into force.

The prospect of an international criminal court and the expectation of international accountability are important factors in the human-rights response to humanitarian emergencies. Such international trials would be instrumental in removing criminal officials and politicians from their positions of power and influence. They would also serve as a warning to those who plan acts of aggression, genocide and crimes against humanity that there are forces with the potential to arrest and punish them. But perhaps the most important aspect of using international humanitarian law and institutions to prosecute war criminals is the contribution that such prosecutions can make for lasting peace and thus prevent another humanitarian emergency. The President of the International Criminal Tribunal for the former Yugoslavia, Judge Antonio Cassese expressed this in his report to the UNGA on 7 November 1995:

> If, at the end of a war, torturers and their victims are treated alike, the war's legacy of hatred, resentment and acrimony will not have been snuffed out; rather it will continue to smoulder. The existence of peace

in such a climate would be precarious indeed. If, however, the Tribunal as an impartial body continues in its work of bringing to justice at least some of the most egregious offenders, those who have suffered through four years of hellish war will be better able to find the forgiveness required for peace to last (1995: 8–9).

12.7 Summary

This chapter has sought to examine a number of stages in any CHE and show how human-rights issues arise. The story has been one of distrust of human rights in the various contexts. The thesis presented here is that human-rights law and monitoring are indispensable tools for preventing and dealing with CHEs. At the preventive stage, it was suggested that human-rights reports and personnel are often overlooked as resources for predicting emergencies. The reason for this is the politically charged atmosphere that surrounds the human-rights debate and the fear that integrating human rights into the humanitarian or security field will lead to unwanted interference in the internal affairs of states. The way forward will be to recognize that human-rights reports are increasingly informational in their approach and that much of the ideological sting of the human-rights debate has evaporated. Secretary-General Kofi Annan articulated the importance of this constructive approach to human rights:

> There is a new realization that ensuring good governance – including securing human rights and the rule of law, assisting with elections and aiding development policies constitute in themselves preventive action. The weakness of these rights and structures are not only the roots of poverty. They are also the causes of conflict and the impediments to post-conflict reconstruction.[18]

In fact, the reforms implemented by Annan have clearly facilitated the integration of human-rights information and policy into other areas of UN activity. In his July 1997 package he explained how he had reorganized the Secretariat's work programme around five core missions of the UN. Four of these core missions now have executive committees that involve the relevant UN departments, programmes and funds. These four committees are: peace and security, economic and social affairs, development cooperation, and humanitarian affairs. The fifth core mission is human rights. This mission does not have an executive committee but is 'designated as cutting across and therefore participating in, each of the other four'.[19] The strengthening of the New York Office of the High Commissioner for Human Rights and the participation of the High Commissioner, Mary Robinson, in these committees represents a most important development in the way in which human-rights issues are being dealt with within the parts of the UN secretariat that deal with peace and security issues.

Approaching the problems of human rights in CHEs along a timeline related to the breaking of the emergency, we have seen how the current arrangements are inadequate and have argued for far-reaching changes. As the emergency breaks, it has to be admitted that, unless the national interest demands it, the UN and the international community do not have the capacity or the will to rapidly deploy personnel to protect civilians or put an end to gross violations of human rights including genocide. Although decisions were taken to send civilian human-rights monitors to Rwanda at the height of the emergency, the operation became operational only months after the genocide erupted. One suggestion is for arrangements to be made for teams of UN personnel to be trained and prepared to leave at short notice for emergency situations. These should be UN personnel sent as a multinational mission and not a collection of national contingents dependent on approval from anxious governments. It remains to be seen whether the European Defence Force could fulfil such a role.

At the height of a humanitarian emergency relief operation, there are a series of human-rights problems facing humanitarian workers. In some cases, it may be unconscionable to continue to supply relief when it seemingly leads to the prolongation of the conflict and sustenance for a party which is flouting respect for basic human rights. The guiding human-rights principle of ensuring accountability for violations of human rights may be of some help if it is combined with some of the established reporting procedures designed to expose international crimes and bring their perpetrators to justice. More generally, the issue of what humanitarian field workers should do with information relating to human-rights violations is now starting to be discussed. Because this information is so sensitive, this is an area that needs to be handled with skill if it is not to put people in even more danger. This kind of information is useful not only for the purposes of attempting to prevent a recurrence of violations by giving publicity to the established facts, it is also useful for short-term planning as refugees and displaced persons return to what may be a dangerous situation. Properly processed, such information can ameliorate and eventually help to end the conflict. Nevertheless, the problem of how to achieve a careful flow of information while retaining access and the cooperation of fighting factions will remain a delicate one.

At all stages of the humanitarian emergency continuum, attention needs to be paid to the position of women and how to address the violence and discrimination they are faced with. CHEs have disproportionate effects on women as they will be the majority of the refugees and displaced persons and have often been the subject of deliberate campaigns of rape and sexual abuse. Negotiated solutions to conflict should ensure the participation of women, and long-term solutions will need to address sex equality as a goal and avoid settlements that entrench women's disadvantaged status in society.

At the time that the terms of a peace agreement are being drafted and negotiated, human-rights standards and verification mechanisms have proved catalytic to forging a final peace agreement. International human-rights law can provide the inspiration for solutions that are principled and fair to all sides. The international nature of these standards will in some contexts have to be adapted to make the norms and principles relevant to the context of a particular conflict. But the same international character of the norms may also help to distance the solution from a particular dominant legal system. The universal nature of human-rights law means that it can sometimes offer reciprocal rights to the parties that national laws based on citizenship and nationality cannot. Moreover, because international human-rights law has been developing to meet the demands of victims from a variety of spheres, it may provide solutions to issues such as language, property or indigenous rights not yet dealt with by national constitutions.

Recent steps to end impunity have included the creation of international criminal tribunals for the former Yugoslavia and Rwanda. The new international criminal court will have jurisdiction over other countries. The determination of states to bring the perpetrators of gross violations of human rights to justice is present, but tempered by short-term aims. It was suggested that an aggressive policy of bringing the violators of human rights to account is a preventive strategy and a long-term solution to the prospect of continuing cycles of violence. The use of truth commissions to assist national reconciliation after years of turmoil in a country has had mixed results. Where naming names is combined with dismissing the perpetrators, there are better chances of reforms having some effect, and actual reconciliation reaching beyond the catharsis of the truth-telling episode.

The costs of reforms designed to protect human rights and thus eliminate the root causes of conflict are high for countries emerging from emergencies. The IFIs have a responsibility to ensure that their demands on fragile governments recognize the importance of such human-rights spending as a future investment for a stable economy and a lasting peace. Furthermore, the human-rights obligations of states involve duties in the economic and social fields with regard to education, healthcare and workers' benefits. Shifting the parameters of the adjustment programmes in order to accommodate a discussion of human-rights obligations need not mean imposing an ideological/political model of how government should be conducted. Including an appreciation of the human-rights recommendations and obligations in the context of post-conflict peace building will ensure that new structures respond to the imperatives of non-discrimination, accountability and the rule of law.

Human-rights monitoring is merely a technique for exposing the structural wrongs in society. For too long, human-rights monitoring has been seen as an ideological battleground rather than part of a methodology for crisis prevention. In fact, used properly, human-rights monitoring has the potential to reveal both problems in the economic sphere and deficiencies in democracy. A human-rights analysis can highlight shortcomings and even provide a framework for reforms and minimum standards. The links between this sort of work and the prevention of emergencies is becoming more and more apparent. There is no better reminder of this than the work of the late Claude Ake, the Nigerian political economist who concluded his contribution to this project in the following way:

> Finally, more than anything else, it is democracy which can reduce responsiveness to ethnic appeal and the belligerence of primary group identity affirmation. For in most developing countries where people respond to ethnic ideologies, they do so because state power is privatized, arbitrary and oppressive. In the worst of them, all but a few citizens encounter the state as ruthless tax collectors, boorish policemen, bullying soldiers, corrupt judges and insensitive officialdom. Everyday, they encounter the state as a maze of regulations through which they have to beg, bribe or cheat their way. In a truly democratic dispensation where there is the rule of law, equal opportunity, accountability of power, a leadership sensitive to social needs because its power depends on consent, and attentive to all interests because every vote counts, primary group identities will be less appealing. In such circumstances humanitarian emergencies are less likely (1997: 9).

Notes

1. See Clapham (2001) for more details.
2. For an up-to-date list, including thematic experts and country experts and representatives reporting to UNCHR in technical cooperation programmes, see http://www.unhchr.ch/.
3. Report of the Special Rapporteur, B. W. Ndiaye, on his mission to Rwanda from 8 to 17 April 1993 (UN Doc. E/CN.4/7/Add.1/11 August 1993, paras 64 and 65).
4. UN Doc. E/CN.4/1994/7, para 171.
5. First included in a document entitled 'Prevention of Racial Discrimination, including Early-Warning and Urgent Procedures: Working Paper Adopted by the Committee on the Elimination of Racial Discrimination' (UN Doc. CERD/C/1993/Misc.1/Rev.2).
6. Report of the Secretary-General on the work of the organization (UN Doc. A/47/1/1992, para 101).
7. The chairpersons of the human rights treaty bodies, at their fourth meeting, expressed full support for the Secretary-General's concept (UN Doc. A/47/628, para 43).
8. See UN Doc. A/CN.4/1997/3/30 September 1996, para 43. See also the report of the independent expert, Philip Alston, to the UNGA on enhancing the long-term effectiveness of the UN human rights treaty system (UN Doc. E/CN.4/1997/74). In para 79, he reflects that, 'It is frustrating for a treaty body to have to remain inactive in the face of massive violations and it risks sending a signal of impotence, perhaps disdain and certainly marginality. On the other hand, the invocation of relatively formalist and inflexible procedures seems unlikely to achieve a great deal'. He goes on to endorse the idea that the thematic mechanisms of the Commission would remain responsible for urgent appeals.

9. Article 1 of the San José Agreement on Human Rights, 26 July 1990 (reproduced in UN Doc S/21541, Annex).
10. General Assembly Resolution (48/267/19 September 1994, preambular para 7).
11. General Comment No. 3, 1990 (UN Doc. E/1991/23, Annex III, para 10).
12. See General Comment No. 12, 1999 (UN Doc. E/C.12/1999/5 CESCR/12 May 1999) on the right to adequate food.
13. The published material on the International Covenant on Economic, Social and Cultural Rights is conveniently summarized in a selective bibliography contained in UN Doc. E/C.12/1997/L.3/Rev.2/11 March 1997.
14. Linkage between Human Rights and Refugee Issues' Statement to the Humanitarian Liaison Group Meeting, 26 November 1997, reiterating a point made to the UNHCR Executive Committee on 14 October 1997.
15. Väyrynen (2000a) categorizes CHEs according to whether people are suffering from all four dimensions of the crisis (war, disease, hunger and displacement) 'strong' cases, as compared to countries where 'people have been severely plagued by war and refugeeism, and either from hunger of disease'. Nafziger and Auvinen (2000) build on this and define a CHE as a man-made crisis in which large numbers of people are dying, suffering or being displaced from war or massive physical violence, and large numbers of people are victims of disease, hunger, or population displacement. The US inter-agency paper 'Global Humanitarian Emergencies, 1997' contains the following definition of a CHE: 'situations in which armed conflict, government repression, and/or natural disasters cause at least 300 000 civilians to depend on international humanitarian assistance'. But the calculation is made by starting with the number of people in need. It is not considered feasible to calculate the number of people who are suffering from armed conflict or government repression so that a meaningful comparison could be made across countries.
16. Statement at the International Conference on Governance for Sustainable Growth and Equity, 28 July 1997 (SG/SM/6291).
17. International Non-Governmental Organizations Joint Policy of Operation (Liberia), 17 April 1997.
18. Address to the Danish Foreign Policy Society, 1 September 1997.
19. 'Renewing the United Nations: A Programme for Reform', Report of the Secretary-General (UN Doc A/51/950/14 July 1997 at para 28).

13
The Geopolitics of Mercy: Humanitarianism in the Age of Globalization

Antonio Donini[1]

13.1 Relief in war zones: what are we doing here?

Internal conflict in LDCs has been one of the characteristics of the last decade. It remains to be seen if the current spate of crisis and conflict is to become a permanent operational reality for the international community or if it is only a transitory phase in the post-Cold War movement of tectonic plates. The inability to deal with such crises is the source of growing uneasiness, if not outright frustration. From Afghanistan to Zaire, for the disparate members of the 'humanitarian international', the writing is on the wall: in the face of massive human-rights violations and deliberate targeting of civilians in conflict situations we are no longer sure we are doing the right thing. More fundamentally, we have no common understanding of why crises occur. The very operating system of the international community's response to crisis and conflict is in a state of flux, if not confusion.

The nature of crises is changing fast but the quality of the response and the nature of the institutions have not kept the pace. During the Cold War era, there was a certain predictability to the way in which political and humanitarian mechanisms could be used to respond to crises, which were shaped by competing bi-polar interests. On the humanitarian front, standard approaches were used to help people who sought asylum across borders. Assistance was provided in the relative security and comfort of camps outside the immediate war zone. Intervention to provide life-saving assistance during conflict, without the acquiescence of the concerned government, was a taboo that only a few NGOs were able to violate.

Today crises have become 'complex' in the sense that many actors (political, humanitarian, human rights) and many dimensions (conflict, displacement, widespread poverty, criminalized economy) are often present at the same time. The majority of people in need are suffering in situations where maximum harm to civilians, and disruption of humanitarian assistance, are often part of the strategy of warring groups. Humanitarian actors are finding it necessary, as a matter of urgency, to reconceptualize the very nature of the imperative that traditionally propelled them into action. While they have become technically and logistically more competent, they are less sure of the impact of what they do. Increasingly, hard questions are being asked about the meaning and functions of humanitarian assistance in the context of North–South relations. Many see it as the most basic safety net for the victims of conflict. But could it be that, by design or by default, it has also become functional to the processes of economic and social globalization?

While the respect for humanitarian norms, and in particular for the fundamental right of victims to receive assistance, has in recent years been tenuous at best, 1994 – the year of genocide in Rwanda – will be remembered as a watershed in the annals of brutality. Rwanda has deeply affected the humanitarian community. It has challenged some of the very concepts of humanitarianism (de Waal and Omaar 1994b).[2] The shadow of genocide is likely to have an important impact on how humanitarians will look upon future crises and, perhaps, even on the shape of the institutions of the international community.[3] For many, a system that results in maintaining an equanimous impartiality between the victims and the executioners is in dire need of reform.[4] Even the ICRC, traditionally a monolithic organization, has engaged in soul searching after the high price paid in Chechnya where six of its delegates were assassinated in early 1997. What values and image do well-paid, well-clad, and well-heeled international officials project in conditions of extreme poverty?

The decade had started on an altogether different footing. The end of bipolarity had ushered in a short-lived period of great expectations. At the UN, for a brief historical moment, both member states and the secretariat felt free to fly. After 45 years the heavy lid of the Cold War was lifted and the Organization's *langue de bois* gave way to more open forms of expression. The ideals of the founding fathers seemed to come to life. Traditionally, the UN regimes for peacekeeping, human rights, humanitarian and development activities had been kept in separate if not watertight compartments and the UNSC, when it was not deadlocked by crossed vetoes, dealt with security and not with humanitarian questions. Issues suddenly refused to remain in neat compartments. The new wave of emergencies became 'complex,' mixing the political, the military, and the humanitarian. The peacekeeping/interventionist approach became the new gospel that the humanitarians were expected to obey. The enthusiasm for peace operations peaked in 1994, when a record number of 80 000 blue helmets were deployed. Bosnia and Somalia have had a sobering effect: extreme caution is likely to be exercised henceforth. Regional coalitions of the willing may selectively pick up the slack. Lighter forms of intervention – limited use of civilian police or of armed guards to protect humanitarian workers – may be the most that the international community is able to consent to.

One of the paradoxical consequences of the end of the Cold War was the sudden appearance of the military in the humanitarian arena, a front where they were seldom seen in the past. For humanitarian agencies, working with the military has not always been easy. Despite efforts to reconcile peacekeeping goals with the imperatives of humanitarian assistance, there is still widespread concern among humanitarian agencies about the appropriateness and the costs of mixing soldiers and relief. From a humanitarian point of view, the pertinence of military intervention is at best doubtful. In Liberia, Somalia and former Yugoslavia, the cynical (or perhaps realist) view is that intervention has prolonged the conflict and has often created obstacles to the provision of humanitarian aid. In Afghanistan and in Sudan, on the other hand, the fact that there was no military intervention allowed some measure of 'humanitarian access' to be negotiated among all factions, thus meeting the urgent humanitarian needs. The risks inherent in the militarization of humanitarian assistance cannot be underestimated. The broad question left unanswered is whether the humanitarians should be better equipped by the international community to do their job or the military trained to take on tasks other than war and security?

Recent experience – and the apparent reluctance of government and military establishments to accept even minimal casualties in operations abroad – leaves the lingering feeling that conflicts have become too complicated and too dangerous for UN-mandated military intervention. In the era of globalization, the international community has more or less consciously given up on active conflict resolution, which is now replaced by 'humanitarian containment'. Relief has clearly become a form of disengagement, or, more precisely, the only form of engagement that the North is willing to finance in peripheral areas. In the face of the cynicism and pusillanimity of the most powerful states in the international community, those which have the means to intervene, the humanitarian agencies, are left to mop up the consequences.

At the same time, however, the humanitarian action in conflict zones appears to be linked to the process of economic globalization. Humanitarian assistance is part of the historical process of homogenization, which inexorably extends its web to the turbulent 'marches' of the world. The exact nature of the relationship between relief and globalization is as yet unclear and further research is required to unscramble it. Is relief simply an indicator of globalization (i.e. the presence of international relief actors is proof that globalization is at work)? Or is there a more direct causal relationship in the sense that relief 'opens up' new areas to the process of globalization and therefore is functional to the development of the economic and social forces driving it?

13.2   The deregulation of North–South relations

The context in which humanitarian assistance is being provided is rapidly changing. War itself is an altogether different reality (van Creveld 1991;

Keen and Wilson 1994; Le Billon 2000). It used to be a matter for states or at least for groups aspiring to statehood and legitimacy. Roles are now increasingly blurred: it is often difficult to distinguish the military from the civilian, the oppressed from the oppressor and even the police force from the firefighters and the ambulance. The red cross and the blue flag, once protecting symbols, have now become fair game and humanitarian workers have paid an increasingly heavy price. Armed bandits are not the best of interlocutors with whom to discuss humanitarian norms and access to victims. Civilians are, in today's wars, pawns and hostages, if not the deliberate targets of violence.

Today, relief agencies have to engage with violence. But the current wave of internal wars is but one of the parameters that define the new environment in which humanitarian actors are compelled to work. In many ways it is intervention itself, whether 'military' or 'humanitarian', that should be seen as the new defining element in the post-bipolar world, rather than conflict which, of course, existed throughout the previous era as wars by proxy or resistance to superpower hegemony. In recent years there has been a kind of double lifting of inhibitions that had been largely suppressed by the rules of the game of the Cold War: the inhibition to wage war and the inhibition to intervene. The changed context, the absence of visible ideological stakes with which to identify, but perhaps more importantly, the lifting of the shackles that constrained diplomacy, have made intervention of the humanitarian variety, that is taking the side of the victims, easier to advocate and more palatable for the international community (and for the purse-holders in donor countries). It has also facilitated intervention of the military variety in support of humanitarian goals. For better or for worse, humanitarian assistance has become an essential ingredient in international relations.

While war and intervention may well be the most visible innovations, other structural changes have accompanied the demise of the old order and the turbulent search for a new one. The environment in which structural breakdown and 'emergencies' occur, and the wider environment of North–South relations, have been radically changed. To begin with, the international community in its response to crises has lifted a number of inhibitions concerning sovereignty. Whether or not it ever existed – and in a world dominated by superpowers – respect for sovereignty was at best relative, and it is now clear that it is no longer sacrosanct. In practice a number of interventions have taken place that would have been unthinkable only a decade ago.

This deregulation of North–South relations raises a number of questions. Could it be that under the alibi of humanitarianism, intervention is simply the clumsy expression of new forms of hegemony? Militarization is a powerful mechanism to force recalcitrant actors to conform and acquiesce. Military intervention is by no means consistent: why Angola and not Afghanistan, why Somalia and not Sudan? This is not to say that militarization of complex emergencies is necessarily guided by ulterior motives. The belated intervention in Rwanda is a case in point. Sometimes Northern powers are shamed into intervening by the pressure of public opinion or by *mediapolitik*. More often than not, however, the eternal rules of *realpolitik* guide the external helping hand.

The limits of the market have been largely dictated by ideological and political barriers rather than by any moral qualms. It is interesting to note the extension of market mechanisms to areas hitherto protected: the privatization of North–South relations and, in particular, of the provision of humanitarian assistance. For half a century, ODA and its junior cousin 'emergency aid' were well within the realm of states. The end of the Cold War emboldened Western governments: the dysfunctionalities inherent in working through governments have led to the application of *laissez-faire* precepts in the conduct of international affairs. The invocation of privatization and of civil society often functions as a smokescreen for the imposition of political conditionality.

The result has been an extraordinary explosion of private-sector intervention in the third world, nowhere more visible than in the provision of relief. Perhaps the most significant innovation in recent years is the extent to which NGOs in weak developing societies have taken over state-type functions in areas like health and education, as well as the bulk of the delivery of relief services in faltering states.[5] In practical terms, this means that the NGO community in the North has benefited significantly from the fact that with the end of superpower confrontation the imperative of political state-to-state support of North to South has all but disappeared. Will this be equally beneficial for the victims of conflict, for local coping mechanisms in crisis areas and for longer-term self-reliance? The answer is less than certain.

A related trend, which is shaping the environment in which humanitarian actors operate, is the diversion of resources and attention from development to relief. The exponential growth of official and private disbursements for humanitarian assistance is unquestionable: from barely US$845 million a year in 1989, these have peaked at over US$7.1 billion in 1995.[6] Both bilateral donors and multilateral organizations have had to 'divert'; just to give one example, the WFP used to be primarily a development organization; now 80 per cent of its resources are being devoted to emergency food aid. In crisis countries, donors naturally tend to focus on the short term. Funds are generally available to save lives in emergencies but seem to be more difficult to come by for recovery and the reconstruction of livelihoods. Moreover, the combination of privatization and diversion of development resources to relief is likely to mean more political conditionality rather than less. For the donor, the reorientation of budgetary priorities towards quick fix emergency relief provides an easy way to flex political muscles when apportioning the residual development assistance funds. Here again, past inhibitions are gone.

Political conditionality – that is, 'human rights and privatization first, development later' – is a practical way of deflecting attention from some of the more disturbing dimensions of North–South relations. Systemic issues have all but disappeared from the debate. The present emphasis on 'managerial' concepts such as sustainable development and global governance,[7] which are neutral with respect to the nature of underdevelopment which perpetuates it, are a manifestation of this. Furthermore, the emphasis on market mechanisms and the privatization of aid allows donors (and to some extent recipient governments) to eschew the issue of the failure of the development strategies of the past, a failure in which the governments and elites of North and South are complicit. There is no accountability for botched development strategies, whatever their consequences.[8] Finally, the fact that both relief and development assistance, because of its privatization, increasingly bypass and therefore weaken state structures, is indicative of the increasing marginalization of the international development discourse.

Powerful new forces are rapidly changing the North–South scene and the context of the debate: 'development' no longer seems to be the mobilizing paradigm.[9] Development as an aspiration for more equality and fraternity not only within but between nations may soon be an idea whose time has passed. Irrespective of the ideological tradition, it is no longer fashionable to advocate structural reform or even social change.[10] A new paradigm has yet to emerge. De facto, in the context of globalization – or more precisely, of the transnationalization of economic processes where the sovereignty of weak states is subordinate to external forces – the new paradigm may well be a combination of intervention in very selected high interest areas and humanitarian assistance as a form of public welfare and containment elsewhere.

13.3   Humanitarianism – the next phase of capitalism?

The Italian proverb *Il diavolo fa le pentole ma non i coperchi* ('the devil makes the saucepans but not lids') aptly reminds us that the bubbling primordial broth kept inside the Cold War pressure cooker is now spilling and spreading in all directions. At the beginning of the 1990s the requirement to contain international politics into blocs suddenly ceased to exist. Parallel but somewhat contradictory pressures for government roll-back, democratization and market expansion became a threat for entrenched authoritarian regimes. This led to a sea of change in the 'politics of economics' worldwide (Pieterse 1997). The fact that these changes were accompanied by a dramatic surge in humanitarian assistance and military intervention raises the 'sinister option' that humanitarian intervention might be the military corollary of neoliberal globalization. A 'replay of imperialism, under the guise of humanitarianism'? (Pieterse 1997: 88, 72). A new global wolf in sheep's clothing? Perhaps not, but the hypothesis that humanitarian assistance is a 'marker' in the processes of globalization deserves to be explored.[11]

Moreover, the notion that conflict may be the result of the turbulence that capitalism creates as it extends its web to its structural limits, deserves another visit.[12] Relief appears to be inescapably intertwined with this historical process: it can either prepare the terrain for market expansion by bringing a semblance of stability and provide the minimal safety nets in areas where the market is temporarily disengaged so that crises and population movements do not spin out of control. In other words, the West is unable or unwilling to assume any global responsibility for alleviating poverty in crisis regions other than in 'welfare terms' through the provision of relief (Duffield 1997). In addition, the deregulation of North–South relations – and the attendant subordination of the historic functions of the nation-state in maintaining internal unity and cohesion to the external forces of globalization – is most likely in itself a root cause of conflict.[13]

In the violent and volatile contexts of internal conflict where the ruthless warlord's monopoly on violence might have replaced the state's monopoly, the fine line of the humanitarian imperative has become difficult to tread. Concepts such as 'impartiality' are no longer immediately understandable, or even pertinent, when humanitarian assistance is massively manipulated, whether by warlords on the ground or by the aidlords and their political masters. Humanitarians are caught between the temptation to fly forward into politics, retreat backwards into logistics or huddle under the cover of military 'humanitarian' interventions. Moreover, it can be argued that if present trends continue, there is an increasing risk that the privatization of war and of relief will mutually reinforce each other.

CHEs are first and foremost political crises that reflect an abuse of power. Relief agencies are reluctant to tackle powerful vested interests even when they are at the root of crises. Humanitarians understand, however, that in order to save lives they must engage 'with' politics. In internal wars this can result in a difficult balancing act between the operational impartiality of the 'political eunuch' ('we are here to save lives, politics is not our business') and the shrewd manoeuvring of the 'humanitarian prostitute' ('we are ready to compromise so that the aid can get through'). The fact that humanitarian assistance is a business complicates things further: agencies have to compete for scarce funds and jockey for position and visibility.

There is mounting evidence, also, that warlords and other de facto entities of governance have learned how to use international humanitarian assistance to their advantage, either directly as a weapon of war (food for fighters) or indirectly (by attracting agencies and projects to areas under their control). Some have become masters in mimicking the language and the latest operational fad of the outsiders: local councils, indigenous NGOs, joint monitoring committees, etc. Elsewhere, where foreigners are seen to be undesirable either as witnesses or because of the values they represent, it is easy enough to equate them with the enemy and to scare them away with terror tactics or worse.[14] From Chechnya to East Timor recent events have shown how dangerous an enterprise humanitarianism can be. Humanitarian workers have paid a high price, a situation made worse by the absence of any protection for gross violations of international humanitarian law.[15]

The humanitarian community is itself rapidly evolving. While many are engaged in constructive debate on how to meet the challenges, others are rushing into new dimensions. Privatization is now spewing 'for-profit NGOs' with attendant trade fairs and marketing strategies. While 'cowboy NGOs' have always existed, the multiplication of small 'truck-by-night NGOs' ready to flock to Goma or Gorazde with a maximum of activism and a minimum of experience deserves to be noted. Perhaps, if the experience of aid agencies in Somalia is any indication, the next logical step in the deregulated aid market is the 'mad max NGO' with a military wing that will ensure that access to victims can be attained, especially in conflict situations where the international community is not intervening. Militarization and privatization have already become frequent bedfellows: private security firms, such as Executive Outcomes in Sierra Leone (Reno 2000)[16] will provide, for a price, the conditions for business pursuits to resume. Others, like Gurkha Security Guards in Mozambique, are involved in de-mining, working closely with humanitarian agencies. It is not unlikely that such rapprochement between 'mercenaries' of the humanitarian and military varieties will continue. This may well add up to the 'futuristic nightmare' foreseen by Duffield (1996) in which the world's dynamic centres are securely ring-fenced while the conflagrations in the periphery that threaten global interests 'are policed by mobile and technologically replete humo-cops' (Duffield 1996).

Some hard thinking is in order to better define the true functions of humanitarian assistance in contemporary crises. The humanitarian international has become a market with its own rules. Containment, appeasement, keeping conflict within state boundaries, stanching the flow of refugees have become key objectives of the powers that shape international relations. Most agencies will be happy to perform these functions for a price. Humanitarian assistance does not address the problems of extreme poverty: it tends to become a palliative that prevents unstable situations from spinning out of control. It has become the preferred response of the international community when it is unable or unwilling to face the fact that the quantum of political will at its disposal is woefully inadequate. It precisely prefers relief, to soothe the pain, because it cannot look at the causes. And, as the latter are not understood, crises appear to be intractable.

As insecurity mounts and institutions of governance break down, 'official' public and private development projects and private investment funds are naturally the first to disappear from conflict zones. What is less clear is how the economy continues to function and what distortions occur (Jean and Rufin 1996; Le Billon 2000). Two trends seem to emerge: the criminalization of the economy to fuel the war effort and the emergence of warlord-affiliated enterprises connected through proxies to the global markets. In the first case, national resources – for example, diamonds in Liberia and Sierra Leone, hardwoods in Cambodia – are being squandered to fuel the war. In the second, private capital is taking advantage of the breakdown of law and order. War becomes a business: in both cases, the privatization of war and of national resources go hand in hand. The fact that huge profits are being reaped by 'reputable' transnational corporations through intermediaries is once again a manifestation of how humanitarian crises are linked to the globalization of the world economy.

With the demise of the state-to-state aid regime, and the corresponding weakening of state structures in the South, governance has thus been reduced to a basic security and welfare function. Humanitarian assistance and the globalization of the capitalist model are not unconnected. Could it be that the former provides the safety net for the latter to thrive? If the unbridled pursuit of profit in countries in crisis – for example, the export of more than US$300 million worth of diamonds per year from Liberia in recent years[17] – can be proved to have fuelled the war and created massive humanitarian needs, does the corporate sector that profited from the war not have a responsibility to contribute towards reconstruction? If it does not, can humanitarian assistance continue to turn a blind eye to the external exploitation of internal conflict? The stripping of a country's natural resources, whether it is by the warlord or the venture capitalist, or their alliance, is a *crime against development* and therefore a violation of the rights of the populations concerned. While the notion of crimes against humanity is slowly coming to haunt the perpetrators of massive human-rights violations, shouldn't a similar justice regime be applied to those who have wilfully compromised the livelihoods of millions of victims of conflict?

An answer to this largely rhetorical question would require the introduction of some form of global accountability. Legitimate corporate entities are heavily involved in reaping profits from crisis countries through warlords or criminalized economic counterparts. We do not know enough about how the drug barons operate in Afghanistan (on its criminalized economy, see Rashid 2000) or the diamond barons in Liberia. At what point does the continuum that extends from the citadels of capitalism to the diamond digger or poppy producer become criminalized? Moral accountability will obviously be difficult to determine, but it is not theoretically inconceivable that exorbitant corporate profits could be identified and a 'reconstruction tax' levied on them. While this tax might actually contribute to preventing conflict, it is unlikely to appear on the global agenda anytime soon. Regrettably, the World State has no black helicopters to deploy for the purpose, nor even a Tobin tax to correct some of the most glaring structural imbalances in countries in or recovering from crisis.

13.4   The political economy of peace

The strains of working in ill-defined and volatile contexts have generated considerable 'unease' in the humanitarian community (Macrae 1996). There is a widespread feeling that humanitarianism should be redefined by recognizing that the contexts in which aid agencies operate are eminently political and so are the uses to which they are put. The obligation to save lives remains intact. But there is no obligation to remain blindfolded. Humanitarian space (access, protection) and humanitarian time (the timeliness of action, and its forward and backward linkages to politics and development) will need constant redefinition in order to minimize unintended negative impacts. Principles will have to be placed up-front, upheld and safeguarded. The long-term implications of practical 'accommodations' with principles will need to be much more carefully considered. The experience in Afghanistan has shown how difficult it is for humanitarian agencies to shift from a situation of 'human rights amnesia', where for years the priority of relief agencies was to get the assistance through, with little regard for the credentials of the particular commanders involved, to an assistance strategy based on human-rights principles (Donini *et al.* 1996).

The humanitarian 'trade' itself will need to be better policed in order to ensure greater effectiveness and accountability. Codes of conduct and clearer standards of operation are welcome developments. Donors, UN agencies and NGOs are slowly coming to realize that more sophisticated mechanisms to ensure accountability and to analyse the impact of programmes are the prerequisites for effectiveness. They are also prerequisites for a better understanding of the functions performed by humanitarian assistance in crisis contexts.

A 'politically alert' approach may well lead to the demise of humanitarianism as we know it: justice and solidarity, rather than impartiality might well become the watchwords. Moreover, there is now widespread recognition that saving lives is not enough. Planting the seeds for the reconstruction of livelihoods is obviously better, but it is easier said than done in situations of conflict and continuing erosion of human rights. Conventional wisdom has it that if we addressed the causes, emergencies would disappear like morning mist. The political economy of peacemaking is not so simple: we must be engaged with the causes and the consequences at the same time. Dealing separately with the political, economic and humanitarian dimension can sometimes provide breathing space, but rarely durable and sustainable solutions. The challenge, therefore, once the context of the crisis and its external ramifications are better understood, is to develop a comprehensive strategy for peacemaking and beyond.

The key problem is political analysis, or the lack thereof. The traditional recipes for peacemaking are no longer adapted to the nature of post-Cold War intrastate conflicts. Yet we continue to apply them. The focus of the international community's conflict resolution efforts remains on the negotiations with parties in conflict to reach a ceasefire, a broad based government, a demobilization plan and elections. A more or less generous assistance programme is thrown in as a sweetener. Such operations are costly: the pressure is to 'vote and forget'. This has worked in high-profile crises where the West has put its might in the balance: Cambodia, Mozambique and, hopefully, Bosnia. But it has not worked in those crises that remain at the periphery of the international community's radar screen.

Afghanistan is a case in point. By focusing exclusively on the apex of the warlord power structure – the political leaders and their military commanders – internationally brokered peace efforts have de facto strengthened the hold of the elites on society. Warlords have been considered as viable interlocutors. This in turn has militated against reconciliation initiatives within the remnants of Afghan civil society, for example the identification of groups or economic forces (businesspeople, traders) who might have an interest in promoting the logic of peace rather than the perpetuation of war. This has resulted in a disconnection between the international community's political and assistance processes that has impacted negatively on both. Because of the lack of a joint analysis that might have illuminated 'what is to be done' in Afghanistan and clearly defined principles which should inform such action, the humanitarian agencies were left to their own disparate programmes, the long-term impact of which was at best doubtful.

In Afghanistan and elsewhere it is slowly being recognized that peacemaking is much too serious a matter to be left within the exclusive purview of political officers. A much more society-oriented perspective on conflict situations is required. As has been recently noted, 'statist perspectives, forever percolating within the orbit of sovereignty, national interest and international security, cannot address society's political problems' (Pieterse 1997: 89). However, there are some signs that this may be changing. The combined pressure of the assistance community, shrinking donor budgets, pressure for accountability and doubts about the pertinence of the traditional peacekeeping approaches are leading to some new thinking and practice. A more holistic approach, the so-called Strategic Framework, has been tested by the UN in Afghanistan. It is premised on the assumption that the only way forward is to start from clearly defined ethical principles and strategic objectives that all external actors should necessarily subscribe to. A common international assistance programme and a more robust coordination mechanism built on the partnership of all actors are the obvious corollaries of this approach.[18]

In order to be able to engage with Afghan society – and not just a small clique of warlords – the international community must speak with one voice. In failed or fragmented states, this is particularly important since de facto external actors, and the UN coordination entity in particular, perform 'surrogate' government functions. In most cases, this will require the international community to funnel its efforts through a 'centre of gravity', which will ensure both a coherent multi-functional approach and a sufficient critical mass of resources capable of ensuring that the logic of peace will overpower the logic of war.

The search for more effective peace-making strategies is complicated by the fact that in the UN, the three 'regimes' or cultures of peacekeeping action, humanitarian assistance and development have traditionally evolved separately. A fourth regime, that of human rights, has recently become an additional ingredient. In internal conflict situations, the humanitarian and the political agendas do not necessarily coincide (Bosnia, Somalia) and the development agenda is nowhere on the radar screen. Advantages and disadvantages of separation, insulation and integration of the political, humanitarian and recovery processes must be carefully weighed (Minear 1995). So far, relative separation and reciprocal mistrust have been the rule. But when peace is in sight, an integrated vision and strategy become vital. The hypothesis being tested in Afghanistan is that an integrated strategy to create alternative livelihoods to those associated with the war and the criminalized economy is the only sensible way forward. The issue of livelihoods – the survival strategies of families and communities – cannot be dissociated from the search for peace.

Conflicts are not aberrations in the linear process of development; their roots are in the politics and economics of the society. These can be exacerbated by external manipulation or the 'inadvertent' effects of international structural adjustment programmes in addition to the 'advertent' effects of divisive political action and warlordism. Similarly, recovery is not linear: it does not start where development stopped. In addition to human, social and economic destruction, conflicts can create huge structural imbalances. Since it is unlikely that in criminalized economies key actors will forego warlordism in the absence of economic alternatives, the challenge, therefore, is to find ways of doing rehabilitative and development work and reviving the economy in a principled and rights-based manner as part of the peace-building strategy.

In addition to being humanitarian emergencies and development emergencies, countries in conflict are also emergencies of governance as institutional props all but disappear. Thus, the failure of the state institutions is a core problem, which has to be addressed as such. One of the lessons of Afghanistan is that a country experiencing an emergency of institutions neither fits neatly within the framework of conventional thinking nor within the current international arrangements for either development or relief. New approaches are required for coping with the grey area between acute humanitarian emergencies and situations in which 'normal' development can be pursued. Such approaches should not be complicated by the conventional relief/development dichotomy, which is institutionalized within the UN and donor bureaucracies.

In LDCs, the national government is the body that coordinates, has the entire picture, and is the final arbiter of conflicting priorities. In a failing state there is a need for some other body to provide a point of stability and coherence in the overall system. In these exceptional circumstances, the UN system is, in some respects, called upon to act as a 'ministry of planning-in-waiting' and to provide, for example, a framework where priorities for the utilization of scarce resources for emergency and development assistance can be set. It also has to develop approaches for dealing with de facto 'entities of governance' at the subnational level, and building capacities for the delivery of essential services at that level. It must also build on what remains of traditional coping mechanisms and local civil society institutions. People affected by crisis modify their behaviour in order to minimize their vulnerability and maximize their chances of survival (Lautze and Hammock 1996). Internal conflict destroys the social fabric, the glue that keeps society together. Healing the wounds means much more than injecting money into the economy and rebuilding institutions. The costs of replacing a culture of war with a culture of peace are formidable. There is no option but to mobilize the necessary resources to help this process along in a coherent manner that keeps the long-term picture in mind.

When all else fails, 'vision' may well be the only and most cost-effective solution left. There is a need for a strategic and holistic approach to internal conflict situations and for orchestrating a response on the basis of clear ethical principles. The new theory will, of course, require a new practice: UN agencies, regional institutions, donors and implementing partners on the ground will have to work together to develop joint strategies for such a response and to ensure a positive relationship between assistance and rights. A more unitary 'managed' approach, built around a single framework and a single set of principles and objectives in a particular country, coupled with a strong international funding strategy, is likely to be required. In 'emergencies of governance' where counterpart institutions are weak or nonexistent, the UN must play a much stronger role and, in some cases, act in lieu of the government on key matters. This type of role will have to continue until such time as more legitimate or recognized national institutions are in a position to take over. The weaker the state, the stronger the UN role will likely need to be.[19]

At the same time, and this is likely to be a herculean challenge because the culture of human rights has yet to percolate fundamentally and profoundly through the international system, a rights-based approach must be introduced. Rights are enshrined in the UN Charter, the Universal Declaration of Human Rights and the precepts of international humanitarian law. Now is the time to apply them to maintain an even keel. The condition for success in countries in crisis is that all actors speak with one voice on issues of principle. What is needed is 'a more concentrated strategy', which integrates 'a human-rights approach to issues of development' (Robinson 1997). We cannot wait for peace in order to start reconstruction. Nor can we afford to provide humanitarian assistance in a policy vacuum. The lesson from emergency situations is that piecemeal or disjointed approaches will not work. We must take conflict for granted and learn to integrate human-rights principles, humanitarian action and development with politics.[20]

A cautionary note is in order, however. While the UN and its agencies, and the international community at large may well get their act together and develop more appropriate and principle-based strategies for countries in crisis, we should recognize that the question of the effectiveness of the response is only a small part of a much wider conundrum. From the perspective of how the processes of globalization are impacting on North–South relations and on the human condition at the extreme periphery of the global system, the question of the response occupies a very small space indeed: that between a rock and a hard place. Humanitarian actors are small players in the larger scheme of things. The obligation to provide assistance, protect victims and alleviate human suffering remains intact, but we should not delude ourselves. We should always be aware of the limits of what we can accomplish.

In this chapter we have argued that conflict and crisis in the periphery, and the attendant humanitarian response that stanches the blood, are intertwined with the processes of economic globalization. These processes have received a massive impulse with the lifting of the inhibitions of the Cold War era and with the demise of any counterweight to the triumphant capitalist model of economic and social organization. The model has become effectively 'transnationalized' when even the most powerful states, or the international institutions they dominate, are unable to exercise any real management or control over its development. The implications of this shift towards metacapitalism are likely to profoundly affect the nature of the state and of state-to-state interactions in the decades to come. Without any form of globalization from below, or even of 'global Keynesianism' (Robinson 1996: 375) to stabilize global capitalism in the same way that national policies used to stabilize national capitalism, the consequences and the dislocations particularly for marginalized groups are likely to be formidable.

One cannot assume that this global juggernaut will be benevolent. It will be driven by its own logic. This may well result in deliberate policies to protect well-fenced citadels of wealth and privilege from the social disruption of disenfranchised groups or from the threats posed by uncontrolled migrations, epidemics, drugs and other plagues. It may well be that humanitarian assistance will play a key role in the containment of the periphery. The international community's humanitarian chain-link fence may well keep crises from spreading to the North. Equally, current efforts to promote 'low intensity democracy' (Robinson 1996: 376) in the periphery through the formality of electoral processes and the promotion of individual civil and political rights (rather than collective socioeconomic rights) can be seen both as a form of containment and as a boost for globalization.

The humanitarians will have to learn to unscramble these unsavoury realities and ask themselves where they stand. For sure they cannot stand on the sidelines. Hopefully, they will be part of the solution because such is the nature of their principles. What is clear is that their relationship with the reality of crises is being transformed by globalization: they are right in the middle of the problem.

Notes

1. Views by the author are expressed in a personal capacity and are not to be attributed to UNOCHA
2. The ethical debate is summarized in Macrae (1996).
3. See the recommendations contained in the synthesis report of the multi-donor evaluation of emergency assistance to Rwanda, *The International Response to Conflict and Genocide: Lessons from the Rwanda Experience* (March 1996). Among the spate of publications issued in conjunction with the fiftieth anniversary of the UN, see Childers and Urquhart (1994), where the authors argue for a consolidation of the UN system relief agencies (UNHCR, WFP, UNICEF) into one single entity. Similar proposals have been made by Evans (1993) and Oxfam. The issue of a single relief agency, or at least of strengthening UNHCR as the prime humanitarian agency, was very much on the agenda of the UNSG's reform team in early 1997 and has resurfaced at regular intervals since, despite the institutional obstacles to such a bold reform. A much more radical proposal for the 'internationalization' of ICRC was made by Ingram (1994)
4. Research on the nature of crises, the humanitarian response and the humanitarian-political nexus has recently mushroomed. The Humanitarianism and War project at Brown University and the publications of the ODI in London illustrate this trend.
5. See Fowler (1992). Mozambique provides a good example of the preponderance of NGOs in the aid system (Hanlon 1993). See Donini (1995).
6. UNDHA estimates, December 1996; see also *Global Humanitarian Emergencies 1997*, US Mission to the UN, New York, April 1997.
7. These concepts contrast with those of the 1970s and 1980s – 'new international economic order', 'basic needs', 'trade, not aid' – which, however ideologically flawed, at least implied that some form of more equitable redistributive justice in North–South relations was called for. In the 1970s and 1980s the banner of development in the UN acted as a powerful 'rallying point' for LDCs, much in the same way as decolonization had mobilized the previous decades.
8. For an analysis of the linkages between development assistance and events leading to the genocide in Rwanda, see Uvin (2000).
9. 'Development' as an ever-growing populist project for the legitimation of third-world governments, supported by the industrial powers, may go the way of

decolonization. Analysts a generation hence may look on it as just another historically significant, but temporary, world political issue, a way of establishing manageable political cleavages among those with more and those with less power...The new cleavages that will replace "development" at the centre of the same politics are not yet clear' (Murphy and Augelli 1993: 82).

10. Absolute concepts such as 'development' and 'underdevelopment' have been replaced by relative concepts such as empowerment, partnership and capacity building (Duffield 1996).

11. Robinson (1996: 4) makes a similar case with respect to the active promotion of democratization in third–world societies, which he sees – much like relief in our argument – as a manifestation of 'the transnationalization of civil society' which is 'inextricably linked to globalization'.

12. A hundred years ago Rosa Luxemburg postulated that the capitalist system needed to feed itself on the non-capitalist periphery in order to develop. When the system reached its structural limits it would collapse. On how Luxemburg's intuitions might apply to present-day crises, see Donini (1996).

13. According to Robinson (1996), hegemony by a superpower is increasingly being replaced by the hegemony of the transnational elite, which has assumed de facto management of the global economy.

14. This is not to exonerate aid agencies for such animosity. Lack of cultural sensitivity, display of wealth (cars, trucks, computers, satellite phones) in the midst of extreme poverty, aggressive or directive behaviour, the lack of visible results, etc., can all contribute to a climate of reciprocal misunderstanding. For more on the 'white car syndrome', see Donini *et al.* (1996).

15. It is a sad reflection on the nature of modern warfare that in recent years, from Afghanistan to Zaire, few individuals responsible for the death of a humanitarian worker have been identified, even fewer tried or punished.

16. See also Rubin (1997). On the changing scene of the provision of private military services, see Isenberg (1997).

17. According to one estimate (Reno 2000), one warlord alone was reaping some US$ 400 million in diamonds per year.

18. The Strategic Framework and related documents are available on the UN Coordinator for Afghanistan's web site at *www.pcp.afg*.

19. The possible elements of a more unitary approach to the UN's involvement in weak or fragmented states is described, in relation to Afghanistan, in Donini *et al.* (1996).

20. We cannot wait for development 'until it is safe'; statement by Jan Pronk (1996).

14
Conclusion: Lessons for Preventive Action

Raimo Väyrynen

Can we prevent complex humanitarian emergencies? A flippant 'yes' indicates self-deception that is hard to defend. The effect of domestic and international factors on political violence and human suffering is partial, delayed, complex and mediated by many other factors. Therefore, the results of preventive strategies are uncertain and unpredictable and may even worsen rather than ameliorate the emergency. The best advice is that of Hippocrates: 'Do no harm'.

Yet, non-action in the face of threatening civil war and humanitarian strategy is not usually an option. Both ethical requirements and utilitarian calculations suggest that preventive action is a recommendable policy. While the minimum goal would be to do no harm, positive aspirations can well save human lives, political institutions and material resources. War always destroys and cannot ever be said to be beneficial for the entire society, although it may benefit individual groups of war profiteers.

14.1 Domestic strategies

The preceding chapters provide some guidelines for policies to contain and mitigate CHEs. The best guarantee against CHEs is durable and balanced economic and social development. Sustained economic growth, the protection of environmental resources, equality in vertical and horizontal social relations and an inclusive and participatory political system create good conditions for social stability. More importantly, they facilitate social change in which conflicts are resolved without recourse to major violence. Prerequisite for stability in politically or ethnically divided societies are institutional arrangements that include accountable and responsible political institutions, independent media and courts and a robust civil society.

Power sharing is usually the most workable approach to consolidating democracy. The most robust finding of empirical research is that democratic countries practically never suffer from CHEs. The issue is less that of formal representative institutions, such as elections and parliaments, than of a national political contract where key players participate and share the benefits and costs of ruling the country. Such a contract facilitates participation, increases transparency and establishes political accountability among rulers.

Power sharing also disseminates information that improves predictability, making long-term planning possible. The lengthening of the time horizon is essential for preventing and recovering from war. Commitment to political cooperation and economic investments become a viable option only if the domestic and foreign actors are assured about the future stability.

Pivotal in sustaining socioeconomic development is not discriminating against individuals or excluding social groups. Adequate basic social services protect vulnerable people from poverty and suffering but also buttress the legitimacy of government. Adequate services require tax reform and a dependable public administration to collect revenue and distribute it effectively and fairly. Taxes should primarily apply to income derived from the market rather than indirect tariffs and excise taxes which provide easily a route to rent-seeking and corruption.

In general, progress towards a welfare state counteracts divisive and unstable political tendencies, such as the exploitation of grievances for political gain. Socioeconomic equity and access to resources are primary in preventing the outbreak and escalation of CHEs. Thus, reform to increase access to land can reduce violent opposition and ameliorate the perception of injustice.

Beyond the physical availability of land is secure and fair property rights, sometimes difficult to establish with competing claims to land, as, for instance, between farmers and pastoralists or different ethnic groups. Too often the pressures of elites establishing commercial farms and cattle ranches take precedent over the interests of traditional communities with longstanding claims to ancestral lands. Also, too often the government tends to favour the demands of one ethnic or political group over the others.

Land reforms and secure usufruct rights raise productivity and thus reduce famine, disease and hunger. Property and usufruct rights are particularly important in countries where population explosion and land deterioration from such causes as erosion and salination make land a scarce resource. Rural populations need to be protected against the urban bias that so often results from the concentration of political influence and mobilization in cities. People in the countryside usually suffer the most from CHEs, partly because they are more difficult to reach by the international relief workers.

The rapid urbanization of LDCs results primarily from population growth and rising expectations, but in some countries may also be due to CHEs, which force people to move from their rural habitats to cities where there are more survival options. Thus, civil wars and CHEs indirectly worsen urban poverty, unemployment and related political tensions and expand the criminal underworld. The urban explosion is conducive to an expanded shadow economy run by organized crime and armed gangs over which the state has only limited control. In fact, the rise of this shadow economy and its criminal, violent underpinnings is a sign of the failure of the state to provide for public order, the lack of which makes CHEs even worse.

Violence and anarchy tend to keep foreign investors, with their capital and technology, away from the country. Without private capital inflows to complement public funds it is virtually impossible to establish a viable infrastructure in transport, communication, energy, education and research. Large-scale violence, by keeping private investment from the country, perpetuates a vicious circle, in which inadequate infrastructure, education and social services spur the continuation of violence that tears the country apart.

Hunger and disease, as components of CHEs, cannot be separated from ecological vulnerability. Environmental factors alone rarely have a direct impact on the outbreak and escalation of CHEs but their negative effects are multiplied by economic and political crises. In fact, the relationship is stronger from emergencies to the environment than vice versa. The main exception is efforts by predatory rulers and warlords to marginalize ethnic communities and their claims to land. In these cases, vulnerable communities, with uncertain land rights, lack incentives to safeguard resources and the environment, thus contributing to the increased risk of a humanitarian disaster.

Both WIDER and WB researchers have found that greed is a key motive for violence that increases human suffering. Violence and CHEs destroy human life and material values, while elites and their allies often benefit from them as a result of the regulated and biased nature of wartime economy. An economy ravaged by a CHE is one in which both political power and economic profits grow out of the barrel of a gun. Undiscriminating economic sanctions may increase the suffering of the people and strengthen the control of the economy by narrow political and military elites.

In this situation, the international community needs concentrated efforts to prevent access by these elites to lucrative transnational business networks through which they can use control of oil wells, hardwood forests, diamonds mines, poaching and cattle trade to accumulate foreign exchange for arms to support their predatory rule. The new international regime, created in 2000, to require a certification process for all the diamonds that enter international markets is an example of efforts at using cooperative action to curtail the access of warlords to funds to finance their military operations.

While it may be impossible to achieve a comprehensive agreement with immediate effect, there is a compelling need to establish international controls of the traffic in small arms. These arms are used to kill more people today than all the major weapons systems combined. As to the general economic sanctions, they could be made 'smarter' and more targeted to misbehaving leaders to minimize the costs to ordinary people.

Rapacious elites can worsen the economic and social situation of the country even if it does not suffer from a civil war. Rent-seeking power-holders can manipulate external tariffs and exchange rates, grant export and import licences to cronies and use the public bureaucracy to their and their allies' benefits. The demand for 'good governance', simplistic as it may sound, contains the truth that without adequate fairness, efficiency and accountability in public administration there cannot be inclusive and sustainable development. In public policy, special emphasis should be put on the health and education of children and their mothers, the most valuable renewable resource of any society.

The common view is that external economic and political conditions seldom cause a CHE but facilitate or become triggers of the crisis. In general, the articles in this volume stress the primacy of adverse domestic factors in increasing the risk of an emergency. In such a degenerative process, the ruling elites are usually the main culprits. Democracy and (if needed) rebellion are the standard means to get rid of rapacious and culpable elites. However, if the 'republic of fear' dominates the country, the domestic means of opposition are limited and often risky to those resorting to them.

The problem of limited means can be partly remedied by creating international institutions that can hold individuals accountable for their crimes and other types of misbehaviour. For this reason, the establishment of the International Criminal Court in Rome is important for preventing future CHEs. The Court, while criticized for being impractical or not in a country's political interest, establishes an international norm that the domestic misdeeds of rulers are not any more beyond reproach.

Most contributions emphasize the importance of long-term strategies instead of improvised rescue operations. Such operations are more often social or economic rather than political in nature. So often when governments and international agencies feel the urgency to do something, it is already too late to start an effective preventive operation. Therefore, individual governments and international organizations must develop forward-looking strategies to tackle the root causes of CHEs early on. The issue is less that of accurate early-warning or the existence of tool boxes that the decision-makers can open but the spread and internalization of the 'culture of prevention' in national and international public policy.

14.2 International strategies

While domestic causes may dominate the outbreak of CHEs, no doubt international factors shape the process of escalation and the outcome of such emergencies. In particular, the economic vulnerability of the country – from low income, high inequality, high indebtedness, lopsided dependence on the global market and high revenue instability – creates an international context in which ethnic and political divisions and the weakness of the state, can open the gates to military conflict and humanitarian crisis.

Development aid and other resource transfers should pay particular attention to ameliorating sudden external shocks, especially for primary-commodity exporters whose purchasing power depends on the amount of export revenue. We also know that not only the decline of raw-material and fuel prices but also their sudden rise (the 'Dutch disease') can bring about long-run economic and political problems as some oil-exporting countries have experienced. In other words, LDCs dependent on these prices may be in a no-win situation unless they design viable practices to use their export earnings.

Perhaps the biggest bone of contention in the study of the causes and preventive strategies of CHEs is the role of international (f)actors. The mainstream argument points to their indirect role in creating or mitigating domestic conditions that are responsible for the emergency. The emphasis on the key role of deep-seated inequities, predatory political rule and gross human rights violations, as catalysts of CHEs, is consistent with this approach. According to this view, while international (f)actors may sustain undemocratic governments, their repression and cruelty are due to domestic decisions and policies which can only be changed with difficulty from outside.

Yet, in the absence of domestic alternatives, there may be no other choice than to use international incentives and/or punishments to alter the local situation. The political goals may include the elimination of a predatory ruler or the containment of his policies to prevent the further deterioration of the humanitarian crisis. A further reason for international preventive reaction is the opportunity to avoid the huge economic and humanitarian costs of a civil war and a CHE. These costs are almost always higher than the expenses of preventive actions. A main political problem is that the main justification of such actions is the counterfactual and therefore imprecise argument that, if successful, they save both human lives and pecuniary resources.

In principle, there are multiple and diverse international strategies to prevent the outbreak and escalation of CHEs. These strategies range from human-rights monitoring and development assistance to economic sanctions and multilateral military responses. Practical experiences indicate, however, that many of these external policies are difficult to initiate, coordinate and implement in an effective and legitimate manner. The interests of governments differ, international institutions are weak and the international system has only a limited capacity at any given time to address multiple crises.

There is ample evidence on how multilateral economic and military responses to civil wars and CHEs have produced unintended or even perverse consequences. For instance, it has been repeatedly noted that responses by IFIs, not heeding the principle of 'do no harm', have often been mechanistic and favoured standardized packages at the expense of more imaginative and flexible strategies. Thus, for example, demands to reduce inflation or deregulate the economy have taken precedence over more comprehensive policies to foster economic development and equity.

Only recently, in the aftermath of the Asian financial crisis, has a serious discussion started on the true nature and consequences of alternative IFI policies. The inflexibility of economic adjustment and financial crisis management strategies reflects the rigid dogma that has prevailed for so long in the global centres of political and economic power. IFI approaches should be modified to encourage greater local initiative and responsibility and to create a more conducive environment for participatory economic development.

Only now have IFIs started to emphasize poverty alleviation and the promotion of equity as equally important to economic growth and financial orthodoxy. Goals of reducing poverty and inequality are linked up with the IMF-WB initiative to reduce the debt of the highly indebted poor countries (HIPCs). Until 1999–2000, with the increasing pressure of NGOs, Jubilee 2000, churches, trade unions and some G8 financial officers, the implementation of debt relief was slow, conditioned on a lengthy programme of IMF-approved stabilization and structural adjustment.

The IFIs, too preoccupied with the costs of moral hazard, failed to emphasize the benefits to poor countries from removing the barrier of high debt-service burdens to investment in social and economic development, the first line of defence against CHEs. The debt relief provided to 22 HIPCs by the end of 2000 may have avoided some moral hazard by mandating the recipients' commitment to allocate the funds released to social development, education and healthcare to reduce poverty and thus improve human security. Achieving these goals is also important in rebuilding wartorn societies into functioning political entities.

The liberalization of national and international economies has become an orthodoxy that has superseded all other social objectives. Even when liberalization benefits the world economy as a whole, its short-term effects, especially on income distribution, can wreak havoc for poor and vulnerable populations. To ensure the progress of globalization and safeguard against its negative consequences, the key national governments and IFIs should consider more carefully their own approaches.

It is important to make sure that abrupt liberalization, which has been more a rule than an exception, does not lead to a crisis of adjustment and decline in living standards for much of the population. Such an advice is particularly problematic if the country is recovering from a civil war or a similar deep crisis. One way to reach this goal is to increase concessional lending to accompany trade liberalization.

Perhaps the most important strategy is to open up the DC markets for the products of the LDCs. The main protectionist barriers exist in the South–North trade, not in trade between DCs. In these countries there are strong lobbies in some sectors, such as agriculture and textiles, that are ready to go at great lengths to block or, if they cannot attain this goal, decelerate the opening up of the domestic markets. Rough estimates are that the annual cost of DC protectionism against LDCs is higher than development assistance to them. If one also adds the cost of debt service, it is clear that LDCs lose in the international economic game.

The problem is not only pecuniary but goes to the heart of international governance – its rules and institutions. The international economic system is structured to favour the well-off and powerful. These rules, which tend to favour powerful vested interests, are difficult to reconfigure. Yet the situation is far from hopeless and progress can be made on two parallel tracks.

On the one hand, existing institutions can be reformed at the insistence of member governments and the non-governmental movements. This is happening, to some extent, in the WB and IMF which are taking the eradication of poverty much more seriously than, say, in the early to mid-1990s. The WTO seems to be slower in rethinking its missions and practices. This can be, in part, due to the fact that it does not dole out funds to LDCs, but aims to provide standards and solve international trade disputes. Actions and reforms are more visible if they are accompanied with tangible resources.

The EU provides a surprisingly remarkable example on how international institutions can change. It has adopted a new and ambitious goal: its internal market must be opened up to all LDC imports except arms. The implementation of this initiative will take time and be fraught with some contradictions, but the commitment of the European Commission appears to be serious. The EU has also repeatedly stressed that the next WTO round of trade liberalization talks can be successful and legitimate only if the developments issues are put at its core and NGO interests are considered.

On the other hand, there is a need to establish alternative structures of global governance and development financing. One should probably abandon any grand designs for global governance and realize that most feasible solutions are partial and hybrid in nature; they bring together governments and their joint organizations, transnational business and NGOs in various ways to collect and assess information, develop alternatives, make decisions and implement and enforce them. In this way, one can gradually develop institutions and practices that gain independence from the established power structures and doctrines.

From the standpoint of CHE prevention, development financing is perhaps the key issue among external strategies. It is encouraging that the UN has recently moved beyond the standard arguments in Secretary-General Kofi Annan's report of January 2001 as a contribution to a summit on financing for development in 2002. The Secretary-General's report contains close to one hundred recommendations on how to improve development financing by reassessing old ideas, combining existing strategies and creating new ones.

The report recommends new ways to handle debt in crisis situations, strengthen cooperation in combating global tax dodging and evasion, improve the effectiveness of aid through donor-recipient dialogues, develop appropriate financial services for the underprivileged and excluded and design effective financial regulations for both DCs and LDCs. In general, the UN is restoring its position as a key player in global economic governance, a move that has been long overdue.

This is reflected in Secretary-General Annan's repeated statements after his Harvard speech in October 1998 about the need to make globalization an inclusive process. He has also pursued the establishment of a Global Compact on corporate accountability and made somewhat unconventional policy interventions. An example of the latter is Annan's call to the EU not to slow down its opening up of markets to LDC imports, even if this move would face the resistance by some member governments.

14.3   Conclusion

A major problem with time-urgent preventive economic and military actions is that they are used by governments as substitutes for long-term commitments to address the root causes of CHEs. Even then, economic and military actions, such as sanctions and various forms of peace maintenance operations, may be poorly planned and executed and their goals inadequately spelled out. There is a need to step out of the box and start rethinking the nature and goals of long-term preventive strategies, including development financing and the role of IFIs. These strategies should primarily touch upon the conduct of domestic economic and social policies.

NGOs have become increasingly central in the conduct of humanitarian operations and new links between these, governments and international agencies are redefining the humanitarian space. NGOs are tangible actors that provide necessary services to the victims in regions suffering from CHEs. Yet, the NGO community, as a system of numerous and diverse actors, suffers from the lack of coordination and clear direction. NGOs cannot help much in the structural prevention of crises as their time horizon and resources are limited; only a handful of organizations have adequate funds and capabilities for simultaneous, sustained humanitarian action in several crisis areas.

The mainstream approach, stressing the inevitable but perhaps secondary nature of international responses, has been challenged by a critical approach, in which CHEs are considered in the context of the globalization of the world economy. The liberalization of trade and capital is regarded as an evil cause of economic vulnerability and social polarization which contribute, in turn, to political and humanitarian crises. Thus, globalization is seen as a cause of CHEs whose amelioration by humanitarian relief may, in turn, have a purpose to save the globalization process from its own contradictions.

The difference between the critical and the mainstream approach is that, in the former, the domestic causes of CHEs are regarded as necessary consequences of global factors instead of being merely conditioned by them as suggested by the latter. Moreover, in the critical approach, the humanitarian responses may be seen as deliberate efforts to maintain the stability of global capitalism and localize the effects of emergencies in the periphery, thus protecting the interests of the centre and its elites.

This interpretation, while valid on its face, is oversimplified. While globalization creates inequities and polarization, there are few, if any, instances in which it has directly caused a CHE. To be sure, emergencies have been common in resource-rich countries because of their lopsided integration into the world economy and the opportunities resources have provided for rent-seeking and predation. However, these situations reflect, the (post-) colonial patterns of development more than recent aspects of globalization based on capital mobility and technology.

Moreover, the CHEs in resource-abundant countries have mostly taken place in closed economic and political systems in which there is neither an efficient capital market nor a competitive allocation of resources. One can argue that it is the closure of the society that permits the misuse of resource rents for the benefit of the ruling elite and at the expense of the common people. From that point of view, humanitarian assistance is not so much a means to patch up the adverse effects of global capitalism as it is a provision for helping victims of unscrupulous political rulers and their abuses of power. The tragedy is that many of these victims cannot be reached without going through the government that has caused the problem in the first place and which often taxes humanitarian relief for additional gain.

In summary, CHEs appear to take place in countries and regions that have experienced a long-term economic and social crisis in which violence has become the dominant medium of politics and public disorder permits unscrupulous behaviour. In this sense, the conditions conducive to CHEs can be pathological. It would be misleading to address the causes of such deterioration and ultimate failure to any single factor, whether it be economic globalization or ethnic conflict. As the causes of CHEs are multiple and complex, the only opportunity is to adjust preventive actions to each particular case; there is no panacea but only trial and error that can, in a successful case, lead to recovery.

More often than not, the focus should be on domestic actions to restructure economic policies, rebuild institutions and share political power. These actions will not succeed without a long-term commitment of the key domestic political actors to reform the society and its power structures. International actions alone cannot prevent or ameliorate humanitarian crises but they can be used to redefine the context in which domestic solutions are sought for. It has become clear that the old financial orthodoxy cannot provide solutions to the predicament of most affected LDCs. Therefore, new thinking is needed on how to assure stability and human worth in the South; fortunately, there are recent signs that progress towards these goals has begun.

Glossary

ACP countries Sixty-six developing countries from Africa, the Caribbean and the Pacific, which had a series of trade and aid agreements, the Lomé conventions, with the EU from 1975 to 2000.

adjustment or structural adjustment Policies of privatization, deregulation, wage and price decontrol, trade and financial liberalization and reforms in agriculture, industry, energy and education intended to increase the economy's efficiency, macroeconomic balance and growth. In context, 'adjustment' may be shorthand for IMF and WB stabilization and adjustment programmes.

aid ODA, which includes non-military development grants or loans made at concessional financial terms (at least a 25 per cent grant element) by official agencies.

backward linkages Links to enterprises that sell inputs to a given firm. These linkages are part of the way society assesses an investment project.

basic social services Education, health, housing and social security and welfare.

bilateral aid Aid given directly by one country to another.

black market premium The extent to which the illegal or unofficial market price of a good or currency exceeds the official market price. For example, if Nigeria's official exchange rate is N0.72=US$1 and the black market rate is N2.95=US$1, then the premium is 310 per cent (2.95–0.72/0.72 = 3.10).

Bretton Woods institutions The IMF and WB, the initial framework of which was established in Bretton Woods, New Hampshire, in 1944.

capital flight Unregistered or illegal private capital outflows by a country's residents and institutions.

Chapter VI International peacekeeping with the consent of the parties involved.

Chapter VII International peacekeeping without the consent of the parties involved.

CHE A man-made crisis, in which large numbers of people die and suffer from war, physical violence (often by the state), or displacement, usually accompanied by widespread disease and hunger.

commoditization The treating of something (e.g. human labour, human life) as if it were a commodity by subjecting it to purchase and sale in a market.

commodity terms of trade The price index of exports divided by the price index of imports. For example, if export prices increase 10 per cent and import prices 22 per cent, the terms of trade would drop 10 per cent, that is 1.10/1.22 = 0.90.

communal tenure Refers to a land system in which some rights to the use of land are shared among members of the community; often the right in question is to graze animals on common property.

concessional funds Grants or loans with a substantial grant component. See also *aid*.

conditionality Conditions that the IMF or WB sets for lending.

crawling peg An exchange-rate system in which a home currency depreciates continuously, rather than abruptly, against foreign currencies.

current account The income component of the international balance of payments, referring to sales and purchases of goods and services separate from the transfer of capital or assets.

debt service   The interest and principal payments due in a given year on external debt.

debt–service ratio   The ratio of annual debt service to exports of goods and services.

economic growth   The rate of growth in gross product per capita.

economic regress   Economic decline or backward movement.

ecu   The notional unit of account, based on a weighted combination of currencies of member nations of the EU, used before the common currency, the euro.

effective rate of protection   Protection as a percentage of value-added by production factors at a processing stage.

ethnic community   A people linked by a special identity, such as race, religion, language, culture or tribe.

exchange control   A government or central bank limitation of citizens' purchase of foreign currency for foreign equipment, materials, consumer goods and travel.

'exit' option   The leaving of a group or withdrawal of membership when dissatisfied with a group or organization yet unable to effect change. In economics, a specific manifestation of 'exit' is the decision not to buy a product of a firm when dissatisfied, leading to a shift to that of another and thus perhaps spurring the management of the firm to search for ways to correct whatever faults have led to an exit (Albert Hirschman).

exogenous shock   A sudden, powerful (economic) disturbance external to the system.

exogenous   External to the system.

external (international) deficit   Exports less than imports of goods and services.

floating exchange rates   Exchange rates that are left free to be determined by supply and demand on the free market without intervention by a country's monetary authorities.

Foggy Bottom   US State Department.

foreign exchange rate   See *exchange rate.*

forward linkages   Links to units that buy output from a given firm. These linkages are part of the way society assesses an investment project.

GDP   A measure of the total output of goods and services in terms of income earned within a country's boundaries.

genocide   Mass murder because of the victims' indelible group membership.

Gini coefficient   An index of inequality (where equality is 0 and maximum inequality is 1), used to measure, say, the distribution of income or land holdings.

GNP   A measure of total output of goods and services in terms of income earned by a country's residents or institutions.

hacienda   The Spanish term for a large farm or estate.

income-elastic tax   A tax that increases as a percentage of GDP as income rises.

inflation tax   Inflationary financing through the government treasury expanding credit or printing money so the government can raise funds in excess of tax revenues. This financing imposes a tax on the holders of money.

informal sector   The part of the LDC urban economy with small-scale individual, family or other firms with less than ten workers, with wages below official minimum wages, with labour-intensive production and few capital, skills and entry barriers. This sector is usually not recorded in official statistics. In many LICs, it provides a major source of urban employment.

infrastructure   Social overhead capital such as that in transport, communication, power and technical research that increases the productivity of investment in directly productive activities.

international balance on goods and services   Exports minus imports of goods and services.

kleptocracy   A government run by thieves.

land consolidation   The grouping together of small plots of land into a larger unit, usually under the assumption that this will allow greater efficiency in the operation of the land.

Langley   US Central Intelligence Agency.

latifundia   Large farms or estates.

LDCs   Low- and middle-income countries, that is, those with a per capita GNP of $9360 or less in 1998, according to the WB. While the margin of error is substantial and the boundary between categories rises each year with inflation, membership in the categories has been relatively stable from 1974 to the 1990s.

liberalism   In economics, a school of thought which stresses freedom from the state's economic restraint. Present-day proponents of this view are often called 'neoliberals', followers in many respects of the English classical economists of the late eighteenth and early nineteenth centuries such as Adam Smith and David Ricardo.

liberalization   A country's movement towards the market, including a reduction in price controls, subsidies, regulations and ownership of land and capital by the state.

LICs   Countries with a per capita GNP of $760 or less in 1998, according to the WB (see *LDCs*).

LLDCs   A statutory UN list of countries based on a low combined score for the following indicators: per capita GDP, human development (life expectancy, per capita calorie consumption, primary and secondary school enrolment and adult literacy rate), economic diversification and population (see UNCTAD's annual *Least Developed Countries Report*). These countries are supposed to receive the majority of the aid provided by industrial countries.

macroeconomics   The economics that concentrates on entire economies, including aggregate income, consumption, investment, expenditures, employment and prices.

market-friendly   Refers to systems or reforms that assign an important role to markets on the grounds that they are expected to allocate resources efficiently.

mean   Average.

MICs   Countries with a per capita GNP of $761 to $9360 in 1998, according to the WB (see *LDCs*).

minifundia   Small farms, usually in both absolute terms and in relation to larger farms in the same agrarian system.

moral hazard   The risk associated with a loan where the borrower has incentives to invest in projects with high risk where the borrower does well if the project succeeds but the lender bears most of the loss if the project fails. The prospect of a 'bail out' of failed projects by the IMF and international community means that borrowers are more likely to shirk or use funds for personal use or power.

multilateral aid   Aid given to a country by an agency with several donor countries.

negative real interest rate   A nominal rate of interest less than the inflation rate.

overvalued currency   Attaining a price of foreign currency (exchange rate) below the market rate through exchange controls and trade restrictions.

parastatal enterprises   Public corporations and statutory boards owned by the state but responsible for day-to-day management to boards of directors, some of whom are appointed by the state.

Paris Club   A venue for LDCs to renegotiate their foreign debts through multilateral agreements with official creditors.

patronage   The establishment by the ruler of clientelist networks to distribute public offices, monopoly rents or other rewards in return for political support.

peasants   Rural cultivators running households whose main concern is survival. Their contrast is to commercial farmers, who run a profit-oriented business enterprise.

politicides   The murder of any person by the state because of the victim's group membership or politics, or for other political purposes.

predatory state   Rule by a personalistic regime ruling through coercion, material inducement and personality politics, a regime which tends to degrade the institutional foundations of the economy and state.

price elasticity (of demand)   The absolute value of the ratio of the percentage change in quantity demanded to the percentage change in price. For example, the increased price of a good, such as sisal used for fibre, by 10 per cent, reduces the amount of sisal demanded by 20 per cent, a price elasticity of 0.20/0.10 or 2.0.

privatization   Policies that include changing at least part of an enterprise's ownership from the public to the private sector, liberalization of entry into activities previously restricted to the public sector and franchising or contracting public services or leasing public assets to the private sector.

real gross product or growth   Inflation-adjusted GDP, GNP or economic growth.

rent-seeking   Unproductive activity to obtain private benefit from public action and resources.

shock therapy   An abrupt transition by a former socialist country to adjustment and the market.

stabilization or macroeconomic stabilization   Monetary, fiscal and exchange-rate policies to attain an optimal tradeoff between domestic economic growth and price stability (internal balance), and between internal balance and external balance, that is the international balance on goods and services.

state failure   The inability of government to produce public goods and/or its capture by a self-interested minority.

state legitimacy   The recognition by the society of the government's right to rule and the inclusion of all its members in decision-making.

structural vulnerability   Economic or ecological weakening of a society to such an extent that its members become exposed to the risk of a complex humanitarian emergency.

surplus   Output minus wages, depreciation and purchases from other units.

tariff rate   The import tax as a percentage of the price of a good. For example if the price of a shirt is US$20 and the import tax on that shirt is US$8, the tariff rate is 8/20 = 40 per cent.

terms of trade   See *commodity terms of trade*.

Tobin tax   A tax on all foreign-exchange transactions, levied to discourage short-term (especially speculative) capital movements, on which the burden of the tax is substantial. The author, James Tobin, suggests that each country tax transactions originating in its country at one-tenth of 1 per cent per dollar per transaction.

Uruguay Round   The 1986–94 (or last) negotiations under GATT before GATT was superseded by the WTO.

usufruct   Right of use, as with land.

variance   A measure of dispersion around the mean.

voice option   Expressing dissatisfaction and attempting to change the practices or products of an organization or firm when unhappy with an objectionable state of affairs. When the 'exit' option is not available, as under a monopolistic market, 'voice' may be the only option (Albert Hirschman).

Washington consensus A basic agreement by Washington-based institutions, the WB, IMF and US Treasury, on international economic policies towards LDCs. This consensus is derived from neoclassical or neoliberal economics, dominated by orthodox economists trained in the US and UK and especially associated with the views of US President Ronald Reagan and UK Prime Minister Margaret Thatcher during the 1980s. See also *liberalism*.

Guide to Readings

In explaining the origins of wars and CHEs, WIDER-QEH's comprehensive two volumes (Nafziger *et al.* 2000) emphasize low GDP per capita, protracted economic stagnation and decline, government exclusion of distinct social groups, state failure, predatory rule and high inequality, especially in access by groups to resources. Collier and Hoeffler (1998), for the WB, also find slow growth and low average GDP but not inequality contributing to wars.

Väyrynen (2000a) discusses the concept of CHEs and their association with failed and declining states. Nafziger and Auvinen (1997, 2000) and Auvinen and Nafziger (1999) use econometrics and politico-economic analysis to examine the sources of CHEs. Keen (1994, 1998, 2000) shows how, amid war and scarcity, ruling elites may benefit from spearheading genocide or tolerating mass murder by allies among militias, war profiteers and ethnic champions. Indeed, some interests derive economic advantage by CHEs, so that stopping them requires changing benefits and costs among rulers and their collaborators (Väyrynen 2000b).

Collier and Hoeffler's econometrics (1998) show that possessing natural resources increases the occurrence and duration of civil war. Contributors to Berdal and Malone (2000) use statistical analysis and case studies to reach similar conclusions. WIDER's contributors also emphasize that the struggle for control over minerals and other natural resources are important sources of conflict. In Angola, Sierra Leone, Liberia and Congo-Kinshasa, rulers and warlords used exclusive contracts with foreign firms for diamonds and other minerals to 'regularize' sources of revenue in lieu of a government agency to collect taxes (Reno 1996, 1998, 2000; Rich 1999).

In contrast to emphasizing the struggle for resource rents, Homer-Dixon and Blitt (1998), Homer-Dixon (1999), Suliman (1999) and Fairhead (2000) argue that scarcity rather than abundance of environmental resources contributes to competition, conflict and human suffering.

Holsti (1996) develops a conceptual framework to study the weakness and legitimacy problems of state in developing countries as an important cause of civil wars. State failure in these countries increases vulnerability to CHEs. Similarly, Cliffe and Luckham (1999) contend that CHEs are often rooted in prior state collapse. Conversely, in a weak or failed state, some rulers, warlords and traders are more likely to profit from war and violence than in peacetime. Indeed, Väyrynen (2000b) argues that CHEs do not result from the incapacity of public institutions but from the fact that rulers, warlords and their clients benefit from the harm thereby befalling a substantial share of the population.

The WB view differs from that of WIDER. Collier (2001) argues: 'Inequality does not seem to effect the risk of conflict'. Since Collier focuses on death inflicted by rebels and not the state, repression can reduce conflict. He contends: 'Conflict is not caused by divisions, rather it actively needs to create them....However, it is the military needs of the rebel organization which have created this political conflict rather than the objective grievances'. UNU/WIDER, however, emphasizes that most deaths from CHEs are from state violence and that objective grievances of poverty and inequality contribute to CHEs (Nafziger *et al.* 2000: vol. 1).

Gurr (1996) and Gurr and Harff (1996) discuss early warning for CHEs; Anderson (1983), Carnegie Commission (1997), Rotberg (1996), Rothchild (1997), Rubin

(1998) and Wallensteen (1998a) preventing or managing conflict; Lund (1996) and Cahill (see Gurr 1996) preventive diplomacy; Gordenker and Weiss (see Cuny 1991) and Minear and Weiss (1995) peacekeeping; and Leatherman *et al.* (1999) breaking cycles of violence. Turton (1997) examines the role of ethnicity in violent conflict and the prospects for prevention in a global context. On democracy and peace, see Ake (1996), Diamond and Plattner (1994), Joseph (1999), Ottaway (1995), Raknerud and Hegre (1997) and Sandbrook (2000). Esman and Herring (2001) discuss the possibility of using development aid to prevent and terminate violence. On rent-seeking and conflict, consult Kuran 1995. On asset transfer during famines, see de Waal (1990) and Duffield (1994a). Macrae and Zwi (1994) examine responses to CHEs. For statistical sources on CHEs, see the annuals from IRC, PRIO, SIPRI and UNHCR.

Bibliography

Abbreviations

FA	*Foreign Affairs*
HRQ	*Human Rights Quarterly*
IHT	*International Herald Tribune*
IPSR	*International Political Science Review*
JAE	*Journal of African Economies*
JD	*Journal of Democracy*
JID	*Journal of International Development*
JMAS	*Journal of Modern African Studies*
JPR	*Journal of Peace Research*
ODS	*Oxford Development Studies*
QEH	Queen Elizabeth House, Oxford University
ROAPE	*Review of African Political Economy*
TWQ	*Third World Quarterly*
USIP	US Institute of Peace
WD	*World Development*

References

Abi-Saab, Georges (1986). 'The Specificities of Humanitarian Law', in C. Swinarski (ed.), 'Studies and Essays on International Humanitarian Law and Red Cross Principles in Honor of Jean Pictet'. *HRQ* 126: 265–80.

Adelman, Howard and Astri Suhrke (with contributions by Bruce Jones) (1996). 'Study 2: Early Warning and Conflict Management', in Howard Adelman and Astri Suhrke (eds), *The International Response to Conflict and Genocide: Lessons from the Rwanda Experience*. Copenhagen: Danish International Development Assistance (DANIDA).

African Rights (1993). *Operation Restore Hope: A Preliminary Assessment*. London: African Rights.

—— (1994a). *Rwanda: Death, Despair and Defiance*. London: African Rights.

—— (1994b). 'Humanitarianism Unbound? Current Dilemmas Facing Multi-Mandate Relief Operations in Political Emergencies'. Discussion Paper No. 5. London: African Rights.

Agénor, Pierre-Richard and Peter J. Montiel (1996). *Development Macroeconomics*. Princeton: Princeton University Press.

Aguilar, Renato (1997). *The Role of Bilateral Donors and the International Financial Institutions in the Structural Adjustment Process: A Study Based on the Experiences of Mozambique, Nicaragua and Tanzania*. Stockholm: Sida.

Ahmed, Ismail I. and Reginald H. Green (1999). 'The Heritage of War and State Collapse in Somalia and Somaliland: Local-level Effects, External Interventions and Reconstruction'. *TWQ* **20**(1): 113–27.

Ake, Claude (1996). *Democracy and Development in Africa.* Washington, DC: Brookings Institution.
—— (1997). 'Why Humanitarian Emergencies Occur: Insights from the Interface of State, Democracy and Civil Society'. RFA 31, WIDER.
Alamgir, Mohammed (1980). *Famine in South Asia.* Cambridge, MA: Oelgeschlager, Gunn and Hain.
Alamgir, Mohiuddin and Poonam Arora (1991). *Providing Food Security for All.* London: Intermediate Technology Publications, for the International Fund for Agricultural Development.
Alesina, Alberto and Roberto Perotti (1996). 'Income Distribution, Political Instability, and Investment'. *European Economic Review* **40**(6) (June).
Alexander, Jocelyn, Jo Ann McGregor and Terence Ranger (2000). 'Ethnicity and the Politics of Conflict: The Case of Matabeleland', in Wayne E. Nafziger, Frances Stewart and Raimo Väyrynen (eds), *War, Hunger, and Displacement: the Origins of Humanitarian Emergencies*, 2 vols. Oxford: Oxford University Press, I.
Ali, Taisier and Robert O. Matthews (1998). 'Civil War and Failed Efforts for Peace in the Sudan', in T. Ali and R. O. Matthews (eds), *Civil Wars in Africa: their Roots and Resolution.* Montreal: Queen's-McGill University Press.
Allison, Graham T. (1971). *The Essence of Decision.* Boston: Little and Brown.
Alston, Philip (1997). 'Statement to the Commission on Human Rights', 18 March. New York.
Amer, Ramses (1993). 'The United Nations' Peacekeeping Operation in Cambodia: Overview and Assessment'. *Contemporary Southeast Asia* **15**(2): 211–31.
Amnesty International (1994). *Peace-keeping and Human Rights.* London: Amnesty International
Amsden, Alice (1997). 'Editorial: Bringing Production Back in – Understanding Government's Economic Role in Late Industrialization'. *WD* **25**(4): 469–80.
Anderson, Benedict (1983). *Imagined Communities: Reflections on the Origin and Spread of Nationalism.* London: Verso.
Anderson, Mary B. (1999). *Do No Harm: How Aid Can Support Peace – or War.* Boulder, CO: Lynne Rienner.
André, Catherine and Jean-Philippe Platteau (1997). 'Land Relations Under Unbearable Stress: Rwanda Caught in the Malthusian Trap'. *Journal of Economic Behaviour and Organization*, summer.
Annan, Kofi (1998). 'Africa Needs Outside Help, and Also Needs to Help Itself'. *IHT*, 2–3 May: 6.
Anonymous (1996). 'Human Rights in Peace Negotiations'. *HRQ*: 249–58.
Aoki, Takeshi (1992). 'Japanese FDI and the Forming of Networks in the Asia-Pacific Region: Experience in Malaysia and Its Implications', in Tokunaga Shojiro (ed.), *Japan's Foreign Investment and Asian Economic Independence.* Tokyo: University of Tokyo Press.
Apthorpe, Raymond (1997). 'Some Relief from Development: Humanitarian Emergency Aid in the Horn of Africa (including Sudan), Rwanda and Liberia'. *The European Journal of Development Research* **9**(2).
Archer, Clive (1994). 'Conflict Prevention in Europe: the Case of the Nordic States and Macedonia'. *Cooperation and Conflict* **29**(4): 367–86.
Aresvik, Oddvar (1976). *The Agricultural Development of Iran.* New York: Praeger.
Aron, Janice (1996). 'The Institutional Foundations of Growth', in S. Ellis (ed.), *Africa Now: Peoples, Policies, Institutions.* London: James Currey, 93–118.
Atwood, J. Brian and Leonard Rogers (1997). 'New US Guidelines for Providing Humanitarian Aid'. *IHT*, 13 March.

Aurik, Johannes and I. William Zartman (1991). 'Power Strategies in De-Escalation', in Louis Kriesberg and Stuart J. Thorson (eds), *Timing in the De-Escalation of International Conflicts*. Syracuse, NY: Syracuse University Press.

Austin, G. (1996). 'The Effects of Government Policy on the Ethnic Distribution of Income and Wealth in Rwanda: a Review of Published Sources'. London: London School of Economics. Mimeo.

Auvinen, Juha (1996a). 'Economic Performance, Adjustment and Political Conflict in the Developing Countries: Cross-National Statistical Analysis of the Determinants of Political Conflict with Case Study on Chile'. University of Sussex. D.Phil. dissertation.

—— (1996b). 'IMF Intervention and Political Protest in the Third World: A Conventional Wisdom Refined'. *TWQ* **17**(3): 377–400.

—— and Timo Kivimäki (1997). 'Towards a More Effective Preventive Diplomacy. Lessons from Conflict Transformation in South Africa'. Publications in International Relations C:4. Rovaniemi, Finland: University of Lapland.

—— and E. Wayne Nafziger (1999). 'Sources of Humanitarian Emergencies'. *Journal of Conflict Resolution* **43**(3): 267–90.

Avramovic, Dragoslav (1991). 'Africa's Debts and Economic Recovery'. Paper presented at the North-South Roundtable, Abidjan, Côte d'Ivoire, 8–9 July.

Ayoob, Mohammed (1995). *The Third World Security Predicament: State Making, Regional Conflict, and the International System*. Boulder, CO: Lynne Rienner.

Baev, Pavel (1994). 'Russia's Experiments and Experience in Conflict Management and Peacemaking'. *International Peacekeeping* **1**(3): 248–52.

Baranyi, Stephen (1995). 'The Challenge in Guatemala: Verifying Human Rights, Strengthening National Institutions and Enhancing an Integrated UN Approach to Peace'. Research Paper 1. London: Centre for the Study of Global Governance, LSE.

Bardhan, Pranab (1997). 'Method in the Madness? A Political-Economy Analysis of the Ethnic Conflicts in Less Developed Countries'. *WD* **25**(9): 1381–98.

Barkan, Joel D. and Njuguna Ng'ethe (1998). 'Kenya Tries Again'. *JD* **9**(2): 32–48.

Bates, Robert H. (1989). *Beyond the Miracle of the Market: the Political Economy of Agrarian Development in Kenya*. Cambridge: Cambridge University Press. MAC-chap-6.

Bayart, Jean-Francois, Achille Mbembe and C. Toulabour (1992). *Le politique par le bas en Afrique Noire*. Paris: Karthala.

Bayliss, Kate and Christopher Cramer (2001). 'Privatization and the Post-Washington Consensus: Between the Lab and the Real World', in Ben Fine, Costas Lapavitsas and Jonathan Pincus (eds), *Development Policy in the Twenty-first Century*. London: Routledge.

Becker, Gary and Casey Mulligan (1998). 'Deadweight Costs and the Size of Government'. NBER Working Paper No. W6789. Cambridge, MA: National Bureau of Economic Research.

Berdal, Mats and David Malone (eds) (2000). *Greed and Grievance. Economic Agendas and Civil Wars*. Boulder, CO: Lynne Rienner.

Berry, R. Albert (1997). 'Agrarian Reform, Land Redistribution, and Small-farm Policy'. Paper prepared for the WIDER project meeting on the Political Economy of Humanitarian Emergencies, 3–5 July, QEH, Oxford University.

—— and William R. Cline (1979). *Agrarian Structure and Productivity in Developing Countries*. Baltimore: Johns Hopkins University Press.

Besley, Timothy and Robin Burgess (2000). 'Land Reform, Poverty Reduction, and Growth: Evidence from India'. *Quarterly Journal of Economics* **112**(2): 389–430.

Best, Geoffrey (1994). *War and Law Since 1945*. New York: Oxford University Press.

Betts, Richard K. (1994). 'The Delusion of Impartial Intervention'. *FA* **73**(6): 20–33.

Bevan, D. (1992). 'How to Pass from a War to a Peace Economy: the Ethiopian Case: Fiscal Aspects of the Ethiopian Transition'. *Développement des Investigations sur L'Ajustement à Longe Terme*, No. 1992–07E. Paris: DIAL.

Binswanger, Hans P. and Klaus Deininger (1997). 'Explaining Agricultural and Agrarian Policies in Developing Countries'. *Journal of Economic Literature* **35**(4): 1958–2005.

——, Klaus Deininger and Gershon Feder (1995). 'Power, Distortions, Revolt, and Reform in Agricultural Land Relations', in Jere Behrman and T. N. Srinivasan (eds), *Handbook of Development Economics*, Vol. 3b. Elsevier: Amsterdam, 2659–772.

Birmingham, David (1992). *Frontline Nationalism in Angola and Mozambique*. London: James Currey.

Blackburn, Robin (1993). 'The Break-Up of Yugoslavia and the Fate of Bosnia'. *New Left Review* 199: 100–19.

Blaikie, Piers and Harold Brookfield (1987). *Land Degradation and Society*. London and New York: Methuen.

Bleaney, M., N. Gemmell and D. Greenaway (1992). 'Tax Revenue Instability in Sub-Saharan Africa: Causes and Consequences'. CREDIT Research Paper 92/2. University of Nottingham.

Boidevaix, Francine (1997). 'Une Diplomatie Informelle pour L'Europe. Le Groupe de Contact Bosnie'. Paris: Foundation pour les Etudes de Défense.

Borton, John (1993). 'Recent Trends in the International Relief System'. *Disasters* **17**(3): 187–201.

Boserup, Ester (1965). *The Conditions of Agricultural Growth: the Economics of Agrarian Change under Population Pressure*. London: Allen and Unwin.

Boutros-Ghali, Boutros (1993). 'Empowering the United Nations'. *FA* 1992/3: 89–102.

—— (1995). *An Agenda for Development 1995*. New York: UN.

—— (1996). 'Foreword', in Thomas G. Weiss and Leon Gordenker (eds), *NGOs, the United Nations, and Global Governance*. Boulder, CO: Lynne Rienner.

Breman, Jan (1997). *Footloose Labour: Working in India's Informal Economy*. Cambridge: Cambridge University Press.

Brilliant, Franca, Frederick C. Cuny, Victor Tanner and Pat Reed (eds) (1992). *Humanitarian Assistance Lessons of 'Operation Provide Comfort': A Study Prepared for the Office of US Foreign Disaster Assistance and US Army Civil Affairs*. Dallas, TX: INTERTECT.

Broad, Robin (1994). 'The Poor and the Environment: Friends or Foes?' *WD* **22**(6): 811–22.

—— and John Cavanagh (1993). *Plundering Paradise: the Struggle for the Environment in the Philippines*. Los Angeles: University of California Press.

Brochmann, Grete (1996). *European Integration and Immigration from Third Countries*. Oslo: Scandinavian University Press.

Bromley, Daniel W. and Devendra P. Chapagain (1989). 'The Village against the Center: Resource Depletion in South Asia'. *American Journal of Agricultural Economics* 66: 869–73.

Brookfield, Harold (1972). 'Intensification and Disintensification in Pacific Agriculture: A Theoretical Approach'. *Pacific Viewpoint* 13: 30–48.

Brown, Gordon (1998). 'Debt and Development, Time to Act Again', *The Economist*, 21 February: 97–98.

Brown, Marion (1971). 'Peasant Organizations of Vehicles of Reform', in Peter Dorner (ed.), *Land Reform in Latin America*. Madison, WI: Land Economics, University of Wisconsin-Madison.

Brown, Michael E. and Richard N. Rosencrance (eds) (1999). *The Costs of Conflict: Prevention and Cure in the Global Arena*. Lanham, MD: Rowman & Littlefield.

Brown, William (2000). 'Restructuring North-South Relations: ACP-EU Development Co-operation in a Liberal International Order'. *ROAPE* 27: 367–84.

Browning, David (1971). *El Salvador: Landscape and Society*. Oxford: Clarendon Press.

Bruce, John W. (1988). 'A Perspective on Indigenous Land Tenure Systems and Land Concentration', in S. P. Reyna and R. E. Downs (eds), *Land and Society in Contemporary Africa*. Hanover, NH: University Press of New England.

Bruck, Connie (1995). 'The World According to Soros'. *The New Yorker*, 23 January: 54–78.

Bruno, Michael and William Easterly (1998). 'Inflation Crises and Long-run Growth'. *Journal of Monetary Economics* **41**(1): 3–24.

Buchanan-Smith, Margaret and Simon Maxwell (1994). 'Linking Relief and Development: An Introduction and Overview'. *IDS Bulletin* **25**(4): 2–16.

—— and Susanna Davies (1995). *Famine Early Warning and Response – the Missing Link*. London: Intermediate Technology Publications.

Buckley, Stephen (1996). 'Zaire Rebels Transform Region's Political Balance'. *IHT*, 16 November.

Burg, Steven L. (1998). 'Nationalism and Civic Identity: Ethnic Models for Macedonia and Kosovo', in Barnett Rubin (ed.), *Cases and Strategies for Preventive Action*. New York: Century Foundations Press, 23–46

Burke, Angela and Gordon Macdonald (1994). 'The Former Yugoslavia Conflict (1991–)', in Michael Cranna (ed.), *The True Costs of Conflict: Seven Recent Wars and their Effects on Society*. New York: New Press, 155–96.

Bush, Kenneth D. (1996). 'Beyond Bungee Cord Humanitarianism: Towards a Developmental Agenda for Peacebuilding'. *Canadian Journal of Development Studies*, Special Issue: 75–92.

Callahan, David (1997). *Unwinnable Wars: American Power and Ethnic Conflict*. New York: Hill and Wang.

Cardeñas, Mauricio and Felipe Barrera (1997). 'On the Effectiveness of Capital Controls: The Experience of Colombia during the 1990s'. *Journal of Development Economics* **54**(1): 27–57.

Carment, David and James Patrick (eds) (1998). *Peace in the Midst of Wars: Preventing and Managing International Ethnic Conflicts*. Columbus, SC: University of South Carolina Press.

Carnegie Commission on Preventing Deadly Conflict (1997). *Preventing Deadly Conflict: Final Report*. Washington, DC: Carnegie Corporation of New York.

Carothers, Thomas (1996). *Assessing Democracy Assistance: The Case of Romania*. Washington, DC: Carnegie Endowment for International Peace.

Carter, Ashton and William Perry (1999). *Preventive Defense: A New Strategy for America*. Washington, DC: Brookings Institution.

Cassese, Antonio (1995). Address to the UN General Assembly. 7 November. New York: UN.

Castel-Branco, Carlos and Christopher Cramer (forthcoming). 'Privatization and Economic Strategy in Mozambique', in Tony Addison (ed.), *From Conflict to Reconstruction in Africa*. Helsinki: UNU/WIDER.

CEC (Commission of the European Communities) (1996a). *Annual Report 1995 on Humanitarian Aid*. Report from the Commission to the Council and the European Parliament. Brussels.

—— (1996b). *Linking Relief, Rehabilitation and Development (LRRD)*. Communication from the Commission to the Council and the European Parliament. Brussels: April.

CGG (Commission on Global Governance) (1995). *Our Global Neighborhood*. New York and Oxford: Oxford University Press.

Chandler, Alfred, F. Amatore and T. Tikino (eds) (1997). *Big Business and the Wealth of Nations*. New York and Cambridge: Cambridge University Press.

Chang, Ha-Joon (1993). *The Political Economy of Industrial Development*. Cambridge: Cambridge University Press.

Chapman, Audrey R. (1996). 'A "Violations Approach" for Monitoring the International Covenant on Economic, Social and Cultural Rights'. *HRQ* **18**(1): 23–66.

Cheru, Fantu (1989). *The Silent Revolution in Africa: Debt, Development and Democracy*. London: Zed Books.

Childers, Erskine and Brian Urquhart (1994). *Renewing the United Nations System*. Uppsala, Sweden: Dag Hammarskjöld Foundation.

Chirot, D. (1995). 'National Liberation and Nationalist Nightmare: the Consequences of the End of Empires in the Twentieth Century', in Beverly Crawford (ed.), *Markets, States and Democracy: the Political Economy of Post-Colonial Transformation*. Boulder, CO: Westview Press.

Chopra, Jarat, Åge Eknes and Toralv Nordbø (1995). *Fighting for Hope in Somalia*. Oslo: NUPI.

Cigar, Norman (1995). *Genocide in Bosnia. The Policy of 'Ethnic Cleansing*. College Station: Texas A&M University Press.

Ciriacy-Wantrup, S. V. and Richard Bishop (1975). 'Common Property as a Concept in Natural Resources Policy'. *Natural Resources Journal* 15: 713–27.

Clapham, Andrew (2001). 'Human Rights and the Prevention of Humanitarian Emergencies'. Working Paper No. 211, WIDER.

Clément, Sophia (1997). 'Conflict Prevention in the Balkans: Case Studies of Kosovo and the FYR of Macedonia'. Chaillot Papers No. 30. Paris: Institute for Security Studies, WEU.

Cliffe, Lionel and Robin Luckham (1999). 'Complex Political Emergencies and the State: Failure and the Fate of the State'. *TWQ* **20**(1): 27–50.

Cohen, Roberta and Jacques Cuenod (1993). *Improving Institutional Arrangements for the Internally Displaced*. Washington, DC: Refugee Policy Group.

Colchester, Marcus (1989). *Pirates, Squatters and Poachers: the Political Ecology of Dispossession of the Native Peoples of Sarawak*. London: Survival International and INSAN.

—— (1992). *Sustaining the Forests: the Community Based Approach in South and East Asia*. Geneva: UNRISD.

Colletta, Nat and Michelle Cullen (2000). *Violent Conflict and the Transformation of Social Capital*. Washington, DC: World Bank.

Collier, Paul (1998). 'The Political Economy of Ethnicity'. Paper presented at the Annual World Bank Conference on Development Economics. Washington, DC, 20–21 April.

—— (2001). 'Economic Causes of Civil Conflict and their Implications for Policy'. *http://www.worldbank.org/research/conflict/papers.civilconflict.htm*. Washington, DC: World Bank.

—— and Anke Hoeffler (1998) 'On Economic Causes of War'. *Oxford Economic Papers* **50**(4): 563–73.

Collins, Cindy and Thomas G. Weiss (1997). 'An Overview and Assessment of 1989–1996 Peace Operations Publications', Occasional Paper no. 28. Providence: Watson Institute.

Committee of Independent Experts (1999). *First Report on Allegations Regarding Fraud, Mismanagement and Nepotism in the European Commission.* Brussels: European Commission, 15 March.

Corbo, Vittorio, Stanley Fischer and Steven B. Webb (1992). *Adjustment Lending Revisited: Policies to Restore Growth.* Washington, DC: World Bank.

Cornia, Giovanni Andrea (1994). 'Neglected Issues in the Decline of Africa's Agriculture: Land Tenure, Land Distribution and R&D Constraints', in Giovanni Andrea Cornia and Gerald K. Helleiner (eds), *From Adjustment to Development in Africa: Conflict, Controversy, Convergence, Consensus?* Basingstoke: St. Martin's Press – now Palgrave, 217–47.

—— and N. H. I. Lipumba (1999). 'The Impact of the Liberalization of the Exchange Rate and Financial Markets in sub-Saharan Africa: Editors' Introduction'. *JID* **11**(3): 317–19.

Cortright, David (1997). 'Incentives and Cooperation in International Affairs', in David Cortright (ed.), *The Price of Peace. Incentives and International Conflict Prevention.* Lanham, MD: Rowman and Littlefield, 3–18.

Côt, Jean (1996). *Dernière Guerre Balkanique?* Paris: l'Edition Harmattan/FED.

Cox, Susan J. (1985). 'No Tragedy of the Commons'. *Environmental Ethics*, 7: 49–61.

Cramer, Christopher (1994). 'A Luta Continua? A Contribution to the Political Economy of War in Angola and Mozambique'. Cambridge: Cambridge University. Ph.D. thesis.

—— (1997). 'Civil War is Not a Stupid Thing: Exploring Growth, Distribution and Conflict Linkages'. Department of Economics Working Paper No. 73. London: School of Oriental and African Studies.

—— and John Weeks (1998). 'Analytical Foundations of Employment and Training Programmes in Conflict-affected Countries'. A report to the ILO under the Action Programme for Countries Emerging from Armed Conflict. Geneva: ILO.

Cranna, Michael (ed.) (1994). *The True Costs of Conflict: Seven Recent Wars and Their Effects on Society.* New York: New Press.

Crocker, Chester A. (1995). 'The Lessons of Somalia'. *FA* **74**(3): 2–8.

—— (1996). 'All Aid is Political'. *New York Times*, 21 November.

——, Fen Osler Hampson and Pamela Aall (eds) (1996). *Managing Global Chaos: Sources of and Responses to International Conflict.* Washington, DC: USIP Press.

Cumberland, Charles C. (1968). *Mexico: the Struggle for Modernity.* Oxford: Oxford University Press.

Cuny, Frederick C. (1983). *Disasters and Development.* New York: Oxford University Press.

—— (1991). 'Dilemmas of Military Involvement in Humanitarian Relief', in Leon Gordenker and Thomas G. Weiss (eds), *Soldiers, Peacekeepers and Disasters.* London: Macmillan Press – now Palgrave, 52–81.

Daalder, Ivo H. (1996). 'Knowing When to Say No: The Development of US Policy for Peace Keeping', in William J. Durch (ed.), *UN Peacekeeping, American Policy, and the Uncivil Wars of the 1990s.* New York: St. Martin's Press – now Palgrave, 35–68.

DAC (1997). *Development Assistance Report 1997.* Paris: OECD Development Assistance Committee.

Darcy, James (1997). 'Human Rights and International Legal Standards: What Do Relief Workers Need to Know?' RR Network Paper 19. London: ODI.

Daudet, Yves (1997). 'Legal Aspects and Financial and Budgetary Processes', in B. Stern (ed.), *United Nations Peacekeeping Operations: A Guide to French Policies.* Tokyo: United Nations University.

Davies, James C. (1962). 'Towards a Theory of Revolution'. *American Sociological Review* **27**(1): 5–19.

DeMars, William (1995). 'Waiting for Early Warning: Humanitarian Action After the Cold War'. *Journal of Refugee Studies* **8**(4): 390–410.

—— (1997). 'Contending Neutralities: Humanitarian Organizations and War in the Horn of Africa', in Jackie Smith, Charles Chatfield and Ron Pagnucco (eds), *Transnational Social Movements and Global Politics: Solidarity Beyond the State*. Syracuse, NY: Syracuse University Press.

—— (2000). 'War and Mercy in Africa'. *World Policy Journal* **17**(2): 1–10.

—— (2001). 'Hazardous Partnership: NGOs and American Intelligence in Small Wars'. *International Journal of Intelligence and Counterintelligence* (forthcoming).

de Nevers, Reneé (1993). 'Democratization and Ethnic Conflict'. *Survival* **35**(2): 31–48.

de Rossanet, Bertrand (1996). *Peacemaking and Peacekeeping in Yugoslavia*. The Hague: Kluwer.

Des Forges, Alison (1996). 'Making Noise Effectively: Lessons from the Rwandan Catastrophe', in Robert I. Rotberg (ed.), *Vigilance and Vengeance: NGOs Preventing Ethnic Conflict in Divided Societies*. Washington, DC: Brookings Institution.

Deshpande, Ashwini (1997). 'The Debt Overhang and the Disincentive to Invest'. *Journal of Development Economics* **52**(1): 169–87.

Dessus, Sébastien, Jean-Dominique Lafay and Christian Morrisson (1998). 'A Politico-economic Model for Stabilization in Africa'. *JAE* **7**(3): 91–119.

Destexhe, Alain (1994–95). 'The Third Genocide'. *Foreign Policy* 97: 3–17 (Winter).

de Tocqueville, Alexis (1955). *The Old Regime and the French Revolution*. Garden City, NY: Doubleday.

de Waal, Alex (1990). 'A Reassessment of Entitlement Theory in the Light of the Recent Famines in Africa'. *Development and Change* 21: 469–90.

—— and Rakiya Omaar (1994a). 'Can Military Intervention be "Humanitarian"?'. *Middle East Report* 187/188: 3–8.

—— (1994b). 'Humanitarianism Unbound: Current Dilemmas Facing Multi-Mandate Relief Operations in Political Emergencies'. Discussion Paper No. 5. London: African Rights.

—— (1995). 'The Genocide in Rwanda and the International Response'. *Current History* 94: 156–61.

Diamond, Larry (1995). *Promoting Democracy in the 1990s: Actors and Instruments, Issues and Imperatives*. A Report to the Carnegie Commission on Preventing Deadly Conflict. Washington, DC: Carnegie Corporation of New York.

—— and Marc F. Plattner (1994). 'Introduction', in Larry Diamond and Marc Plattner (eds), *Nationalism, Ethnic Conflict and Democracy*. Baltimore: Johns Hopkins University Press, ix–xxx.

Dixit, Avinash K. and Robert S. Pindyck (1994). *Investment under Uncertainty*. Princeton, NJ: Princeton University Press.

Donini, Antonio (1995). 'The Bureaucracy and the Free Spirits, Stagnation and Innovation in the Relationship between the UN and NGOs'. *TWQ* **16**(3): 421–39.

—— (1996). 'Surfing on the Crest of the Wave until it Crashes: Intervention and the South'. *Journal of Humanitarian Assistance*, Cambridge University (available through *www.gsp.cam.ac.uk/jha.html*).

—— Eric Dudley and Ron Ockwell (1996). 'Afghanistan: Coordination in a Fragmented State'. A lessons-learned report prepared for UNDHA, New York, December.

Dorner, Peter and William Theisenhusen (1992). 'Land Tenure and Deforestation: Interactions and Environmental Implications'. Discussion Paper No. 34. Geneva: UNRISD.

Downing, T. E. (1991). 'Assessing Socio-economic Vulnerability to Famine: Frameworks, Concept and Application'. Famine and Early Warning System (FEWS) Working Paper 2.1. Washington, DC: USAID, 102 pp.

Downs, George W. (ed.) (1994). *Collective Security Beyond the Cold War*. Ann Arbor, MI: University of Michigan Press.

Doyle, Michael (1996). 'Strategies of Enhanced Consent', in Abram Chayes and Antonia Handler Chayes (eds), *Preventing Conflict in the Post-Communist World. Mobilizing International and Regional Organizations*. Washington, DC: Brookings Institution, 483–505.

Drèze, Jean and Amartya Sen (1989). *Hunger and Public Action*. Oxford: Clarendon Press.

Duffield, Mark (1994a). 'The Political Economy of Internal War: Asset Transfer, Complex Emergencies and International Aid', in Joanna Macrae and Anthony Zwi (eds), *War and Hunger: Rethinking International Responses to Complex Emergencies*. London: Zed Books.

—— (1994b). 'Complex Emergencies and the Crisis in Developmentalism'. *IDS Bulletin* **25**(4): 37–45.

—— (1996). 'The Symphony of the Damned: Racial Discourse, Complex Political Emergencies and Humanitarian Aid. *Disasters* **20**(3): 173–93.

—— (1997). 'NGO Relief in War Zones: Toward an Analysis of the New Aid Paradigm'. *TWQ* **18**(3): 527–42.

—— (1998). 'Aid Policy and Post-Modern Conflict'. Occasional Paper 19. Birmingham: School of Public Policy.

Durch, William J. and James A. Schear (1996). 'Faultlines: UN Operations in the Former Yugoslavia', in William J. Durch (ed.), *UN Peacekeeping, American Policy, and the Uncivil Wars of the 1990s*. New York: St. Martin's Press – now Palgrave, 193–274.

Durning, Alan B. (1989). 'Poverty and the Environment: Reversing the Downward Spiral'. Worldwatch Paper. Washington, DC: Worldwatch Institute.

Eagleburger, Lawrence and Robert Barry (1996). 'Dollars and Sense Diplomacy: A Better Foreign Policy for Less Money'. *FA* **75**(4): 2–8.

Easterlin, Richard and Nauro Campos (1997). 'A Note on Mortality Reduction in East Asia and Latin America'. Paper presented at the Rethinking Development in East Asia and Latin America workshop, University of Southern California, Los Angeles, 11–12 April.

Easterly, William and Ross Levine (1997). 'Africa's Growth Tragedy: Policies and Ethnic Divisions'. *Quarterly Journal of Economics* **112**(4): 1203–50.

ECA (1989). *South African Destabilization: The Economic Cost of Frontline Resistance to Apartheid*. Addis Ababa: UN Economic Commission for Africa.

Eckholm, Erik P. (1982). *Down to Earth: Environment and Human Needs*. London: Pluto Press.

Edgren, Gus (1996). 'A Challenge to the Aid Relationship', in *Aid Dependency: Causes, Symptoms, and Remedies*. Stockholm: Sida, 9–21.

Egeland, Jan (1988). *Impotent Superpower – Potent Small Power*. Oslo: Norwegian University Press.

Ehrenpreis, Dag (1997). 'Preface', in Renato Aguilar (ed.), *The Role of Bilateral Donors and the International Financial Institutions in the Structural Adjustment Process: A Study Based on the Experiences of Mozambique, Nicaragua and Tanzania*. Stockholm: Sida.

Eicher, Carl K. and D. C. Baker (1982). 'Research on Agricultural Development in Sub-Saharan Africa: A Critical Survey'. International Development Paper No. 1. East Lansing: Michigan State University.

Eide, Asbjorn (1989). 'Realization of Social and Economic Rights and the Minimum Threshold Approach'. *Human Rights Law Journal* 10: 35–51.

Ekins, Paul (1992). *A New World Order: Grassroots Movements for Global Change.* London: Routledge.

Ellman, Michael (1979). *Socialist Planning.* Cambridge: Cambridge University Press.

Emizet, Kisangani N. F. (2000). 'Congo (Zaire): Corruption, Disintegration, and State Failure', in Wayne E. Nafziger, Frances Stewart and Raimo Väyrynen (eds), *War, Hunger and Displacement: the Origins of Humanitarian Emergencies*, 2 vols. Oxford: Oxford University Press, I.

Esman, Milton (1996). 'A Survey of Interventions', in Milton Esman and Shibley Telhami (eds), *International Organizations and Ethnic Conflict.* Ithaca, NY: Cornell University Press, 21–45.

—— (1997). 'Can Foreign Aid Moderate Ethnic Conflict?' *Peaceworks* 13. Washington, DC: USIP.

—— and Ronald Herring (eds) (2001). *Carrots, Sticks, and Ethnic Conflict: Rethinking Development Assistance.* Ann Arbor, MI: University of Michigan Press.

European Commission Humanitarian Office (ECHO) (1993). *ECHO Annual Review 1993.* Brussels: European Commission.

—— (1994). *ECHO Annual Review 1994.* Brussels: European Commission.

—— (1996). *ECHO Annual Review 1996.* Brussels: European Commission.

—— (1997). *ECHO Statistics 1997.* Brussels: European Commission.

Evans, Gareth (1993). *Cooperating for Peace. The Global Agenda for the 1990s and Beyond.* St. Leonards, Australia: Allen and Unwin.

—— Evans, Glynne (1997). 'Responding to Crises in the African Great Lakes'. *Adelphi Paper* 311. London: IISS.

Fairhead, James (2000). 'The Conflict over Natural and Environmental Resources', in Wayne E. Nafziger, Frances Stewart and Raimo Väyrynen (eds), *War, Hunger and Displacement: the Origins of Humanitarian Emergencies*, 2 vols. Oxford: Oxford University Press, I.

—— and Melissa Leach (1996). *Misreading the African Landscape: Society and Ecology in a Forest-Savanna Mosaic.* Cambridge: Cambridge University Press.

Falk, Richard (1993). 'Human Rights, Humanitarian Assistance, and the Sovereignty of States', in K. M. Cahill (ed.), *A Framework for Survival: Health, Human Rights, and Humanitarian Assistance in Conflicts and Disasters.* London: Basic Books, 27–40.

Fall, Bernard B. (1967). *The Two Viet-Nams.* New York. Praeger.

FAO (1991). *The State of Food and Agriculture, 1990.* Rome: FAO.

Farrell, Theo (1995). 'Sliding Into War: the Somalia Imbroglio and US Army Peace Operations Doctrine'. *International Peacekeeping* 2(2): 194–214.

Felipe, Jesus (2000). 'Convergence, Catch-up and Growth Sustainability in Asia: Some Pitfalls'. *ODS* 28(1): 51–69.

Fields, Gary S. (1994). 'Poverty and Income Distribution: Data for Measuring Poverty and Inequality Changes in Developing Countries'. *Journal of Development Economics* 44(1): 87–102.

Fine, Ben (1994). 'To What Are We Adjusting – the World Bank, the IMF and Economic Theory'. London: School of Oriental and African Studies. Mimeo.

Fischer, Stanley (1997). 'Capital Account Liberalization and the Role of the IMF'. *IMF Survey* 26(19): 321–24.

—— (1998). 'IMF and Crisis Prevention'. *Financial Times*, 30 March: 12.

Fisher, Ronald J. (1997). *Interactive Conflict Resolution*. Syracuse, NY: Syracuse University Press.

FitzGerald, Valpy and Frances Stewart (eds) (1997). 'War, Economy and Society'. *ODS* **25**(1): 1–10.

Fondation pour les Études de Defense Nationale (1995). *Operations des Nations Unies, leVons de terrain*. Paris: La Documentation Française.

Forsythe, David (1991). *The Internationalization of Human Rights*. Lexington, MA: Lexington Books for the Free Press.

Foundation on Inter-ethnic Relations (1997). *The Role of the High Commissioner on Natural Minorities in OSCE Conflict Prevention, An Introduction*. The Hague: Foundation on Inter-ethnic Relations.

Fowler, Allan (1992). 'Distant Obligations: Speculations on NGO Funding and the Global Market'. *ROAPE*, N 55.

Frankel, Jeffrey A. and David Romer (1999). 'Does Trade Cause Growth?' *American Economic Review* **89**(3): 379–99.

Freedman, Lawrence (1994–95). 'Why the West Failed'. *Foreign Policy* 97: 53–69 (Winter).

Friedmann, John and Haripriya Rangan (eds) (1993). *In Defense of Livelihood: Comparative Studies in Environmental Action*. West Hartford, CT: Kumarian.

Gaer, Felice D. (1997). 'UN-Anonymous: Reflections on Human Rights in Peace Negotiations'. *HRQ* **19**(1): 1–8.

Galtung, Johan (1971). 'A Structural Theory of Imperialism'. *JPR* 2: 81–99.

García-Sayán, D. (1995). 'The Experience of ONUSAL in El Salvador', in A. Henkin (ed.), *Honoring Human Rights and Keeping the Peace: Lessons from El Salvador, Cambodia and Haiti – Recommendations for the United Nations*. Washington, DC: Aspen Institute, 31–55.

Gellman, Barton (1999). 'The Path to Crisis: How the United States and Its Allies Went to War. *IHT*, 19 April.

George, Alexander (1999). 'Strategies for Preventive Diplomacy and Conflict Resolution. Scholarship for Policy-making'. *Cooperation and Conflict* **34**(1): 9–19.

—— and Jane Holl (1997). 'The Warning-Response Problem and Missed Opportunities in Preventive Diplomacy'. A Report to the Carnegie Commission on Preventing Deadly Conflict. Washington, DC: Carnegie Corporation of New York.

Gerschenkron, Alexander (1962). *Economic Backwardness in Historical Perspective: A Book of Essays*. Oxford: Oxford University Press.

Ghai, Dharam (1994). 'Environment, Livelihood and Empowerment', in Dharam Ghai (ed.), *Development and Environment: Sustaining People and Nature*. Oxford: Blackwell.

—— and Jessica M. Vivian (1992). *Grassroots Environmental Action: People's Participation in Sustainable Development*. London: Routledge.

Gibbs, Christopher J. N. and Daniel Bromley (1989). 'Institutional Arrangements for Management of Rural Resources: Common Property Regimes', in Fikret Birkes (ed.), *Common Property Resources*. London: Belhaven, 22–32.

Gilhodes, Pierre (1974). 'La Question Agraire en Colombie, 1958–71'. Paris: Librarie Armand Colin et Fondation Nationale des Sciences Politiques.

Gillis, Malcolm, Carl Shoup and Gerardo Sicat (eds) (1990). *Value Added Taxation in Developing Countries*. Washington, DC: World Bank.

Girardet, Edward (ed.) (1995). *Somalia, Rwanda, and Beyond: the Role of the International Media in Wars and Humanitarian Crises*. Crosslines Special Report 1. Dublin: Crosslines Communications Ltd.

Glantz, M. H. (1987). 'Drought, Famine and the Seasons in Sub-Saharan Africa', in R. Huss-Ashmore and S. Katz (eds), *Anthropological Perspectives on the African Famine*. New York: Gordon and Breach Science Publishers.

Gluckman, Max (1955). *The Judicial Process among the Barotse of Northern Rhodesia.* Manchester: Manchester University Press, reprinted 1980.

Goodpaster, Andrew J. (1996). *When Diplomacy Is Not Enough: Managing Multinational Military Interventions.* New York: Carnegie Corporation.

Goulding, Marrack (1996). 'The Use of Force by the United Nations'. *International Peacekeeping* 3(1): 1–18.

Government of Canada (1995). *United Nations Peacekeeping Operations: Toward a Rapid Reaction Capability for the United Nations.* Report by the Government of Canada (joint Foreign Affairs and National Defence), Ottawa.

Gowing, Nik (1994). *Real-Time Television Coverage of Armed Conflicts and Diplomatic Crises.* Cambridge, MA: Harvard University Shorenstein Center.

Grainger, Alan (1990). *The Threatening Desert: Controlling Desertification.* London: Earthscan Publications.

Green, Joy (1986). *Evaluating the Impact of Consolidation of Holdings, Individualization of Tenure, and Registration of Title: Lessons from Kenya.* Madison, WI: Land Tenure Center, University of Wisconsin.

Green, Reginald H. (1986). 'Hunger, Poverty and Food Aid in Sub-Saharan Africa: Retrospect and Potential'. *Disasters* 10(4): 288–310.

—— (1994). 'The Course of Four Horsemen: Costs of War and its Aftermath in Sub-Saharan Africa', in Joanna Macrae and Anthony Zwi (eds), *War and Hunger: Rethinking International Responses to Complex Emergencies.* London: Zed Books.

Greenaway, David, Wyn Morgan and Peter Wright (1997) 'Trade Liberalization and Growth in Developing Countries: Some New Evidence'. *WD* 25(11): 1885–92.

Greene, Joshua and Delano Villanueva (1991). 'Private Investment in Developing Countries'. *IMF Staff Papers* 38(1): 33–58.

Guillaumont, Patrick and Sylviane Guillaumont (eds) (1994). 'Adjustment and Development: the Experience of the ACP countries'. A study conducted at the request of, and in collaboration with the EC. Paris: Economica.

Gunther, Richard and Anthony Mughan (1993). 'Political Institutions and Cleavage Management', in R. K. Weaver and B. A. Rockman (eds), *Do Institutions Matter?* Washington, DC: Brookings Institution, 273–300.

Gurr, Ted Robert (1970). *Why Men Rebel.* Princeton, NJ: Princeton University Press.

—— (1996) 'Early Warning Systems: From Surveillance to Assessment to Action', in Kevin M. Cahill (ed.), *Preventive Diplomacy: Stopping Wars Before They Start.* London and New York: Basic Books, 123–43.

—— and Barbara Harff (1996). *Early Warning of Communal Conflicts and Genocide: Linking Empirical Research to International Responses.* Tokyo: United Nations University.

Gyimah-Boadi, E. (1996). 'Civil Society in Africa'. *JD* 7(2): 118-32.

—— (1998). 'The Rebirth of African Liberalism'. *JD* 9(2): 18–31.

Hampton, Jamie (ed.) (1998). *Internally Displaced People: A Global Survey.* London: Earthscan Publications.

Hanisch, Rolf and Peter Mossmann (eds) (1996). *Katastrophen und ihre Bewältigung in den Ländern des Südens.* Hamburg: Deutsche Ubersee-Institut.

Hanlon, Joseph (1993). *Mozambique, Who Calls the Shots?* Bloomington: Indiana University Press.

Hansen, Peter (1996). 'Old Concepts and New Approaches. Three Stages of Positive Prevention', in Kevin M. Cahill (ed.), *Preventive Diplomacy: Stopping Wars Before They Start.* New York: Basic Books, 285–302.

Hara, Fabienne (1999). 'Burundi: A Case of Parallel Diplomacy', in Chester Crocker *et al.* (eds), *Herding Cats. Multiparty Mediation in a Complex World.* Washington, DC: USIP Press, 139–58.

Hardin, Garrett (1968). 'The Tragedy of the Commons'. *Science* 162(3859): 1243–8.

Harriss, John (ed.) (1995). *The Politics of Humanitarian Intervention*. London: Pinter.

Harriss-White, Barbara and Gordon White (1996). 'Corruption, Liberalization and Democracy'. *IDS Bulletin* 27(2): 1–5.

Hayner, P. B. (1994). 'Fifteen Truth Commissions – 1974 to 1994: A Comparative Survey'. *HRQ* 16: 567–655.

Henderson, Errol A. and J. David Singer (2000). 'Civil War in the Post-Colonial World, 1946–92'. *JPR* 17(3): 275–99.

Hendricksen, Dylan, Robin Mearns and Jeremy Armon (1996). 'Livestock Raiding among the Pastoral Turkana of Kenya'. *IDS Bulletin* 27(3): 17–30.

Henkin, Alice (ed.) (1995). *Honoring Human Rights and Keeping the Peace. Lessons from El Salvador, Cambodia, and Haiti*. Washington, DC: Aspen Institute.

Herbst, Jeffrey (1996/97). 'Responding to State Failure in Africa'. *International Security* 21(3): 120–44.

Hertel, Thomas W., William A. Masters and Aziz Elbehri (1998). 'The Uruguay Round and Africa: A Global, General Equilibrium Analysis'. *JAE* 7(2): 208–36.

Hibou, Beatrice (1999). 'The "Social Capital" of the State as an Agent of Deception', in Jean-Francois Bayart, S. Ellis and B. Hibou (eds), *The Criminalization of the State in Africa*. London: James Curry.

Hirschman, Albert O. (1970). *Exit, Voice, and Loyalty: Responses to Decline in Firms, Organisations and States*. Cambridge, MA: Harvard University Press.

—— (1995). *A Propensity to Self-Subversion*. Cambridge, MA and London: Harvard University Press.

Hoben, Allan (1988). 'The Political Economy of Land Tenure in Somalia', in S. P. Reyna and R. E. Downs (eds), *Land and Society in Contemporary Africa*. Hanover, NH: University Press of New England.

—— (1995). 'Paradigms and Politics: the Cultural Construction of Environmental Policy in Ethiopia'. *WD* 23(6): 1007–21.

Hoffmann, Stanley (1995/96). 'The Politics and Ethics of Military Intervention'. *Survival* 37(4): 29–51.

Holm, John D. and Richard G. Morgan (1985). 'Coping with Drought in Botswana: An African Success'. *JMAS* 23(3): 463–82.

Holsti, Kalevi (1996). *The State, War, and the State of War*. Cambridge: Cambridge University Press.

—— (2000). 'Political Causes of Humanitarian Emergencies', in Wayne E. Nafziger, Frances Stewart and Raimo Väyrynen (eds), *War, Hunger and Displacement: the Origins of Humanitarian Emergencies*, 2 vols. Oxford: Oxford University Press, I.

Homer-Dixon, Thomas (1994). 'Environmental Scarcities and Violent Conflict: Evidence from Cases'. *International Security* 19(1): 25.

—— (1995). 'Strategies for Studying Causation in Complex Ecological Political Systems'. Toronto: University College. Unpublished.

—— (1999). *Environment, Scarcity, and Violence*. Princeton, NJ: Princeton University Press.

—— and Jessica Blitt (eds) (1998). *Ecoviolence. Links among Environment, Population, and Security*. Lanham, MD: Rowman & Littlefield.

Horowitz, Donald (1991). 'Ethnic Conflict Management for Policymakers', in Joseph Montville (ed.), *Conflict and Peacemaking in Multiethnic Societies*. New York: Lexington.

—— (1992). 'Comparing Democratic Systems', in A. Lijphart (ed.), *Parliamentary versus Presidential Government*. Oxford: Oxford University Press, 203–6.

—— (1994). 'Democracy in Divided Societies', in Larry Diamond and M. F. Plattner (eds), *Nationalism, Ethnic Conflict and Democracy*. Baltimore: Johns Hopkins University Press, 35–57.

HRFOR (Human Rights Field Operation in Rwanda) (1995). 'The Strategies and Priorities of HRFOR in 1996'. 19 December. New York: UNHCR.

Hroch, Miroslav (1993). 'From National Movement to the Fully-formed Nation: the Nation-building Process in Europe'. *New Left Review* 198: 3–20.

Hulme, David and Michael Edwards (eds) (1997). *NGOs, States and Donors: Too Close for Comfort?* New York: St. Martin's Press – now Palgrave.

Human Rights Watch (1993). *The Lost Agenda: Human Rights and UN Field Operations.* New York: Human Rights Watch.

Hveem, Helge (1994). *Internasjonalisering og Politikk (Internationalization and Politics).* Oslo: TANO.

—— (1997). 'Policies of Adjustment – National Coordination or Sectoral Logic? The Case of Norway'. Paper presented at the IPSA Congress, Seoul, August.

ICRC (1997). *World Disasters Report.* Oxford: Oxford University Press.

—— (2000). *World Disasters Report.* Oxford: Oxford University Press.

IDS-IDR (1996). *An Evaluation of Development Co-operation between the European Union and Ethiopia, 1976–1994.* Brighton and Addis Ababa: Institute of Development Studies (IDS) and Institute of Development Research.

Ignatieff, Michael (1997). 'Unarmed Warriors'. *The New Yorker.* 24 March: 54–71.

ILO (1997). *Guidelines for Employment and Skills Training in Conflict-Affected Countries.* ILO Action Programme on Skills and Entrepreneurship Training for Countries Emerging from Armed Conflict. Geneva: ILO.

IMF (1995). 'Unproductive Public Expenditures. A Pragmatic Approach to Policy Analysis'. IMF Fiscal Affairs Department Pamphlet No. 48. Washington, DC: IMF.

—— (1997). *World Economic Outlook, May 1997.* Washington, DC: IMF.

Independent Commission on International Humanitarian Issues (1988). *Winning the Human Race?.* London: Zed Books.

Ingram, James (1994). 'The Future Architecture for International Humanitarian Assistance', in Thomas G. Weiss and Larry Minear (eds), *Humanitarianism across Borders. Sustaining Civilians in Times of War.* Boulder, CO and London: Lynne Rienner.

Inoguchi, Takashi (1993). *Japan's Foreign Policy in an Era of Change.* London: Pinter.

IPA (International Peace Academy) (1996). *Civil Society and Conflict Management in Africa.* New York: IPA.

Isenberg, David (1997). *Soldiers of Fortune Ltd. A Profile of Today's Private Sector Corporate Mercenary Firms.* Center for Defence Information Monograph, November (*http://www.cdi.org/issues/mercenaries*).

Jaberg, Sabine (1997). 'Unvermeidbare Gewalt? Chancen und Grenzen Präventiver Friedenssicherung', in Friedhelm Solms *et al.* (eds), *Friedensgutachten.* Münster. LIT Verlag, 171–84.

Jackson, Robert H. (1991). *Quasi-States: Sovereignty, International Relations and the Third World.* New York: Cambridge University Press.

—— (1993). 'Armed Humanitarianism'. *International Journal* 68(4): 579–606.

Jacobs, Dan (1987). *The Brutality of Nations.* New York: Alfred A. Knopf.

Jakobsen, M. (1996). 'La Paix et Prosperité ou le Chaos Démocratique? Changements de Régime et Querres Civiles entre 1945 et 1992'. *Internasjonal Politikk* 54(2): 237–52.

Jakobsen, Peter Viggo (1996). 'National Interest, Humanitarianism, or CNN: What Triggers UN Peace Enforcement?'. *JPR* 33: 205–15 (May).

—— (1998). *Western Use of Coercive Diplomacy after the Cold War. A Challenge for Theory and Practice.* London: Macmillan Press – now Palgrave.

Jean, François and Jean-Cristopher Rufin (eds) (1996). *Economie des Guerres Civiles.* Paris: Hachette.

JEEAR (Joint Evaluation of Emergency Assistance to Rwanda) (1995). *Synthesis Report of the International Response to Conflict and Genocide: Lessons from the Rwandan Experience*. Copenhagen: JEEAR.

Jentleson, Bruce (2000). *Coercive Prevention. Normative, Political, and Policy Dilemmas*. Washington, DC: USIP.

Jervis, Robert (1997). *System Effects. Complexity in Political and Social Life*. Princeton, NJ: Princeton University Press.

Jetschke, Anja, Thomas Risse-Kappen and Hans Peter Schmitz (1996). 'Principled Ideas, International Institutions, and Domestic Political Change: Human Rights in Uganda and the Philippines'. Paper presented at the Annual Convention of the International Studies Association, San Diego, 16–20 April.

Jodha, Narpat S. (1986). 'Common Property Resources and Rural Poor in Dry Regions of India'. *Economic and Political Weekly* **XXX**(27): 1169–81.

Joseph, Richard (1987). *Democracy and Prebendal Politics in Nigeria: the Rise and Fall of the Second Republic*. Cambridge: Cambridge University Press.

—— (1998). 'Africa, 1990–1997: From *Abertura* to Closure'. *JD* **9**(2): 3–17.

—— (ed.) (1999). *State, Conflict, and Democracy in Africa*. Boulder, CO: Lynne Rienner.

Jungk, M. (1999). 'A Practical Guide to Addressing Human Rights Concerns for Companies Operating Abroad', in Michael K. Addo (ed.), *Human Rights Standards and the Responsibility of Transnational Corporations*. The Hague: Kluwer Law International, 171–86.

Kaiser, Paul J. (1996). 'Structural Adjustment and the Fragile Nation: the Demise of Social Unity in Tanzania'. *JMAS* **34**(2): 227-37.

Kaplan, Robert D. (1994). 'The Coming Anarchy'. *Atlantic Monthly* **273**(2): 44 ff.

Katz, Friedrich (1988). 'Rural Rebellions After 1810', in F. Katz (ed.), *Riot, Rebellion and Revolution: Rural Social Conflict in Mexico*. Princeton, NJ: Princeton University Press.

Kaufmann, Chaim (1996). 'Possible and Impossible Solutions to Ethnic Civil Wars'. *International Security*, **20**(4): 136–75.

—— (1999). 'When All Else Fails: Evaluating Population Transfers and Partition as Solutions to Ethnic Conflict', in Barbara F. Walter and Jack Snyder (eds), *Civil Wars, Insecurity, and Intervention*. New York: Columbia University Press, 221–60.

Keck, Margaret and Kathryn Sikkink (1998). *Activists Beyond Borders: Advocacy Networks in International Politics*. Ithaca, NY: Cornell University Press.

Keen, David (1994). *The Benefits of Famine: A Political Economy of Famine and Relief in Southwestern Sudan, 1983–1989*. Princeton, NJ: Princeton University Press.

—— (1997). 'A Rational Kind of Madness'. *ODS* , **25**(1): 67–74.

—— (1998). 'The Economic Functions of Violence in Civil Wars'. *Adelphi Paper* 320, Oxford: Oxford University Press.

—— (2000). 'War, Crime, and Access to Resources', in Wayne E. Nafziger, Frances Stewart and Raimo Väyrynen (eds), *War, Hunger, and Displacement: the Origins of Humanitarian Emergencies*, 2 vols, Oxford: Oxford University Press, I.

—— and Ken Wilson (1994). 'Engaging with Violence: A Reassessment of Relief in Wartime', in Joanna Macrae and Anthony Zwi (eds), *War and Hunger: Rethinking International Responses to Complex Emergencies*. London: Zed Books.

Keller, Gabriel (1992). 'La France et le Conseil de Sécurité'. *Le Trimèstre du Monde*, 4. trimèstre.

Kent, Randolph (1987). *Anatomy of Disaster Relief: the International Network in Action*. London: Pinter.

—— (1989). 'The United Nations Disaster Relief and Preparedness Role in Ethiopia: An Evaluation of the UN Emergency Prevention and Preparedness Group, 1987–1989'. Addis Ababa: UNEPPG. Mimeo.

Khan, M. (1987). 'Macroeconomic Adjustment in Developing Countries: A Policy Perspective'. *World Bank Research Observer* **2** (1): 23–39.

Kibreab, Gaim (1996). *People on the Edge in the Horn: Displacement, Land Use and the Environment*. London: James Currey.

—— (1997). 'Environmental Causes and Impact of Refugee Movements: A Critique of the Current Debate'. *The Journal of Disaster Studies, Policy and Management*, **21**(1):20–38.

—— (2000). 'Common Property Resources and Resettlement', in M. Cernea and C. McDowell (eds), *Risks and Reconstruction*. Washington, DC: World Bank, 293–331.

King, Charles (1997). 'Ending Civil Wars'. *Adelphi Paper* 308. Oxford: Oxford University Press.

Kleine-Ahlbrandt, S. T. E. (1996). 'The Protection Gap in the International protection of Internally Displaced Persons: the Case of Rwanda'. Geneva: HEI, Université de Genève.

Klugman, Jeni (2000). 'Kenya: Economic Decline and Ethnic Politics', in Wayne E. Nafziger, Frances Stewart and Raimo Väyrynen (eds) *War, Hunger, and Displacement: the Origins of Humanitarian Emergencies*, 2 vols. Oxford University Press, II.

Kohli, Atul (1993). 'Democracy amid Economic Orthodoxy: Trends in Developing Countries'. *TWQ*, **14**(4): 671–89.

—— (1997). 'Introduction: Community Conflicts and the State in India'. *Journal of Asian Studies* **56**(2): 320–4.

Korey, William (1998). *NGOs and the Universal Declaration of Human Rights*. New York: St. Martin's Press – now Palgrave.

Kriesberg, Louis (1997). 'Preventing and Resolving Destructive Communal Conflict', in David Carment and Patrick James (eds), *Wars in the Midst of Peace*. Pittsburgh: University of Pittsburgh Press, 232–51

Kumar, B. G. (1990). 'Ethiopian Famines 1973–1985: A Case Study', in Jean Drèze and Amartya K. Sen (eds), *The Political Economy of Hunger*, Vol. 2: *Famine Prevention*. Oxford: Clarendon Press.

Kuran, Timur (1995). *Private Truths, Public Lies*. Cambridge, MA: Harvard University Press.

Lake, Anthony (1994). Speech by the Assistant to the President for Security Affairs at a press briefing on PDD 25. 5 May.

Lake, David and Donald Rothchild (1996). 'Containing Fear: the Origins and Management of Ethnic Conflict'. *International Security* **21**(2): 41–75.

Lall, Sanjaya (1995). 'Structural Adjustment and African Industry'. *WD* **23**(12): 2019–31.

Lanxade, Jacques (1995). 'L'operation Turquoise'. *Defense Nationale* 51: 7–15.

Lautze, Sue and John Hammock (1996). 'Coping with Crisis, Coping with Aid'. Paper prepared for UNDHA, New York.

Lawyers Committee for Human Rights (1995). *Improvising History: A Critical Evaluation of the United Nations Observer Mission in El Salvador*. New York: LCHR.

Leach, Melissa, Robin Mearns and Ian Scoones (1997). 'Community-Based Sustainable Development: Consensus or Conflict?' *IDS Bulletin* **28**(4): 1–3.

Leatherman, Janie, William DeMars, Patrick D. Gaffney and Raimo Väyrynen (1999). *Breaking Cycles of Violence. Conflict Prevention in Interstate Crises*. West Hartford, CT: Kumarian Press.

Le Billon, Philippe (with Joanna Macrae, Nick Leader and Roger East) (2000). *The Political Economy of War: What Relief Agencies Need to Know*. London: Overseas Development Institute (ODI).

Leftwich, Adrian (1993). 'Governance, Democracy and Development in the Third World'. *TWQ* **14**(3): 605–24.

Legrand, Catherine (1986). *Frontier Expansion and Peasant Protest in Colombia, 1850–1936*. Albuquerque: University of New Mexico Press.

Lehman, John F. Jnr and Harvey Sicherman (eds) (1997). *The Demilitarization of the Military*. Washington, DC: Foreign Policy Research Institute.

Lemarchand, René (1998). 'Genocide in the Great Lakes: Which Genocide? Whose Genocide?' *African Studies Review*, **41**(1): 3–16.

Lepgold, Joseph S. and Thomas G. Weiss (eds) (1998). *Collective Conflict Management and Changing World Politics*. Albany, NY: State University Press of New York.

Levine, Alice (1996). 'Political Accommodation and the Prevention of Secessionist Violence', in Michael E. Brown (ed.), *The International Dimensions of Internal Conflict*. Cambridge, MA: MIT Press, 311–40.

Lijphart, Arend (1977). *Democracy in Plural Societies*. New Haven: Yale University Press.

—— (1991). 'Constitutional Choices for New Democracies'. *JD* **2**(1): 72–84.

—— and C. H. Waisman (1996). 'The Design of Democracies and Markets: Generalizing Across Regions', in A. Lijphart and C. H. Waisman (eds), *Institutional Design in New Democracies*. Boulder, CO: Westview Press, 235–48.

Lin, Justin Yifu and Jeffrey B. Nugent (1995). 'Institutions and Economic Development', in Jere Behrman and T. N. Srinivasan (eds), *Handbook of Development Economics*, Vol. 3. Amsterdam: Elsevier, 2301–70.

Linz, Juan (1990). 'The Perils of Presidentialism'. *JD* **1**: 51–69.

Lipton, Michael (1993a). 'Land Reform as Unfinished Business: the Evidence Against Stopping'. *WD* **21**(4): April.

—— (1993b). *Land Reform*. London: Routledge.

Loescher, Gil (1993). *Beyond Charity: International Cooperation and the Global Refugee Crisis*. New York: Oxford University Press.

—— (1994). 'The International Refugee Regime: stretched to the Limit? *Journal of International Affairs* **47**(2): 351–77.

Lonsdale, J. (1989). 'Introduction', in David Anderson and Richard Grove (eds), *Conservation in Africa: People, Policies and Practice*. Cambridge: Cambridge University Press.

López, Alejandro (1927). *Problemas Colombianas*. Paris: Editorial Paris-America.

Lopez, George and Michael Stohl (1991). 'Problems of Concept and Measurement in the Study of Human Rights', in Thomas Jabine and Richard Claude (eds), *Statistics and Human Rights*. Philadelphia: University of Pennsylvania Press.

Luck, Edward C. (1999). *Mixed Messages: American Politics and International Organization 1919–1999*. Washington, DC: Brookings Institution.

Lund, Michael (1996). *Preventing Violent Conflicts. A Strategy for Preventive Diplomacy*. Washington, DC: USIP Press.

—— (1997). *Preventing and Mitigating Violent Conflicts: A Revised Guide for Practitioners*. Prepared for the Greater Horn of Africa Initiative, US Department of State and USAID. Washington, DC: Creative Associates International.

—— (1998). 'Not Only When to Act, But How: From Early Warning to Rolling Prevention', in Peter Wallensteen (ed.), *Preventing Violent Conflicts. Past Record and Future Challenges*. Uppsala, Sweden: Uppsala University, 155–66.

——, Barnett Rubin and Fabienne Hara (1998). 'Learning from Burundi's Failed Democratic Transition, 1993–96: Did International Initiatives Match the Problem?', in Barnett Rubin (ed.), *Cases and Strategies for Preventive Action*. New York: Century Foundation Press, 47–91.

Lundberg, Lars and Lyn Squire (1999). 'Inequality and Growth: Lessons for Policy'. Washington, DC: World Bank. Mimeo.

Maastricht Guidelines (1997). 'Guidelines on Violations of Economic, Social and Cultural Rights, Adopted 27 January 1997'. *HRQ*, 20: 691–705.

Mackinlay, John and Randolph Kent (1997). 'A New Approach to Complex Emergencies'. *International Peacekeeping* 4(4): 31–49.

Macrae, Joanna (1996). 'The Origins of Unease'. Paper presented at a seminar on Ethics in Humanitarian Aid, Dublin, 9–10 December.

—— and Anthony Zwi (eds) (1994). *War and Hunger: Rethinking International Responses to Complex Emergencies*. London: Zed Books.

Maguire, Robert, Edwige Balutansky, Jacques Fomerand, Larry Minear, William O'Neill and Thomas G. Weiss (1996). 'Haiti Held Hostage: International Responses to the Quest for Nationhood 1986 to 1996'. Occasional Paper No. 23. Providence, RI: Watson Institute.

Malthus, Thomas (1798). *An Essay on the Principle of Population*. Published in Penguin Classics Edition (1970).

Mandela, Nelson (1995). *Long Walk to Freedom*. London: Abacus.

Martin, Ian (1994). 'Haiti Mangled Multilateralism'. *Foreign Policy* 95: 72–89.

—— (1997). 'How Can Human Rights Be Better Integrated Into Peace Processes?'. Paper presented at The Fund for Peace on 24–25 September. Washington, DC: Fund for Peace.

Mathews, Jessica (1997). 'Power Shift'. *FA* 76(1): 50–66.

Mauro, Paolo (1997). 'The Effects of Corruption on Growth, Investment and Government Expenditure: A Cross-Country Analysis', in K. A. Elliott (ed.), *Corruption and the Global Economy*. Washington, DC: Institute for International Economics.

McCann, James (1995). *People of the Plow: An Agricultural History of Ethiopia 1800–1990*. Madison, WI: University of Wisconsin Press.

McLeod, Alex (1995). 'La France à la Recherche du Leadership International'. *Relations Internationales et Stratégiques,* 19 (automne).

McNeill, Terry (1997). 'Humanitarian Intervention and Peacekeeping in the Former Soviet Union and Eastern Europe'. *IPSR* 18(1): 95–113.

Médard, Jean-Francois (1982). 'The Underdeveloped State in Tropical Africa: Political Clientelism or Neo-Partimonialism?', in Christopher Clapham (ed.), *Private Patronage and Public Power: Political Clientelism in the Modern State*. London: Frances Pinter.

Melkas, Helinä (1996). 'Humanitarian Emergencies: Indicators, Measurements, and Data Considerations'. Research in Progress 5. WIDER.

Melvern, Linda (1997). 'Genocide Behind the Thin Blue Line'. *Security Dialogue* 28(3): 333–46.

Meron, Theodore (1997) 'Answering for War Crimes: Lessons from the Balkans'. *FA* 76(1): 1–7.

Mesfin, Wolde-Marian (1991). *Suffering under God's Environment: A Vertical Study of the Predicament of Peasants in North-Central Ethiopia*. Berne: African Mountains Association.

Miall, Hugh (1992). *The Peacemakers. Peaceful Settlement of Disputes Since 1945*. New York: St. Martin's Press – now Palgrave.

Milne, Seamus (1997). 'Making Markets Work – Contracts, Competition and Cooperation'. Pamphlet available from Department of Management, Birkbeck College, University of London.

Minear, Larry (1995). 'The Evolving Humanitarian Enterprise', in Thomas G. Weiss (ed.), *The United Nations and Civil Wars*. Boulder, CO: Lynne Rienner.

——, in collaboration with T. A. Abuom, E. Chole, K. Manibe, A. Mohammed, J. Sebstad and Thomas G. Weiss (1991). *Humanitarianism under Siege: A Critical Review of Operation Lifeline Sudan*. Trenton, NJ: Red Sea Press.

——, U. B. P. Chelliah, Jeff Crisp, John MacKinlay and Thomas G. Weiss (1992). 'United Nations Coordination of the International Humanitarian Response to the Gulf Crisis 1990–1992'. Occasional Paper No. 13. Providence, RI: Watson Institute.

—— and Thomas G. Weiss (1993). *Humanitarian Action in Times of War*. Boulder, CO: Lynne Rienner.

—— and Thomas G. Weiss (1995). *Mercy under Fire. War and the Global Humanitarian Community*. Boulder, CO: Westview Press.

—— and Philippe Guillot (1996). *Soldiers to the Rescue: Humanitarian Lessons from Rwanda*. Paris: OECD.

Mitchell, Edward J. (1967). *Land Tenure and Rebellion: A Statistical Analysis of Factors Affecting Government Control in South Vietnam*. Memorandum RM-5181–ARPA (abridged), prepared for the advanced Research Projects Agency, ARPA order No. 189–1, June, Rand Corporation, Santa Monica, California.

Mkandawire, Thandika (1999). 'The Political Economy of Financial Reform in Africa'. *JID* **11**(3): 321–42.

Mokyr, Joel (1983). *Why Ireland Starved*. London: Allen and Unwin.

Molvaer, Reidulf K. (1991). 'Environmentally Induced Conflicts? A Discussion Based on Studies from the Horn of Africa'. *Bulletin of Peace Proposals* 22: 175–88.

Moore, Barrington, Jr. (1966). *Social Origins of Dictatorship and Democracy: Lord and Peasant in the Making of the Modern World*. Boston, MA: Beacon Press.

Morillon, Philippe (1997). 'Military and Civilian Aspects of Field Operations', in Brigitte Stern (ed.), *United Nations Peacekeeping Operations: A Guide to French Policies*. Tokyo: United Nations University.

Morrisson, Christian (2000). 'Stabilization Programmes, Social Costs, Violence, and Humanitarian Emergencies', in Wayne E. Nafziger, Frances Stewart and Raimo Väyrynen (eds), *War, Hunger, and Displacement: the Origins of Humanitarian Emergencies*, 2 vols. Oxford: Oxford University Press, I.

——, Jean-Dominique Lafay and Sébastien Dessus (1994) 'Adjustment Programmes and Politico-Economic Interactions in Developing Countries: Lessons from Empirical Analysis of Africa in the 1980s', in Giovanni Andrea Cornia and Gerald K. Helleiner (eds), *From Adjustment to Development in Africa: Conflict, Controversy, Convergence, Consensus?* Basingstoke: St. Martin's Press – now Palgrave.

Morris-Suzuki, Tessa (1992). 'Japanese Technology and the New International Division of Knowledge in Asia', in Tokunga Shojiro (ed.), *Japan's Foreign Investment and Asian Economic Interdependence*. Tokyo: University of Tokyo Press.

Morss, Elliot R. (1984). 'Institutional Destruction Resulting from Donor and Project Proliferation in Sub-Saharan African Countries'. *WD* **12**(4): 465–70.

Mosley, Paul (1999). 'Micro-macro Linkages in Financial Markets: the Impact of Financial Liberalization on Access to Rural Credit in Four African Countries'. *JID* **11**(3): 367–84.

——, Jane Harrigan and John Toye (1991). *Aid and Power: the World Bank and Policy-based Lending*, Vol. 1. London: Routledge.

—— and John Weeks (1993). 'Has Recovery Begun? Africa's Adjustment in the 1980s Revisited'. *WD* **21**(10): 1583–1606.

——, Turan Subasat and John Weeks (1995). 'Assessing Adjustment in Africa'. *WD* **23**(9): 1459–73.

MSF (Médecins Sans Frontières) (1996). 'Conference on the Cooperation between Humanitarian Organizations and Human Rights Organizations'. Final report of the Conference held in Amsterdam, The Netherlands, 9 February.

Mulaga, Geoffrey and John Weiss (1996). 'Trade Reform and Manufacturing Performance in Malawi 1970–91'. *WD* **24**(7): 1267–78.

Murphy, Craig (1994). *International Organizations and Industrial Change: Global Governance Since 1850*. New York: Oxford University Press.

—— and Enrico Augelli (1993). 'International Institutions, Decolonization and Development'. *IPSR* **14**(1): 82.

Mussa, Michael, Alexander Swoboda, Jeromin Zettelmeyer, and Olivier Jeanne (1999). 'Moderating Fluctuations in Capital Flows to Emerging Market Economies'. *Finance and Development* **36**(3): 9–12

Nadel, N. S. (1946). 'Land Tenure in the Eritrean Plateau'. *Africa* **16**(1): 1–22.

Nafziger, E. Wayne (1983). *The Economics of Political Instability*. Boulder, CO: Westview Press.

—— (1988). *Inequality in Africa: Political Elites, Proletariat, Peasants, and the Poor*. Cambridge: Cambridge University Press.

—— (1993). *The Debt Crisis in Africa*. Baltimore, MD: Johns Hopkins University Press.

—— (1995). *Learning from the Japanese: Japan's Pre-war Development and the Third World*. Armonk, NY: M. E. Sharpe.

—— (1996). 'The Economics of Complex Humanitarian Emergencies: Preliminary Approaches and Findings'. Working Paper No. 119. WIDER.

—— (1997). *The Economics of Developing Countries*, 3rd edition. Upper Saddle River, NJ: Prentice Hall.

—— and William L. Richter (1976). 'Biafra and Bangladesh: the Political Economy of Secessionist Conflict'. *JPR* **13**(2): 91-109.

—— and Juha Auvinen (1997). 'War, Hunger, and Displacement: An Econometric Investigation into the Sources of Humanitarian Emergencies'. Working Paper No. 141. WIDER.

—— and Raimo Väyrynen (1998). 'The Wave of Emergencies of the Last Decade: Causes, Extent, Predictability and Response'.WIDER. Mimeo.

—— and Juha Auvinen (2000). 'The Economic Causes of Humanitarian Emergencies', in Wayne E. Nafziger, Frances Stewart and Raimo Väyrynen (eds), *War, Hunger, and Displacement: the Origins of Humanitarian Emergencies*, 2 vols, Oxford: Oxford University Press, I.

——, Frances Stewart and Raimo Väyrynen (eds) (2000). *War, Hunger, and Displacement: the Origins of Humanitarian Emergencies*, 2 vols, Oxford: Oxford University Press.

Nathanson, Stephen (1998). *Economic Justice*. New Jersey: Prentice Hall.

National Security Council (1994). *The Clinton Administration's Policy on Reforming Multilateral Peace Operations*. Washington, DC: May.

Natsios, Andrew (1996). 'Humanitarian Relief Interventions: the Economics of Chaos'. *International Peacekeeping* **3**(1): 68–91.

—— (1997). 'US Foreign Policy and the Four Horsemen of the Apocalypse: Humanitarian Relief in Complex Emergencies'. CSIS Washington Papers. Washington, DC: Center for Strategic and International Studies.

Ndikumana, Leonce (1998). 'Institutional Failure and Ethnic Conflict in Burundi'. *African Studies Review* **41**(1): 29–47.

—— and James K. Boyce (1998). 'Congo's Odious Debt: External Borrowing and Capital Flight in Zaire'. *Development and Change* **29**(1): 195–217.

New York Times (1998). Various issues, in particular 28 February: A4; 25 March: A11; 26 March: A11.

Nikolaïdis, Kalypso (1996). 'International Preventive Action: Developing a Strategic Framework', in Robert I. Rotberg (ed.), *Vigilance and Vengeance. NGOs Preventing Ethnic Conflict in Divided Societies*. Washington, DC: Brookings Institution, 23–69.

Nordic UN Project (1990). 'Responding to Emergencies. The Role of the UN in Emergencies and ad hoc Operations'. Report no. 14. Stockholm.

North, Douglass C. (1990). *Institutions, Institutional Change and Economic Performance*. Cambridge: Cambridge University Press.

—— (1997). 'The Process of Economic Change'. Working Paper No. 128. WIDER.

Norwegian Institute for International Affairs (1998). *Development Assistance as a Means of Conflict Prevention*. Oslo: Norwegian Institute of International Relations.

Noy-Meir, I. (1982). 'Stability of Plant Herbivore Models and Possible Applications to Savanna'. *Ecological Studies* 42: 591–609.

OAU (First Economic Summit of the Assembly of Heads of State and Government) (1980). Plan of Action for the Implementation of the Monrovia Strategy for the Economic Development of Africa. Lagos.

ODI (1997). 'Foreign Direct Investment Flows to Low-Income Countries: A Review of the Evidence'. ODI Briefing Paper No. 3 (September): 1–4.

O'Donnell, Guillermo (1994). 'Delegative Democracy'. *JD* 5(1): 55–69.

—— (1996). 'Illusions about Consolidation'. *JD* 7(2): 34–51.

OECD (1997a). *Development Co-operation: Efforts and Policies of the Members of the Development Assistance Committee*. Paris: OECD.

—— (1997b). *Development Assistance Report 1997*. Paris: OECD/DAC.

Ogata, Sadako (1994). 'Role of Humanitarian Action in Peacekeeping Operations'. Keynote address given in Vienna, 5 July.

O'Neill, William G. (1995). 'Human Rights Monitoring vs. Political Expediency: the Experience of the OAS/UN Mission in Haiti'. *Harvard Human Rights Journal* 8: 101–28.

Ottaway, Marina (1995). 'Democratization in Collapsed States', in I. W. Zartman (ed.), *Collapsed States: the Disintegration and Restoration of Legitimate Authority*. Boulder, CO: Lynne Rienner, 235–49.

Oxfam (1995). Paper circulated in January 1995 now re-posted in the electronic *Journal of Humanitarian Assistance,* Cambridge University, *http://www.gsp.cam.ac.uk/ jha.html*.

Packenham, Robert (1973). *Liberal America and the Third World: Political Development Ideas in Foreign Aid and Social Science*. Princeton, NJ: Princeton University Press.

Palda, Filip (1993). 'Can Repressive Regimes Be Moderated Through Foreign Aid?'. *Public Choice* 77(3): 535–50.

Pape, Robert A. (1997). 'Why Economic Sanctions Do Not Work?'. *International Security* 22(2): 90–136.

Parekh, Bhikhu (1997). 'Rethinking Humanitarian Intervention'. *IPSR* 18 (1): 49–69.

Pastor, Manuel and James Boyce (2000). 'El Salvador: Economic Disparities, External Intervention, and Civil Conflict', in Wayne E. Nafziger, Frances Stewart and Raimo Väyrynen (eds), *War, Hunger, and Displacement: the Origins of Humanitarian Emergencies,* 2 vols. Oxford: Oxford University Press, II.

Paus, Eva (1995). 'Exports, Economic Growth and the Consolidation of Peace in El Salvador'. *WD* 23(12): 2173–93.

Pearse, Andrew (1975). *The Latin American Peasant*. London: Frank Cass.

Pellet, Alain (1995). *Droit d'Ingérence ou Devoir d'Assistance Humanitaire?*. Paris La Documentation Française.

Pieterse, Jan Nederveen (1997). 'Sociology of Humanitarian Intervention: Bosnia, Rwanda and Somalia Compared'. *IPSR* **18**(1):71–93.

Pinstrup-Andersen, Per, Rajul Pandya-Lorch and Mark W. Rosegrant (1997). *The World Food Situation: Recent Developments, Emerging Issues, and Long-term Prospects.* Washington, DC: IFPRI.

Platteau, J. P. (1996). 'The Evolutionary Theory of Land Rights as Applied to Sub-Saharan Africa: A Critical Assessment'. *Development and Change* **27** (1): 29–86.

Posen, Barry (1993). 'The Security Dilemma in Ethnic Conflict', in Michael E. Brown (ed.), *Ethnic Conflict and International Security.* Princeton, NJ: Princeton University Press, 103–24.

Posner, Richard A. (1998). 'Creating a Legal Framework for Economic Development'. *World Bank Research Observer* 13 (1): 1–11.

Prendergast, John (1996a). *Crisis and Hope in Africa.* Washington, DC: Center of Concern.

—— (1996b). *Frontline Diplomacy: Humanitarian Aid and Conflict in Africa.* Boulder, CO: Lynne Rienner.

PRIO (International Peace Research Institute, Oslo) (1997). *The State of War and Peace Atlas.* London: Penguin.

PRIO/NUPI (1997). *Engaging the Challenges of Tomorrow: Adjusting Humanitarian Interventions to the Character of Future Conflicts.* Final Report. Oslo: PRIO/NUPI (March).

Pritchett, Lant (1996). 'Measuring Outward Orientation in LDCs: Can It Be Done?' *Journal of Development Economics* 49: 307–35.

Pronk, Jan (1996). 'Development in Conflict'. Speech by the Minister of Development Cooperation of the Netherlands at the UNHCRA/IPA Conference on Healing the Wounds: Refugees, Reconstruction and Reconciliation, July, Princeton.

Prunier, Gérard (1995a). *The Rwanda Crisis: History of Genocide.* New York: Columbia University Press.

—— (1995b). 'Somalia: Civil War, Intervention and Withdrawal 1990–1995'. WRITENET Country Papers. UK.

Putnam, Robert D. (1988). 'Diplomacy and Domestic Politics: the Logic of Two-Level Games'. *International Organization* **45**(3): 427–60.

Radelet, S. and J. Sachs (1998). 'The Onset of the East Asian Financial Crisis'. Harvard Institute for International Development, 30 March. Mimeo.

Raknerud, Arvid and Havard Hegre (1997). 'The Hazard of War: Reassessing the Evidence for the Democratic Peace'. *JPR* **34**(4): 385–404.

Ramcharan, B. G. (1991). *The International Law and Practice of Early-Warning and Preventive Diplomacy: the Emerging Global Watch.* The Hague: Martinus Nijhoff.

—— (1996). 'Lawyers and Peace Negotiations'. *Review of the International Commission of Jurists* 56: 15–22.

Ramsbotham, Oliver and Tom Woodhouse (1996). *Humanitarian Intervention in Contemporary Conflict.* Cambridge: Polity Press.

Randel, Judith and Tony German (1996). *The Reality of Aid 1996. An Independent Review of International Aid.* ICVA, Eurostep Report. London: Earthscan Publications.

Ranis, G. and F. Stewart (1987). 'Rural Linkages in the Philippines and Taiwan', in F. Stewart (ed.), *Macro-Policies for Appropriate Technology in Developing Countries.* Boulder, CO: Westview Press.

Rashid, Ahmad (2000). *Taliban. Islam, Oil, and the New Great Game in Central Asia.* New York: I. B. Tauris.

Ravallion, Martin (1987). *Markets and Famines*. Oxford: Clarendon Press.

Rawson, David (1994). 'Dealing with Disintegration: US Assistance and the Somali State', in Ahmed I. Sattar (ed.), *The Somali Challenge. From Catastrophe to Renewal?*. Boulder, CO: Lynne Rienner, 147–87.

Refugee Policy Group (1994a). *Challenges of Demobilization and Reintegration*. Background Paper and Conference Summary. Washington, DC: Refugee Policy Group.

—— (1994b). *Lives Lost, Lives Saved: Excess Mortality and the Impact of Health Interventions in the Somalia Emergency*. Washington, DC: Refugee Policy Group.

Reilly, Charles (1995). 'Balancing State, Market and Civil Society: NGOs for a New Development Consensus'. Paper prepared for Notre Dame Conference on Poverty, University of Notre Dame, September.

Reinecke, Wolfgang H. (1996). 'Can International Financial Institutions Prevent Internal Violence?', in Abram Chayes and Antonia Handler Chayes (eds), *Preventing Conflict in the Post-Communist World. Mobilizing International and Regional Organizations*. Washington, DC: Brookings Institution, 281–337.

Reno, William (1996). 'Ironies of Post-Cold War Structural Adjustment in Sierra Leone'. *ROAPE* 67: 7–18;

—— (1998). *Warlord Politics and African States*. Boulder, CO: Lynne Rienner.

—— (2000). 'Liberia and Sierra Leone: the Competition for Patronage in Resource-Rich Economies', in Wayne E. Nafziger, Frances Stewart and Raimo Väyrynen (eds), *War, Hunger, and Displacement: the Origin of Humanitarian Emergencies*. 2 vols. Oxford: Oxford University Press, II.

Reychler, Luc (1997). 'Les Conflits en Afrique: Comment les Gérer ou les Prévenir?', in *Conflits en Afrique. Analyse des Crises et Pistes pour une Prévention*. Brussels: GRIP, 15–38.

Reyna, S. P. and R. E. Downs (eds) (1988). *Land and Society in Contemporary Africa*. Hanover, NH: University Press of New England, Vol. 3, ch. 5.

Reynolds, Andrew (1995). 'Constitutional Engineering in Southern Africa'. *JD* 6(2): 86–99.

Reynolds, Clark W. (1970). *The Mexican Economy: Twentieth Century Structure and Growth*. New Haven, CT: Yale University Press.

Richards, Paul (1996). *Fighting for the Rainforest: War, Youth and Resources in Sierra Leone*. London: Heinemann/James Currey.

Rich, Oaul (1999). *Warlords in International Relations*. London: Macmillan Press – now Palgrave.

Riddell, Roger C. (1996). 'Aid Dependency', in *Aid Dependency: Causes, Symptoms, and Remedies*. Stockholm: Sida, 23–110.

Risse-Kappen, Thomas (ed.) (1995). *Bringing Transnational Relations Back In*. Cambridge: Cambridge University Press.

Rittberger, Volker and Gabriele Kittel (1996). 'Föderalistische Konfliktbewältigung. Der Beitrag Föderalistischer Strukturen zur konstruktiven Bearbeitung innerstaatlicher Konflikte'. *Die Friedens Warte*, **71**(4): 373–94.

Roberts, Adam (1993). 'Humanitarian War: Military Intervention and Human Rights'. *International Affairs* 69: 429–49.

—— (1996). 'Humanitarian Action in War: Aid, Protection and Impartiality in a Policy Vacuum'. *Adelphi Paper* 305. Oxford: Oxford University Press.

Robinson, Mary (1997). 'Statement of the High Commissioner for Human Rights' in Kigali, Rwanda, 7 December. UNCHR: Mission to Rwanda.

Robinson, William (1996). *Promoting Polyarchy. Globalization, US Intervention and Hegemony*. Cambridge: Cambridge University Press.

Rodriguez, Francisco and Dani Rodrik (1999). 'Trade Policy and Economic Growth: A Skeptic's Guide to the Cross-National Evidence'. NBER Working Paper No. 7081. Cambridge, MA: National Bureau of Economic Research.

Roe, Paul (1999). 'The Intrastate Security Dilemma: Ethnic Conflict as a "Tragedy" '. *JPR* **36**(2): 183–202.

Rondos, Alex (1994). 'The Collapsing State and International Security', in Janne Nolan (ed.), *Global Engagement: Cooperation and Security in the 21st Century*. Washington, DC: Brookings Institution.

Ronfeldt, David and Cathryn L. Thorup (1995). 'North America in the Era of Citizen Networks: State, Society, and Security'. Santa Monica, CA: RAND.

Ropers, Norbert (1997). 'Prävention und Friedenskonsolidierung als Aufgabe für gesellschaftliche Akteure', in Dieter Senghaas (ed.), *Frieden Machen*. Frankfurt am Main: Suhrkamp, 219–42.

Rosenau, James (ed.) (1967). *Domestic Sources of Foreign Policy*. New York: The Free Press.

Rosenfeld, Stephen (1997). 'The Essential Humanitarians are Imperiled Professionals'. *IHT*, 19–20 April.

Rotberg, Robert I. (ed.) (1996). *Vigilance and Vengeance: NGOs Preventing Ethnic Conflict in Divided Societies*. Washington, DC: Brookings Institution.

—— and Thomas G. Weiss (eds) (1996). *From Massacres to Genocide: the Media, Public Policy, and Humanitarian Crises*. Washington, DC: Brookings Institution.

Rothchild, Donald (1997). *Managing Ethnic Conflict in Africa. Pressures and Incentives for Cooperation*. Washington, DC: Brookings Institution.

Rubin, Barnett (ed.) (1996). *Toward Comprehensive Peace in Southeast Europe: Conflict Prevention in the South Balkans*. New York: Twentieth Century Fund Press.

—— (ed.) (1998). *Cases and Strategies for Preventive Action*. New York: Century Foundation Press.

Rubin, Elizabeth (1997). 'An Army of One's Own'. *Harper's Magazine*, February.

Runge, C. F. (1983). 'Common Property Externalities – Isolation, Assurance, and Resource Depletion in a Traditional Grazing Context. *American Journal of Agricultural Economics* **63**(4): 596–606.

Sachs, Jeffrey D. and Andrew M. Warner (1997). 'Sources of Slow Growth in African Economies'. *JAE* **6**(3): 335–76.

Sahnoun, Mohamed (1994). *Somalia: the Missed Opportunities*. Washington, DC: USIP Press.

Salamon, Lester and Helmut Anheier (1994). *The Emerging Sector: An Overview*. Baltimore, MD: The Johns Hopkins University Institute for Policy Studies.

Salih, Kamal O. (1991). 'The Sudan, 1985–89: the Fading Democracy', in Peter Woodward (ed.), *Sudan after Nimeiri*. London: Routledge, 45–75.

Samatar, Ahmed I. (2000). 'The Somali Catastrophe: Explanation and Implications', in Morten Bøås, Einar Braathen and Gjermund Sæter (eds), *Ethnicity Kills? The Politics of War, Peace and Ethnicity in Sub-Saharan Africa*. London: Macmillan Press – now Palgrave, 37–67

Sandbrook, Richard (1993). *The Politics of Africa's Economic Recovery*. Cambridge: Cambridge University Press, ch. 3.

—— (2000). *Closing the Circle: Democratization and Development in Africa*. London and New York: Zed Books, ch. 6.

—— and Jay Oelbaum (1997). 'Reforming Dysfunctional Institutions through Democratization? Reflections on Ghana'. *JMAS* **35**(4): 603–46.

Sapir, Deborati G. and Hedwig Deconnick (1995). 'The Paradox of Humanitarian Assistance and Military Intervention in Somalia', in Thomas G. Weiss (ed.), *The United Nations and Civil Wars*. Boulder, CO: Lynne Rienner, 151–72.

Scherrer, Christian (1999). 'Conflict Management and the Process of Escalation: Timing and Types of Responses', in Håkan Wiberg and Christian Scherrer (eds), *Ethnicity and Intra-State Conflict*. Aldershot: Ashgate, 165–84.

Schierup, Carl-Ulrich (1992). 'Quasi-proletarians and a Patriarchal Bureaucracy: Aspects of Yugoslavia's Re-peripheralization'. *Soviet Studies* **44**(1): 79–99.

—— (1993a). 'Eurobalkanism: Ethnic Cleansing and the Post-Cold War Order'. Paper prepared for the international conference on The Yugoslav War and Security in the Balkans and in Europe, Bologna, 10–11 December.

—— (1993b). 'Prelude to the Inferno: Economic Disintegration and the Political Fragmentation of Yugoslavia'. *Balkan Forum* **1**(8): March.

Scott, James C. (1976). *The Moral Economy of the Peasant: Rebellion and Subsistence in Southeast Asia*. New Haven, CT: Yale University Press.

Seiple, Chris (1996). *The US Military/NGO Relationship in Humanitarian Interventions*. Carlisle, PA: US Army War College.

Sen, Amartya K. (1981). *Poverty and Famines*. Oxford: Clarendon Press.

—— (1994). 'Economic Regress: Concepts and Features'. *Proceedings of the World Bank Annual Conference on Development Economics*. Washington, DC: World Bank.

Shaw, R. Paul (1989). 'Rapid Population Growth and Environmental Degradation: Ultimate Versus Proximate Factors'. *Environmental Conservation* **16**(3): 1999–2008.

Shinn, James (1996). 'Japan as an "Ordinary Country"'. *Current History* **95**(605) (December).

Shiras, Peter (1996). 'Big Problems, Small Print: A Guide to the Complexity of Humanitarian Emergencies and the Media', in Robert I. Rotberg and Thomas G. Weiss (eds), *From Massacres to Genocide. The Media, Public Policy, and Humanitarian Crises*. Washington, DC: Brookings Institution.

Shojiro, Tokunaga (1992). 'Japan's FDI-Promoting Systems and Intra-Asia Networks: New Investment and Trade Systems Created by the Borderless Economy', in Tokunaga Shojiro (ed.), *Japan's Foreign Investment and Asian Economic Interdependence*. Tokyo: University of Tokyo Press.

Simpson, M. and A. H. Khalifa (1976). 'A Study of Agricultural Development in the Central Rainlands of the Sudan: An Interim Report'. Occasional Paper No. 5. Khartoum: Economic and Social Research Council, National Council for Research.

Singer, J. David and Melvyn Small (1994 and update). *Correlates of War Project: International Civil War Data*. Pt. 2, The Civil Wars File. New Haven, CT: http://biscu.its.yale.edu/cgi-bin/s-despires/925.spires.

Singh, Ajit (1999). 'Should Africa Promote Stock Market Capitalism?' *JID* **11**(3): 343–65.

SIPRI (1996). *SIPRI Yearbook, 1996: Armaments, Disarmament and International Security*. Oxford: Oxford University Press.

Sisk, Timothy D. (1996). *Power Sharing and International Mediation in Ethnic Conflicts*. Washington, DC: USIP Press.

Slim, Hugo (1995). 'The Continuing Metamorphosis of the Humanitarian Practitioner: Some New Colours for an Endangered Chameleon'. *Disasters*, **19**(2): 110–26.

Smith, Adam (1961). *An Inquiry into the Causes of the Wealth of Nation*. London: Methuen.

Smith, Brian (1990). *More Than Altruism: the Politics of Private Foreign Aid*. Princeton, NY: Princeton University Press.

Smith, Dan (1999). 'Preventing Conflict Escalation: Uncertainty and Knowledge', in Ho-Won Jeong (ed.), *The New Agenda for Peace Research*. Aldershot: Ashgate, 161–78.

Smith, Jackie, Charles Chatfield and Ron Pagnucco (eds) (1997). *Transnational Social Movements and Global Politics: Solidarity Beyond the State*. Syracuse, NY: Syracuse University Press.

Smock, David R. (1997). 'Creative Approaches to Managing Conflict in Africa'. Peaceworks No. 15. Washington, DC: USIP Press.

Smoke, Richard (1977). *War: Controlling Escalation*. Cambridge, MA: Harvard University Press.

Smouts, Marie-Claude (1997). 'Political Environment', in Brigitte Stern (ed.), *United Nations Peacekeeping Operations: A Guide to French Policies*. Tokyo: United Nations University.

Snyder, Jack (1993). 'Nationalism and the Crisis of the Post-Soviet State'. *Survival* **35**(1).

Sobhan, Rehman (1996). 'Aid Dependence and Donor Policy: the Case of Tanzania, with Lessons from Bangladesh's Experience', in *Aid Dependency: Causes, Symptoms, and Remedies*. Stockholm: Sida, 111–245.

Sollom, Richard and Darren Kew (1996). 'Humanitarian Assistance and Conflict Prevention in Burundi', in Robert I. Rotberg (ed.), *Vigilance and Vengeance: NGOs Preventing Ethnic Conflict in Divided Societies*. Washington, DC: Brookings Institution.

Sommer, John (1994). *Hope Restored? Humanitarian Aid in Somalia 1990–1994*. Washington, DC: Refugee Policy Group.

Sood, Krishnalekha (1995). 'Trends in International Cooperation and Net Resource Transfers to Developing Countries'. RFA 19. IDER.

Soros, George (1996). 'Conflict Prevention: Can We Meet the Challenge?', in *Conflict Prevention Strategies to Sustain Peace in the Post-Cold War World*. Washington, DC: Aspen Institute, 77–81.

Sparks, Allister (1995). *Tomorrow is Another Country. The Inside Story of South Africa's Road to Change*. New York: Hill and Wang.

Stavropoulou, M. (1996). 'Human Rights and "Early Warning" in the United Nations' Netherlands'. *Netherlands' Quarterly of Human Rights* **14**(4): 419–33.

Stedman, Stephen John (1995). 'Alchemy for a New World Order: Overselling Preventive Diplomacy'. *FA* **74**(3): 14–20.

Stern, Brigitte (ed.) (1997). *United Nations Peacekeeping Operations: A Guide to French Policies*. Tokyo: United Nations University.

Stevenson, Jonathan (2000). 'Preventing Conflict: the Role of the Bretton Woods Institutions'. *Adelphi Paper* 336. London: IISS.

Stewart, Frances, Frank P. Humphreys and Nick Lea (1997). 'Civil Conflict in Developing Countries over the Last Quarter of a Century: An Empirical Overview of Economic and Social Consequences'. *ODS* **25**(1): 11–40.

—— and Willem van der Geest (1998). 'Adjustment and Social Funds: Political Panacea or Effective Poverty Reduction?' Working Paper. Oxford: QEH, Oxford University.

——, Valpy Fitzgerald and Associates (2000a). *War and Underdevelopment*, 2 vols. Oxford: Oxford University Press.

——, Cindy Huang and Michael Wang (2000b). 'Internal Wars in Developing Countries: An Empirical Overview of Economic and Social Consequences', in Frances Stewart, Valpy Fitzgerald and Associates (eds), *War and Underdevelopment*, Vol. 1. Oxford: Oxford University Press.

Stiglitz, Joseph E. (1998). 'More Instruments and Broader Goals: Moving toward the Post-Washington Consensus'. WIDER Annual Lectures, 2. Helsinki: UNU/WIDER.

Suliman, Mohamed (1999). *Ecology, Politics, and Violent Conflict*. London: Zed Books.

Summers, Lawrence (1998). 'Go with the Flow'. *Financial Times*, 11 March: 14.

Swain, Ashok (1996). 'Environmental Migration and Conflict Dynamics: Focus on Developing Regions'. *TWQ* **17**(5): 959–73.

Thacker, Strom C. (1999). 'The High Politics of IMF Lending'. *World Politics* **52**(1): 38–75.

Thornberry, Cedric (1996). 'Saving the War Crimes Tribunal'. *Foreign Policy* (104): 72–85.

Tiffen, Mary, Michael Mortimore and Francis Gichuki (eds) (1994). *More People, Less Erosion: Environmental Recovery in Kenya*. Chichester: John Wiley & Sons.

Tilly, Charles (ed.) (1990). *Coercion, Capital and European States, AD 990–1992*. Cambridge and Oxford: Blackwell.

Timberlake, Lloyd (1985). *Africa in Crisis: the Causes, the Cures of Environmental Bankruptcy*. London: Earthscan Publications.

Torelli, Maurice (1993). 'Les Missions Humanitaires de L'armée Française'. *Défense Nationale* 3.

—— (1995). 'Les Zones de Sécurité'. *Revue Générale de Droit Internationale Public* 4.

Toronto Globe and Mail (1997), 23 March, p. 20.

Trotsky, Leon (1996). *Revolution Betrayed: What is the Soviet Union and Where is it Going?* Translated for the Internet by Zodiac *(http://csf.colorado.edu/mirrors/marxists.org/archive/trotsky/work/1936-rev/index.htm#00)*.

Turton, David (1989). 'The Mursi and National Park Development in the Lower Omo Valley', in David Anderson and Richard Grove (eds), *Conservation in Africa: People, Policies and Practice*. Cambridge: Cambridge University Press, 169–86.

Turton, David (ed.) (1997). *War and Ethnicity. Global Connections and Local Violence*. Rochester, NY: University of Rochester Press.

Uche, Chibuike Ugochukwu (1997). 'Does Nigeria Need an Independent Central Bank?' *Savings and Development* 1–2: 141–55.

UNCTAD (1994). *Trade and Development Report, 1994*. New York/Geneva: UN.

—— (1996). *The Least Developed Countries Report 1996*. Geneva: UNCTAD.

—— (1997a). *Trade and Development Report, 1997*. New York/Geneva: UN.

—— (1997b). *World Investment Report, 1997: Transnational Corporations, Market Structure and Competition Policy*. New York/Geneva: UN.

UNDHA (1996). *Analysis of Total Humanitarian Assistance Reported to DHA for Complex Emergencies in 1995*. Geneva: UN Complex Emergency Support Unit, Financial Tracking Sub-Unit.

UNDP (1994). 'The Relief to Development Continuum'. Draft Position Paper, February. New York: UN.

—— (1997). *Human Development Report, 1997*. New York: Oxford University Press.

—— (1998). *Human Development Report, 1998*. New York: Oxford University Press.

UNHCR (1995). *The State of the World's Refugees 1995: In Search of Solutions*. New York: Oxford University Press.

—— (1997). *The State of the World's Refugees 1997–98: A Humanitarian Agenda*. New York: Oxford University Press.

United Nations (1996). 'Report on the Situation of Human Rights in Rwanda'. New York: UN.

—— (1999). Srebrenica Report: The Secretary-General's Report (S/25939). Pursuant to General Assembly Resolution 1998/53/35. New York: UN.

UNRISD (1995). *States of Disarray: the Social Effects of Globalization*. Geneva: UNRISD.

USAID (1989). 'Evaluation of the 1988 Ethiopian Drought Assistance Program'. (Nancy Metcalf, Ellen Patterson Brown, Michael Glantz and Hope Sukin for Devres, Inc.). Addis Ababa: USAID.

—— (1996). *Humanitarian and Transition Assistance*. Washington, DC: USAID.

US General Accounting Office (1995). *Peace Operations: Update on the Situation in the Former Yugoslavia*. Washington, DC: General Accounting Office.

US Mission to the UN (1996). *Global Humanitarian Emergencies 1996*. New York: US Mission to the UN.

Uvin, Peter (1998). *Aiding Violence: the Development Enterprise in Rwanda*. West Hartford, CT: Kumarian Press.

—— (2000). 'Rwanda: the Social Roots of Genocide', in Wayne E. Nafziger, Frances Stewart and Raimo Väyrynen (eds), *War, Hunger, and Displacement: the Origins of Humanitarian Emergencies*. 2 vols. Oxford: Oxford University Press, II.

—— and Isabelle Biagiotti (1996). 'Global Governance and the "New" Political Conditionality'. *Global Governance* 2(4): 377–400.

van Creveld, Martin (1991). *On Future War*. Washington, DC: Brassey's.

van de Walle, Nicolas (1995). 'Crisis and Opportunity in Africa', in L. Diamond and M. F. Plattner (eds), *Economic Reform and Democracy*. Baltimore, MD: The Johns Hopkins University Press, 153–66.

Väyrynen, Raimo (1991). 'To Settle or to Transform? Perspectives on the Resolution of National and International Conflicts', in Raimo Väyrynen (ed.), *New Directions in Conflict Theory. Conflict Resolution and Conflict Transformation*. London: Sage, 1–25.

—— (1996). 'Preventive Action: Failure in Yugoslavia'. *International Peacekeeping* 3(4): 21–42.

—— (1999). 'From Conflict Resolution to Conflict Transformation: A Critical Review', in Ho-Won Jeong (ed.), *The New Agenda for Peace Research*. Aldershot: Ashgate, 135–60.

—— (2000a). 'Complex Humanitarian Emergencies: Concepts and Issues', in Wayne E. Nafziger, Frances Stewart and Raimo Väyrynen (eds), *War, Hunger, and Displacement: the Origins of Humanitarian Emergencies*. 2 vols. Oxford: Oxford University Press, I.

—— (2000b). 'Weak States and Humanitarian Emergencies: Failure, Predation, and Rent-Seeking', in Wayne E. Nafziger, Frances Stewart and Raimo Väyrynen (eds), *War, Hunger, and Displacement: the Origins of Humanitarian Emergencies*. 2 vols. Oxford: Oxford University Press, II.

—— (2000c). 'Preventing Deadly Conflicts: Failures in Iraq and Yugoslavia'. *Global Society* 14(1): 5–33.

Vivian, Jessica M. (1992). 'Greening at the Grassroots: People's Participation in Sustainable Development', in Dharam Ghai and Jessica M. Vivian (eds), *Grassroots Environmental Action: People's Participation in Sustainable Development*. London: Routledge.

Walker, B. H., D. Ludwig, C. S. Holling and R. M. Peterman (1981). 'Stability of Semi-Arid Savanna Grazing Systems'. *Journal of Ecology* 69: 473–98.

Wallensteen, Peter (1998a). 'Preventive Security: Direct and Structural Prevention of Violent Conflicts', in Peter Wallensteen (ed.), *Preventing Violent Conflicts. Past Record and Future Challenges*. Uppsala, Sweden: University of Uppsala, 9–38.

—— (1998b). *Preventing Violent Conflict*. Uppsala, Sweden: University of Uppsala.

Waller, R. (1988). 'Emutai: Crisis and Response in Maasailand 1883–1902', in D. H. Johnson and D. M. Anderson (eds), *The Ecology of Survival: Case Studies from Northeast African History*. London: Lester Crook, 73–112.

Warren, Bill (1980). *Imperialism: Pioneer of Capitalism*. London: Verso. B

Watts, Michael (1991). 'Entitlements or Empowerment? Famine and Starvation in Africa'. *ROAPE* 19(51): 9–26.

Weber, Max (1968). *Economy and Society*, Vol. 2 (edited by G. Roth and C. Wittieh). Los Angeles: University of California Press.

Wedel, Janine R. (1998). *Collision and Collusion: the Strange Case of Western Aid to Eastern Europe 1989–1998*. New York: St. Martin's Press – now Palgrave.

Weeks, John (1992). *Development Strategy and the Economy of Sierra Leone*. London: Macmillan Press – now Palgrave.

—— (1997). 'Macroeconomic Imbalances and Unsustainable Growth in Mozambique'. London: School of Oriental and African Studies. Manuscript.

—— (2001). 'Orthodox and Heterodox Policy for Growth for Africa South of the Sahara', in Terry McKinley (ed.), *Growth, Employment and Poverty in Africa*. Forthcoming. London: Macmillan Press – now Palgrave.

Weiss, Thomas G. (1996). 'Collective Spinelessness: UN Actions in the Former Yugoslavia', in Richard H. Ullman (ed.), *The World and Yugoslavia's Wars*. New York: Council on Foreign Relations, 59–96.

—— (1997). 'A Research Note about Military-Civilian Humanitarianism: More Questions than Answers'. *Disasters* **21**(2): 95–117.

—— (1999a). *Military-Civilian Interactions: Intervening in Humanitarian Crises*. Boulder, CO: Rowman & Littlefield.

—— (1999b). 'Principles, Politics, and Humanitarian Action'. *Ethics & International Affairs* 13: 1–22.

—— and Leon Gordenker (eds) (1996). *NGOs, the United Nations, and Global Governance*. Boulder, CO: Lynne Rienner.

—— and Amir Pasic (1997). 'Reinventing UNHCR: Enterprising Humanitarians in the Former Yugoslavia, 1991–1995'. *Global Governance* **3**(1): 41–57.

—— and Cindy Collins (2000). *Humanitarian Challenges and Intervention: World Politics and the Dilemmas of Help*, 2nd edn. Boulder, CO: Westview Press.

Welsh, David (1993). 'Domestic Politics and Ethnic Conflict'. *Survival* **35**(1): 63–80.

Wendt, Alexander and Michael Barnett (1993). 'Dependent State Formation and Third World Militarization'. *Review of International Studies* 19: 321–47.

Wheeler, Nicholas J. (1997). 'Agency, Humanitarianism and Intervention'. *IPSR* **18**(1): 9–26.

White, Gordon (1995). 'Towards a Democratic Developmental State'. *IDS Bulletin* **26**(2): 27–36.

White, Howard (1996). 'Review Article: Adjustment in Africa'. *Development and Change* 27: 785–815.

Wiener, Myron (1998). 'The Clash of Norms: Dilemmas in Refugee Politics'. *Journal of Refugee Studies* **11**(4): 1–21.

Willetts, Peter (ed.) (1996). *The Conscience of the World: the Influence of Non-Governmental Organizations in the UN System*. Washington, DC: Brookings Institution.

Winn, Neil (1996). *European Crisis Management in the 1980s*. Aldershot: Dartmouth.

Wolf, Eric R. (1969). *Peasant Wars of the Twentieth Century*. New York: Harper and Row.

Woodham-Smith, Cecil (1962). *The Great Hunger: Ireland, 1845–1849*. Hamish, UK: Hamilton.

Woodhouse, Philip (1997). 'Governance and Local Environmental Management in Africa'. *ROAPE* **24**(74): 537–47.

Woodward, Susan (1995). *Balkan Tragedy: Chaos and Dissolution after the Cold War*. Washington, DC: Brookings Institution.

World Bank (1990). *World Development Report, 1990: Poverty*. New York: Oxford University Press.

—— (1992a). *World Bank Structural and Sectoral Adjustment Operations: The Second OED Overview.* Washington, DC: World Bank.

—— (1992b). *Governance and Development.* Washington, DC: World Bank.

—— (1994). *Adjustment in Africa: Reforms, Results, and the Road Ahead.* New York: Oxford University Press.

—— (1996a). *Poverty Reduction and the World Bank: Progress and Challenges in the 1990s.* Washington, DC: World Bank.

—— (1996b). *World Development Report 1996: From Plan to Market.* New York: Oxford University Press.

—— (1997a). *Global Economic Prospects and the Developing Countries.* Washington, DC: World Bank.

—— (1997b). *World Development Report 1997: The State in a Changing World.* Oxford: Oxford University Press.

—— (1997c). *A Framework for World Bank Involvement in Post-Conflict Reconstruction.* Washington, DC: World Bank.

—— (2000). *Can Africa Claim the 21st Century.* Washington, DC: World Bank.

—— (2001). *Global Economic Prospects and the Developing Countries.* Washington, DC: World Bank.

World Commission on Environment and Development (1987). *Our Common Future.* New York: Oxford University Press.

Wylde, Augustus (1901). *Modern Abyssinia.* London: Methuen.

Zaidi, Sarah (1997). 'Humanitarian Effects of the Coup and Sanctions in Haiti', in Thomas G. Weiss, David Cortright, George A. Lopez and Larry Minear (eds), *Political Gain and Civilian Pain: Humanitarian Impacts of Economic Sanctions.* Lanham, MD: Rowman & Littlefield, 189–212.

Zakaria, Fareed (1997). 'The Rise of Illiberal Democracy'. *FA* **76**(6): 22–43.

Zamosc, Leon (1986). *The Agrarian Question and the Peasant Movement in Colombia: Struggles of the National Peasant Association 1967–1981.* Cambridge: Cambridge University Press.

Zevallos, José Vicente (1989). 'Agrarian Reform and Structural Change: Ecuador since 1964', in W. C. Thiesenhusen (ed.), *Searching for Agrarian Reform in Latin America.* Boston: Unwin Hyman.

Index